A PATTERN OF
GOVERNMENT GROWTH
1800–1860

A PATTERN OF
Government Growth
1800-60

=====

The Passenger Acts and their Enforcement

=====

by

OLIVER MACDONAGH

*Fellow of St Catharine's College,
Cambridge*

LONDON
MACGIBBON & KEE
1961

FIRST PUBLISHED 1961 BY MACGIBBON AND KEE
© OLIVER MACDONAGH 1961
PRINTED IN GREAT BRITAIN BY
EBENEZER BAYLIS AND SON LTD
LONDON AND WORCESTER

FOR CARMEL

FOR CARMEL

PREFACE

THIS book is a case study in the origins of modern government in the United Kingdom. It also provides an account of the greatest population movement of its day, and of its concommitant sufferings.

The North Atlantic emigration of 1800–60 is an apt subject for an inquiry into the beginnings of collectivism. Few of the first great detonators of the new sort of state activity is missing from its history. The essential problems of voluntary emigration at that time were seven: the inequality of bargaining power between the parties to the basic contract, and absolute misrepresentation: the supplying of large numbers of persons, outside the settled life of the community, with necessities: deficiency and contagious diseases, and malnutrition: a dirty, overcrowded and insanitary state of living: the sexual promiscuity and offences against decency arising from contiguity: the physical dangers which sprang from poor equipment and careless management: and the technical issues which both derived from new practices and inventions, and were successively raised by advances in the natural sciences. These were also general mainsprings of the reluctant, but also extensive, intervention of the central power in the ordinary lives of people in the first three-quarters of the nineteenth century. Whether we seek to explain the regulation of coal mines or of Irish land tenure; of public health or sanitation or merchant shipping; of merchandise marks or industrial waste or hours of labour, we are always driven back to one or several of these sources. In short, the emigrant trade and the passenger vessel involved, in one way or another, a most important range of the forces which brought the early modern state into existence.

Equally important for the purpose of a case study, emigrant protection is a comparatively simple and unadulterated subject. No Wilberforce or Shaftesbury, no Chadwick or Trevelyan, directed its reform. No League or Association was dedicated to its Amelioration. No political party or parliamentary interest took it up. No jealous local authority or powerful trade society succeeded here in holding back the tide of centralization and official regulation. All this makes it possible for us to study the

7

indigenous developments of government in as 'pure' and un-
complicated a state as is likely to be found. It may also have the
secondary value of helping to redress the balance in certain lesser,
but by no means insignificant aspects of nineteenth-century
history. Even in the present state of early and mid-Victorian
studies, it may be well worth bringing into high relief—as this
book does—such elemental facts as these: that reform did not
always depend upon master-reformers or agitation: that bureaucracy could develop without any assistance from master-bureaucrats: that much, if not the absolute majority, of the new
administrative system was presented and accepted as a-political:
that pressure from the localities was often in favour of, and not
against, the enlargement of the central power: that economical
reform might be the foremost enemy of social—and, by a converse
irony, breed 'despotism' in the state: or that lobbies and interests
(even very powerful ones, as in the case of coal mines or the
mercantile marine) might be emasculated by the mere establishment of a field-executive.

The plan of the book is simple. The first two chapters discuss,
respectively, the methods and materials employed, and the social
problem under review. The last two attempt to draw general
conclusions from the analysis, and to place them in their appropriate contexts. The intervening chapters describe (so far as
practicable, in chronological sequence) the growth of the remedial legislation and the increasing efficiency, or otherwise, of its
enforcement. Generally speaking, the process traced in these
middle chapters falls into two parts. The first consists of the
enactment of remedial legislation, the appointment of an executive corps to enforce it and the adjustment of central government
to accommodate the innovations. In the second part, the emphasis
shifts to the gathering of internal momentum, and self-exten-
sions, within government itself—a process periodically refreshed
by further catastrophes and disclosures. In time, in this field,
the dividing line is 1840.

In the first case I have made comparisons with other fields of
administration. In the second case I have not. There is a simple
reason for the distinction. The first is a plain and palpable, logical
and also often chronological, progression. Even if the writers
themselves are not concerned with them, these divisions may

readily be discerned in descriptions of the earlier phases of other social reforms. But in the second case, not only (so far as I am aware) has no real counterpart to the present study been published: unless the complex interaction of executive practice and legislation is specifically and exhaustively analysed—and that over a considerable period of time—our type of governmental dynamic can scarcely be disclosed. The loss, however, is probably more formal than real. The full pattern exposed by this study is no more likely to have been repeated elsewhere than one set of fingerprints to have a duplicate. But almost certainly substantial or partial counterparts are plentiful. Almost every development which took place in emigrant protection was a matter of the most ordinary and everyday reactions (see below, pp. 349–50). In fact, the whole process required little more than that men should have reacted reasonably intelligently to established facts, and with reasonable compassion for the sufferings of others. Given similar circumstances and stimuli—and similar circumstances and stimuli abounded in the nineteenth century—it is a safe assumption that things fell out in essentially the same fashion in many other areas of life.

Where more than one form of a term was employed by contemporaries, I have standardized, for the purposes of this book, what seemed the most common usage, e.g., 'passenger act', otherwise 'passenger regulation act' or 'passengers' act'; or 'emigration officer', otherwise 'emigration agent' or 'emigration inspector'. I have also adopted some abbreviations for purposes of citation, e.g. 'B.N.A.' for 'British North America'; or 'C.L.E.C.' for 'colonial land and emigration commission'.

Of the many people who have helped me, I must thank especially Professors W. L. Burn, S. R. Dennison and R. M. Titmuss, Drs G. Kitson Clark and R. J. Lambert, and Mr R. N. Gooderson. I have greatly profited not only from their advice but also their encouragement to persist in what is, in some ways, an experimental work. I am also very grateful to Mr P. Grierson and Professor T. W. Moody (representing the Royal Historical Society and the Irish Historical Society respectively) and to the editors of *Victorian Studies* and *The Historical Journal* for permission to use material which has appeared in their publications.

As to the rest, I do not know how to better what R. C. K.

Ensor wrote when launching a much greater book upon the world, 'My greatest debt, however, is to my wife; and the fact that that is a common experience among authors, shall not dissuade me from saying so.'

St Catharine's College O. MacD.
Cambridge

CONTENTS

A PATTERN OF
GOVERNMENT GROWTH
1800–1860

1

INTRODUCTORY

THE subject of this book is the formulation and execution of an obscure and all but forgotten body of legislation, the passenger acts of 1803–72. But though these laws were obscure in their own day and are all but forgotten now, they were matters of great moment to the seven and a half million people who emigrated from the United Kingdom during the first three-quarters of the nineteenth century. Whatever the intrinsic interest of such a story, however, this book is not written merely to chronicle the successive statutes, or to describe the trade which they attempted to control. Its fundamental purpose is to elucidate, in one particular field, the operation of certain pressures and tendencies working in the early and mid-nineteenth century towards the development of the modern state; and to establish (so far as may be) some principles of governmental growth in this period. The main emphasis will be on law and executive practice—or rather upon their unintended and unexpected consequences. 'Because it is true', as Mr Plamenatz has written, 'that society is nothing except men and their habits and laws, it does not follow that men make societies. For to make is to contrive for a purpose, and implies a conscious end and a knowledge of means. It is only because we use words that suggest purposes to describe nearly all the consequences of human activities that it comes natural to us to describe social and political institutions as if they were made by men . . . Men are always trying to adapt their institutions to their desires, and to some extent they succeed. But all this makes it no less true that these institutions are not the realizations of human purposes, and that they affect these purposes just as much (and perhaps much more) than they are affected by them'.[1] This is as true of government as of any other human activity; and to no period is it more applicable than the middle quarters of the nineteenth century when (contrary to all expectation and desire) the collectivist system of the present day began to take its shape.

[1] J. Plamenatz, *The English utilitarians* (Oxford, 1949), p. 151.

15

The study of the origins of collectivism in the United Kingdom is a relatively young subject. In terms of the stages of historical inquiry, we are still, to an extent, in the heroic age. Even yet we tend to seek explanations of the change in the nineteenth-century state almost exclusively in terms of the great individuals and ideas and events. There is also (it seems fair to say) a tendency to regard administration as a passive end- or by-product of the dynamic forces, social, political and economic. Government is explained in terms of other factors, not regarded as itself explanatory. This book is meant as a corrective, however small, to these views. Somewhere a beginning must be made in the study of inherent structures and patterns of development. In particular, it needs to be shown that within the field of government, no less than others, a genuine historical process was at work, moulding men and ideas just as it was moulded by them. We can easily see how this last is true in the sense in which all administration tends towards bureaucracy. 'The forms acquire an independent life of their own, and the original purpose or meaning is forgotten; the Thibetans are not the only people to employ praying wheels'.[1] But it is also true in a less obvious and much more important sense. In some circumstances— in the peculiar circumstances of the nineteenth century, at any rate —administration may be, so to speak, creative and self-generating. It may be independent, not in the sense of congealing into forms, but in the sense of growing and breaking out in character and scope. It may gather its own momentum; it may turn unexpectedly in new directions; it may reach beyond the control or comprehension of anyone in particular. No doubt such a process is always both initiated and affected by external forces. But it is a grave error to treat it altogether as their creature.

One means of confirming the existence of this independent process, and understanding something of its nature, is the close analysis of one particular governmental growth. This method has its drawbacks. It is laborious and exact. It does not perhaps lend itself to lively or graceful treatment, and certainly not to the rapid multiplication of cases. But it has one extraordinary and important advantage. Concentrating attention upon a single, continuous line enables us to span a sufficiently long and varied period of development,

---

[1] L. B. Namier, *The structure of politics at the accession of George III* (London, 1929), i, p. 164.

and at the same time to examine the matter in sufficient detail to understand the most intimate causes and connexions, and the cumulative effects, of the complete range of changes. This illuminates, as I think no other procedure can, the hidden pressures working within society towards collectivism, and the self-generating qualities of administration. Despite the considerable fortune in descriptive, biographical and philosophic material which the history of nineteenth-century government has already accumulated, it is far from rich in either exhaustive or consecutive analyses. Yet there is so much which minute dissection may discover but no alternative method can extract; and there is so much locked away in the material, awaiting the framing and pursuit of the appropriate questions. This, at any rate, is what the present history sets out to show.

The particular problem with which we are concerned, emigrant protection, arose like so many others from the prodigious increase in, and the new mobility of population. It never gained considerable public attention. In fact, it gained none at all until, through the characteristic nineteenth-century media of catastrophes, official inspections and investigations by commissioners and select committees, there issued terrible disclosures of mortality, privation, gross imposition upon poor and ignorant men, and sexual immorality. But these disclosures were acting, wherever they did act, upon a sensitive and generally humanitarian opinion. This led to irresistible demands for remedies. Little thought was given, except in the earliest and least informed stages, to the philosophic, commercial or political implications of what was being proposed. Increasingly, the downright contradiction of laissez faire and individualism which the remedies involved was ignored or explained away sophistically. Without the slightest spur from doctrinaires or any other *a priori* influence, experience and the brute facts of the situation forced those who were concerned with emigration towards centralization, autonomy and the delegation of legislation; towards demands for discretionary powers and the direct management of certain aspects of a private trade; towards fluidity and experimentation in regulations; towards a division and a specialization in administrative labour—in a word, towards the sort of state we recognize as modern. With surprising speed and ease an extraordinary governmental revolution was accomplished. The change was not, of course, premeditated or well-recognized. The executive officers and their parliamentary and other superiors mirrored the confusion of the half-century, 1825–75, and shared in the general failure to observe the cumulative effect of piecemeal measures. But throughout the whole haphazard and unconsidered process, throughout the extension of passenger legislation and of a multitude of similar expedients, a new sort of state was being born. As for the practical limit to its interference, this was fixed only—or at least fixed in the main—by the current hostility to public spending.

This book moves far at times from the multitudes who passed, almost tracelessly, across the Atlantic during the first three-quarters of the nineteenth century. But the subject would lose much, not only of its interest, but also of its meaning, if we do not remember them to have been real persons, liable to suffer hunger, pain and fear just as we may do. Not, of course, that they were in any sense heroic. Had the opportunities been offered, many emigrants would have equalled the worst of masters, brokers and runners in rapacity. In fact, the dockland hangers-on of Liverpool and New York were themselves 'spoiled' emigrants or immigrants, as the case might be; and there is much evidence of 'contributory cupidity' on the part of emigrants seeking to improve upon their passage contracts. But however we apportion turpitude or heap blame on 'that terrible Nobody'[1] of Samuel Smiles, the plain fact still remains that millions of the nineteenth-century emigrants were liable from their very situation to suffer injustice and distress.

Precisely what proportion of the passenger trade was corrupt is, of course, impossible to decide. There are no clear criteria here; nor can we expect really telling evidence of the quantities of good, bad and indifferent amongst the vessels, masters, brokers and so on. It is in the nature of this book to be engrossed with the 'bad', to concentrate attention almost exclusively upon the defects of the passenger trade and the defencelessness of the emigrants. But it is no part of its purpose to pontificate upon the trade or emigration as a whole. To all appearances, the honest broker, the self-reliant emigrant and the well-appointed vessel seem to have been exceptional. But, in the inevitable absence of relevant statistics, this cannot

---

[1] ' "That terrible Nobody". How much he has to answer for. More mischief is done by Nobody than by all the world besides. Nobody adulterates our food. Nobody leaves our towns undrained. Nobody fills jails, penitentiaries and convict stations'.

be absolutely demonstrated. But our thesis does not depend upon establishing any particular preponderance of iniquity or ignorance. All it asserts is that there were from first to last a very large number of grievous evils in the passenger trade, and a very large number of emigrants who indisputably required a protection by the state— sufficient and more than sufficient in either case to generate the most powerful demands for interference, come what might. Even statistically, we have here firm ground beneath our feet. An emigrant mortality which reached as high as 15 per cent in one large season, and as high as 50 per cent on many individual vessels from time to time; an Irish passenger business in which the average tonnage of the vessels never exceeded 250; an emigration of, for the most part, illiterates, and, for a great part, persons who knew no English; a total of nearly 4,000 complaints of, and nearly 1,000 successful prosecutions for, breaches of contract and other abuses in a Liverpool emigration of some 20,000 in 1837[1]—such facts as these constituted a sound prima facie case (to say the least) for the necessity of reform. All this apart, nineteenth-century bluebooks and public records contain several hundred testimonies from seamen, philanthropists, merchants, journalists, priests, lodging-keepers and emigrants themselves, testimonies of their first-hand experience of the traffic in the ports of embarkation, at sea or on arrival in the new world. The bluebooks and public records also include several thousand reports from the United Kingdom and colonial emigration officers, again very largely of their own direct experience of the trade. This very considerable body of primary evidence makes it quite clear that at no stage within our period was the passenger trade as yet sufficiently controlled or the emigrants sufficiently protected. On the contrary, regardless of its date, nearly every piece of testimony either asserted or implied that the trade was still marked by great abuses and that many of the emigrants were still too vulnerable. There can be no doubt that these were the essential facts of the situation.

Had the handful of philanthropists, members of parliament and public servants, who concerned themselves or found themselves

[1] To realize the significance of these proportions, we must understand that the requirements of the passenger acts in 1837 were, by later standards, very few and difficult to enforce, and that at all times a very large number of emigrants did not, for one reason or another, make the complaints or press the charges which they might have done.

concerned in the matter, not been moved by some feeling of common humanity there would have been small improvement, at any rate before 1850.[1] Hence the importance of trying to enter into their reactions. It is hard to break the great blur of the nameless, transient emigrants into fellow beings. But just as a workman's scribble on a slate may suddenly reinvoke a buried culture, so there survives in the bluebooks, family papers and the fragments of the local press, a handful of letters and depositions which can transmute the mere, anonymous mass of numbers into immediate and contingent life. One example will serve as well—or as ill—as many in attempting to convey this reality. In March 1848, a railroad labourer, Thomas Garry, who had emigrated at the end of 1847, sent £6 (three months' savings) to his wife and children still in Ireland. They had been very ill in the winter of 1847, and the money could not be used, as had been intended, for prepaid passages. 'i consider,' he wrote, 'yous could not stand the wracking of the sea till yous be nourished for a time'. This letter accompanied the remittance:

'My dear and loveing wife and children, I Received yours of January 20th 1848 which gave me to understand that yous were attacked by a severe Fever but thanks be God that yous are re-ceovered. . . . Be on the watch at the Post Office day after day I wont delay relieving yous as it is a duty Encumbered on me by the law of Church and I hope God will Relieve me. I work on a Railway at 6 shillings per day and pays 18 shillings per week for my Boarding. . . . So I will be able to pay yours passage with the help of God on the First of August next. The sending of this sum of money to yous Compells me to let it be Back tel them and i long to see that long wished for hour that I will Embrace yous in my arms. There is nothing in this world gives me trouble but yous and my dear Children whoom I loved as my life. Be Pleased to let me know how my two Sons is Patrick and Franciss and not forgetting my Father and mother . . . and not forgetting your

---

[1] The coming of steam to the Atlantic emigrant trade and the construction of vessels specifically designed for passengers (both of which date from about 1850), would, of course, have wrought very great improvements even had there been no protective legislation. But even this would have taken time. Steam passenger vessels and specially designed passenger vessels did not predominate in the trade until after the end of the American civil war. See below, chapter 14.

sister Bridget, thank God she was to mind yous in your sickness
and sorrows which I will never forget to her . . . Keep your
heart as god spareed you, you will be shortly in the lands of
promise"[1].

[1] *3rd rep. select comm. colonization 1st.*, 129, H.C. 1849 (86), xi. Appendix X of
this report contains a considerable number of emigrants' letters and is a rare and
very valuable source of material in this field. The *Monteagle papers* in the
National Library of Ireland also contain an interesting collection of emigrants'
letters.

2

THE PROBLEM

IT was the Irish emigration which set the pace for imperial legislation and administration in the period 1815–60. Not only did it greatly exceed in magnitude the combined British emigrations in these years;[1] it was also in much the greater need of protection and regulation. The Irish emigrants, wrote the colonial land and emigration commissioners in a review of the great pre-famine and famine exodus, 'are the most ignorant and helpless of their class'.[2] This does not mean that the Irish emigrants belonged to the lowest stratum of Irish society. Even in 1847, the 'worst' year of Irish emigration, the chief emigration officer at Liverpool went out of his way to distinguish clearly between the Irish emigrants and the 'poorest Irish'.[3] But more than five-sixths of the Irish emigrants were of rural origin, and the gradations in the Irish agrarian economy were minute, and its static, hierarchical system all-enveloping. Smallholders and even 'warm' men holding twenty acres possessed very little capital, and needed much the same protection as cottiers or labourers. In each case, the worldly experience of the departing was more or less confined to the sullen decay of the immediate neighbourhood in which they lived.[4] The chief emigration officer at Liverpool observed that 90 per cent of the cases of fraud and imposition which came to his attention concerned the Irish: they were, he added, 'frequently taken in by the runners of agents, who lay

[1] Over 75 per cent of the emigrants from the United Kingdom during these forty-five years were Irish, *International migrations*, ed. I. Ferenczi (New York, 1929), vol. i, p. 99.

[2] P.R.O., C.O. 384/89, 6006 North America, 28 June 1852.

[3] i.e., those who intended to remain in Great Britain, C.O. 384/80, 163 Emigration, 5 Feb. 1847. For a fuller analysis of this question, see O. Mac-Donagh, 'Irish emigration to the United States of America and the British colonies during the famine', sec. 1, in *The great famine*, a symposium (Dublin, 1956), pp. 319–31.

[4] There were other reasons for the peculiar helplessness of the Irish, e.g. the high rate of illiteracy, the fact that some spoke only Gaelic, and, on occasions, lack of adequate preparations for the voyage.

themselves in their way for that purpose. On these occasions they show great ignorance and gullibility, and indeed appear to want common sense in making a bargain'.[1] Both because of their extreme poverty and ignorance, and because of the scale and pace of their population movement as a whole, it is to the Irish almost exclusively that the interference and regulation of the period 1815–60 must be attributed.

Ironically enough, then, they were the creative force. But they not only created: they also retarded. Passenger legislation could never leave their desperate poverty out of account. Shillings and even pence were great matters for almost all. Thus we find the Londonderry shipping agents observing in 1849 that a current minor increase in fares—it amounted to 8s. 3d. in all—would check the Irish outflow very sharply.[2] Similarly, a Liverpool shipping agent testified in 1834, 'We find it difficult to please an Englishman or a Scotchman, with respect to the accommodation on board ships, where an Irishman would be perfectly satisfied. The Irish would prefer to be three in a berth to save expense in the article of bedding'.[3] In 1854, the emigration commissioners wrote that their object since their inception had been 'to interfere with the usual course of trade no farther than was indispensable for the protection of the more ignorant and helpless of the emigrants. Consequently as nine-tenths of the emigration then consisted of the Irish peasantry, the minimum allowance which would suffice for them became the standard . . . to be enforced by law. Anything more it was considered would unnecessarily enhance the price of passage and obstruct the transfer of the poorest classes'.[4] Hence it was the Irish who provided both spur and curb throughout the greater

[1] Rep. poor inquiry commrs Ire., Appendix G, 34–5, H.C. 1836, xxxiv.

[2] Londonderry Sentinel, 29 Mar. 1849. The occasion of the increase was the raising of the statutory food allowance for the passage from a diet costing 8s. 9d. to one costing 17s., C.O. 384/84, 361 Miscellaneous, commissioners: Merivale, 13 Jan. 1849.

[3] Rep. poor inquiry commrs Ire., Appendix G, 34, H.C. 1836, xxxiv (evidence of W. S. Fitzhugh).

[4] C.O. 384/92, 449 North America, 10 Jan. 1854. Actually, this statement over-simplified the issue; many other factors were operative in fixing the limit of restrictive legislation. But the need to keep fares low did exercise a considerable influence upon the acts. See also 2nd rep. select comm. emigrant ships, 139–40, Q.5573–80, H.C. 1854 (349), xiii; Earl Grey, The colonial policy of Lord John Russell's administration (London, 1853), i, pp. 236–42.

portion of the nineteenth century, and hence it is to them,[1] to their main ports of departure and arrival, Liverpool and New York, and to the time of their heaviest emigration, 1840–55, that we shall direct most of our attention in the following survey of the trade.

Down to 1815, Irish emigration, though regular, was on a very small scale. It is doubtful whether it exceeded 5,000 in any single season in the eighteenth century. This emigration was, moreover, predominantly one of Ulster presbyterian smallholders and townsmen. These emigrants were poor. Although political and religious discontent did play some part, the essential motivation (as is usual with emigration) was economic. But they were by no means paupers. Generally they took some small capital, perhaps £50 to £100, to the new world; often they joined relatives who secured employment or land for them or in other ways smoothed their path.[2] This 'Scots-Irish' emigration continued throughout the nineteenth century. But after 1815 it was accompanied and after 1835 quite dwarfed by a very different movement of Irish population, that of the catholic peasantry of the other three Irish provinces and of the poor lands and mountain farms of Ulster.[3] The demands of the revolutionary and Napoleonic wars had masked very dangerous developments in the Irish economy and society in the closing decades of the eighteenth century. But peace exposed them suddenly and dreadfully. After Waterloo, Ireland (the north-east corner to some extent excepted) rapidly became a land without employment for wages. As Nassau Senior put the point, the landlords lived by rent, 'the farmers worked for themselves and the labourers worked for nobody': almost everyone had to hold land in order to survive, and the struggle to possess it was like that 'to buy bread in a besieged town,

---

[1] Fortunately, the Irish are clearly distinguishable from the other emigrants by their ports of departure. Everyone who sailed from an Irish port and (from about 1830 till the mid-1850s) almost everyone who sailed from Liverpool and one in three of those who sailed from Glasgow and Greenock was Irish, *10th rep. C.L.E.C.*, 5 [1204], H.C. 1850, xxxii; *11th rep. C.L.E.C.*, 1 [1383], H.C. 1851, xxii. (C.L.E.C. is used in references throughout the book as an abbreviation for colonial land and emigration commissioners.)

[2] For a general description of the presbyterian emigration, see W. F. Dunaway, *The Scotch-Irish of colonial Pennsylvania* (Chapel Hill, 1944). For a discussion of the number involved, see W. F. Adams, *Ireland and Irish emigration to the new world from 1815 to the famine* (Yale, 1932), pp. 68–70.

[3] See Adams, op. cit., chapters, iii, iv and v.

or to buy water in an African caravan'.[1] The incentives to postpone marriage disappeared with the growing hopelessness of improving one's position, and population mounted in a geometrical progression. In its turn, the increase in population steadily reduced the size of holdings and the peasant's margin of safety, and at the same time, rendered ever more complete his dependence upon a single weakening crop, the potato. After 1820 the desperation of the cottiers led increasingly to the employment of their only defence against eviction, agrarian intimidation and outrage; and, again in turn, this facilitated further subdivision and the multiplication of squatters. The upshot was failing rents, falling productivity and dwindling capital, as the Irish economy rushed towards self-destruction and a more or less common ruin.

In these circumstances, and given a large demand for labour in both Great Britain and North America, a very heavy exodus was to be expected. To some extent it came. Almost 400,000 Irish emigrated overseas in the twenty years 1815–34;[2] and in 1842 the annual total reached 90,000. But, when the state of pre-famine Ireland is borne in mind, we are astonished not by the magnitude but by the smallness of the emigration. Cobbett's comment on the English farmers in 1821, 'they hang on, like sailors to the masts or hull of a wreck', could have been applied with much more force to the Irish peasants in the years 1815–45. As late as 1843 and 1844, that is to say, on the very eve of the ultimate catastrophe, several witnesses before the Devon commission testified to the stubbornness of the resistance to emigration. As one land agent, J. Lynch, put it, 'There's such a clinging to the country that they would live on anything rather than go'.[3] It is true that emigration was thoroughly established in many districts in Ulster, the north midlands and the counties of Cork and Limerick, and that resistance was weakening amongst the young. But by and large Lynch's observation well described the common disposition.

All this was revolutionized by the potato blights of 1845–51. The long succession of failures and partial failures, accompanied as they were by scenes of unutterable desolation and despair, wrought a

[1] N. Senior, *Journals, conversations and essays relating to Ireland* (London, 1868), vol. i, p. 28.

[2] For a discussion of the volume of Irish emigration during these years, and the various statistical sources which illuminate it, see Adams, op. cit., pp. 410–27.

[3] *Devon commission*, i, 153–4.

volte face in the general attitude to emigration. 'Those farmers,' the *Limerick Chronicle* noted in 1848, 'who could manage to prepare the land for tillage have not the courage to encounter a third or fourth adverse season. Such a climax of social disorganization is without parallel'.[1] The failures deprived the cottiers of their last stay, and 'the poor law acted on the small farmer much as the potato-failure acted on the cottar'.[2] Henceforth, an immense and continuous outflow was accepted as inevitable, and emigration became a regular, indispensable element in the familial structure. In a sense, the economy simply disintegrated. We might almost say that in the place of one, there now emerged two closely interacting Irish societies poised on the opposite seaboards of the Atlantic. In Ireland itself, the old and apparently ineradicable trends towards subdivision and early marriage were, almost overnight, reversed; while constant emigration and the remittance became (as they have ever since remained) integral parts of the Irish patterns of behaviour and economics. Relatively speaking, the famine emigration was one of the greatest voluntary movements of population that the world has ever seen. Over 20 per cent of the entire population left the island permanently in a single decade. During the five years, 1847–51, nearly one-third of the population of the province of Connacht and more than one-quarter of the population of the province of Munster emigrated overseas. In the single season of 1851, the total emigration exceeded one-quarter of a million—out of a population of, by then, less than seven millions. No other nineteenth-century emigration was on nearly so great or so terrible a scale. In fact, we may perhaps best catch its character if we regard it not as an emigration proper but rather as a desperate outrush of economic refugees.[3]

The composition of nineteenth-century Irish emigration was a matter of some dispute amongst contemporaries and must remain a matter of some uncertainty to historians. Naturally, the main conflict of evidence arises from the discrepancy between Irish and American accounts. Those at home saw 'the life-blood of the coun-

---

[1] *Limerick Chronicle*, 18 Nov. 1848.

[2] *Quarterly Review*, vol. xc, p. 193. From 1847 on, the notorious Gregory or 'quarter-acre' clause forced small farmers in distress to throw up their holdings by refusing them poor relief unless they surrendered all but a quarter of an acre.

[3] For a description in detail of the famine emigration, see MacDonagh, op. cit., in *The great famine*.

try', 'its bone and sinew', the young and the enterprising, depart; Americans saw the 'refuse' and 'off-scourings', paupers and disease, arrive. Doubtless, the difference in living standards—American wages being four or five times as large as Irish—accounts for much of the divergence; and it scarcely needs saying that each party tended to observe only that which worked to its own disadvantage. But while exactitude is impossible, the main facts are clear enough. Even if we allow the benefit of every doubt to go against poverty and ignorance, it is still quite certain that the Irish was the most destitute and defenceless of all nineteenth-century emigrations.[1] Down to 1830 a considerable proportion of the Irish emigration consisted of small farmers and artisans who, though poor, stood well above the extremes of poverty which characterized the cottiers and labourers. But the pre-1830 emigration was comparatively small, and from 1830 onwards (that is to say, from the time when really large-scale emigration got under way) the great majority of Irish emigrants lacked almost entirely both capital and knowledge of the world. Protestant emigration, and the emigration of those who passed for 'strong' farmers in the wretched countryside never ceased: even in some famine seasons, during 1849–51 particularly, it appears to have been unusually large. But to keep the matter in perspective we must recollect that from 1830 to 1845 at least one-third of the entire body of Irish emigrants were incapable of paying even their bare Atlantic fare, £5 at most, from their own resources; that after 1845 this proportion was considerably increased; and that taking nineteenth-century Irish emigration as a whole we may safely assume that more than one-half of its participants were in this state of destitution.

The majority of nineteenth-century Irish emigration was financed by remittances or prepaid passages from North America. Even before 1820 prepaid passages were not uncommon and by the early 1830s the proportion of Irish emigration financed from overseas was very large. W. S. Fitzhugh, a leading Liverpool shipping agent, estimated in 1834 that some 45 per cent of the 3,000 passages which his firm booked every year were prepaid or paid for by remittance;

---

[1] The conditions of the passenger trade and of passenger protection under which the Mediterranean and eastern European emigrations of the closing decades of the century took place were, of course, vastly different to those obtaining before 1855.

and in many cases additional moneys were furnished to buy 'sea-stock' or provisions for the voyage. 'Generally', Fitzhugh concluded, 'someone goes out first to feel the way, and, if he succeeds, he either advises his friends to come out or pays their passage if they cannot pay for it themselves . . . The experience of ten years enables me to say that the disposition to assist relations and friends in this manner exists much more strongly amongst the Irish than amongst the English'.[1] Two Belfast agents observed in the same year that at least one-third of their passages were paid for either in or from America: 'the most enterprising of a family goes first, he sends home for part of his family, and then in some time longer for more of them, until the whole are brought out'.[2] Clearly the effects were cumulative; the proportion of remittance and prepaid emigration increased naturally and steadily by chain-reaction. In 1848 some 40 per cent of the £400,000 remitted to Liverpool was in the form of prepaid passages,[3] and a very large number of the remaining drafts and orders must also have been sent to finance emigration.[4] The emigration commissioners reported that some 75 per cent of the Irish emigrants of the following season, 1849, had received their fares in one form or another from North America;[5] and after this date the flow of money (though not necessarily the proportion of emigrants assisted) from the new world increased prodigiously year by year.[6] For nineteenth-century Irish emigration to the new world

[1] *Rep. poor inquiry commrs Ire.*, Appendix G, 33, H.C. 1836, xxxiv. Fitzhugh added that 75 per cent of the prepaid passages were on behalf of Irish people living in Ireland, and a further 12½ per cent on behalf of Irish people living in Great Britain.

[2] *1st rep. poor inquiry commrs Ire.*, Appendix C, part I, 18, H.C. 1836, xxx (evidence of G. Ash and J. H. Shaw).

[3] *Papers rel. emigration B.N.A.—part II*, 75-6, H.C. 1849 (593–II), xxxviii. One Liverpool firm, Harndon's, received almost £120,000 in prepaid passages during 1848. (B.N.A. is used throughout as an abbreviation for British North America.)

[4] It was a common practice at this time to send money orders or drafts to the local parish priests, trusted landlords or similar educated persons to buy passages and outfits on behalf of relatives or friends, *Rep. select comm. colonization Ire.*, 248, [737], H.C. 1847, vi; *3rd rep. select comm. colonization Ire.*, Appendix X, 125-32, H.C. 1849 (86), xi.

[5] *9th rep. C.L.E.C.*, 1–2 [1082], H.C. 1849, xxii. See also *Hans.*, 3rd, ciii, 1145, 22 Feb. 1849 (Sir Charles Wood).

[6] It was calculated in 1867 that more than $120,000,000 had been remitted from the United States by Irish immigrants during the preceding twenty years, J. F. Maguire, *The Irish in America* (London, 1868), p. 313. This is a reasonable,

was a peculiarly filial and co-operative venture. As the chief emigration officer of New Brunswick once observed, the average Irish
immigrant's first and whole effort was directed towards saving
money to send for his friends and to provide for their coming.[1] No
other immigrant group adopted this practice, and the sustained self-
denial which it necessitated, to anything like the same extent or with
the same regularity. As to its operation, two cases of which he had
direct knowledge which J. R. Stewart, an Ulster landowner, described may serve as typical. In one instance, a priest in Letterkenny
lent six guineas to a girl in 1846; in 1847 she remitted enough to
repay the loan and to enable one of her sisters to join her in the
United States; and in the following year the two sent prepaid
passages to two other girls. A second case concerned a woman with
six children whose husband died, reducing her to pauperdom, in
1845. She persuaded her brother to furnish her eldest boy with a
passage; and by 1848 he had succeeded in bringing out the entire
family.[2] Commonly those who remained behind entered workhouses to await release; one poor law union reported that five or
six of its paupers emigrated weekly throughout 1849 by means of
American remittances.[3] Nor was the assistance to emigrate confined
to one's immediate family or even near kin. A Liverpool ship-
master told of two Irish maid-servants formerly in his employment
who had brought out thirteen persons within a few years, some of
them remote or no relations; and many similar accounts are to be
found.[4] Indeed, so widely was the duty recognized and so generously

or at any rate not greatly exaggerated, estimate. Maguire, an Irish M.P., consulted bankers and brokers in all the leading cities in the United States, and his
conclusion was supported by the figures returned by the emigration commissioners in their annual reports. The commissioners' figures, although they do
not reach in sum so high a total, approach it nearly; and although they also include remittances from British North America, this is doubtless offset by the
facts that some important brokers such as Baring Bros made no returns, and that
there was no record of the large sums which Irish corn-importing merchants
were directed to pay to persons in Ireland by the American exporters, *Rep.
comm. select colonization Ire.*, 110–11 [737], H.C. 1847, vi. A considerable portion of the money remitted from North America was of course spent on purposes
other than emigration.

[1] *Rep. select comm. colonization Ire.*, 33, Q.299–500 [737], H.C. 1847, vi
(evidence of M. Perley). See also Maguire, op. cit., pp. 324–9.

[2] *7th rep. select comm. poor laws Ire.*, 31, H.C. 1849 (237), xv, part I. See also
W. S. Trench, *The realities of Irish life* (London, 1868), pp. 136–51.

[3] *Morning Chronicle*, 15 July 1850, p. 5.

[4] Ibid.; *Nation*, 22 Mar. 1851; *Limerick Chronicle*, 17 Feb. 1847; &c.

was its extent regarded that landlords could depend upon assisted emigration from their estates leading ultimately to a clearance several times larger than the original undertaking. Within eighteen months of Palmerston's sending 2,000 of his tenants to America in 1847, 4,000 others had been brought out by the remittances of the first wave.[1]

Hence in a very real sense, *ce n'est que le premier pas qui conte*: it was the first breach in the wall with which poverty surrounded the cottiers and the labourers which mattered. Aubrey de Vere testified that in his own country—the Clare-Limerick region—the prevailing custom was that funds for emigration should be supplied partly by landlords, and partly from a collection in the locality in which even the poorest contributed their shillings to purchase passages for some. De Vere, himself a landlord, added that one could not speak too highly of the practice: a loan to one poor man meant that the whole family would emigrate within two or three seasons as a consequence of his endeavours.[2] Loans and collections of this type were to be found in all parts of Ireland, although they do not appear to have been as systematically established elsewhere. Another method of finance was credit. The Canadian quarantine physician noted in his annual report for 1843, 'Many of those who did emigrate came out on the credit of friends at home who made themselves responsible for the payment of the passage money within twelve months after the arrival of the emigrants in this country. On board of one vessel, the bark *Anne* of New Ross, out of sixty-four passengers I was assured by the master that only one family had paid their passage money before leaving, all the others having come out in the manner just described'.[3] Similarly, we find, in the case of the *Faithful* in 1850, that one passenger had arranged with the master to work his passage out and a second to pay for his sister's fare by labour in British North America, and that others had made corresponding bargains for various sums and considerations.[4] Not least

---

[1] *Further papers rel. emigration B.N.A.*, 40 [932], H.C. 1847–8, xlvii; *Hans.*, 3rd, cv, 500–12, 15 May 1849 (W. Monsell).

[2] *Rep. select comm. colonization Ire.*, 536–7, Q.4858–62 [737], H.C. 1847, vi; *7th rep. select comm. poor laws Ire.*, 89–90, Q.5682–3, H.C. 1849 (237), xv, part I. See also *Monteagle papers* (National Library of Ireland), Lady Monteagle: T. Spring Rice, 10 July 1847. The Clare-Limerick region was one in which a number of benevolent landlords were interested in the promotion of emigration.

[3] *Annual rep. agents emigration Canada*, 25, H.C. 1844 (181), xxxv.

[4] *Papers rel. emigration B.N.A.*, 1–2, H.C. 1851 (348), xl; *12th rep. C.L.E.C.*, 84 [1499], H.C. 1852, xviii.

important in breaking through the barrier of poverty were landlord-assisted and (to a lesser extent) poor law emigration. Possibly as many as 100,000 persons, most of whom could not pay for their passages from their own resources, were sent out by these methods during the nineteenth century.[1] Hundreds of thousands, of course, never possessed the connexions in the new world or the influence or fortune in the old to raise sufficient money for their fares. Much of the permanent immigration into Great Britain before 1850 was of this class; and there were besides multitudes whom even a cross-channel fare defeated. Scores of instances of men and women deliberately committing felonies in the hope of transportation to Van Diemen's Land were recorded during the worst years, 1847–9.

Remittances and resources have been considered at such length to establish clearly that much of Irish emigration, although not reaching deeply into the ranks of the poorest of all, was nonetheless a movement of very destitute and vulnerable people, and to indicate the circumstances and state of preparation in which the departure was commonly undertaken. We shall now turn to the emigrant trade in so far as it concerned the passage contract and the ports of embarkation; and on both counts Liverpool takes pride of place.

II

'Of all the seaports in the world', wrote Herman Melville in 1849,[2] 'Liverpool perhaps most abounds in all the variety of land-sharks, land-rats and other vermin which make the helpless mariner their prey. In the shape of landlords, barkeepers, clothiers, crimps and boarding-house lodgers, the land-sharks devour him limb by limb'. Melville spoke of sailors, but what he said applied with still greater force to the emigrants. If Liverpool showed the passenger trade in its highest form of development, it also showed the abuses which it led to on their grandest scale. It was by far the most important outlet in the United Kingdom for emigration to North America in the nineteenth century. During the years 1830–45 more than half of the Irish emigrants for North America embarked there, and in the

[1] Cf. MacDonagh, op. cit. in *The great famine*, sec. ii and O. MacDonagh, 'The poor law, emigration and the Irish question, 1830–55', *Christus Rex*, xii, 1.
[2] In *Redburn*, chap. xxix.

decade which followed the proportion rose to four in five. Irish newspapers and Irish shippers might deplore the loss of trade, but the fact was that emigration had to follow the established lanes of transatlantic commerce, and Ireland had neither the shipping nor the imports to capture the new movement. Liverpool alone could provide the vessels in sufficient numbers. Liverpool alone could build up packet lines in half a decade, and cope with the immense business in remittances and prepaid passages which followed in the wake of Irish and (to a much lesser extent so far as Liverpool was concerned) of German and British mass emigration.[1]

Nevertheless, the port had many disadvantages. Firstly, to embark there exposed the Irish emigrants at least to the additional discomfort of a preliminary steamer passage. This usually meant twenty-four to thirty hours on the open deck of a cross-channel packet, quite without cover, and often washed over by heavy seas.[2] It was also a hazardous undertaking. Accidents were common, especially in the dank and crowded Mersey estuary, and the numbers aboard the packets were, practically speaking, unregulated: it was said that the Cork steamers carried lifeboats sufficient only for 3 per cent or 4 per cent of their passengers. Nevertheless, the packet companies demanded ten shillings for deck passage: 'they do not get half that money for the pigs, and yet the pigs are comfortably lodged between decks, while these poor people are not looked after at all'.[3] So horrible were the conditions that the housing of cross-channel passengers in the horse-stalls was spoken of, quite seriously, as an improvement.[4] Secondly, whatever Liverpool's merits as a commercial *entrepôt*, it was thoroughly unsuitable as an emigration port. It was both large and busy and often fogbound; its sandbars were always dangerous to shipping; its passenger vessels had to be boarded from the dock; and the times during which embarkations

[1] *Rep. select comm. passenger acts*, v–vi, H.C. 1851 (632), xix.

[2] C.O. 384/46, 637 Miscellaneous, 9 Mar. 1838; 384/49, board of trade: Stephen, 27 Feb. 1838; *1st rep. select comm. emigrant ships*, 88–89, Q.1515–45, H.C. 1854 (163), xiii.

[3] *Rep. select comm. passenger acts*, 712–14, Q.6658–72, H.C. 1851 (632), xix (evidence of J. Besnard). The emigrant ships committee of 1854 expressed its indignation that livestock should be covered and cared for during the voyage while human beings were exposed in such a way, *2nd rep. select comm. emigrant ships*, vii, H.C. 1854 (349), xiii.

[4] *1st rep. select comm. colonization Ire.*, 179, Q.1915–18, H.C. 1847–8 (415), xvii.

might take place were very short.[1] Dock regulations forbade the use
of fire or lights on vessels, and the practice of the port was to stow
cargo up to the last minute. Consequently, no passenger was permitted to go aboard his vessel until it was almost time to sail,[2] and
vessels commonly cast off in the midst of wild confusion, passengers
and luggage being thrown aboard as the ship moved from the quay.[3]
Moreover, Liverpool was growing rapidly, and the spread of foul
slums along its docklands laid it open to every infection. This was
of prime importance for our subject because, as a result of the prohibition upon early embarkation, almost every emigrant had to spend
at least two nights in lodgings before he might go aboard.[4] This in
turn compelled emigrants to stay in houses where they were likely
to contract infectious diseases, and provided excellent opportunities
for those who made it their business to defraud them. The actual
charges for lodgings were not high—they ranged from twopence to
fourpence a night[5]—but the places themselves were invariably foul.
People lay packed together on straw or cellar floors, with neither
fire nor light.[6] Moreover, assemblies of this kind invited 'American
wakes' and embarkation celebrations. A journalist who knew the
Liverpool trade thoroughly described emigrants on the eve of sailing
as alternately weeping and singing, 'dancing, hurraing, shouting and
drinking whiskey, supplied to them by the lodging keeper for his
own profit'.[7] Such living conditions and such practices were poor
preparation for the voyage; and there is no doubt that many of the
epidemics which ravaged emigration at sea had their origins in these
surroundings.

But the danger of infection was but one evil, and the lodging

[1] *Rep. select comm. passenger acts*, 272, Q.2633-7, H.C. 1851 (632), xix; *1st
rep. select comm. emigrant ships*, 27, Q.416-19, H.C. 1854 (163), xiii.

[2] C.O. 384/86, 6983 Emigration, 30 July 1851. See also *Morning Chronicle*,
15 July 1850, which contains an excellent account of the Liverpool passenger
trade generally.

[3] *Rep. select comm. passenger acts*, xiv, H.C. 1851 (632), xix.

[4] C.O. 384/84, 4584, Emigration, commissioners: Merivale, 22 May 1849.
This report discusses in detail the Liverpool abuses mentioned below.

[5] *Rep. select comm. passenger acts*, vi, H.C. 1851 (632), xix.

[6] Ibid., 287, 301-2, Q.2765-6, 2870-3. The municipal sanitary board did fix
the numbers which each lodging house might accommodate, but even if obeyed
in the letter this regulation was usually evaded in spirit by crowding all the
lodgers into one room or two, ibid., viii-ix.

[7] *1st rep. select comm. emigrant ships*, 91-2, Q.1583-9, H.C. 1854 (163), xiii
(evidence of S. Redmond).

house but one link in the chain of imposition. It is difficult to say where precisely the centre of the system of abuses lay. A select committee appointed in 1851 to investigate the working of the passenger acts placed it at the runners who were employed by shipping agents and lodging keepers. Certainly it was the runners who initiated the process, it was they who led emigrants into the traps which had been prepared.[1] Much of their effectiveness derived from close organization. They worked in bodies resembling trade unions, the most powerful of which was known as the 'Forty Thieves'. These bands met every Irish steamer as it docked and laid hands upon the disembarking passengers. It may seem surprising that the runners made 'captures' with great ease, for the Irish newspapers and (after 1833) the Liverpool emigration officers constantly issued warnings against their activities. But in fact they were favoured by every circumstance. We must remember the ignorance and bewilderment of the emigrants (the great majority of whom were countrymen), the ordeal on the steamer which they had just endured and the noise and confusion of arrival. According to eye-witnesses, the emigrants were 'actually driven from the ship with sticks into the hands of . . . so many pirates'; those who would not submit were 'almost torn to pieces'.[2] One runner crudely but graphically described the scene: a tumult of solicitation went up as the vessel docked, and the 'Greatest Robber' shouted loudest, 'he payed us or payed the Master make heast your ship is just going out'.[3] The pandemonium played into the runner's hands. Before he could understand what was happening, the emigrant, or his baggage, was seized. Occasionally, the 'mancatchers' went to greater lengths to achieve their object. It was not uncommon for one of a gang to travel on the cross-channel steamer to Liverpool; he would mix with a particular group of passengers and extract from them all the gossip of their parish; this he would impart, on arrival, to a confederate, who could then rush up to the party as a long-lost connexion; and once their confidence was won, wholesale imposition was easy.[4] Similarly, several had correspondents in Ireland who would send them the names of

[1] *Rep. select comm. passenger acts*, 216–17, Q.2098–110, H.C. 1851 (632), xix (evidence of Lieut. Prior).

[2] Ibid., 300–1, 408–9, Q.3732–5, 3866–9 (evidence of Sir George Stephen and F. Sabell). Sabell concluded, 'it is really a horrible thing'.

[3] *Morning Chronicle*, 15 July 1850; *Liverpool Courier*, 29 Mar. 1848.

[4] C.O. 384/91, 361 North America, 14 Jan. 1853.

persons who were emigrating from their particular districts.[1] A final factor which worked in the same direction was the peasant's fatal passion for bargaining for himself and seeking to improve upon the terms he had got. A few were really shrewd but generally it was the lamb offering itself for the slaughter.

Once he was in the runner's hands, it was almost inevitable that the emigrant should be cheated. As James Stephen, permanent under-secretary of the colonial office, put it, 'The effect of Lying, on the one hand, and Credulity on the other, must, as it would seem, be that of the perpetual generation of frauds'.[2] The runner could then 'dollar', or exchange, the emigrant's little stock of gold greatly to his own advantage, or persuade the emigrant that he would not be allowed aboard without liquor, telescopes, bowie knives or whatever rubbish he had to trade.[3] But worse than individual and petty fraud was the fact that runners worked hand-in-glove with brokers and lodging and shop keepers, and extorted a commission from them on all transactions in which an emigrant whom they had introduced took part. Most shipping agents maintained provision stores and paid the runners well for enticing customers; and the 'slops' or clothing shops were worked on the same basis. Tapscott, one of the main shippers at Liverpool and New York, admitted that runners received at least 7½ per cent from brokers, and a great deal more from chandlers and ordinary dealers.[4] Obviously, this commission

[1] C.O. 384/73, 162 Emigration, circular from Brown, Shipley & Co., 15 Jan. 1842; *1st rep. select comm. emigrant ships*, 92, Q.1594-7, H.C. 1854 (163), xiii. Most of the runners were themselves Irish.

[2] C.O. 384/83, 63 Emigration, Stephen: Gladstone, 15 Apr. 1835.

[3] Circular from the Irish Emigration Society printed in *Limerick Chronicle*, 13 May 1848: *Morning Chronicle*, 15 July 1850.

[4] *Rep. select comm. passenger acts*, 287-9, Q.2767-88, H.C. 1851 (632), xix. Tapscott argued that the cut-throat competition—the term was not inapposite—of the runner system provided some safeguard for the emigrant. Correspondingly, it might have been argued that the runner provided a useful economic function either as middleman or as advertiser. Had emigrants been the equals of runners in experience and knowledge, had the connexion between them been an ordinary continuing commercial relationship, had there been no or a fixed or regularized commission, and had there been no city or dock police or emigration officers to direct or guide, this might have been the case. As things were, however, all the testimony of disinterested parties tells against both Tapscott's and our hypothetical contention. It was universally agreed that the runner was at best a useless intermediary and much more commonly a heartless rogue, and that the main consequence of the runner system was swindling and imposition —petty doubtless in absolute terms, but grave and terrible in its effects upon the very poor. It is interesting to note, moreover, that when the New York civic

lay at the bottom of much of the abuses. It had once unfortunately been upheld in court; and thereafter runners had regarded, and by their organization compelled brokers and shopkeepers to accept it as a matter of right.[1] An attempt was made in 1849 to break the stranglehold, when an act of parliament was passed withdrawing the right to commission unless a runner had acted under written authority.[2] Early in the following year, at a time of particularly heavy demand for passages, the chief emigration officer at Liverpool persuaded the shipping brokers of the city to agree under bonds of £200 to abandon the commission system, increase the salaries of their own runners and work through them alone. Within a month or two, however, shipping became plentiful again; one agent broke the terms of the combination; and the whole arrangement instantly dissolved.[3] The old freelance warfare was thereupon resumed and with it the systematic extortion of the clothing and provision and other stores.[4]

All this represented one aspect of the imposition, that of the runner, the lodging keeper and the merchant. Another concerned shipping, passages, fares and remittances. Frauds of the second sort generally took the form of breach of contract. The Irish custom was to buy tickets, or obtain them on receipt of a deposit, from the agents of the Liverpool houses who were stationed in the various country towns. These agents would then advertise the sailing dates of the vessels contracted for in the local newspapers, and instruct passengers to reach Liverpool by a particular time.[5] As the emigrants were leaving Ireland once for all, this procedure obviously opened the way for great abuses. When they arrived at Liverpool, emigrants often found themselves compelled to delay for days or even weeks beyond

authorities condemned outright the system of 'private enterprise' emigrant homes and hospital which operated in that city, they selected Tapscott's firm for particular opprobrium, and described the operation of Tapscott's home in terms reminiscent of the scandals of Andover workhouse, cf. D. M. Schneider, *The history of public welfare in New York state, 1609–1866* (New York, 1938), p. 305.

[1] Ibid., 127–8, Q.1224–31 (evidence of Lieut. Hodder).

[2] 12 & 13 Vic., c. 33.

[3] *Rep. select comm. passenger acts*, 217–18, 289, 334–5, Q.2111–27, 2789–90, 3191–5, H.C. 1851 (632), xix.

[4] C.O. 384/28, unmarked, 25 June 1831; C.O. 384/84, 4584 Emigration, 22 May 1849; *1st rep. select comm. emigrant ships*, 90, Q.1551–63, H.C. 1854 (163), xiii.

[5] Priests were often asked in these advertisements to communicate the sailing dates to their 'poorer neighbours'.

their appointed sailing day, or packed off on a vessel other than that contracted for,[1] or even robbed completely of their money. Not one emigrant in a hundred knew anything of ships or shipping.[2] The remittance trade, of course, almost invited abuses. Sir George Stephen, who claimed a long acquaintance with the Liverpool passage business, said in 1851 that the evasion of money orders and drafts by shipping houses, and receiving prepaid fares and deposits for passages under false pretences, were probably the most common means of all of defrauding emigrants.[3] In the same year, the Irish Emigrant Protection Society observed a great increase in this evil, and begged Irish people in America to prevent the loss of great sums of money every year by using only reputable banks and agents, and by purchasing no sailing tickets whatsoever in the United States.[4]

The consequences of breaches of contract were often serious. Vessels varied greatly in safety and comfort, and every delay meant that the emigrant and his dependants were eating into their little sea-stock, which was often insufficient to keep them in good health even during a favourable voyage. Sometimes a man's whole project of emigrating was defeated. As the Liverpool Dock Committee put it in one execrable but all too accurate sentence, 'The heartless plunder of which these poor people are, in almost every case, the victims may be said to double the criminality because it more than so multiplies the suffering consequent upon ordinary robbery, by not only stripping them of the little means which the sacrifice of what most men hold dearest may have put them in possession of, but also disqualifying them from pursuing successfully the new path in life which that sacrifice has been incurred to promote'.[5] An extreme instance of this type of abuse, which occurred in 1846, concerned 150 passengers from Cork who arrived at Liverpool with tickets on

[1] This jobbing in passages was due to the fluctuations in the demand on shipping, the considerable variations in fares, and the amount of private bargaining.
[2] 2nd rep. select comm. emigrant ships, 52, Q.3899–906, H.C. 1854 (349), xiii.
[3] Rep. select comm. passenger acts, 299–300, Q.2861–4, H.C. 1851 (632), xix.
[4] 2nd rep. Emigrant Society, pp. 5–6. It was suggested, also in 1851, that the remittance business was developing on such a scale and respectable houses and agents were becoming so firmly established that abuses in this field were on the decline, Rep. select comm. passenger acts, v–vi, H.C. 1851 (632), xix. This was undoubtedly the long-run development, but the remittance trade was subject to many abuses throughout the 1850s.
[5] C.O. 384/85, 7384 Emigration, 24 Aug. 1850. See also C.O. 384/41, 629 Emigration, 15 Jan. 1842.

which they had already paid a pound; they were to give the balance to Messrs Shaw, the firm with whom the contract had been made. Upon disembarkation they were seized by a runner in the pay of Keenan, another agent, who led them to Keenan's office under the pretence that it was Shaw's. Here they each paid the remaining £4, and in the event were unable to obtain redress and actually lost their passages to America.[1]

To prevent long detentions and to husband the tiny capital of the emigrants, the passenger acts from 1835 on entitled them to receive one shilling for every day they were delayed beyond their appointed sailing date.[2] This requirement was a useful check. But sailing dates and contract tickets could not always be determined at law, and in any event the sum was an inadequate compensation: maintenance at Liverpool cost considerably more.[3] As often as not, moreover, emigrants made no efforts to recover their money. In general they were, according to experienced witnesses, 'exceedingly thoughtless and confiding', 'very simple', 'with no craft at all'.[4] Frequently they knew nothing of their rights or were easily cajoled to surrender them by the agent or his runner.[5] Moreover, the temptation to be off as quickly as possible and to have done with all the preliminaries to embarkation was very great. It was extremely difficult to persuade passengers to bring an action or even tender evidence in court.[6] For legal proceedings usually meant delays which they could not afford, and, however good their case, a successful prosecution was rarely certain. By the 1840s brokers and runners had had long experience of the petty sessions, and knew to a nicety just how close to the wind they might safely sail.

Over and above sharp practice in tickets, sailing dates and detention money, there was a multitude of absolute frauds. Shipping houses refused to honour orders drawn upon them by their New

---

[1] *Nation*, 23 May 1846. For other descriptions of this type of abuse see C.O. 384/41, 524, 583 and 605 Emigration, 2, 11 and 14 Apr. 1836; *8th rep. C.L.E.C.*, 18 [961], H.C. 1847–8, xxvi.

[2] 5 & 6 Will., IV, c.53, sec. 14 and 5 & 6 Vic., c. 107, sec. 22.

[3] *2nd rep. select comm. emigrant ships*, 25, 160, Q.3571–7, 5927–39, H.C. 1854 (349), xiii (evidence of Capt. Schomberg and Lieut. de Courcy).

[4] Ibid., 87, 95, Q.4612, 4749–51 (evidence of J. Besnard and J. Duross). See also ibid., 56–7, Q.4014–61.

[5] *1st rep. select comm. emigrant ships*, 126, Q.2299–320, H.C. 1854 (163), xiii.

[6] C.O. 384/35, 2101 Emigration, 14 May 1834; *Rep. select comm. passenger acts*, 478–81, 492–3, Q.4232–47, 4355–9, H.C. 1851 (632), xix.

York agents;[1] brokers suddenly declared themselves bankrupt,
leaving tens or even hundreds of emigrant-creditors in despair;[2]
agents played upon the ignorance of the departing passengers and
sent them a thousand miles north or south of their ultimate destination;[3] confidence men sold them holdings in the state of Texas.[4]
Such things happened almost daily during the season, and a large
proportion of them never came to light. Small wonder, then, that the
reputation of Liverpool should have sunk so low that several German governments attempted to ban it altogether to their emigrants.[5]
Even the mayor admitted in 1849 that the 'Emigrants are all
strangers . . . with whom there is no kindly sympathy, and the
maxim appears to be to get all out of them they can'.[6] But these
abuses would, of course, have grown up in any great mid-nineteenth-
century city with docklands and a comparable volume of emigration.
The fact that, as we shall see, they were matched almost exactly,
both in event and in particulars, by the system then obtaining in
New York is sufficient proof of this. Only in two respects, the preliminary steamer passage and the prohibition upon early embarkation, had Liverpool peculiar disadvantages. Otherwise, the relative
freedom of the Irish and the other British ports can be attributed
solely to the smallness of their emigrations.

III

The difference in scale between Liverpool and the other ports of
departure can be seen clearly from the embarkation statistics for the
years 1834–6 and 1840–72, published by the agent-general for emigration and the colonial land and emigration commissioners.[7] The
agent-general's figures show that both Liverpool and the combined
Irish ports averaged some 22,000 annually in the mid-1830s; that at
this time, four Irish ports, Cork, Dublin, Londonderry and Belfast,

[1] *2nd rep. Emigrant Society*, pp. 2–8; C.O. 386/20, 21 Nov. 1837; C.O. 386/21,
30 Nov. 1837.
[2] E.g., C.O. 384/86, 4035 North American Emigration, 5 May 1851.
[3] E.g., *11th rep. C.L.E.C.*, 8–9, [1383], H.C. 1851, xxii.
[4] E.g., *Morning Chronicle*, 15 July 1850; *Tipperary Vindicator*, 4 Aug. 1847.
[5] *2nd rep. select comm. emigrant ships*, 40, Q.3767, H.C. 1854, (349), xiii.
[6] C.O. 384/83, 9485 Emigration, 31 Oct. 1849.
[7] For the agent-general's statistics, see *Rep. agent-general emigration U.K.*
14–15, H.C. 1837–8 (388), xl; for the commissioners' statistics, see their annual
reports published in the parliamentary papers from 1842 onwards.

fell into the 3,000–5,000 category, and three others, Sligo, Limerick and Waterford, into the 1,000–3,000 category; and that, London and Glasgow excepted, no other port in the United Kingdom contributed significantly to the emigration. The commissioners' figures show that during the years 1840–60, Liverpool averaged nearly 150,000 annually, rising in a few seasons almost to 200,000, whereas no other United Kingdom port ever exceeded Cork's 17,000 in 1847. Generally speaking, the Irish trade was well distributed and consisted mainly of emigrants drawn from the immediate vicinity of the particular ports. In the commissioners' tables, either Cork or Limerick came first in most seasons.[1] Each of these ports could count on seven to ten thousand persons annually in the decade 1845–54. Next came the lesser ports serving other regions; Sligo, which drained north Connacht; Belfast and Londonderry, the former outlets for the presbyterian emigration, which now served most of Ulster between them; and Waterford and New Ross, which covered the counties of Wexford and Kilkenny and the south-east tip of Munster. They averaged between three and six thousand during the years of heaviest Irish emigration. Dublin drew emigrants from all parts, but its own total was usually small.[2] Apart from these 'regular' emigration ports, Galway, Wexford, Tralee and Donegal were the only others of any significance, though emigration took place, from time to time, from many smaller harbours and inlets, when shipping happened to be available, or the demand for passages was so keen that the masters of the little vessels felt that the Atlantic crossing was worth gambling on.[3]

Thus, the passenger trade in Ireland was on a very small scale, and essentially local and traditional in character. This was its best guarantee against systematic fraud. For, firstly, there was relatively little profit to be made from four or five thousand emigrants, or even

---

[1] Sligo was second in importance amongst Irish ports in the early 1840s, but sank rapidly in the scale after 1845. In the first phase of nineteenth-century Irish emigration, 1815–30, when Ulster and the north midlands still predominated, Belfast, Dublin and Londonderry were the leading Irish ports. Before about 1825 Irish emigration via Liverpool was very small.

[2] Greenock must be counted amongst the 'regular' ports of Irish emigration. Two to three thousand Irish emigrants embarked there annually during the years of heavy emigration.

[3] For the geographical distribution of Irish emigration between 1846 and 1851, see S. H. Cousens, 'The regional pattern of emigration during the great Irish famine, 1846–51', *Trans. Institute British Geographers, 1960*, pp. 119–34.

ten. Then again, the passengers would probably have known something of their own localities; many doubtless derived from the ports
in question or had relatives who dwelt there. And finally, the
emigration officers could cope with, and, if necessary, intimidate
the small group of brokers and shippers within their jurisdiction.
When the officers were first appointed in 1834, they found, as we
shall see, the Irish trade riddled with abuses. Yet within a decade
much of this had been checked. There were still habitual offenders
under the passenger acts, who detained passengers beyond the
appointed sailing date, or overcrowded their vessels, or provided
bad food and water. But, on the whole, the embarkations went off
smoothly once an officer had learnt his way about an Irish port. In
what was usually a small community, he could use his personal
authority and private information in a way that was not possible at
Liverpool,[1] and he often exercised an extraordinary influence over
the local trade. He could also assist emigrants in informal ways,
such as mobilizing public opinion against abuses, or enlisting the
support of the clergy and inhabitants for the relief of occasional
distress.[2] Moreover, his task was rendered easy by the general Irish
custom of permitting passengers, if they wished, to board their
vessels when they came to town.[3]

But Cork, the first emigration port of Ireland, was a partial exception
to these generalizations. Three reasons may be suggested for this:
first, that if we include the Cork emigration via Liverpool, which
averaged at least 25,000 a year in the mid-century, its total volume[4]
of emigration was much larger than that of any other Irish port;
second, that its passenger trade appears to have been in particularly
bad hands during the 1830s and 1840s;[5] and third, that a very high

---

[1] *2nd rep. select comm. emigrant ships*, 132, Q.5469, H.C. 1854 (349), xiii
(evidence of Capt. Kerr); ibid., 159–60, Q.5910–26 (evidence of Lieut. de
Courcy); C.O. 384/35, 3608 Emigration, 8 Sept. 1834. See also *Cork Constitution*, 21 Nov. 1846 and 30 Mar. 1847; *Nation*, 11 Apr. 1846, p. 412.

[2] Cf. *1st rep. select comm. emigrant ships*, 116, H.C. 1854 (163), xiii; C.O.
384/69, 574 Emigration, 23 Mar. 1842. The catholic clergy had, of course, an
extraordinary social and civic influence in Ireland in the nineteenth century, and
this naturally affected emigration, see O. MacDonagh, 'The Irish catholic clergy
and emigration during the great famine', *Irish Hist. Stud.* (1947), pp. 287–302.

[3] *Rep. select comm. passenger acts*, 626–7, Q.5717–26, H.C. 1851 (632), xix.

[4] *2nd rep. select comm. emigrant ships*, 85, Q.4568–86, H.C. 1854 (349), xiii.

[5] C.O. 384/35, 1626 and 1931 Emigration, 12 Apr. and 4 May 1834; C.O.
386/34, pp. 49–50, 18 Aug. 1834; C.O. 384/80, 1364 Emigration, circular of
J. Besnard; *Southern Reporter*, 16 May 1843; *Limerick Chronicle*, 17 Aug. 1844.

proportion of the direct emigrants spent some time in lodgings before their embarkation. John Besnard, who had twenty years' experience of the Cork emigration, estimated the average stay of emigrants in the city before the sailing at no less than nine or ten days. They lodged, he said, in the 'lowest and filthiest' houses on the north side of Lee, where they were freely imposed upon. The lodgings were not regulated, inspected or licensed; the charge was a mere three-pence a night; but the keepers made their profits by impositions upon the poor country people. Besnard considered that the system in Cork differed from that of Liverpool in scale alone. Though the runners were not, of course, nearly so numerous at Cork, they were equally 'unprincipled' and their methods were identical.[1] Duross, the constable in charge of passenger regulation at the port from 1849 to 1854, corroborated Besnard's testimony completely. Just as at Liverpool, he said, the runners received commissions on all trans-actions, and the emigrants were induced to buy trashy goods and utensils and bad provisions. Duross's general conclusion was that the Cork passengers were 'defrauded from the day they start from their homes until they are at sea'.[2]

Significantly, the Cork trade appears to have been at its worst during the year of largest emigration, 1847. According to Fr Mathew, the temperance 'apostle', who knew the city well, 'the rogues called brokers' were adding two shillings to the cost of every pound of sea-stock in the spring,[3] and other abuses were so scandalous that the city magistrates 'declared war' upon the 'trafficking' in human be-ings, and the emigration officer threatened to withdraw a large number of licences if such behaviour continued, and actually publi-cized some of the worst offences in the hope of shaming the Cork trade into decent conduct.[4] For the consequences of postponed passages, decayed provisions and ticket frauds were very tragic in 1847. 'No tongue can describe, no understanding can conceive', said Mathew, 'the misery and wretchedness that flowed into Cork'

[1] *Rep. select comm. passenger acts*, 694–5, 707–8, Q.6468–70, 6596–609, H.C. 1851, (632), xix. Besnard had acted as an agent for the government in organizing assisted emigration from Cork to Australia, and he was also the manager of an emigrants' home.

[2] *2nd rep. select comm. emigrant ships*, 80–2, Q.4474–515, H.C. 1854 (349), xiii.

[3] *Rep. select comm. colonization Ire.*, 243, Q.2359–61 [737], H.C. 1847, vi.

[4] *Cork Constitution*, 27 Mar. and 1 May 1847; *Cork Examiner*, 5 Apr. 1847; *Limerick Chronicle*, 1, 5 and 26 May 1847; *Nation*, 13 Mar. 1847.

from Kerry and the west. Hundreds had to wait patiently for vessels until their funds were completely exhausted; and when fever broke out amongst them, they were turned out of their lodgings to die miserably in the narrow streets, alleys and cellars. Those who did secure passages were scarcely more fortunate. Bernard testified that people who had contracted typhus in lodgings went aboard almost every Cork vessel of the season, and that the medical inspection was negligible, and the emigration officer's scarcely more effective.[1] All this was paralleled, though on a lesser scale, in Limerick.[2] Because of the number of complaints in the first six months of 1847, the magistrates of the city resolved to renew no broker's licence unless he were approved by a general meeting of the shipping trade at which the local emigration officer was also present.[3] Here we have an instance of what could occur in Ireland, when the emigration became unusually large and the demand on shipping unusually keen. Together with the first part of our sketch of the passenger trade in Cork, it bears out the conclusion that it was only the smallness and regularity of their emigrations which preserved the lesser ports from the worst abuses of Liverpool and New York.

IV

The next stage of the problem was the ocean crossing. Down to 1850, emigration was a subordinate interest of the Atlantic merchantmen, and suffered accordingly. The trade had grown up haphazardly. An experienced emigration officer described its development at Liverpool as follows. At first emigrants came to the port from all quarters without bookings. They relied for advice on lodging-keepers, who soon fell to extracting commissions from the masters for introductions to their vessels. Around 1817, with emigration 'tolerably regular', 'speculators' began chartering between-decks space for passengers. They paid a fixed sum for the space: their profit depended on the number they could cram into it. Most were brokers and merchants together, and gained from supplying the passengers for the voyage as well as from the passage contracts. 'The evils arising out of this state of things were soon developed. 1st. The

---

[1] *1st rep. select comm. colonization Ire.*, 181, Q.1934–9, H.C. 1847–8 (415), xvii.
[2] *Limerick Chronicle*, 8, 19, and 22 May 1847.
[3] Ibid., 14 July 1847.

detention of the emigrants at their own cost and at considerable expense in a strange place . . . 2d. The insufficiency of the vessels . . . many inferior and second-class vessels being chartered for that purpose, while the ignorance of the emigrants prevented them from ascertaining or attempting to ascertain the charterers of them. 3d. The want of sufficient space, there being no effective regulating control. 4th. The engaging of a greater number than the vessel could legally carry; in consequence of which many were frequently turned on shore by the masters . . . and the poor creatures were left without any redress'.[1] The chief immigration physician of Canada confirmed that many of these early practices survived (and in the Irish ports as well as Liverpool) as late as 1840. The common practice, he wrote, was for groups of speculating brokers to charter the space on out-going timber vessels for a small sum, in return for which the owners provided berths and water. Sub-agents were then sent through the country to 'ferret out' passengers. Paid by commission to drum up trade, the sub-agents naturally told prospective emigrants that the voyage was short, that they would need little food at sea, that the master would take care of everything, and so on. 'Thus, hundreds of Irish labourers are induced to embark for this country with but a scanty supply of oatmeal and potatoes for the voyage; often with no clothes but what they have on, and a bundle of straw for a bed'. The customs officers almost always accepted the captain's word that enough provisions had been put aboard. But the captain had not made the contract, and 'though, like most seamen, he invariably declares that his passengers have a confounded lot of baggage', he actually knew nothing and cared less about his unwanted charges; and was usually quite wrong.[2] All this helps to explain why so many passengers set sail in circumstances which invited hunger, cold and death.

The extreme hardships of the years 1800–35 were slowly mitigated in the late 1830s and especially after 1842. But even down to 1855 the inherent evils of a trade which had grown out of chartering remained. Worst of all perhaps was the fact that the emigrants were accepted by owners and captains (who had often no direct responsibility for the passage contracts) only with the utmost reluctance and as a necessary evil. Freights were occasionally too high and

[1] *Rep. poor inquiry commrs Ire.*, Appendix G, 34–35, H.C. 1836, xxxiv.
[2] *Corres. rel. emigration Canada*, 57 [298], H.C. 1841, xv.

speed too important for owners to undergo the irritations and restrictions which carrying passengers involved.[1] But in general they were indispensable. The Irish Atlantic vessels were principally engaged in the timber, potash and grain trades, and predominantly the first; the Liverpool vessels depended upon cotton and timber.[2] These imports demanded ships with large, broad holds, for which there were either no outward cargoes at all or insufficient outward cargoes to fill the space.[3] In consequence, the shippers were forced to turn to emigrants. None wanted them as such; but the alternative was to sail in ballast and at a total loss. All this engendered in owners an indifference to the discomforts of the emigrants, and in masters a hostility and contempt which survived even to the days when passengers constituted a trade in their own right. From first to last it was the root of many of the troubles.

This casual traffic had advantages for emigrants. Only at times of the most extraordinary pressure did shipping run short; and even then the deficiencies were rapidly supplied.[4] The low standards meant that almost anything above eighty tons which floated could be diverted to the carriage of passengers in an emergency. It also meant that fares were low, because of the sharp competition amongst merchantmen and the shipper's want of access to alternatives. 'The

[1] *Rep. select comm. colonization Ire.*, 482–3, appendix iii, 16, [737], H.C. 1847, vi.
[2] By 1848, a three-cornered traffic, New Orleans or some other southern port to Liverpool with cotton, Liverpool to the Atlantic states with emigrants, and New York to the south with manufactured goods, coals or hard cargoes, was an established pattern, *Liverpool Mercury*, quoted by *Freeman's Journal*, 4 Apr. 1849. To give an example of an Irish port, all Limerick's transatlantic vessels were engaged in the import of timber, staves and deal. As the port had nothing to send out but human beings, every ship was regularly employed in carrying them to Quebec or St John (or Boston or New York before proceeding northwards) in the spring and summer. The Limerick ships spent the winter months in the coastal trade in provisions, coal and iron with Glasgow, Liverpool or South Wales, *Rep. select comm. colonization Ire.*, 213–14, 332–4 [737], H.C. 1847, vi; *Shipping Intelligence* in the *Limerick Chronicle* and *Limerick Reporter*. Derry had a similar pattern of trade with Philadelphia, whence she had imported flour and maize for several decades, sending for the most part only emigrants in return, *Rep. select comm. passenger acts*, 618–23, Q.5625–87, H.C. 1851 (632), xix.
[3] The only exports of significance were manufactured goods, chemicals and, in the later years, pig and bar iron and rails. The Irish ports sent out very little even of these.
[4] C.O. 384/79, 660 Emigration, 22 Apr. 1847. The emigration commissioners always maintained, rightly in event, that 'the ordinary course of Trade would supply vessels'.

Irish Timber Vessels', wrote Wilmot Horton, the tireless colonizer, in 1825, 'necessarily go without freight and can therefore . . . transport Emigrants much below the price of a vessel expressly chartered for the purpose'.[1] At this stage, when an organized trade scarcely existed, a passage might cost as little as 30s. or as much as 90s., according to the equally erratic demand and supply of shipping space and clients.[2] By the early 1830s rates had settled down to roughly 70s. from Liverpool, 55s. from Dublin and Cork and 45s. from the western Irish ports, with provisions for the voyage standing (in theory, at least) at about 40s. more at Liverpool, and 30s. in Ireland.[3] In the mid-1840s, when owners had to spend something on preparing the vessels for the emigrants and also to furnish a portion of the provisions, the fares rose only to a £3–£5 bracket.[4] They increased for a time to £5–£7 during the Irish famine crisis;[5] but soon relapsed to £3 10s.–£5, at which level they remained despite increasingly heavy burdens upon the shippers, including the provision of all the food for passengers.[6] Eventually, they fell still lower. As Carter, a leading London shipper, had prophesied in 1847, when the trade became fixed and certain on a large scale, rates tended to decline and vessels to improve.[7] These fares may have been beyond the reach of hundreds of thousands who wished to emigrate, and may for many years have given the emigrants little in return. But at no stage could they have been accounted dear.

[1] C.O. 324/95, pp. 13–14, 5 Feb. 1825.
[2] The actual fares charged always varied of course according to individual circumstances and bargaining, and the original contracts were often broken and 'revised', C.O. 384/80, 1333 Emigration; *2nd rep. select comm. emigrant ships*, 45–6, H.C. 1854 (349), xiii.
[3] *Rep. Mr. Richards respecting waste lands Canadas*, 23–26, H.C. 1833 (334), xxxii; *Rep. poor inquiry commrs Ire.*, Appendix G, 33–4, H.C. 1836, xxxiv.
[4] *Rep. select comm. colonization Ire.*, 446, Q.4427 [737], H.C. 1847, vi.
[5] Ibid., 210, 249, 446, Q.2045, 2419, 4427; C.O. 384/79, 660 Emigration, 22 Apr. 1847.
[6] C.O. 384/88, 158 Canada Emigration, 8 Jan. 1850; *Correspondence rel. emigration N.A. colonies*, 12, H.C. 1857 (14), x; ibid., 6–7, H.C. 1857 (125), xxviii.
[7] *Rep. select comm. colonization Ire.*, 482–3, Q.4507–18 [737], H.C. 1847, vi. There was another secular change in the structure of the trade. Down to 1850 or so, the fares on vessels sailing from Irish ports, on British vessels generally and on vessels bound for British North America tended to be cheaper, respectively, than the fares on vessels from Liverpool, on American vessels and on vessels bound for the United States. In each case the relationship was gradually reversed during the 1850s.

But here the merits of the passenger trade in the first fifty years of the nineteenth century began and ended. The primacy of commerce meant that the emigrants had to follow shipping wherever it was concentrated, and this led the majority to Liverpool and New York. It also meant the use of vessels which were thoroughly unsuitable for passengers. Down to 1850 few drew over 400 tons.[1] In fact, the average tonnage of the vessels employed in the carriage of passengers between 1800 and 1850 was probably about 300. Yet these little ships carried 200 to 250 passengers, and in the early years much more. There were many cases in which the number of the people aboard equalled or even exceeded the tonnage of the vessel. The shallow draught and breadth of timber and cotton ships rendered them heavy-rolling 'sailers'.[2] Their wide holds precluded the use of permanent upper decks; and the substitutes or 'temporaries' were no more than bare planks laid across the ship's beams, never sealed or cleansed.[3] Finally, they were slow, often adding a week or fortnight to the crossing which proved fatal to the weak and hungry passengers. All this was true of the run-of-the-mill cargo ships; but some were still more disgraceful. Wooden brigs built in the 1760s were still plying to the St Lawrence in 1845; one ship regularly employed in the New Brunswick run was officially described as a 'mere tub, altogether unfit for the passenger trade';[4] another was found in 1847 to have a leaking hull and rigging rotted through;[5] and these are but a few of many instances. The years 1815–50 marked, moreover, the nadir of the British mercantile marine. Generally, there was an over-supply of transatlantic shipping, and the Americans were steadily gaining ground. The only response of the British ship-owners was to cut costs, even at the expense of safety and seamanship. 'They spent too little on the construction of a ship, on its maintenance, and on the training and welfare of the crew. The result was a general deterioration . . . . Masters and mates were unqualified;

---

[1] *7th rep. C.L.E.C.*, 63 [809], H.C. 1847, xxxiii; *Rep. select. comm. passenger acts*, 494–5, H.C. 1851 (632), xix. There are a large number of partial statistics on the size of vessels scattered through the official papers.

[2] They were sometimes known as 'kettle bottoms' in the trade, *Papers rel. emigration B.N.A.*, 34, H.C. 1851 (348), xl. See also *Further papers emigration B.N.A.*, 8–17, 42–50 [964], H.C. 1847–8, xlvii.

[3] *2nd rep. select comm. colonization Ire.*, 345, Q.3306, H.C. 1847–8, (593), xvii.

[4] *Papers rel. emigration B.N.A.*, 53, 58 [1474], H.C. 1852, xxxiii.

[5] *Cork Constitution*, 8 May 1847.

they received little or no schooling, had too little experience and were not examined for competence or knowledge, even of navigation. Sailors were even more the subject of complaint'.[1] The sad consequences bore this out. Down to 1840 shipwrecks and putting back in distress were almost everyday occurrences, with bad vessels, bad navigation and drunken ship's officers sharing the blame in more or less equal parts. Even in the 1850s, when all these matters had improved incomparably, more than forty emigrant ships perished in the Atlantic. American vessels enjoyed, and deserved, a better reputation.[2] They were superior in speed, accommodation and design[3]—in all in fact except the humanity of their masters and crews—and were usually sought after despite their higher fares. But to the pre-1850 emigrants the difference between the average and best vessels was only marginal—a barely perceptible distinction in the degree of misery to be endured at sea.

'How, then', wrote Melville of his *Highlander* (incidentally a first-rank New England merchantman), 'with the friendless emigrants, stowed away like bales of cotton, and packed like slaves in a slave ship; confined in a place that during storm time, must be closed against both light and air, who can do no cooking, nor warm so much as a cup of water? . . . Nor is this all . . . passengers are cut off from the most indispensable conveniences of a civilized dwelling. . . . We had not been at sea one week, when to hold your head down the fore-hatchway was like holding it down a suddenly opened cess pool'. Melville scarcely exaggerated. Even after the reforming legislation of 1842 there was little more than two square feet of clear space for each passenger, in the quarters in which he would have to dwell for forty days or more. Only a child could stand upright in the usual low-ceilinged steerage. There was little, or perhaps no ventilation except through the open hatchways; there was none at all when the between-decks was battened in bad weather.

[1] R. Prouty, *The transformation of the board of trade* (London, 1957), pp. 32–33.

[2] C.O. 384/35, 2800 Canada, 14 June 1834; C.O. 384/82, 1768 Emigration, 9 Sept. 1848; C.O. 384/88, 158 Canada, 8 Jan. 1850.

[3] R. G. Albion, *The rise of New York port* (New York, 1939), pp. 330–40; Prouty, op. cit., p. 32. The one superiority claimed for British vessels was the absence of the elaborate superstructure which often precluded exercise on American ships, *Rep. select comm. passenger acts*, 485–6, Q.4288–93, H.C. 1851 (632), xix. But this was relatively unimportant.

There was no sanitary system whatsoever on most vessels before 1850, and never one which worked; and there was no privacy. Men and women had to clothe and unclothe (if they did), and 'relieve nature', as it was delicately put, in sight of one another. Some did not even bring 'utensils' aboard, and more or less filth (and with it dangerous bacteria) accumulated on the floors, and especially beneath the bottom row of berths. The wooden berths, in layers little more than two feet high, and only six square feet in area, bedded at least four people—often more. On nine vessels out of ten no attempt was made to separate the sexes before it was made obligatory to do so in 1849; and as late as 1860 the separation was not effectively enforced. Even young girls travelling alone were allotted beds at random with other passengers. Some sat on their bundles night after night rather than expose themselves to molestation. *The Times*, discussing accounts of the crossing collected from newly arrived immigrants in New York in 1853, observed, 'There is a disgusting and repulsive uniformity in the process. . . . The emigrant is shown a berth, a shelf of coarse pinewood, situated in a noisome dungeon, airless and lightless, in which several hundred persons of both sexes and all ages are stowed away on shelves two feet one inch above the other, three feet wide[1] and six feet long, still reeking from the ineradicable stench left by the emigrants of the last voyage'.[2]

The first two or three days out were usually marred by sea-sickness. This in small, unstable cargo ships, was not so trivial as it might seem. Several observers emphasized that it might even determine the whole subsequent fate of the emigrants. The steerage was fouled; the passengers were weakened; and in reaction they ate 'extravagantly'. By the time the vessel reached the region of the Newfoundland banks many had exhausted their stocks of food just as the weather turned cold and damp. Thus commonly began a vicious circle of malnutrition, inertia and disease.[3] So long as the passengers supplied themselves entirely—that is, down to 1842—they were always liable to hunger in the end; and for the first few years after the vessels were compelled to furnish a little breadstuffs, the

---

[1] By 1853 only two adult passengers were permitted by law to share each berth: hence the width was halved.
[2] *The Times*, 27 Dec. 1853.
[3] *Corres. rel. emigration Canada*, 57 [298], H.C. 1841, xv; *Rep. select comm. passenger acts*, xxiii, 417-20, H.C. 1851 (632), xix; *1st rep. select comm. emigrant ships*, 83, Q.1400-15, H.C. 1854 (163), xiii.

standard of their provisions was disgraceful.[1] Some ships provided no means of cooking whatsoever; and even the best left hordes of passengers to brawl and struggle around one, or at most two stoves. Water was always the owner's responsibility, and from first to last a likely source of infectious disease. An investigation in 1848 disclosed that at nearly half the Irish ports ordinary river water was taken aboard for the passengers to drink[2]—and no attempt was made subsequently to remedy this evil. The casks (often old rum or molasses puncheons) were sweetened by being soaked in quicklime; and water commonly ran short because of leakages.

Inevitably, the fear of sickness overhung the vessels. Even the most ignorant emigrant knew the consequences if an epidemic, typhus or cholera, broke out at sea. Once an infectious disease struck, there was no knowing how it might be arrested. Medicines were crude and scanty; and not one vessel in fifty carried a medical officer on board. This hopelessness often bred a fatal apathy in passengers which led them to sink without resistance into disease, and to neglect the simplest precautions.[3] Sometimes the sick were shunned from fear; there were even cases where the dead were left for hours, or days, between-decks until someone took courage and cast them overboard.[4] If the disease spread to the officers and crew, the misfortunes and the terror multiplied. This is no melodramatic representation: more horrifying accounts abound amongst the official papers; and while thousands of passenger vessels did cross the Atlantic in the years 1800–60 without loss of life, there were hundreds on which the scenes which we have outlined were reproduced. Down to 1840 a very great number of vessels—perhaps even a majority—suffered mortalities from deficiency and other diseases on the crossing. Even thereafter terrible epidemics swept the trade, especially during 1846–9, 1851 and 1853–4. Death-rates at sea of 10 per cent or more of all the passengers on particular vessels were

[1] As late as 1848 the bread on one vessel was described by the New Brunswick emigration officer as mouldered, dirty and crawling with maggots, *Papers rel. emigration B.N.A.*, 19–20, [985], H.C. 1847–8, xlvii. See also *Papers rel. emigration B.N.A.*, 110–15, 181 in (50) and 14 in [932], H.C. 1847–8, xlvii; *2nd rep. select comm. colonization Ire.*, 490–1, H.C. 1847–8 (593), xvii; Albion, op. cit., p. 343.

[2] *Papers rel. emigration B.N.A.*, 183–5, H.C. 1847–8 (50), xlvii.

[3] *Papers rel. emigration B.N.A.*, 13–14 in (50) and 17 in [964], H.C. 1847–8, xlvii; C.O. 384/79, 535 Canada, 1848.

[4] There were also examples of dignity and heroism, e.g., *3rd rep. select colonization Ire.*, Appendix X, 125–32, H.C. 1849 (86), xi.

not uncommon in the worst seasons; death-rates of 40 per cent and upwards were not unknown. Then there followed the mortalities upon disembarkation.

All this constituted, in outline, the problem of the Atlantic passage.[1]

V

The last stage in the emigrant's journey, his arrival in the new world, does not concern us directly. For the most part, it lay outside the scope of the legislation and executive control of the United Kingdom. But because the British and American protective systems impinged on one another, and because it was the same victims who were involved at every stage, it may not be irrelevant to give at least some indication of the ulterior difficulties. Here we may take New York, where more than half the total immigration entered the United States, as the counterpart of Liverpool. New York was, in this respect, Liverpool through the looking glass. The sequence was reversed but the abuses were virtually the same. Down to 1847 all masters of emigrant vessels arriving at New York had to enter bonds indemnifying the state against expenses arising from the illness or indigence of their passengers. Doubtless this irritated masters and (perhaps its real purpose) held down direct immigration to New York. But it also exposed sick and distressed immigrants to barbarous treatment. The masters almost invariably transferred their liability under the bonds to brokers with little money and no scruples: the so-called homes maintained by the brokers were, one and all, inhumanly conducted.[2] This particular evil was eradicated by 1848, the bond arrangement having been altered in the preceding year. But the remaining system of abuses still defied reform. The first problem was to convey the passengers from the vessels to the docks without their falling into the clutches of the boatmen in league with runners. The second was to safeguard the immigrants on the docks themselves. The third was to keep them out of evil lodgings and saloons. The runners (mostly Gaelic- or German-, as well as English-speaking) played essentially the same role as their counterparts at Liverpool. Having seized the immigrants (or what

[1] Where no references have been given in the section above for particular aspects of the passage, they will be provided below when these features are discussed in greater detail.

[2] Schneider, op. cit., pp. 300–10.

amounted to the same thing, their baggage) they led them to the lodging-keepers, travel agents, provisioners, money-changers and the rest, with whom they were in collusion and from whom they received commissions for the introductions. The subsequent fraud and imposition exceeded, if anything, that at Liverpool. Official inquiries of the New York state legislature and the New York emigration commission in the late 1840s disclosed cases of immigrants being manhandled and robbed upon landing; of lodging-keepers, in the worst slums of the slum-ridden city, extorting money from the ignorant or stealing their few belongings; and of moral turpitude. Short of these extremities, abuses amongst the transport and forwarding agencies, which sold rail and canal tickets to the interior, were widespread; and, according to the emigration commissioners, very serious in their results. 'I and others engaged in the business', one ticket-broker admitted, 'get all we can from the passengers, except that I never shave a lady when travelling alone. . . . I have all I can get over a certain amount which is paid to the transportation companies'.[1] Other common sources of fraud included the sale of western lands, the procuring of employment and the 'dollaring' of sterling and continental currencies. In short, New York was already a city of 'rackets', even if on a petty scale; and for many of them the immigrant was a natural victim. The counter-measures undertaken by the city and state of New York between 1848 and 1858 radically changed the pattern, and provided immigrants with a higher degree of protection than they were ever to enjoy at the ports of embarkation. But as late as 1866, after nearly twenty years of labour, the New York emigration commissioners could still report, 'The work never ceases; new schemes of fraud spring up whenever occasion offers'.[2] No other port in North America was subject to

[1] *State of New York in assembly no. 46*, 8 Jan. 1848, evidence of C. Webb.
[2] This account of the abuses in New York is based on ibid.; *2nd rep. select comm. colonization Ire.*, 333–48 (evidence of R. B. Minturn, a New York emigration commissioner) and *3rd rep.*, Appendix Q (extracts of evidence before the New York legislature), H.C. 1847–8 (593), xvii and H.C. 1849 (86), xi; *1st, 2nd* and *20th annual reports of the New York commissioners of emigration*, 1847, 1848 and 1866; *Papers rel. emigration B.N.A.*, 78–90 (text of New York regulations), H.C. 1849 (593.–II), xxxviii; *Nation*, 14 Aug. and 27 Oct. 1849, pp. 712 and 135 respectively; C.O. 384/88, 9004 Emigration, 25 Sept. 1851; A. J. Peyton, *The emigrant's friend* (Cork, 1853), p. 15; Maguire, op. cit., pp. 184–210. See also R. J. Purcell, 'The Irish Emigration Society of New York' and 'The New York commissioners of emigration 1847–60', *Studies*, xxvii, pp. 587–94 and xxxvii, pp. 28–42.

the same complex of social evils as New York. But according to the volume of immigration which they attracted, Boston, Philadelphia, Baltimore and New Orleans all suffered, more or less, from the extortioners.

3

THE FIRST LEGISLATION
1803-28

THE laborious process of improving the conditions of voluntary emigration began—formally, at any rate—with the passenger act of 1803. The background to this, the first of a long line of statutes, was very curious. Generally speaking, eighteenth-century emigration was extremely small both in terms of the total number involved and in terms of the number of passengers on each vessel. In the two decades before the French Revolutionary wars, however, there was some foreshadowing of the things to come. The new British North America and the newly independent states had each particular attractions for certain classes; and, perhaps more important for our purpose, the clearances in the Scottish highlands and to a lesser extent in Ireland tended to swell greatly the numbers emigrating in particular seasons and also to provide extraordinarily large complements of passengers on particular vessels. Such a 'density' was to be the crux of the emigrant problem in the nineteenth century; but in so far as the occasional increases in emigration engaged public attention at all before 1793, it was not this but the time-honoured 'threat of depopulation' which was canvassed.

The main agitator of the question was the Highland Society of Scotland, founded in 1787 to preserve the population and culture of that region. This was an influential body, composed mainly of landed proprietors who, through Henry Dundas, possessed the ear of government[1]—and possessed it to such effect as to obtain a parliamentary grant for the restitution of highland estates. The society was, of course, firmly opposed to emigration; but its activities had scarcely begun before the outflow was checked by the opening of hostilities with France. The situation changed dramatically with the signing of the Peace of Amiens. Even in 1801, several hundred highlanders sailed for North America; in the following year 3,000 did

---

[1] H. I. Cowan, *British emigration to British North America, 1783-1837* (Toronto, 1928), pp. 22-23.

so; and it was believed on every side that these movements were but a prelude to a much vaster exodus in the coming season. So threatened, the Highland Society, in conjunction and possibly in collusion with Charles Hope, lord-advocate of Scotland and M.P. for Edinburgh, began to press the government strongly to take some deterrent action.[1] They were rewarded by the appointment of Thomas Telford, the civil engineer, to conduct a survey of 'the coasts and central highlands of Scotland' in the autumn of 1802. Telford was instructed to investigate both the possibilities of opening up the region by new communications and the development of indigenous industries, and 'the causes of emigration and the means of preventing it'.[2]

Telford's report on communications, industries and emigration was printed in April 1803. As to the last, Telford agreed with the common, though not undisputed, opinion that the main cause of highland emigration was the conversion of settled lands to sheepwalks. He went on to say that 'regulations might be made to prevent landowners lessening population below a certain proportion', but he himself considered that the emigration would very probably prove beneficial in the long run.[3] He added that almost 10,000 highlanders might be expected to emigrate in 1803. This report was referred at once to a select committee of the house of commons, which included Hope amongst its members. The committee in turn reported with extraordinary dispatch—within five weeks—but it reported only upon emigration in the first instance upon the ground that this was a matter of extraordinary urgency and interest. Yet its recommendation was not concerned at all with the original subject of inquiry, depopulation, but to the effect that the very great distress which was being caused by overcrowding and inadequate provisioning on the emigrant ships should be checked at once by regulation.[4] Thus, to all appearances fortuitously, did the first of the passenger acts come into being.

How is the extraordinary diversion in the select committee's

[1] In support of its campaign, the society sent copies of its report on the regulation of emigration and on highland improvement to Henry Dundas, several members of the cabinet and other influential people, *Trans. Highland Soc. Scotland* (1803), vol. ii, pp. viii–ix.

[2] *Survey and report by Thomas Telford*, 3, H.C. 1802–3, iv.

[3] Ibid., 15–16. Telford admitted that the dispossessed crofters suffered hardship, but argued that 'the empire' would benefit by the increased production of food consequent on their removal.

[4] *1st rep. comm. survey and report Scotland*, 4–5, H.C., 1802–3, iv.

interest to be explained? The answer lies in the original agitation of the Highland Society for government intervention. In the course of its campaign in 1801–2, the society had conducted its own investigation into the 'momentous' subject of emigration; and in the course of this inquiry there had come to light, doubtless unexpectedly, some very dreadful instances of suffering and imposition in the passenger trade.[1] When the select committee of the commons was deliberating the same matter in April and May 1803, the evidence, oral and documentary, which the society had gathered and some at least of the witnesses whom they had seen, were forwarded or presented. And just as the society had reacted to the evidence of terrifying hardships and mortality by resolving that, since the emigrant trade was still more cruel and iniquitous than the slave, it, too, should be subject to protective regulations;[2] so also did the select committee react to the same evidence by demanding immediate legislation. While we do not know the testimony in full, enough has survived to make such reactions appear very natural, and to establish that it was but plain truth to assert that the slave trade was superior in many aspects. As to the 'size and tonnage of the vessels, a striking comparison was drawn under this head between the ships which the law obliges traders to use for the transportation of slaves and the preferable accommodation which was afforded to the latter'.[3] The committee learnt of a Scottish vessel which had carried three passengers for every two tons burden. Each passenger was allowed but two square feet of deck space in the hold, and twenty-five lacked berths altogether, until sleeping places were vacated by the deaths at sea of the same number of their fellow-emigrants: all this on a voyage of almost three months' duration. It learnt of another Scottish vessel of 270 tons which had sailed with 400 passengers in 1791, on which the berths were only eighteen inches wide and two feet high and on which only two small cooking vessels had been provided. It learnt of an Irish vessel on which three out of every five passengers died at sea or upon disembarkation, and on which more than thirty corpses lay putrefying on the upper deck when the ship arrived in port. It learnt that the water allowance—fouled in

---

[1] These were, according to the Highland Society, 'ascertained beyond possibility of doubt, by authentic papers and documents', *Trans. Highland Soc. Scotland* (1803), vol. ii, p. vii.

[2] Ibid., pp. vii–ix.

[3] Ibid., p. ix.

uncleansed containers into the bargain—might be as little as one pint daily for all uses. Perhaps worst of all because so close in time, the committee was informed that only two years before 700 highlanders had emigrated on two vessels which would have been forbidden by statute to carry even 500 slaves, and that fifty-three persons (one-seventh of the total complement) had perished on one of these vessels during a miserable and terrifying voyage.[1]

I have described the evidence before the Highland Society and the select committee in some detail, because without these brutal particulars we can scarcely appreciate the shock which such disclosures—authenticated and incontrovertible, as they were—must have administered to those who heard them. But once we do appreciate their impact it seems not merely natural but inevitable that the society and committee should have immediately demanded that these evils be crushed out, so far as law could crush them. It was later suggested that, since the regulations which were ultimately imposed would have increased the cost of passage three- or fourfold (had they ever been enforced), the demand for such legislation might have been a circuitous method of prohibiting emigration altogether.[2] It is certainly true that a £10 or £12 passage would have put emigration beyond the reach of the great majority of likely emigrants. It is also true that the passenger act was accompanied by a parliamentary grant for the rehabilitation of the highlands. It is even possible, though unlikely, that some of the members of the Highland Society recognized the tendency of the passenger act to reduce emigration absolutely.[3] But this is not to say that the demand

---

[1] *1st rep. comm. survey and report Scotland*, 7–9, H.C., 1802–3, iv and K. A. Walpole, 'The humanitarian movement of the early nineteenth century to remedy abuses on emigrant vessels to America', *Trans. Royal Hist. Soc.*, 4th ser., xiv, pp. 199–200. Miss Walpole added some details to those contained in the blue-book by examining the Sederunt Book of the Highland Society.

[2] A later critic (who was also a warm advocate of increased emigration) hinted at this interpretation in the *Edinburgh Review* (1806), vol. vii, pp. 195–8. But his grounds for the insinuation—that the passenger-tonnage ratio of 1:2 was absurdly large and that salt meat was required during the voyage for highlanders, who ate practically none at home—are not convincing. Subsequent experience showed that the 1:2 ratio was much too low, and the ordinary highland diet was impracticable at sea, whereas salt meat was a normal part of sea diet.

[3] It is most improbable that the effect of increased costs was foreseen by the society. These costs would have arisen not directly but obliquely. Even the critic mentioned in the preceding note believed—though it destroyed his earlier argument—that the society did not realize the financial implications of its proposals, ibid., p. 198.

for humane standards in the trade was disingenuous. In the absence of any positive evidence whatsoever of machiavellianism, the sufficient and overwhelmingly probable explanation seems to be, simply, that the demand was a normal reaction to the facts of suffering and mortality as disclosed.[1] Over and over again, the same or equivalent facts were to produce precisely this reaction in their auditors during the course of the next half-century.

The resolution of the select committee took concrete shape in the hands of Charles Hope, who quickly prepared a bill upon the basis of recommendations made by the Highland Society. Hope's bill was extraordinarily comprehensive and severe. It limited the numbers who might be carried to one for every two tons of *clear space* on British vessels and one for every five tons on foreign. It required the daily issue of $1\frac{1}{2}$ lb. of breadstuffs, $\frac{1}{2}$ lb. of meal and $\frac{1}{2}$ pint of 'melasses' to every passenger of whatever age; and the daily airing of bedding and bi-weekly fumigation of vessels with vinegar, unless bad weather intervened. Every vessel with fifty passengers or more had to carry a 'properly supplied' medicine chest and a surgeon qualified at the London, Dublin or Edinburgh schools. Before any vessel might be cleared by customs officers, all passengers were to be mustered before an officer and a justice of the peace who might detain the vessel for any breach of the act or false representation. Copies of the act were to be displayed at each customs house and aboard ship; and masters and surgeons were required to keep journals during the voyage and deposit them with the commissioners of customs upon their return. Finally, naval officers might stop and search passenger vessels on the high seas, and send any offending vessel back to port. The penalties prescribed were extremely, indeed absurdly, harsh. Fines of £20 were to be imposed in every case of insufficient issue of food or water, of failure to cleanse or fumigate

---

[1] The society's own account in 1803 of its motives was as follows: to 'prevent the unjust and tempting gains now accruing to the traders in, and encouragers of emigration', and to 'afford to the country losing part of its inhabitants, the consolation of their being carried in safety for the culture and improvement of another, instead of being, as now, delivered over by numberless privations, and the want of comfort and of care, to disease and destruction', *Trans. Highland Soc. Scotland* (1803), vol. ii, p. ix. Four years later, the society said of the 1803 act that 'it was . . . a consideration of humanity that the transportation of such as were ultimately obliged to emigrate, should be made in such a manner, as to land them . . . in health and strength', ibid., (1807), vol. iii, p. xix. These observations can, I think, be accepted at their full face value.

the ship and of failure to display a copy of the act in the scheduled places; and fines of £50 were to be imposed for all other infringements except those of re-landing provisions or taking on passengers at a place where no customs officer was stationed, in which cases the penalties were to be £200 and £500 respectively. Two further coercive devices were a requirement that masters enter bonds for seaworthiness and the landing of their passengers at the ports contracted for, and a provision for the dismissal of any customs officer who disobeyed the statute, salt to be rubbed into such an unfortunate's wounds by a fine of £50. Hope's hand may be seen in a shrewd and considerable legal section upon the recovery and payment of penalties, and the jurisdictions under which the act might be enforced. Perhaps it is also to be seen in such precautions as the retention of one certified copy of the muster roll in the customs house concerned, and in the various testaments upon oath which were demanded of surgeons and masters.

Despite the scope and severity of Hope's bill, it passed quietly and quickly into law.[1] Not a single voice was raised in protest as it wended its way through parliament in May and June 1803. Yet, it is interesting to observe, the new act was introducing a revolutionary principle to English law, a principle of first importance which was to have no true counterpart in other fields for thirty years to come. This innovation was the interference of the legislature with freedom of contract—for to buy a passage was after all to make a contract—upon the ground that the free, sane and adult citizens concerned required a peculiar statutory protection in these transactions. The recent and more modest interferences with the slave trade and with infant factory labour[2] provided some resemblances to, but no precedent for passenger regulation. From reasons of subjection or parentless youth,[3] the classes dealt with in the earlier measures were clearly powerless to protect themselves. In the case of the emigrants, however,

[1] 43 Geo III, c. 56.
[2] 42 Geo. III, c. 73, generally known as Sir Robert Peel's 'The health and morals act'. Cf. A. V. Dicey, *Lectures on the relation between law and public opinion in England during the nineteenth century*, 2nd ed. (London, 1914), pp. 108–10.
[3] The operation of the health and morals act was restricted not only to the cotton industry, but also to pauper apprentices. In fact, it was justified on the ground that there was no parental protection in these cases. Cf. M. W. Thomas, *The early factory legislation* (Leigh-on-Sea, 1948), pp. 8–10.

the presumption on which a whole branch of common law had rested for centuries, namely, that adult persons of sound mind were entirely responsible for and free in making their own contracts, was effortlessly, almost casually, overthrown.

How is the general acquiescence in such a radical departure to be explained? The answer is, very probably, that the revolutionary implications of Hope's bill were quite unrecognized. There are several good reasons why this should have been so. First, we should note that during the time when the bill might have been examined the attention of parliament was engrossed by the resumption of hostilities with France. The introduction of the bill coincided with the king's message on the ending of the French discussions, while it passed through committee on the very days of the full-dress commons debate upon the renewal of the war, 25 and 26 May.[1] It was but natural in these circumstances that an obscure measure of regulation should slip by unnoticed. Secondly, the shibboleths of free trade and laissez faire had not as yet formed clearly or found many advocates in parliament. These concepts (we might even say, these phrases) were to prove sharp and effective scalpels in exposing the inner meaning of legislation in such matters as free contract or the intervention of the state. So, at any rate, those who wielded them believed, and, within their own terms of reference, believed with reason. Certainly, regulatory legislation was much more likely to escape attention in the relative absence of these simple but searching tests and of doctrinaires to apply them. Thirdly, the passenger trade was at this time much too small and disreputable to possess a parliamentary interest or even influence with the important shippers. The business scarcely deserved to be called a 'trade' in 1803. It consisted of nothing more than the occasional charterings—as an alternative to sending vessels out in ballast—of a handful of Scottish and Irish shipping agents and owners. Such men and such a traffic were commercially and politically insignificant. That they should muster, or even attempt to muster, a parliamentary protest against the new regulations was out of the question; and they were the only parties who were likely from self-interest to draw attention to the very great severity of Hope's bill. These three factors in conjunction provide a very probable explanation of the ease with which the bill reached the statute book; although it was, of course, fortuitous that no

[1] Walpole, op. cit., *Trans. Royal Hist. Soc.*, 4th ser., xiv, p. 201.

lawyer, constitutional 'watchdog' or other member critically disposed happened to scrutinize the measure.

Over and above its contractual aspect, the passenger act of 1803
was a remarkable measure. As against its immediate successors, as
against any other statute in this field for almost forty years, it had
many merits. It was shrewdly concerned with the problem of enforcement at law. To an extraordinary degree, it anticipated the
difficulties of application and the possibilities of evasion, down to
such minutiae (but all-important minutiae) as the presence of justices of the peace at musterings, or the rejection of surgeons who
had not qualified at one of the three reputable colleges in the United
Kingdom, or the calculation of the passenger ratio in terms of space
free from cargo and encumbrance. It laid down, as we shall see,
several guiding principles of regulation which later dropped out of
sight only to be laboriously rediscovered. All these merits, all this
practicality, comprehension and anticipation, probably derived
from the relatively intimate knowledge of the trade and law of those
who prepared the bill; from the fact that the Highland Society had
been in long and close contact with witnesses who had actually
sailed on emigrant vessels or were engaged in shipping; and from
the fact that the draftsman of the bill was a practising barrister of
the first rank. Many years were to pass before another passenger bill
was drawn up by persons so well informed.

This is, however, but half or less than half the story. It is hardly
too much to say that the 1803 act failed and was bound to fail. In the
first place, it was much too complex, burdensome and repressive
for an original measure of regulation. Had it been carried thoroughly
into effect, the passenger trade of the first half of the nineteenth
century could never have come into being. The numbers and foodstuffs clauses alone would have raised the price of passages to
£10–£12 or perhaps even more; and only a small proportion of those
who did in fact emigrate could have afforded so high a fare. Again,
had the act been thoroughly enforced it would not have needed
(by the common standards of the trade) very grievous malpractices to render masters and owners liable to fines running into hundreds, or even thousands of pounds. Now down to 1845, as we have
seen, scarcely any of the Atlantic vessels really depended upon the
passenger trade. It often appeared more profitable, and it certainly
saved much time and trouble, to sail in ballast. This being so, we

may safely say that, had the 1803 act been enforced, few shippers would have engaged at all in a business of uncertain profit in which total ruin might so easily fall upon them. In short, the trade would lack, to a very considerable extent, both passengers and vessels. The natural corollary, if emigration ever appeared to be desirable, was, simply, that the 1803 act should not be enforced; and this is in effect what happened.[1] Apart from an initial flurry of instructions from the board of customs in 1803, there is but one instance of the act ever being invoked or acted on.[2]

This leads us to a second weakness of the statute, the lack of
√ direction from above and of instruments of execution. It is true that the treasury was soon in control *de facto*. It is also true that regular agencies of legal enforcement, the customs and naval services and the justices of the peace, were charged with certain duties. But the passenger trade was clearly outside the sphere of treasury knowledge and interest, and customs officers already bore other, sufficient and very different obligations. As for the admiralty and the magistrates, we may safely assume that neither was even apprised of its role in the projected regulation. In fact, it was a fatal mischance that the statute, down to its very drafting, came altogether from outside the ordinary branches of government. This meant that no one within the public service knew its background or purpose or the conditions of the trade; and that no administrator or branch of the administration was concerned with what would nowadays be termed its 'implementation'. The failure to understand the likely consequences of this, or of involving so many unconnected departments in the matter, may perhaps seem a serious error on the part of those who prepared the bill. But it was also the inevitable result of reform being still regarded as the business of members in their private capacity rather than of government as such. In this respect, the act shows one form of state struggling into existence before the mechanism of another form had been superseded.

---

[1] Newfoundland was almost immediately exempted from all the provisions of the act by 44 Geo. III, c. 44. This was a very important concession as it was easy to ship from Newfoundland to Nova Scotia, Prince Edward Island and the United States. Cf. Cowan, op. cit., p. 131, n. 3.

[2] This was in the case of the earl of Selkirk's assisted emigration of 1812, Cowan, op. cit., p. 35. On the other hand, the Highland Society observed in 1807 that the 1803 act was 'sometimes censured for going beyond the necessity of the case', *Trans. Highland Soc. Scotland* (1807), vol. iii, p. xx.

A third significant weakness of the 1803 act was its excursions beyond the limits of what was at all practicable. Just as it dealt extensively and in many ways sensibly with enforcement yet failed to see how much depended on some governmental agency being interested in enforcing, so too the act tended to condemn all that was iniquitous without discriminating between iniquities which could be dealt with by law and iniquities which, in the existing circumstances, could not. It would almost seem as if some of the clauses (like the penalties of Star Chamber) expressed horror and reprobation of the evil rather than executive intention. Thus, the regulations governing the actual sea-passage, the daily issue of provisions and the periodic cleansing of berths and holds were bound, in the nature of things, to be dead letters. Experience was to show that even if there were some persons at the port of arrival to make inquiries (and this was not to be the case anywhere till 1829), it was virtually impossible to gather evidence which would secure a conviction on these points. Almost invariably, the matter reached an impasse of assertion and counter-assertion, and was then dropped. Again, it was all very well to require vessels with more than fifty passengers to take a surgeon, qualified at one of the three leading colleges, aboard; but was it considered whether any such surgeons were available? Once more, experience was to show that respectable surgeons simply could not be tempted to make an Atlantic crossing with a horde of emigrants. Again, how were such matters as the 'unseaworthiness' of vessels or the 'unsuitability' of medicine chests to be established at law, when the statute said nothing of criteria or adjudicators? Or of what value was a master's journal likely to be (and this was its only conceivable use) as evidence against himself? It is clear from these criticisms that the framers of the 1803 act did not consider at all the 'upper limit' of enforceability, and secondly that the only context into which the act fitted was one in which emigration was positively discouraged.

A final observation on the 1803 act is that it was, as the last remark suggests, cradled in mercantilism. There is no reason to doubt that the measure was substantially and honestly what it purported to be, humanitarian in intention. But the general economic purpose which surrounds the act—the Highland Society's hostility to emigration, the corresponding directives to Telford and the select committee, and the grant for the preservation of the highlands which accompanied the statute—certainly helps to explain the ease with which monstrous penalties and reckless prohibitions and injunctions were piled up. Moreover, one object of the important numbers clause was that, if emigration were inevitable, British shipping and British North America, rather than American shipping and the United States, should gain whatever benefit was going. The trade of the St Lawrence and the maritime provinces was distinctly favoured by the restriction of the passenger quota on foreign vessels bound for North America to one passenger for every five tons burden, but the allowance of one passenger for every two tons burden on British vessels. Like the general desire to check the loss of manpower from the United Kingdom, this discrimination was in part at least a dying flicker of mercantilism. It may also have been motivated by the reawakened fears of American designs upon the ill-defended northern provinces.[1] For in so far as the Old Tories had a policy which favoured emigration in any way, it was to build up the Canadian and other frontiers with soldier settlers.

All these sentiments and objects were quickly replaced by their opposites in the years which followed Waterloo. Even before 1815 the economist Patrick Colquhoun had sounded a new note in looking forward, first, to colonial demand for British manufactures, and secondly, to emigration from the distressed areas as partial solutions to the coming economic difficulties.[2] With peace came heavy unemployment, trade depression and consequent Malthusian forebodings which soon wrought a corresponding change in the general attitude. By 1819 we find a select committee on the poor laws virtually recommending emigration to the workless. In the same year, the first parliamentary grant for state-assisted colonization was made.[3] Meanwhile, the spread of the new doctrines of political economy, together with certain changes in the interests of the shipping and timber merchants, undermined both the desire to maintain the old colonial system and suspicion of the United States as a competitor for immigration. As a consequence of this general reversal of policies and of the prodigious increase in the numbers

[1] Cf. Adams, op. cit., pp. 254–66.
[2] P. Colquhoun, *A treatise on the wealth, power and resources of the British empire* (London, 1814).
[3] In this case, the Cape of Good Hope was the area for settlement.

seeking to emigrate,[1] the 1803 act was steadily pared down. During the years 1815-20 it needed no more than an application from any reasonably responsible person to the treasury to produce an amending statute.[2] Between them, one such amendment in 1817, one in 1818 and one in 1820[3] reduced the heaviest penalties and several of the restrictive requirements of the 1803 act, and weakened its executive clauses. Meanwhile, the treasury used an apparently self-assumed power of dispensation to reduce the scale of foodstuffs to be issued.

This trend was temporarily reversed in 1823 when several of the harsh regulations of 1803 were reimposed, and two new clauses added.[4] The 1823 act[5] was mainly humanitarian in purpose, for the scandalous condition of the British North American emigrant trade had received some publicity in the two preceding seasons. But it was also inspired by a new object, that of destroying trade restrictions and discriminations;[6] and from 1823 to 1828 it was the free trade motive which held the field. The last survivals of the ancien regime fell in 1824 and 1825, when the archaic ban on the emigration of artisans and seamen was swept away, and various minor regulations affecting emigrants and their possessions, which were scattered through the customs acts, were pruned and consolidated. The 1825 act[7] also relaxed the severe regulations of 1823

[1] The actual numbers emigrating from the United Kingdom were, by official calculation, as follows:

1815 : 2,081	1817 : 20,634	1819 : 34,787
1816 : 12,510	1818 : 27,787	

[2] Cf. Walpole, op. cit., in *Trans. Royal Hist. Soc.*, 4th ser., xiv, p. 203.

[3] 57 Geo. III, c. 10, 58 Geo. III, c. 89 and 1 Geo. IV, c. 7. The 1817 act, which began the paring-down of requirements, allowed one adult or three children under fourteen years for every ton and a half, slightly reduced the food requirements, considerably reduced certain of the penalties and otherwise retained but two of the many restrictive or preventive clauses of the 1803 act. This relaxation, however, applied only to emigration from the United Kingdom to British North America.

[4] These were that passenger vessels be marked by a large 'P' so that revenue and warships might stop them for inspections, and that the minimum height between decks should be 5½ feet. The first was not repeated in any subsequent passenger act, although it did represent the only scheme ever proposed for providing a 'spot-check' during the voyage. It is extremely unlikely that it was ever put into practice during the two years of its operation.

[5] 4 Geo. IV, c. 84.

[6] Cf. Adams, op. cit., pp. 270-3.

[7] 6 Geo. IV, c. 116.

and exempted Irish vessels bound for British North America from its operation. For by the mid-1820s the protest of the shipowners that legislation much more harsh than the federal passenger act of 1819 was handing over their trade to the Americans, and would soon end all emigration to the British colonies, was being supported by campaigns in the *Edinburgh Review*[1] and other journals for the removal of all restraints upon the outflow.

The 1825 act, which did not come into force until the beginning of 1826, survived but a year. The select committee on emigration which sat under Wilmot Horton's chairmanship in 1826–7 strongly favoured both state-assisted and private colonization, and came eventually to advocate the total repeal of the passenger acts upon the grounds that legislative restrictions raised the cost of passages and retarded the full exodus from the United Kingdom. The committee also contended that restraints on trade were *per se* vexatious—this was a seed which fell, of course, on ready ground in 1827—and contrary evidence from other witnesses notwithstanding, it accepted the contention of the Nova Scotian attorney-general that 'though calculated upon principles of humanity and principles of great benevolence', the laws 'operated the reverse of what the legislature intended, for they have kept people at home in a state of actual starvation'.[2] Accordingly, on the day after the final report of the 1827 committee had been tabled, a bill was presented to repeal the 1825 act and to leave the passenger trade altogether uncontrolled.[3] This bill became law in April, 1827,[4] and for the remainder of that season the trade was entirely 'free'.

This venture proved disastrous. A stream of protests flowed in at once to the colonial office from the North American provinces and the more reputable shipowners of the United Kingdom.[5] The fears

[1] *Edinburgh Review* (1824), vol. xxxi, pp. 315–46. See also Cowan, op. cit., pp. 134–5.

[2] *Rep. select comm. emigration, 1826*, 38, H.C. 1826 (404), iv (evidence of R. J. Uniacke). Uniacke added, 'They [the passengers] would have perhaps encountered much difficulty in the outward voyage but it would at least have taken them away to a country where they would have been removed from any kind of starvation'.

[3] Originally, it had been intended merely to reduce still further the requirements of the passenger act, but the final report led to the proposal of total repeal, *House of Commons Journals*, 1826–8, pp. 359–60, 368, 385, 391, 401.

[4] As 7 & 8 Geo. IV, c. 19.

[5] The Dublin chamber of commerce also protested, C.O. 384/20, 399 Emigration, 26 Apr. 1827.

expressed in these complaints were all too well justified by events, for the year produced unprecedented shipwreck, sickness and even starvation at sea.[1] On one vessel some of the hungry passengers attacked the master and had to be imprisoned, while he guarded his provisions under arms from the remainder until the ship arrived in Newfoundland.[2] On the brig *James* from Waterford, typhus broke out at sea, and when she berthed at Halifax and the contagion spread to the port, 800 of its 11,000 inhabitants fell victims.[3] The secretary of the New Brunswick Emigrant Society wrote in his autumn report for 1827: 'It is notorious that many of the poor emigrants were deluded from their homes by false but specious statements of brokers and ship masters whose sole object in prosecuting the inhuman traffic appears to be, that of collecting as large cargoes as possible of their unsuspecting fellow subjects; and as the passage money is paid in advance, it is of little consequence to them in a pecuniary point of view, whether the helpless victims of their cupidity perish on the voyage, or live to spread disease and death among the people on whose shores they may be landed.'[4]

It was these experiences and the resulting colonial recriminations which made a renewal of regulation inevitable. When a measure to restore the trade to its old footing was being proposed in 1828, Huskisson, who introduced the new bill,[5] and E. G. Stanley,[6] Sir James Graham and Wortley (three other free traders who had been members of the 1826–7 emigration committee but who now advocated a retreat from laissez faire) all justified their change about upon the ground that the 1827 season had demonstrated that some minimum requirements for the voyage must be secured by law.[7] This was poetic rather than exact justice. Almost certainly, the absence of a passenger act was not the sole or even the main cause

[1] For a full account of the season see Cowan, op. cit., pp. 206–7.
[2] *7th rep. C.L.E.C.*, 2 [809], H.C. 1847, xxxiii.
[3] *Hans.*, 3rd, 962, 4 Mar. 1828 (Huskisson).
[4] Quoted in Cowan, op. cit., pp. 207–8.
[5] The bill was introduced during Huskisson's short period as secretary of state for war and the colonies in Wellington's government, January to May 1828.
[6] Later Lord Stanley and earl of Derby and three times prime minister.
[7] They were supported by several passenger brokers and others concerned with the trade, all of whom argued upon the same line. One Cork broker, who was also a Quaker, wrote that the mortality in 1827 had been immense, and believed that some 1,500 had perished in one group of 3,500 emigrants, C.O. 384/20, 395, 677 and 863 Emigration and 412 North America, 21 Mar., 9 Feb., 1 Mar. and 8 Jan. 1828.

of the calamities of the second half of 1827. Doubtless, such legislation did, to some extent, restrain or at least produce a 'scaling-
down' of the malpractices. But the fact that no prosecutions were
undertaken during the 1820s and the revelation of the ineffectiveness of the 1828 act which were to come in the 1830s show clearly
that legislation could only have worked a very marginal improvement. What was really important in 1827 was the coincidence of
three more or less fortuitous factors. First, the very large scale of
that season's emigration,[1] for difficulties tended to increase geo-
metrically rather than arithmetically with size. Second, the typhus
outbreak of the spring and summer, one of the occasional epidemics
which struck the passenger trade perhaps twice or three times in
every decade. Third, the arrival of reports on the condition of emigrants from the governor-generals of British North America at
almost the same time as Huskisson took up charge at the colonial
office: Wilmot Horton had happened to call for these reports before
his resignation. The free traders, however, had no notion of how
strong a case might have been presented against connecting the
repeal of the 1825 act and the disasters of 1827. For once, chance and
circumstance facilitated social legislation.

The debates on the 1828 bill[2] deserve some examination as this
was the first (and indeed the last) occasion within our period on
which the principle of regulating the passenger trade at all was discussed openly and in general terms in parliament. On the face of
things, it was difficult to justify the replacement of shackles which
had been removed but a year before. Was it not a wilful return to
obscurantism? Here it was Huskisson, both as colonial secretary
and as a celebrated convert to free trade, who bore the brunt of the
attack. Both Joseph Hume and Poullett Thomson, the leading parliamentary radicals, accused him of treachery. *Video meliora pro-
boque, deteriora sequor.* Hume went on to say that 'every arrangement by legislation was injurious', that Huskisson wished to erect
false standards of comfort for the lower classes, and that the earlier
passenger acts had been wholly mischievous and would have destroyed a profitable trade had they not been altogether evaded; while
Thomson argued that a comparison which Huskisson had made with

[1] The emigration for 1827 exceeded 28,000; it was the second highest total to
be reached up to that time.
[2] *Hans.*, 2nd, xviii, 961–5, 4 Mar. 1828, 1208–20, 18 Mar. 1828.

the slave trade was misleading because slaves were not free agents but compelled to undertake the voyage. Others—for the most part spokesmen of shipping and timber interests[1]—brought forward the argument which had earlier influenced Horton's committees, that regulation would impede emigration by raising fares; and the bill was also denounced as being but pseudo-humanitarian, and in reality a sop to appease angry colonists. Finally, one radical, Warburton, denied that the new requirements would check typhus and ship fever. He argued that contagious diseases were generated not by the conditions at sea, but by the embarkation of even a single infected person, and that this would be impossible to avoid so long as the poor Irish emigrated in such numbers.

Huskisson was sensitive to the charges of inconsistency, and ready to go very far in order to elude them. He allowed that only the 'barest minimum' of regulation should be imposed; that the obnoxious clauses of the old acts should not be revived; that anything superfluous in the current measure should be lopped off; and that commercial interests should be consulted. But the reports reaching the colonial office had left him with no doubt that some action or other must be taken. It was intolerable, he said, that passengers should be without enough food for survival or water fit for human beings to drink, or that a naval officer engaged for years in the preventive slave service could report that emigrant vessels arrived in British North America in worse condition than any slaver he had ever seen. It must be the state's duty 'to put a stop to these enormities . . . even in the teeth of science and philosophy . . . He was unable to understand the meaning of those pure abstract principles which were to prevent them from interfering where the interests of humanity were at stake. He could not conceive the meaning of those general principles which were never to bend to circumstances'. To the more specific arguments against interference, Huskisson replied that so far from reducing emigration, protection would augment it, and that Warburton's theory of infection was contradicted by the colonial reports, all of which blamed dirt, malnutrition and overcrowding during the voyage.

Stanley took up the same position. 'Though he remained a warm

[1] Sir John Newport, member for Waterford and one of the representatives of the Irish timber and shipping interests, was, for example, another advocate of the pure freedom of trade.

advocate of the general principles of free trade, he thought a special case of exemption could be made out in this instance', where a trade lay in the hands of greedy and unscrupulous adventurers. If regulations were needed to safeguard the comfort and possessions of stage-coach travellers, how much more imperative was it to apply some settled rules to the taking out of emigrants?[1] 'The ships selected for this purpose were old vessels, specially taken up for the occasion, and never used again. They were crammed with human beings, badly provided with necessaries, and the consequences were disease and death. The persons who carried on this system were left to play the game over and over again with fresh victims'. Wilmot Horton was yet another free trader who denied—though he gave no reasons for denying—that true free trade principles were being violated. He added roundly that members should be ashamed to raise a cry of 'free trade' where such plain necessities were in question, that common decency demanded that men and women who were ignorant of the requirements of the voyage should be guaranteed enough food and water.[2] Most of the ordinary members who spoke in favour of the bill echoed this common sense. One simply quoted an account of emigrants who had starved at sea because of the misrepresentations of a broker, and asked 'was there any black slavery equal to this?' Another, Villiers Stuart, put the matter still more plainly: 'As to the Irish ship-owners, if they meant to do what was right, they could have no objection to do it under an act of parliament, and if they did not, the sooner they were made to do it the better'.

We can distinguish at least three lines of conflict in the debates. At first sight the major contest might appear to have lain between humanitarians and free traders. But this is, perhaps, a retrospective and misleading categorization. To contemporaries, at any rate, the clash was rather one of doctrinaires and 'practical men'. Harcourt's famous aphorism on the 1890s might be applied, topsy-turvy, to the 1820s—we are all free traders now. However powerful as a sentiment or an impulse, humanitarianism was not an articulate creed, and those with pretensions to being thinking men had to justify

[1] Huskisson used a similar argument: even in the old slave trade there were regulations; even for packages forms had to be filled out; was it too much to ask the same for fellow-countrymen?

[2] Horton had never followed his select committee to the length of advocating total repeal. As usual, his heart was stronger than his head. See also Walpole, op. cit., *Trans. Royal Hist. Soc.*, 4th ser., xiv, pp. 203–5.

their impulse by reference to exceptional cases or conditions, or by some other form of special pleading. The three main arguments by which the advocates of the bill defended their deviation were these: that since the existing state of the passenger trade had been shown to be intolerable, principle could not be applied rigorously in this field; that there were precedents in corresponding spheres for government intervention; and that the passenger trade was exceptional amongst commercial transactions in that it involved single, unrepeatable bargains with each contractee.

The first of these arguments was to prove the master card throughout. In the form in which it had been presented by Villiers Stuart, for example, it was incontrovertible. Time was to show that no wall of laissez faire could permanently withstand the trumpet cry, 'intolerable'. In this respect, it was the doctrinaires who were justified by events. As they had feared, free trade as it was conceived of in the 1820s was swiftly eaten through by the 'exceptions' and 'peculiar cases', But it is also true that this concept was an unmeaning abstraction, whose emptiness and irrelevance might have been exposed had the second line of argument been extended. For only if they were blind to the realities of life about them could men contend that society existed, or ever might exist, upon a basis of private contractual relationships, or that such relationships were necessarily free, in anything beyond the most formal sense. If they observed at all, they would have seen a hundred 'contractual' activities in contemporary society in which the absence of all regulation was unthinkable, or in which the assumption that the parties were equal or nearly equal in knowledge and bargaining power was absurd. It was easy for the supporters of the bill to point out that even for packages forms had to be completed, that even for stagecoach travelling rules had to be prescribed; and the still more important argument, that on a true consideration of the circumstances emigrants could not be regarded as 'free' contracting agents, was at least partially implied. In reality, then, the observations of the supporters of the passenger bill, casual and piecemeal though they were, opened up the way for a fundamental criticism of anarchic laissez faire. But it is equally significant that the criticism was oblique and unexplored. Even under the provocation of Poullett Thomson's logic, which reached the perverse conclusion that free citizens, who plainly required it, should be denied the protection

which was afforded to slaves at sea—even under this provocation,
no one suggested that a theory which might end in such barbarity
must be unsound. To sum up on this particular point, two back-
doors, those of 'exceptional circumstances' and 'flexibility' in
applying principle, had been opened, and these were doors which
might be pushed outwards almost indefinitely. But free trade, un-
critically accepted as a concept and a goal, was yet a brake and was
for some time to remain a brake upon common sense and humanity
alike. The third argument might well have been contested on its own
terms. There were many other branches of commerce in which
transactions were 'unrepeatable', and to some extent the reputation
of particular vessels, masters and shipping firms affected the choice
of emigrants.[1] What is, however, interesting in this and similar
apologies is the implied respect for trade as a consideration. I do not
mean here, of course, particular parliamentary interests or lobbies,
but the general and deepening acquiescence in the supremacy of
commercial norms and ethics. This too, was to persist, grow and
exercise a powerful influence throughout our period.

The second conflict concerned the practical effects of what was to
be enacted. Here the debates were remarkably inconclusive. In the
first place, all members were more or less ignorant of the real conditions in the trade, and of the methods of enforcing social legislation. Though first-hand descriptions made it indisputable that
dreadful scandals existed, there were no authoritative statistics or
systematic collections of evidence concerning the passage. Consequently, the argument could shuttle backwards and forwards
endlessly in a blur of contradictory assertions. Correspondingly, the
1828 act was a feeble measure, much more a gesture than a regulation, because no thought was given to its execution. As we shall see,
whatever teeth the bill originally possessed were drawn before it
reached the statute book. Secondly, as Professor Finer points out
in another connexion,[2] social legislation was bedevilled at this time
and for many years to come by the fact that the technical sciences
were still largely unexperimental. The debate between Warburton
and Huskisson as to the source of infection is a case in point. For

[1] Such a choice existed only during the slack periods of emigration, or at the
Irish ports which had a small, regular transatlantic traffic and where there was
widespread local knowledge of the masters and vessels involved.
[2] S. E. Finer, *The life and times of Sir Edwin Chadwick* (London, 1952),
pp. 439–46.

what it was worth, Warburton's assertion that infections were brought aboard ships from the shore was probably the more correct. The colonial authorities who attributed their generation to conditions at sea were doubtless building upon the erroneous atmospheric theory of contagion. But on either side the argument was altogether abstract and *a priori*.

The third conflict centred about the promotion of emigration. Even a decade before, the desirability of emigration had been hotly disputed, but in 1828, with the spectres of over-population and economic ruin again overshadowing men's minds, the 'emigrationists' were virtually unchallenged. But there was now a cleavage between the 'emigrationists' who believed that a passenger act would promote emigration by improving conditions at sea, and those who still contended that legislative restrictions must impede it by raising fares. The colonies added a further complication. In theory, they favoured immigration, but in practice it was only the immigration of those whom the mother country least wanted, and was least likely, to lose; and the attitude of any particular colony might be suddenly reversed by a collapse in her sensitive economy. This last applied particularly to the British North American provinces in the 1830s and 1840s, when depression in the lumber trade was never far away.

I have described these issues at some length because (with the later addition of other factors) they formed a more or less constant background to passenger legislation. If from the vantage point of the twentieth century the arguments seem amateur, irrelevant or inhuman, three main reasons can be ascribed for the discordance: the indiscriminate and inappropriate use of notions and images such as laissez faire, the sacrosanctity which surrounded trade and contract, and the lack of experience in analysing social problems and in mastering the technical matters which they involved.

4

AN ANATOMY OF TWO ACTS

1828-35

IN examining the new legislation we must first observe that although the 1828 act was a much more modest measure than that of 1803, it was also more truly revolutionary. Whereas the latter had slipped through parliament at a time when emigration was insignificant, the former ran the gauntlet in the bright noon of both the 'emigrationists' and the protagonists of total laissez faire. The second decision was conscious in a sense in which the first was not, and correspondingly it formed a powerful precedent. Eleven years later we find G. F. Young, president of the General Shipowners Society and a diehard opponent of state regulation, testifying before an inquiry into the carrying of timber on the decks of merchant vessels in these terms: 'The interference of the legislature with the transaction of commercial affairs I hold in principle to be exceedingly objectionable; but I think that where the interests of humanity are concerned, that general principle might have to give way . . . I find, that in the conveyance of passengers in ships, the legislature has, by the Passengers' Act, expressly interfered to determine the quantity of cargo, the state of the ship, as to the sufficiency for the voyage and the quantity and quality of the provisions supplied; I think, therefore, that equally on principle, and under the authority of precedent, the legislature is both justified in interfering and bound to interfere'.[1] A whole generation after this, we find Gladstone justifying the Irish land bill of 1870 (in many respects the turning point of later nineteenth-century politics) upon the ground that 'English legislation is full of interferences', and then going on to cite the passenger acts, together with factory legislation, as precedents.[2] Moreover, it is

[1] *Rep. sel. comm. shipwrecks of timber ships*, 57, H.C. 1839 (333), ix. Young also mentioned the much less certain and relevant precedents of stagecoach and building regulations. See also Prouty, op. cit., pp. 36–39.

[2] *Hans.*, 3rd, cxcix, 333. Although the Irish land act of 1870 was presented as still within the pale of 'property rights', and although the conservative party did not oppose it outright in the commons, its 'finality' and its 'moderation' were as

74

difficult to believe that even those who spoke in 1828 of regulations governing packages, luggage and the like had no inkling or uneasy sense that rules of this sort, albeit a limitation on 'free contract', were no true precedent for the positive statutory protection of a whole class of adults in certain dealings. The real model was the regulation of the slave trade, but the extension of protection of this type to free men constituted an essential innovation. But even if *per impossibile* all the contestants in 1828 were altogether unconscious of the novelty of what was being done, this would, in the circumstances of the second quarter of the nineteenth century, have robbed the change of principle of little of its revolutionary power. As Dicey has so well observed, 'People often, indeed, fancy that . . . random legislation, because it is called "practical" is not based on any principle, and therefore does not affect legislative opinion. But this is a delusion. Every law must of necessity be based on some general idea . . . and to this principle or idea, it inevitably gives more or less of prestige'.[1]

Apart from its significance as a hidden leaven in these respects, the 1828 act was, to speak mildly, an unambitious measure. It merely limited the numbers who might be carried to three persons for every four tons burden;[2] prescribed a minimum height of $5\frac{1}{2}$ feet between-decks;[3] obliged vessels to take aboard 50 gallons of water and 50 lb. of breadstuffs (the latter provided and paid for by the passengers themselves) for every person making the voyage; and required masters to furnish passenger lists to the collectors of customs at the ports of departure and arrival,[4] to dock at their appointed destinations and to enter bonds of £1,000 for the seaworthiness of their vessels and due performance of the act. The only penalty which was summarily recoverable was that for setting passengers ashore at places other than those which they had contracted for.

illusory as those of the reform act of 1832. Both measures were proposed as 'final' reconstructions within the traditional framework of 'rights', but both, in retrospect, take on a very different appearance.

[1] Dicey, op. cit., p. 44.

[2] Two children under fourteen years or three under seven years were counted as one adult passenger, sec. 1.

[3] For every passenger below the full complement, three cubic feet of the space between-decks might be filled with cargo, sec. 3.

[4] The list presented to the customs officer at the home port was to be countersigned by him so that there would be a check at the port of arrival upon the number with which the vessel had legally cleared, sec. 4.

For other breaches of the act, the passengers had no redress except for their ordinary rights at common law. Throughout, the 'minimum requirements' concept had been busily at work, both in the eclectic choice which had been made from amongst the provisions of the 1803 and 1823 acts, and in the paring down of the few requirements which were revived.

The 1828 bill was originally prepared by A. C. Buchanan, a member of a Londonderry shipping family, who had settled in Quebec and later given evidence before Wilmot Horton's committee. Although Buchanan was a fervent 'emigrationist', his heads for a bill were much more severe and realistic than those subsequently enacted. He had suggested 2 : 3 as the numbers ratio in place of 3 : 4; 75 lb. of breadstuffs in place of fifty; regulations for the cleansing of the passengers' quarters and bedding; an official mustering and inspection of passengers and provisions before each vessel sailed; and that all penalties under the act be special and summarily recoverable before two justices of the peace. The last two clauses showed a very sensible concern with the execution of the law. Only the first and last of Buchanan's proposals survived intact in the bill which was drafted for parliament by James Stephen; and while the former was changed mysteriously before the bill reached the commons, the latter was struck out by Tenterden, a 'pig-tail' law lord remarkable even in the upper house for his unflinching resistance to all reform. Buchanan protested vigorously to Huskisson and the parliamentary under-secretary, Lord Frederick Leveson Gower, against these last omissions. The first, he justly observed, would legalize gross over-crowding,[1] and the second would render it impossible to impose any penalties whatever for most clauses. Huskisson and Leveson Gower agreed, but decided to let the bill catch the 1828 session as it stood, and amend it in 1829.[2] In fact, seven years were to pass before the act was altered. This extraordinary delay was due in part to the growing pressure on government time in parliament (a factor of considerable if ill-recognized importance in retarding and mutilating

[1] The 3 : 4 ratio made it possible to run an additional row of berths down the centre of the between-decks space, and thus deprive the emigrants of a passage way.

[2] *Corres. with governors of colonies*, 15–16, H.C. 1835 (87), xxxix. Buchanan claimed that he had consulted in drawing up his proposals the chambers of commerce of Dublin, Londonderry, Belfast and Bristol and some leading London shippers, and that all approved.

social legislation), but mostly to respect for and fear of the laissez faire opposition. In 1832, T. F. Elliot, secretary to the emigration commission of 1831-2, remarked that the badly needed remedial legislation could scarcely be pushed through a parliament where it would be bitterly contested 'as well by the advocates of conflicting theories in political economy as by the representatives of opposing interests in commerce'.[1] A year later, when Buchanan pressed a list of proposed amendments on the colonial secretary, Goderich replied that though the changes were most desirable, 'I doubt whether . . . the advantage to be expected from them outweighs the inconvenience and difficulty of altering the existing law'.[2]

More specifically, the weaknesses of the 1828 act, other than those concerning penalties, were as follows. Water, even where it was sufficient in quantity at the outset, was usually carried in foul and leaky casks,[3] there being no regulation governing containers. Though 50 lb. of breadstuffs for each passenger was quite inadequate, both in quantity and for the lack of variety in the diet,[4] vessels very rarely took as much aboard. The customs officers paid little attention to the enforcement of the clause. At Belfast, for instance, they made no pretence of inspection, but merely warned masters that it was dangerous to sail without enough food and water.[5] Again, shippers commonly sold bad or damaged provisions to their clients, and it was the dangerous practice of the trade that masters sold food to emigrants at sea when their own stock was exhausted. This was dangerous both because of the extortionate prices which the masters charged, and because of the interest which it gave them in seeing that passengers embarked with inadequate supplies.[6] The

---

[1] C.O. 42/239, memorandum by Elliot, 17 Feb. 1832.

[2] Corres. with governors of colonies, 22, H.C. 1833 (141), xxvi. Goderich added, 'at any rate, it is certain that the state of public business would not admit of it being brought forward under the consideration of parliament during the present session'.

[3] Old salt hide, oil and molasses casks were used to carry drinking water, Hans., 2nd, xviii, 1213, 18 Mar. 1828 (Huskisson).

[4] A typical entry in the Canadian emigration returns runs, 'The Bellona from Dublin, seventy-nine days' passage, the emigrants by this ship suffered much from the want of provisions. We had them supplied on arrival with tea, sugar and bread,' Corres. with governors of colonies, H.C. 1833 (141), xxvi.

[5] C.O. 384/27, 3567 New Brunswick, commissioners of customs: treasury, 19 Aug. 1831.

[6] Rep. commissioners of emigration, 9, 18-19, H.C. 1831-2 (724), xxxii.

3 : 4 ratio for numbers was simply barbarous. One broker calculated that on some cargo vessels this might mean an allowance of less than two square feet of surface space for every passenger.[1] But, once more, even so lax a regulation was not observed. The majority of vessels regularly exceeded the statutory limit. Amongst the arrivals at Quebec in 1831 were three Irish ships with tonnages of 229, 334 and 378, which carried respectively 300, 505 and 447 passengers.[2] Again it was the absence of machinery for enforcement that made possible such shameless violations of the act. No inspections of the type proposed by Buchanan had been set out. Presumably it was intended that the customs officers at the ports of embarkation, to whom the passenger lists were to be first delivered, should satisfy themselves that the lists had not been falsified. But, if this were their duty, it was habitually neglected. There were even instances in which it was left to the masters themselves to sign their own clearances.[3] Finally, there is no record of a master's bond ever being enforced; in fact it was found later to have been virtually unenforceable under the existing conditions. The only provision of the 1828 act which was neither impotent nor violated as a matter of course was that requiring a minimum height of $5\frac{1}{2}$ feet between decks. In general, masters, agents and owners stood to gain nothing by disobedience in this particular.

The first forward step was the appointment of A. C. Buchanan as agent-general for emigration in Canada. This took place at the same time as the passage of the 1828 act, though there was no connexion in the first instance between the two events. It is not quite certain why Buchanan was selected. Very probably, he owed his appointment to a combination of services rendered and family influence. He had been useful for some time to Wilmot Horton, and his brother James, an unwearying busybody in emigration matters whose rashness and folly had not yet been revealed to Whitehall, was consul at New York. The original purpose of the office appears to have been the promotion and facilitation of parish, landlord and other emigration to the North American colonies. It was with this in view that Wilmot Horton's emigration committee of 1827 had

[1] C.O. 384/20. Todhunter: Huskisson, 1 Apr. 1828.
[2] C.O. 42/233, list drawn up by the grand jury of Quebec, enclosure in Aylmer: Goderich, 12 Oct. 1831.
[3] Cowan, op. cit., p. 221.

recommended the institution of the agency.[1] The office may also
have been quasi-political in intention. Certainly, if the current
example of his brother went for anything, the agent-general would
have striven to attract emigration to British North America at the
expense of the United States. Again, there may have been some
notion that the agent-general should mitigate, so far as he could by
advice and management, the ill-effects of immigration in Lower
Canada. At the time this task was being undertaken by the Quebec
Emigrant Society, a voluntary organization which had been in
receipt of an annual grant of £1,000 from the imperial treasury
since 1824.[2] The money was spent on transportation grants, 'settlement' and 'the relief of indigence', and according to Buchanan's
later accounts, spent in a very extravagant and even harmful fashion.[3]

Buchanan's appointment had one unlooked-for consequence of
great importance to our subject. At last there was someone with
some authority who possessed an interest in the enforcement and
improvement of passenger legislation. Not only did Buchanan,
through having drafted the original bill, know more than any other
person of the background and deficiencies of the 1828 act, but the
question continued to arouse and engross him. From 1830 onwards
he regularly prosecuted for breaches of the passenger act whenever
evidence could be assembled; he endeavoured to win recompense
for passengers who had suffered losses through such malpractices as
their being landed prematurely or at the wrong places; and he
remonstrated with masters who had ill-treated their passengers or
endangered their lives.[4] Buchanan undertook this work—which
altogether transcended the sort of 'emigrant welfare' which the
Quebec voluntary society had in view—entirely on his own initiative; and in doing so he foreshadowed in many ways the regulation
exercised by emigration officers in the United Kingdom after 1833.

A second indirect and unintended step was taken towards

[1] Huskisson's instruction to Buchanan on his appointn.ent was merely to
afford information to immigrants on land for purchase and opportunities for
employment, C.O. 43/27, 29, Huskisson: Dalhousie, 8 May 1828. Buchanan's
salary was paid from the colonial land and timber fund.

[2] For the earlier history of the society and the circumstances of the authoriza-
tion of the yearly grant, see Cowan, op. cit., pp. 138-9.

[3] Since Buchanan's work to some extent overlapped that of the society he
may not have been an altogether impartial witness.

[4] For an example of Buchanan's work in this field over a season, see *Corres.
with governors of colonies*, 14-19, H.C. 1833 (141), xxvi.

reform when a commission on emigration was appointed in 1831. Its main purpose was to consider the now threadbare subjects of over-population and relief by colonization—it was the first fruit of Wakefield's machinations. But it also investigated in a cursory way the circumstances of the voluntary movement. On the whole, the commissioners inclined towards laissez faire. Their report on the abuses in the passenger trade ended on a chilling note, 'we think their [the emigrants'] comfort must continue to depend chiefly on their own prudence'. But it was at least recognized that very grave abuses existed: in fact, the commissioners issued a public warning to all emigrants against them. Moreover, the report concluded by commending warmly 'the vigilance lately excited in the colonies, and . . . the desire of the colonial authorities to concert measures with those at home for the more effectual enforcement of the law'.[1] Not only was the report an advertisement of the grievances, however slight; it also set off a gradual process of publicity and inquiry. From this time onwards, Buchanan's reports and other writings relating to emigration were published annually in the parliamentary papers; while R. W. Hay, the permanent under-secretary to the colonial office, continued the collection of material on the conditions of the trade which was originally undertaken to enlighten the commissioners.[2]

Perhaps more important in precipitating change than either of the factors described above was the mere scale and character of the emigration of the early 1830s. The emigration of 1831 to Canada was extraordinarily heavy, probably 55,000 in all,[3] and it was marked by many scandals and misfortunes. In answer to the inevitable colonial protests, Goderich proposed that the various provincial legislatures should impose an immigration tax of 5s. for every passenger within the statutory quota, and 10s. for every passenger above it.[4] His main object was to secure some indirect reform

[1] Rep. commissioners of emigration, 6, H.C. 1831–2 (724), xxxii.
[2] Rep. agent general emigration, 1837, 4, H.C. 1837–8 (388), xl; C.O. 43/80, Hay: Baring, 12 Feb. 1835.
[3] Buchanan arrived at this figure by the addition of some 10 per cent for illegal entries and false passenger returns, Corres. with governors of colonies, 5, H.C. 1833 (141), xxvi. Cf. Adams, op. cit., pp. 410–23. This was in the circumstances of the time not an unreasonable augmentation.
[4] Miss Cowan repeats Goderich's misleading phrases, 'with government advice' and 'without the sanction of government', Cowan, op. cit., p. 214. But it is clear that the distinction relates to the quota allowed by the passenger act.

(particularly of overcrowding) without exposing the passenger act itself to the lions of the parliamentary arena; and it is interesting to note that a year before tutelary Benthamism, in the person of Edwin Chadwick, entered the public service, Goderich was proposing what amounted to an artificial identification of self and public interest by a system of rewards and penalties. 'Any positive law', he wrote, 'defining beforehand what is required of masters . . . would not be framed without much difficulty, and would be always liable to evasion, while by appealing to their pecuniary interest, it may, by making misconduct no longer answer as a matter of profit, I think, be effectually prevented'.[1] The immigrant tax would also have the advantage of providing funds for the relief of the sick and indigent arrivals, thus sparing the colonies those occasional financial burdens under which they groaned so loudly. But the trade was not deceived by the new provincial legislation. The tax was vigorously opposed by ship-owners as well as by the doctrinaires, emigrants[2] and, strangely enough Buchanan himself.[3] As a consequence of these and other pressures, the tax was suspended in the following season. But with a recurrence of cholera in 1834,[4] it had to be speedily reimposed, and though never successful in its primary object of persuading masters to obey the law, it was later to form the basis of an important extension in government interference. In fact, in the very first season of its operation, 1832, it provided money for the setting up of a quarantine station at Grosse Isle, some miles up-river from Quebec, a step of great consequence for the future.

The 1832 season equalled 1831 in magnitude and greatly exceeded it in distress. Buchanan estimated that the net Canadian immigration was again some 55,000.[5] Apart from the uncounted numbers who perished at sea, almost 5 per cent of these immigrants died of cholera or kindred diseases in Quebec, Montreal and the interior.[6]

[1] *Acts levying tax on emigrants*, 3, H.C. 1831-2 (730), xxxii.

[2] The emigrants naturally opposed the tax because the amount was simply added to their fares by the passage brokers.

[3] Buchanan's objection was mainly to the fact that the relief funds were in the hands, not of the government agency, but of the Emigrant Societies of Quebec and Montreal, who, he alleged, distributed them so recklessly as to undermine the immigrants' self-reliance, *Corres. with governors of colonies*, 6-8, H.C. 1833 (141), xxvi.

[4] The first serious outbreak of cholera occurred in 1832.

[5] Ibid., 5.

[6] Buchanan's estimate of the deaths amongst immigrants was 2,350, ibid., 6.

Hundreds of the inhabitants of the ports and inland towns also fell victims. Compared with the visitation that was to come in 1847, the epidemics might almost be described as mild. The season was good in other respects, and the bulk of the early emigration had fortunately passed up-river before cholera broke out. None the less, so large a mortality was arresting, and the colonists were naturally frightened and resentful.[1] Buchanan's annual report, now published in the parliamentary papers, and other official accounts of the immigration showed clearly the inadequacy of the existing statute and arrangements, the foul state of the vessels, the miseries of overcrowding and hunger, the extortions of masters, the frauds of brokers and the wretchedly inadequate character of the new quarantine station at Grosse Isle. As to the enforcement of the 1828 act, Buchanan wrote: 'I will here remark the bad effects of the penalties in the Passenger Regulation Act not being special; it is out of the question to think that emigrants can remain here to abide the issue of a law-suit for non-fulfilment of a contract on the part of the captain; besides the form of law proceedings in this city are [sic] so exceedingly expensive and tedious that it is better to submit to any loss, than to have anything to do with it . . . I had very great trouble last summer with captains and their passengers, in disputed cases; and unless some satisfactory plan can be adopted, I anticipate a great increase to the existing abuses'.[2]

The cholera outbreak amongst emigrants also aroused considerable interest and alarm in the United Kingdom. This was important because it directed attention at home in a very sensational fashion to the weakness of the current regulation, thereby loosening the defences of laissez faire to an extent which more colonial fulminations could never hope to do. During the spring there were several serious demands that the state should take vigorous action,[3] and on 28 March 1832 an order-in-council reimposed the clauses of the 1803 act which had required that every vessel with more than fifty passengers aboard should carry a qualified surgeon and a medicine chest, and that passengers' bedding should be aired daily on deck during the voyage. In practice, the order-in-council could have

---

[1] Buchanan reported that hundreds of the inhabitants of the Canadian towns fled before the immigrants in terror, C.O. 384/30, 2266 Lower Canada, 14 June 1832.

[2] *Corres. with governors of colonies*, 19, H.C. 1833 (141), xxvi.

[3] C.O. 384/30, 977 and 1534 North America, 10 Mar. and 17 Apr. 1832.

achieved little, perhaps nothing whatsoever. There were no quarantine arrangements at the ports of embarkation; no means of disciplining passengers at sea was devised or even considered; no attempt was made to ensure that vessels with more than fifty passengers carried surgeons; and, in any event, the surgeons would not have been available in nearly sufficient numbers, if indeed any would have been available at all. None the less, the order was a significant gesture. We should note, first, that under pressure, the 'minimum requirements' line had simply fallen back, and secondly, the resort to order-in-council, which avoided the parliamentary process altogether.

The most important event of the season was the putting back in distress of two Liverpool vessels, the *Brutus* and the *City of Rochester*. The mortality on the former, after a fortnight's voyage, was eighty-three; and the latter had been notoriously unseaworthy before she sailed. Both had been grossly overcrowded and were probably short in provisions; and in each case the surviving passengers were stranded at Liverpool almost without food or money. The *Brutus* emigrants, moreover, had no prospect of resuming their voyage.[1] These flagrant violations of the law, and the attendant notoriety, stirred the colonial office to a belated desire to make an example of the delinquents. But it was found impossible to institute a prosecution. Though the act had been openly flouted, no evidence to substantiate this at law could possibly be brought forward without grave scandal since the vessels had already cleared the customs.[2] Here was a clear demonstration of the futility of the existing legislation, at any rate so long as its enforcement was left to customs officers or, as sometimes happened, to tide surveyors or other members of the uninterested bumbledom of the ports. The colonial office was shaken by the revelation of its impotence, and the Liverpool corporation insistent upon some reform. As we shall see, it was this perturbation and pressure which eventually bore fruit in the appointment of a special officer at Liverpool to enforce the statute, probably the most important single step in the entire progress of reform.

The disasters of 1832 dampened the emigrating spirit, and in the

[1] The 1828 act did not provide for compensation for passengers on vessels putting back to ports in the United Kingdom.

[2] C.O. 384/30, 2331 and 2938 Lower Canada, 19 June and 25 July 1832, and unmarked memoranda by Elliot and Stephen, dated 1 and 31 July respectively.

following year emigration was both small and quiet, though Lieut. Low, the newly appointed officer at Liverpool, gradually uncovered throughout the season an almost unbelievable system of mismanagement, deceit and imposition at that great port. But the cholera returned in 1834. In that year, apart from those who died at sea, 800 immigrants fell victims to the disease in Canada. There was, moreover, a fresh source of scandal. No less than seventeen vessels, the majority of them Irish, foundered on the Canadian run alone. Seven hundred and thirty-one lives were lost as well as the possessions of all survivors.[1] Shipwrecks were common every season, but they had never been so numerous before. The main cause now was drunkenness amongst ships' officers, and Buchanan said that in this respect the Canadian trade had for some time presented a disgraceful contrast to the American.[2] After these latest provocations, a public meeting was held in Quebec in August 1834, to demand the immediate amendment of the passenger act. Buchanan appears to have dominated the proceedings, for the proposals which were adopted included the substance of his 1828 recommendations, together with five new clauses requiring that the sale of spirits on emigrant ships be prohibited; that masters be liable for contracts entered into by brokers or charterers with their passengers; that an allowance be made to each passenger of 9d. per diem, or victuals, whenever the sailing of a vessel were delayed for any reason other than accident or weather; that a copy of the act be carried on all vessels for open inspection by the passengers; and that passengers be maintained on board ship for forty-eight hours after arrival at their destination.[3] Meanwhile, many other proposals were being sent in by the newly appointed emigration officers, who also contributed richly to the growing body of evidence at the colonial office on the inadequacy and ineffectiveness of the current statute. Under this accumulating pressure, it was decided that the act must be amended in 1835.

It was unfortunate that the telling pressure had not been exercised a little earlier. Had the amending act been passed in the

---

[1] *Corres. with governors of colonies*, 4, H.C. 1835 (87), xxxix.
[2] Ibid., 7.
[3] Ibid., 15–16. Two years before, Buchanan had recommended some of these additional clauses in his annual report, *Corres. with governors of colonies*, 11, H.C. 1833 (141), xxvi.

preceding session it would have fallen to E. G. Stanley and not to
Gladstone to supervise the passenger bill and steer it through the
house of commons.[1] By and large, so far as our subject and period
are concerned, Stanley was the most sympathetic and effective of all
the colonial secretaries and under-secretaries of state. After his *volte
face* over the passenger bill of 1828, he saw but one side—or some
might say the essence—of the question. The fact that a multitude of
poor and defenceless people were suffering great hardship and injustice overshadowed all else. Stanley at the colonial office has been
decried as a dilettante, a mere Prince Rupert of debate.[2] However
that may have been, he was within this particular field a Rupert of
action, original and bold. Immediately after his appointment as
colonial secretary in 1833, he took it upon himself, perhaps exor-
bitantly, to appoint an emigration officer at Liverpool. He supported
this officer firmly in his early struggles with the trade, and went on
to increase the number of these officers to seven in the spring of
1834. The immediate significance of all this is that, had Stanley had
charge of the amending bill, he would almost certainly have sub-
ordinated all other interests so far as possible to the main purpose
of protecting emigrants. It is also likely that he would have incor-
porated as many as possible of the specific recommendations of the
emigration officers for reform. In both respects, Gladstone disappointed.[3] He was, of course, very young and without previous
experience of office or even breathing space in which to learn something of emigration before the preparation of the bill.[4] Besides, the
permanent officials, on whom he would in the circumstances naturally
rely,[5] were unsatisfactory advisers on this subject. There is no

[1] Gladstone's chief, Aberdeen, was in the house of lords. Aberdeen does
not appear to have taken any part in the preparation of the passenger bill: the
only 'parliamentary' memoranda and endorsements to be found amongst the
colonial office papers on this matter were written by Gladstone. Gladstone left
office in April 1835, before the passenger bill had finally cleared the commons.
[2] W. P. Morrell, *British colonial policy in the age of Peel and Russell* (Oxford,
1930), pp. 32–36.
[3] It is impossible to agree with Miss Walpole's judgment that Gladstone
'tackled the difficulties of this Bill, which seems to have been the first public
measure for which he was responsible, with characteristic thoroughness',
Walpole, op. cit., in *Trans. Royal Hist. Soc.*, 4th ser., xiv, p. 215.
[4] Gladstone became under-secretary in December, 1834, and the bill was
introduced to the commons in March, 1835.
[5] Cf. E. Halévy, *The age of Peel and Cobden* (London, 1947), p. 14.

evidence that R. W. Hay ever went beyond the mere collection of material in an 'Emigration Room'; and on all questions of emigrant protection the great James Stephen (soon to succeed Hay as under-secretary) more or less contented himself with a melancholy con-templation of the folly and hopeless misery of mortals. As to the 1835 bill, moreover, Stephen's advice to Gladstone was to follow the guidance of experts on these technical matters;[1] but, unfortunately, the 'experts' proved to be, not the emigration officers, but for the most part shippers' trade societies, consuls and the like.[2] Generally, Stephen's influence was dispiriting. 'I fear', he told Gladstone, 'that when you bring in this Bill, you will be pressed for more reasons than you will have to give and more authority than you will be able to advance'. He added, 'I confess myself so ignorant about these Subjects, as not to understand the meaning of some of the technical terms employed in these papers, as I certainly am quite incompetent to calculate the probable working of many of the Provisions which I do understand'.[3] But Stephen's scruples did not prevent him from replying to a request to frame a provision to safeguard emigrants against runners' misrepresentations, in this strain: 'Nor can I per-ceive how you would remedy this, except by a Law of so compre-hensive a nature as to be productive of more and greater Evils than it could cure'.[4] The upshot of Stanley's departure, Gladstone's ineptitude, Hay's inactivity and Stephen's gloom was, as we shall see, a patchwork and inadequate amending statute.

None the less, the new bill met with much less opposition in parliament than its predecessor. Gladstone argued that it introduced no new principle but merely modified an existing interference; that experience had shown that humanity and 'good feeling towards the poor' alike required it; and that the three- or fourfold increase in the volume of the outflow since 1828 had proved decisively that pro-tection encouraged rather than retarded emigration.[5] In the course of a vague and desultory speech, Gladstone threw out two further sug-gestions, that the act be extended to vessels bound for the United States and that all vessels be surveyed for seaworthiness by customs

[1] C.O. 384/35, 900 Lower Canada, Stephen: Gladstone, 16 Mar. 1835.
[2] C.O. 384/39, 1333 and 1350 North America, 17 and 18 Mar. 1835.
[3] C.O. 384/35, 900 Lower Canada, Stephen: Gladstone, 16 Mar. 1835.
[4] C.O. 384/38, 63 Emigration, Stephen: Gladstone, 15 Apr. 1835.
[5] *Hans.*, 3rd, xxvi, 1235–6, 19 Mar. 1835.

officers, without, however, pressing either in the least.[1] But the house needed little persuasion.[2] Only one member still challenged directly the need for protective legislation, and the bill was warmly supported by those who had connexions with or knowledge of the trade. Baring, who knew something of shipping through his family business, pointed out that drunkenness led not only to shipwrecks but also to brutality and extortion. Smith O'Brien, destined to lead the tragi-comic Irish rising of 1848 but at this stage a 'mere' philanthropist and one who had for some years striven to improve the Limerick passenger trade, testified that this trade was still disgracful. Five hundred, or 20 per cent, of the passengers who had embarked at Limerick during the preceding season had died at sea. Lord Sandon, member for Liverpool, stated boldly that it was only 'a just principle of legislation when parliament interposed for the protection of the weak and ignorant', and went on to say that he could corroborate the worst descriptions of emigrant suffering with a hundred cases from his own experience. Even Hume by now admitted that it was the state's duty to see that vessels were seaworthy, provisions sufficient and contracts fair; and he and Warburton confined their energies, not unsuccessfully, to weakening the particular clauses.[3]

Though there was, then, no longer an open opposition 'in principle' to interference, the powers to be granted to customs officers (now that they were specifically named as the executors of the act) provided a new bone of contention. Here there was much disagreement. Hume advocated throughout that as much as possible should be left to the officers' discretion, and not become the subject of 'minute and vexatious' legislation. Possibly he anticipated that this would tend towards laxity in practice. But his fellow radical, Warburton, strongly opposed such a course upon the ground that powers for officials bred favouritism and corruption. Correspondingly, some humanitarians desired wide discretions, others exact legislation, the disagreement being solely as to which would prove the more

[1] Ibid., 1237.
[2] For the debates on the passenger bill, see ibid., 1235-8, 19 Mar. 1835, and ibid., xxviii, 856-8, 17 June 1835.
[3] The timber interest offered little opposition on this occasion, partly because the merchants had some larger fish to fry at that time and were anxious not to alienate public opinion, partly because the emigrant trade was no longer very important to them financially, Adams, op. cit., pp. 308-9.

effective.[1] Though at this stage in the development of passenger legislation, exactitude was much more desirable than discretions, the question was later to prove one of infinite difficulty and complexity.

The new act[2] greatly extended the range of the requirements. The numbers ratio was reduced from three passengers for every four tons burden to three passengers for every five,[3] and the quantity of breadstuffs increased from 50 to 70 lb. Customs officers were entrusted with the duty of inspecting food, water and berths, and deciding seaworthiness.[4] If they were not satisfied as to the last, they might order a survey of the vessel by two 'competent persons'. Several of the Quebec recommendations were also adopted: detention money (1s. per diem instead of 9d.) was to be paid if vessels were delayed otherwise than 'unavoidably' or by stress of weather; passengers were to be maintained for forty-eight hours after their arrival; and masters were required to have an abstract of the act available for the scrutiny of passengers. Some of the other changes, too, were clearly inspired by the colonial reports. Masters were required to post up and adhere to a list of charges for their provisions, and while spirits were not prohibited the amount which might be carried was severely limited. The main clause of the order-in-council of 1832 was not renewed, but it now became statutory for vessels to carry medicines of a 'sufficient' kind and quantity.

Though the sweep and number of the changes were imposing, and though some decided improvements had been made, the 1835 act was an unsatisfactory measure. Throughout it compromised unintelligently between humanitarian instinct and free trade persuasion. On the numbers ratio, Gladstone informed the commons with evident satisfaction that he had struck an exact mean between the proportion recommended by Bonham, the British consul at New York, and that recommended by the London Shipowners

[1] *Hans.*, 3rd, xxviii, 856–8, 17 June 1835. When Hume objected to one requirement that it would be as logical to order the inspection of a packet's steam boiler before each trip on the ground that it might blow up, Goulburn replied that in the latter case the self interest of the owner operated, where as in the passenger trade it did not.

[2] 5 & 6 Will. IV, c. 53.

[3] Sec. 2. There was a further requirement that at least ten square feet of surface space were to be allowed for every passenger and his belongings, but the inclusion of baggage, provisions &c. in the calculation made it virtually worthless.

[4] This last was added to the bill while it was before the house of commons.

Society;[1] and this spirit typifies the act and explains the concessions made in consultation and committee. For the concessions betrayed the hands of amateurs, who did not understand which points might be yielded and which must be held. This weakness was shown above all in the failure to utilize the new corps of emigration officers. Not only was the fruit of their early experience largely wasted, and the substance of their recommendations rejected or but half-accepted;[2] but worst of all, the enforcement of the new act was placed not in their hands, but in those of the customs officers who had proved themselves many times over to be incompetent to fulfil such a duty.

More specifically, neither of the main improvements, in space and food, was as yet nearly sufficient, while the majority of the new requirements were either trivial in their value to passengers or unenforceable or both. The most important innovations were those which introduced detention money and surveys for seaworthiness. But neither was very useful as first enacted. The qualifications 'unavoidably' and 'by stress of weather' opened many loopholes in the matter of detentions, while customs officers were not to be depended on to reject unseaworthy vessels. Again, for practical purposes, such clauses as those obliging masters to adhere to a price list for provisions, or to keep an abstract of the act for passengers, were worthless. Had emigrants been literate, moneyed, spirited and thoroughly grounded in law, they would have gained, but this, of course, was far from being the case. A major weakness of the act was, once more, the machinery for imposing penalties. In the first place, penalities themselves were so small[3] that in several instances it was actually profitable to disobey the law. Secondly, the pleas of Buchanan, Low and others for the introduction of effective summary processes had been ignored. Finally other clauses which had been designed by the officers to facilitate the enforcement of the act, such as that rendering masters liable under contracts entered into by brokers or charterers with their passengers, were rejected. A last fatal concession to the trade was the exemption of vessels carrying less than one passenger for every five tons burden from the requirements of

[1] *Hans.*, 3rd, xxvi, 1236, 19 Mar. 1835.
[2] In so far as professional advice was taken, it was taken from Buchanan rather than the United Kingdom officers. This was, as we shall see, something of an error.
[3] The maximum fine was in all cases £20, sec. 16.

the statute.[1] As soon as the new law came into force brokers began to charter only small portions of the between-decks space in order to avoid coming within the act; and passengers on such ships were to suffer the most dreadful hardships through detentions before sailing, and to be sent to sea with foul and dangerously insufficient food and water.[2]

The emigration officers on either side of the Atlantic were bitterly disappointed with the new act. Low observed that decent standards in the trade could not be hoped for with such minute allowances of food and space and in the absence of summary powers to stamp out fraud.[3] Buchanan appealed at the eleventh hour to Gladstone for the insertion of the omitted clauses, and spoke with regret of his failure in his annual report. He still trusted that much might be accomplished if the act were rigorously enforced.[4] But the hope was forlorn. Earlier in the year, he himself had to report to Hay 'the want of proper attention on the part of the officers of the customs at many ports in Ireland. I would respectfully suggest that a remonstrance from the Colonial office to the collectors of customs generally would have a very desirable effect'.[5]

[1] Sec. 20. These vessels were known as 'short ships'.
[2] C.O. 384/38, 703 and 741 North America, 23 July and 3 Aug. 1835. The passengers were also compelled to sleep in berths arranged in three tiers, instead of the usual and now statutory two.
[3] Ibid., 214 Emigration, 25 Apr. 1835.
[4] *Corres. with governors of colonies*, 5, H.C. 1836.
[5] Ibid., 23.

5

LIEUTENANT LOW AT LIVERPOOL

1833–40

IT is not easy to determine the purposes with which the corps of emigration officers in the United Kingdom was formed. One element in its casual origin was the general, if ill-defined, desire to relieve 'over-population'. Widespread interest had been aroused in Wakefield's systematic colonization, particularly when it was proposed as a partial solution to the looming problem of a new poor law; and even after the more grandiose schemes had been rejected in 1832, it was still hoped that something might be done for parish and landlord emigration.[1] The voluntary movement, moreover, was still rapidly increasing in importance. The annual average had risen from some 25,000 in the years between 1815 and 1820 to over 70,000 in the early 'thirties; and there was a growing feeling that so useful a safety valve might be judiciously prised further open. It is interesting to note that Stanley later justified the expenditure on the emigration corps upon the ground that it 'would be ten-thousand-fold repaid by the effect it would have in assisting the progress of spontaneous emigration'.[2] But undoubtedly the most important and immediate cause lay in the scandals and misfortunes of 1831–2, or, to narrow it even further, in those particular cases which aroused such interest and compassion in Liverpool in the cholera year.

A special superintendence of emigration was first suggested in 1831,[3] when it was proposed independently, and in the name of humanity, by a Liverpool philanthropist, Rowland Edwards,[4] and

[1] See C.O. 384/27, unmarked, instruction of Goderich, 1 July 1831, and 3887 Emigration, 20 July 1831. In fact, the first proposal was that the emigration officer's salary should be met by a tax of 1s. on each parish emigrant.
[2] *Hans.*, 3rd, xxii, 964, 18 Apr. 1834.
[3] It may possibly have been implied, however, in A. C. Buchanan's recommendation in 1828 of an 'official' mustering and inspection of passengers and provisions.
[4] C.O. 384/28, unmarked, 25 June 1831.

in a report from the British consul at New York.[1] After the return to port in 1832 of the *Brutus* and the *City of Rochester*, fresh appeals were made by the mayor and various citizens of Liverpool;[2] and when at the beginning of 1833 the mayor specifically requested a naval officer to furnish emigrants with information, advice and 'protection', the government at last succumbed. 'Emigration is now becoming so extensive and so systematic', Stanley told Althorp, 'that it is very desirable to afford any facilities for it on the part of the government, and to check, as far as we can, the frauds which are practised on the lower description of emigrants by the agents . . . Their interest being to secure as many passengers as they can for the ships for which they are engaged, they deceive them by all sorts of misrepresentations as to the time of vessels sailing, &c. and keep them loitering about the port till the whole of their little stock of money is exhausted . . . There is every reason to believe that . . . advantages would result from appointing a responsible person to whom individuals, and parishes, might apply for correct information and for forwarding the parties. The experiment might be tried at Liverpool, and if found to answer might be applied to Bristol, Dublin &c. . . . The expense would be very trifling—a lieut. of the navy, as suggested by the mayor, would perform the service for the difference between his half and full pay, with a small allowance for a clerk &c'.[3] Within a fortnight of this letter, one Robert Low, a half-pay naval lieutenant and possibly the mayor's own nominee, was appointed emigration officer[4] at Liverpool.

As might be expected from such a modest and ad hoc beginning, the purpose of the corps and the duties of the officers were ill-defined. According to the surviving official memorandum, the officer was to look to the seaworthiness of vessels and the enforcement of the passenger act; to receive money for, and to advise in the securing of passages; to direct emigrants to respectable lodgings, once he knew the port; and to work with the local magistrates in

---

[1] Ibid., 3238 Emigration, 8 Nov. 1831.
[2] C.O. 384/30, 2375 North America and 2844 Canada, 19 June and 21 July 1832.
[3] C.O. 384/33, C. Horsfall: Goderich, and endorsements, 4 Jan. 1833. In the event, Low was allowed full pay and £100 for expenses.
[4] The terms 'emigration officer' and 'emigration agent' were both used commonly in the early years of the corps. Later, the first became the established mode of description.

securing rapid and summary justice.[1] Clearly, the office was not well considered. No new legislation had been contemplated, though the old statute did not cover such a service. The emigration officer had no *locus standi*. Customs officers could, and at some ports did, clear vessels which had not been submitted to his inspection. Moreover, to charge him with selecting vessels and lodgings for private individuals was to place him in the dangerous situation of discriminating between ordinary merchants in competitive trades; and to burden him with working rough justice without any promise to stand over his extra-legal actions was, to say the least of it, ungenerous. To what extent would the colonial office support him when he worked outside the statute? A host of difficulties sprang from the failure to answer this question clearly. Again, although there was no specific instruction on the point, the officer appears to have been expected to carry out a sort of government policy in such matters as the encouragement of landlord undertakings or the diversion of emigration to British colonies. Not only was this unsatisfactory in being both vague and tacit. It was also difficult to reconcile with the impartiality towards all interests which the main duty of enforcing protective legislation should have demanded. Finally, we may note that the public advertisement which announced the appointment of an officer at Liverpool was, to say the least of it, tendentious. 'It is notorious', it began, 'that ships are advertized to sail on a particular day and are kept in port many weeks after their time. The emigrants arrive with their families and are waylaid by the agents for these vessels; are conducted to lodgings or public houses; are provided with clothes, bedding, provisions etc. by persons all connected in the same concern and in the end are generally plundered of every farthing which they brought with them'.[2] If this was not an open declaration of war upon the trade, it was at least a firm assertion that the government had ranged itself upon the side of the emigrant.

From the first Low was shocked by the state of the emigrant trade

[1] C.O. 384/39, unmarked memorandum, 4 Mar. 1833. The account which Stanley gave the commons of the officer's duties was still more vague. 'His duties were to receive applications from emigrants, to give them advice as to the course they should pursue, to see that no frauds were practised on them, and, if the provisions of the law were not complied with by the merchants, to direct the emigrants to the quarters in which they could obtain redress', *Hans.*, 3rd, xxii, 964, 18 Apr. 1834.

[2] *Rep. poor inquiry commrs Ire.*, Appendix G, 34, H.C. 1836, xxxiv.

in Liverpool and the inadequacy of the passenger act.[1] The great majority of vessels were unfit for emigrants, many being in disrepair, unseaworthy or recklessly stowed. Most were short of water and provisions; and almost all lacked kitchens, sanitation and adequate lifeboats. Worst of all, the act allowed far too many passengers aboard; and even the insufficient limitation of the statute was illusory, both because it was rarely observed and because the between-decks space was 'blocked up with chests, buoys, water casks and provisions'. Finally, Low caustically observed, the 1828 act was 'to a great extent inoperative, the officers of the customs, to whom the execution of it was delegated, being generally otherwise employed on what they conceived matters of more importance to the revenue'. Low's early experience with two vessels belonging to the firm of Robinson Brothers will suffice to illustrate his difficulties and the appalling conditions which must have prevailed at sea on voyages of five, six or seven weeks, during which passengers were often battened down for days on end in foul weather.

The first vessel, the *General Brown*, sailed despite Low's protests with fifty-four passengers in a living space of 250 square feet by 5 feet 7 inches high, which was moreover choked with luggage and sea-stock, and without any partition to divide it from the cargo.[2] The other vessel, the *Cumberland*, 336 tons burden, carried eighty-six passengers and their luggage and provisions in a room of some 600 square feet by $5\frac{1}{2}$ feet high. 'The remainder of the space of this vessel', Low's report ran, 'was taken up with the cabin, and forecastle for the crew, beside which she was filled with a cargo consisting of the following articles, viz., 126 tons of iron stowed close to the ceiling, 292 tons of salt in cargo, 17 tons of earthenware and 44 tons of water, provisions and coals, making together 479 tons'. Since the vessel was so grossly overloaded, and unseaworthy and dangerously stowed into the bargain, Low tried to prevent her

---

[1] The following account of Low's early activity in Liverpool is based (unless otherwise stated) on his eighteen reports to the colonial office contained in C.O. 384/32, covering the period May–Nov. 1833; and his twelve reports contained in C.O. 384/35, covering the period Jan.–Nov. 1834; and the endorsements upon these reports.

[2] The *General Brown* was by no means exceptional in her overcrowding. Of the other vessels which sailed at the same time, the *Rolla* carried seventy-eight passengers and their possessions in a space of 28 feet × 23 feet, and the *Devereaux* 178 passengers in a space of 48 feet × 48 feet.

departure by withholding a certificate of clearance. But Robinsons refused point-blank to provide an alternative passage, and as the emigrants were all the while eating into their little sea-stock, Low had finally to let her sail. A fortnight later, she put back in 'a crazy state', all cargo, provisions and luggage having been thrown over-board to save the ship; and Robinsons, taking their stand upon the law, remained indifferent to the sufferings of the penniless and ragged emigrants when they returned to Liverpool.[1]

What could Low do in such cases? Even his refusal to grant a clearance was of very doubtful legality. All it rested upon was a discretion as to seaworthiness possibly implied in the 1828 act, and this would scarcely have sustained him in a court of law. In any event, if anyone were empowered to exercise such a discretion, it was the controller of customs and his subordinates, not the emigra-tion officer, who had no statutory authority to detain vessels for his clearance.[2] It was fortunate for Low that his understanding with the customs officers at Liverpool was good, and that no master was shrewd enough to challenge him at common law. As to the other matters at issue, the passenger act had no remedy to offer. Masters were not required to keep the between-decks space clear of encum-brances or to limit the amount of their cargo, and there was no clause governing the stowage of vessels, or providing compensation for emigrants who had been returned to port.

From these cases, which were typical of a great deal of the Liver-pool trade, we can readily appreciate the magnitude of Low's task. Except for those few matters which the statute, often uncertainly, covered, his only weapons were what he called 'threats and remon-strances' and the refusal to grant a clearance. However effective in some cases, the former were obviously unsatisfactory as a procedure. Inevitably, they led to bad relations with the trade; and as a general rule the worse the broker the less likely was he to be persuaded or

[1] Ultimately, as a result of repeated denunciations by Low and many appeals from the magistracy, Robinson Brothers furnished the emigrants with a second passage. Low had meantime got up a public subscription to restock them with provisions. But the second vessel was even worse than the *Cumberland*; and when it foundered, the passengers were again returned to Liverpool, by now altogether destitute and in many cases sick. At this point, Robinsons washed their hands of the whole affair.
[2] The departmental instruction to Low to 'see to' the seaworthiness of vessels had, of course, no significance in law.

intimidated.[1] Nor was refusal to grant clearances a very reliable support. Quite apart from the difficulties which we have already noted, it was at best a two-edged weapon. So long as passengers suffered through the delays, the officer dared not detain a vessel beyond the point where they ran the risk of starving during the passage. In this matter, too, Robinsons and their like soon realized that the officer's bluff could eventually be called. In short, as matters stood an emigration officer could do relatively little to improve the trade; and what he did achieve depended largely, and most unfairly, not upon his legitimate powers or the provisions of statute, but upon the brokers' ignorance of the law and his own capacity to browbeat and cajole. It was no coincidence that Low's first demand, for a boat, should have been couched in these terms: 'It was absolutely essential . . . as the very sight of a King's boat commands respect and ensures obedience to any recommendation'. Nor was it a coincidence that within a few weeks of his appointment he drew up a long series of recommendations for a new passenger act.

Finding that the worst of all the evils and the source of many others was overcrowding, Low first pressed strongly for a reduction in the numbers ratio to three for every five tons of *unoccupied* space, and asked that this requirement should be extended to American vessels. Though he granted that the American act, which allowed only two passengers for every five tons, was 'liberal in spirit', he found it ineffective in practice so long as water, cargo and provisions could be crowded into the space ostensibly reserved for emigrants.[2] He next recommended an increase in the water allowance and in the minimum height between decks; the provision of adequate lifeboats and cooking places; segregation of the sexes by means of bulkheads; a minimum area of six feet square for berths (which usually held four persons); and a limitation of the deadweight which might be carried to half the registered tonnage. Low

[1] Robinsons, for example, long continued to use unseaworthy vessels despite Low's remonstrances. In 1834, they sent out the *Herald*, which had not been repaired since 1816 and was in disgraceful condition, although Low and the customs officers, at Low's request, objected vigorously. In such disputes, Robinsons always referred Low to the statute, and he rightly concluded that the only remedy was new legislation.

[2] Low reported that 'in the hands of the passenger agents' the American act was 'a means of crowding their vessels to a greater excess even than vessels to which no law applies'.

went on to deal with the enforcement of these measures. First he suggested very wide discretions for the emigration officer, who was to be the sole judge of the quantity and the quality of the victuals, of the seaworthiness, berths and fittings of the vessels and of the stowage of cargo and provisions. He then drew up complicated regulations for maintaining order and discipline at sea,[1] and proposed that passenger lists would be sent on ahead to the ports of arrival where the colonial emigration agent or the British consul (as the case might be) could check the emigrants as they disembarked. Finally, he asked for much heavier penalties for breaches of the act, particularly for overcrowding.

So much for conditions at sea. Low now turned to breaches of contract and impositions in the port of embarkation. These were often ruinous to emigrants, as most did not come within the jurisdiction of the mayor's court, and the ordinary processes of common law were quite inaccessible to intending passengers. Low's first suggestion was, of course, a special form of summary process to be dispatched immediately before two justices of the peace. He next recommended that 'all passenger agents should be licensed by government, or by the local magistrates at the port where the emigration takes place, so that, in the event of their, or of any of their people committing a fraud, on any of their emigrants, their licence should be withdrawn and even a fine or imprisonment imposed upon them'. But his master stroke was perhaps his proposal that brokers be compelled to furnish emigrants with all provisions needed for the voyage.[2] One advantage of this device was that passengers might be guaranteed a full and balanced diet; another, that if food were shipped in bulk proper inspections would be practicable. But most important, the measure would strike at the delays in sailing which led to so much suffering during the voyage, and even to passages being thrown up altogether because emigrants could not afford to lay in fresh sea-stock. If brokers were bound to furnish

---

[1] Low wanted a daily airing of the bedding and passengers' quarters; all emigrants to be dressed by 7 a.m.; women to be obliged to clean up after their children &c. This type of naval discipline could not, as a matter of fact, be realized on passenger vessels, though it was frequently proposed in one form or another in later years.

[2] The cost of the provisions was to be added to the fares. Low estimated that with bulk buying this should not amount to more than 30s. a head. If this were so, emigrants would not have lost financially.

passengers with provisions from the moment that the vessel should have sailed, the source of many frauds would have been stopped, and a new statutory power to refuse clearances could be used to full advantage.

It is noteworthy that almost every recommendation made by Low was sooner or later adopted; that many were extended in severity after their utility had been established; and that in almost every field he touched he adumbrated a type of regulation that was to prove successful.[1] He was right in marking out the complements of vessels as the key problem; and most of the other aspects of the passage which he stressed, kitchens, berthing, segregation of the sexes, life-boats and deadweight, were later shown to be of critical importance. Discretionary powers for the emigration officer, and the furnishing of early information to the ports of arrival, were essential for the enforcement of the statute. The summary process was eventually recognized as the only effective counter to breaches of contract; and the requirement that brokers provide some at least of the foodstuffs for the voyage was to be a cornerstone of the important reform act of 1842.

What is interesting here is that Low was no solitary genius. We have already seen how the 1803 act foreshadowed several of his proposals albeit in an ineffective or indiscriminate form. More significant still, although none of the Irish officers who was appointed in the following season,[2] made such extensive or intelligent recommendations as Low, all diagnosed substantially the weaknesses and advocated substantially the same improvements. This last establishes clearly that what was hitherto lacking was responsible persons with a technical understanding of ships and sailing, a first-hand knowledge of the trade and a professional interest in its amendment. The appointment of an emigration agent in Canada in 1828 had done something to fill this gap. But although his early experience as a passage broker had taught him something of the trade, Buchanan

----

[1] There were, of course, some exceptions. Overcrowding was eventually countered not by Low's impracticable suggestion of measuring 'unoccupied space' but by a simple reduction in the ratio and by effective machinery for enforcing the law; and neither the problem of discipline and cleanliness at sea, nor that of emigrant physicians, was ever solved, though this was due to the difficulties inherent in each case and not to failure to search for a solution.

[2] Officers were appointed to four of the Irish ports early in 1834, see below, Chapter 6.

was no sailor. In contrast to the total ignorance of the colonial office and the politicians, his recommendations of the late 1820s and the early 1830s might have seemed almost professional. But a comparison of these recommendations with the proposals of the United Kingdom officers on all matters concerning vessels or the voyage reveals at once that he was an amateur, though interested and, up to a point, informed. It was, moreover, in the ports of embarkation that the sources of the evils lay. In Canada, Buchanan could see only a medley concatenation of their effects.

The other portion of Low's duties, the putting down of pre-embarkation abuses, proved as difficult as his dealings with the vessels. Soon after his arrival at Liverpool he reported, 'with the better sort of agent I have not a great deal of trouble, but there are so many disreputable in this traffic that I will find some difficulty in overcoming them'. So it was to be. Within a few weeks Low had uncovered a very cruel and complex system of deception. Emigrants were being led to the wrong agent and thereby losing their deposits; or dispatched on vessels, or to ports, other than those contracted for; or despoiled in their lodgings, or charged extortionate prices for their provisions, or sold foul bread. If they tried to leave their lodgings or to change their ships, their baggage was seized. If by chance they learned that they might have a legal remedy, they were usually intimidated or bribed to return the contract ticket. With the blessing and support of the mayor's court, Low at once began a vigorous attack upon these abuses. In his first two months of office he undertook twenty prosecutions; and at the end of that time he made a division of the Liverpool brokers into sheep and goats, chief amongst the latter being P. W. Byrnes & Co., O'Beckett & Co., Robinson Brothers, Grimshaw's and Walkinshaw's. He followed this up by persuading the mayor to remonstrate officially with some of these firms; by securing the committal of Byrnes himself for assault upon an emigrant; and by prosecuting two of Byrnes' runners for receiving money under false pretences from intending passengers. The trial of the runners gives us a glimpse of the dockland underworld into which Low intruded. On the day set for the hearing, the main witness was abducted, and the brokers responsible for the kidnapping celebrated their victory with a dinner. Meanwhile, however, Low persuaded the magistrates to postpone the hearing, rescued the witness and lodged him in gaol for safekeeping. When the trial came off, Low, with a view to example, asked for and obtained heavy sentences of imprisonment.

Low, then, was dealing with rough, unscrupulous men, and considering the true weakness of his position he was extraordinarily successful. Apart from his actual prosecutions, the very threat of the mayor's court, once it was known that the municipal authorities, whom he consulted before each prosecution,[1] would back him to the last, was often enough to win substantial justice—the passages contracted for, or a return of fares, or compensation in the form of sea-stock. But there was another side to the story. In the first place, the trade was not prepared for Low's appointment. No new legislation had been passed, and no public or political discussion had taken place. For the most part, the brokers were ignorant of the particular requirements of the passenger act, as virtually no attempt had been made to execute them before 1833. Now established practices and conventions were suddenly and violently assailed. A ship-owner's letter published in the *Liverpool Mercury* about this time expresses the general reaction. Low, complained the writer with some justice, was enforcing unknown and unknowable regulations. Vessels were being detained on all sides for alleged deficiencies in provisioning, berthing, stowage or accommodation. The panic-stricken emigrants were flying about in search of other ships not threatened with delays. In short, the entire trade was upset by the uncertainties. The letter ended with a not unreasonable demand that the law's requirements should be clearly defined and published.[2]

Secondly, Low's division of the Liverpool trade into 'respectable' and 'disreputable' brokers proved an important and unfortunate feature of his policy. He soon put forward a request for a system of special licences for the 'respectable' to place them on a superior footing to their brethren. Such an attitude inevitably bred an opposition party amongst those who believed that they were being victimized. A complaint made by Sherlock & Co., a long-established firm, in the autumn of 1833, was typical. While they were in partnership with another agency, Fitzhugh's, they wrote, Low took no action against them. But since the firms had recently parted company, he had pestered them with petty interferences, and used his official position

---

[1] Low justified this upon the ground that unsuccessful prosecutions 'tended to weaken' his authority.

[2] Undated cutting of 1834 contained in C.O. 384/33.

to divert their clients to Fitzhugh's. The complaint added that Low's partiality for the latter was notorious: he always recommended emigrants to deal with them, and though their vessels were frequently delayed never brought a charge against them.[1] Low's defence was revealing. He attributed the complaint to a conspiracy against him, and to a suggestion which he had made to the mayor that Sherlock's trading licence should be withdrawn in the following year. He admitted frankly that he discriminated against brokers who had been fined, and recommended emigrants to deal only with those firms which were 'most deserving of any sort of countenance'; and he added that Sherlock had been so insolent to him personally that he adjudged him to be 'amongst those passenger agents who would not scruple to commit a fraud'. He ended by threatening to prosecute Sherlock if he complained again. Shortly after this episode, Low reported that he had followed up his practice of recommending particular brokers by drawing up a list of 'respectable' lodgings which he advised all emigrants to frequent. He had also issued instructions to the town and dock police to direct all strange passengers to his office: he himself met as many of the Irish steamers as possible.[2] Clearly Low was riding for a fall. It is true that down to the end of 1833, despite some early protests such as Sherlock's, only the beneficial consequences of his work had engaged attention.[3] This was so partly because of the striking impression made by Low's early reports, partly because he had a warm and courageous sympathizer in his ultimate superior, Stanley, who saw the issue in simple terms of right and wrong.[4] But so reckless an assumption and so contumacious an application of discretionary and discriminatory powers could only end in trouble for Low himself.

In the early summer of 1834, trouble came, as the repercussions of Low's early actions began to reach the surface. First he was severely reprimanded by the treasury for having spent without prior permission £130 upon prosecutions and the maintenance of and the provision of new passages for witnesses.[5] This was an important setback. Had Low been able to spend public money upon ensuring

[1] C.O. 384/32, 4703 and 5002 Emigration, 19 Sept. and 11 Oct. 1833.
[2] Low also had placards concerning the emigration office and posters directing the emigrants to the more 'respectable' lodgings displayed on the Irish steamers.
[3] *Hans.*, 3rd, xii, 964, 18 Apr. 1834 (Stanley).
[4] Cf. C.O. 384/36, 137 Emigration, 6 Jan. 1834, Stanley's endorsement.
[5] C.O. 384/36, 2041 Emigration, treasury: Hay, 14 May 1834.

that the evidence needed for prosecutions was available, his position *vis-à-vis* the trade would have been strong indeed—strong, at any rate, up to the limits of his own abilities and of the meagre regulations of 1828. It was, however, scarcely thinkable that a government of the mid-1830s would have sanctioned such a course. Not only was a new public expenditure proposed—and this in itself raised difficulties—but its object represented a very revolutionary concept of public policy. For the idea implicit in Low's use of 'crown witnesses' was that the state should, of its own initiative (and incidentally without recourse to its own legal officers) use litigation and support litigants to achieve an accepted social good.[1] Moreover, because of the exigencies of sailings and embarkations, Low's programme would necessarily have involved a 'forward' sanctioning of expenditure. Thus objectionable at every point, the policy was quite chimerical in 1833; and it is not at all surprising that Stephen should have denounced it a little later. What is remarkable is that the inner logic of the situation should have impelled an ordinary executive officer to adumbrate so radical and 'modern' a project in the very first stages of his attempt to fulfil his duties.

Hard upon the heels of the treasury rebuke came a complaint by a Liverpool ship-owner, Froste, that Low behaved 'most offensively both in the manner and nature of his interference'. This was pressed upon the colonial office by Lord Sandon and could not be treated as lightly as the several earlier protests by individual brokers or firms. When called upon for an explanation, Low denied that his remonstrances were anything but 'mild' and 'patient', and characteristically accused Froste of belonging to the conspiracy against him. But he was none the less cautioned not to threaten where he could not perform.[2] Meanwhile, he had become involved in a much more serious dispute. His opponent was a broker Edward Walkinshaw, of whom James Stephen observed at a later stage, 'Mr Walkinshaw is (I can hardly find an expression at once decorous and appropriate)

---

[1] The powers of the first factory inspectors under the 1833 act (3 & 4 Will. *IV*, c. 103, see especially secs 17, 33–38) tended in some respects in this direction. But there is no true parallel. These inspectors were, in effect, constituted magistrates for offences under the statute, and were to act *pro tanto* as justices of the peace rather than executive officers. The questions of test cases and state expenditure for litigation and the support of litigants were never, apparently, considered; and probably would not have arisen in the circumstances.

[2] C.O. 384/35, 2253 and 2254 Emigration, 30 May 1834.

a knave'.[1] Low and he had first come to grips over a group of pauper emigrants from Dublin, who had been detained for months on end, sent trekking from vessel to vessel to suit Walkinshaw's convenience, and threatened with having their rations stopped if they complained. Through Low's efforts the paupers received their passages at last,[2] and this intervention was followed by others[3] until, at the close of 1833, Walkinshaw was forced to declare himself a bankrupt. Naturally, if unreasonably, blaming Low for the disaster, Walkinshaw proceeded to denounce him by pamphlet[4] and in the press for haughtiness, partiality and the use of his official position to divert trade to his favoured firms.[5] The affair received considerable publicity, with some of the national newspapers publishing Walkinshaw's complaint, and the Liverpool *Albion* and *Standard* taking opposite sides in the quarrel. Low returned the fire with spirit. He wrote to each of the newly appointed emigration officers asking them to expose Walkinshaw and to 'Caution all emigrants, applying to you, against being imposed on by that person'.[6] In conjunction with the mayor of Liverpool, he requested that similar placards be sent to the local authorities of all ports without emigration officers.[7] Finally, he pressed the government to support a group of penniless emigrants in a legal action against Walkinshaw with the object of 'breaking' him once for all.

At this point, Stephen intervened decisively. He insisted that Walkinshaw be treated courteously, not from respect for the man himself 'but from respect for the "Public" (that irritable and sensitive abstraction) of which he is a member and we are the servants'. 'As to proclaiming Walkinshaw's character to the world at large', Stephen continued, 'I hold that by any such quixotism more harm would be done than good. Walkinshaw would forthwith pass from

[1] Ibid, 3605 Emigration, 8 Sept. 1834, Stephen's endorsement.
[2] C.O. 384/33, 2837 Emigration, 10 June 1833; C.O. 384/35, 47 Emigration, 17 June 1833.
[3] C.O. 384/35, 585 Emigration, 15 Feb. 1834.
[4] E. Walkinshaw, *A vindication of Edward Walkinshaw* (Liverpool, 1834).
[5] C.O. 384/36, 1754 Emigration, 21 Apr. 1834. The most serious charge was that Low appropriated passengers' money, but no evidence to substantiate it was produced. By Low's own account, Walkinshaw sent him, under various false names, letters containing sovereigns, in the hope that he might be incriminated, C.O. 384/35, 3506 Emigration, 8 Sept. 1834.
[6] A copy of the circular letter was published in the *Limerick Times*, 3 July 1834.
[7] C.O. 384/35, 2535 Emigration, 21 June 1834.

his present character of an obscure swindler, into the dignified position of a man oppressed by persons in high place and power. You would have the whole radical press, in full cry against you'. Stephen concluded that Low had been hotheaded and indiscreet, and Hay agreed that he had 'indulged in rather too great an assumption of power, and attached too much importance to his functions . . . although he had very likely done so to control one, of whose conduct towards emigrants he has had much reason to complain'.[1] All Low's proposals were rejected,[2] and he himself was reprimanded for excess of zeal. He was ordered not to discriminate in future amongst the brokers, *'not to talk too much . . .* and not to assume even in word, much less in deed, any extraordinary power'.[3] These reprimands were delivered at the end of the 1834 emigration season.

Clearly Low's conduct as a public servant had been deplorable. Nor can it be doubted that his personal failings contributed to the deficiency. The Sherlock and Walkinshaw cases show clearly that he dramatized his own behaviour, and was self-important, petty and rash;[4] and every complainant emphasized his aggressiveness and partiality. But however much Low's vanity and manners may have sharpened the conflicts, we must recollect that the fault lay fundamentally with his conditions of appointment. The memorandum setting out the emigration officer's duties had clearly envisaged discrimination against particular brokers, chandlers, lodging-keepers and the rest. It had assumed that a certain proportion was 'disreputable' and more or less enjoined the officer to remove as much of the trade as possible from its hands. All Low's partisanship was merely in tune with this principle. Even his exaggeration of his office, his truculence and his collusions with the mayor and magistrates had been virtually sanctioned by the obligation to secure 'substantial justice' and the instruction to work with the local authorities to this end. And to direct the officer to stamp out abuses by his own

[1] Ibid., 3605 Emigration, 8 Sept. 1834, Stephen's endorsement; and Hay's endorsement of the same.

[2] The publication of Low's circular to the emigration officers was stopped in time everywhere except Limerick, ibid., 3191 Emigration 4 Aug. 1834.

[3] For Low's justifications of his conduct see ibid., 2861 and 3432 Emigration, 14 July and 25 Aug. 1834.

[4] All these qualities were exemplified in the case of Low's dispute with a broker, Salmon, who was also an ordance out-pensioner. Low went to the length of demanding that the pension be withdrawn, in the hope of ruining Salmon. See below, pp. 112–13.

'authority' without defining his discretions or amending the statute was surely to invite exorbitance and disputes. In short, the colonial office must take the blame for its failure to consider really seriously at the start—or for that matter at any later stage—the implications and necessary consequences of establishing the agency.

On paper, at any rate, the decisions taken in the Walkinshaw case represented at once a clarification and a reversal of policy. When Stephen stated roundly that an emigration officer, as a servant of the public, owed a duty of impartiality and courtesy to every member of that body, and when Low was ordered not to discriminate amongst the brokers, the original concept of reform, through the removal of the trade from the hands of disreputable persons, was being thrown overboard. When Low was told not to threaten where he could not perform, and not to assert his authority gratuitously, the idea of securing substantial justice through 'remonstrances' was being in effect abandoned. Moreover, the request that the government should back a group of emigrants too poor to undertake a legal action on their own behalf had provoked a minute from Stephen, which confined the activities of emigration officers to the strictest limits. 'The function of an emigration agent', he wrote, 'is, I apprehend, to assist emigrants with his advice and aid: and to enforce the penalties of the passengers' act, when necessary. . . . But I do not suppose that the emigration agent is further intended to undertake the redress of those wrongs which, in the progress of their mutual dealing respecting emigration, individuals may inflict on each other. . . . Lieut. Low desires to engage in this action with a view, not so much as to damages, as to example; grounding himself on the defectiveness of the passengers' act, as an apology for not resorting to the remedies which it provides. Without disputing the justice of these opinions, I should say that the general maxim must prevail; that the executive government, and those whom it employs, must enforce the law as they find it, looking to the legislature for further powers when necessary, but acquiescing in the defectiveness of the law, so long as it continues unremedied by Parliament'.

At first sight, all this may appear to have been a wholly desirable correction of initial errors. But while it is true that if the new 'policy' had been literally interpreted and consistently applied, the emigration officers might have conducted themselves with the decorum and impartiality which befitted public servants, it is also true that

4*

they could have achieved little or nothing for the passengers. There was no gainsaying the fact that Low had been relatively successful in the vital work of emigrant protection, or that it was his extra-legal methods which had been responsible for the success. Nor can we withhold sympathy from a man who, perceiving acute and unmeritea sufferings, struck without regard to his weapons at the inhuman ruffians who were responsible. Low probably spoke the truth when he said that he never interfered with a broker 'except I perceive a gross dereliction from acting fairly and honestly towards emigrants'.[1] When on another occasion Low was reprimanded by the admiralty for dealing insolently with an agent, Stanley reminded the reprimanders that the agent in question had twice been convicted of participation 'in a system of imposition on poor and ignorant men'.[2]

Without haters of iniquity there would have been no improvement. Stephen's definition of the emigration officer's function was constitutionally correct, but it was also, in effect, unreal and callous. Outside his dedicated task of eradicating slavery, Stephen was no reformer. The family trait of melancholy and his first profession, law, had combined to render him, in practice, a supporter of the status quo. Invariably, his influence was on the side of restricting the volume of legislation; invariably, he advised against courses of action which might issue in expensive litigation. 'I see in this correspondence the material of many 6/8 charges'[3] was a characteristically irresponsible, if amusing, observation. However keenly he may have understood, in an abstract fashion, the desirability of change, Stephen was always so conscious of the difficulties in the way, and so wanting in adventurous imagination that he despaired before the sword was drawn. 'These Irishmen', ran a typical minute, 'are not the first, nor will they be the last, to make the discovery that a man may starve and yet have the best right of action that a special pleader could wish for'.[4] The colonial office papers for these years abound in clever, tart endorsements to this effect; but in no case did Stephen go on to say that such a state of things was intolerable, or even to consider anything more needed to be said or done. It is not,

---

[1] Ibid., 3432 Emigration, 25 Aug. 1834.
[2] C.O. 384/36, 137 Emigration, 6 Jan. 1834, Stanley's endorsement.
[3] C.O. 384/35, unmarked, 27 Sept. 1834, Stephen's endorsement.
[4] C.O. 384/30, unmarked, Stephen: Elliot, 31 July 1832.

perhaps, irrelevant to recall that long after he had left the public service, Stephen told the Northcote–Trevelyan commissioners that although the majority of the civil service was unbelievably brainless and inefficient, the world was not yet ripe for an overthrow of the system which was responsible for their recruitment.[1]

Stephen's cast of mind was ever legal rather than bureaucratic. He could diagnose unerringly the matters of principle involved in Low's concept of a public office. But extraordinary powers of analysis and a thorough grasp of accepted constitutional theory were dangerous qualities in a public servant of the 1830s, unless they were accompanied by sympathy and creativeness. Stephen's attitude towards the cases which came before him was depersonalized and fatalistic. To him, emigrants no less than brokers or the remainder of poor mankind appeared as 'parties' rather than human beings. The underlying assumption of his judgments in the Walkinshaw and similar cases was that the state and its officers must be not only impartial in deciding upon the facts, and in their dealings with individuals of the same class, but also neutral as between all classes of person whatsoever. But every passenger act and the very creation of the corps, not to say a multitude of similar undertakings of the same period, implied the opposite principle, that all persons were not equal in capacity and that some required a peculiar protection from the state. Ironically enough, it was Stephen's own son, Fitzjames, who made this latter principle—or perhaps we should say, these facts—the basis of a proposal for criminal law reform. 'It [the present procedure]', he wrote in 1857, 'is an admirable system if it is fully worked out, but this only happens when the accused person has money enough to avail himself of all the privileges which the law gives him. . . . It throws a very heavy task indeed upon the poor and ignorant. . . . It allows a man ample opportunities for defending himself, but it does nothing whatever to help him in doing so'.[2]

All this is not to justify the original instructions to the emigration officer or Low's régime at Liverpool. Unquestionably, both were mistaken. But they did represent an attempt, however injudicious

[1] *Rep. reorganization civil service*, 71–80 [1870], H.C. 1854–5, xx.

[2] F. Stephen, 'The characteristics of English criminal law', *Cambridge Essays, 1857* (London, 1857), pp. 54–55. Fitzjames Stephen was a comparatively young man when he made this comment. As he grew older, his attitudes increasingly resembled his father's.

and unworthy, to fulfil the main purpose for which emigration officers had been appointed. It was not enough to detect errors and to order that improper modes of action be discontinued. Some alternative method of reform should have been concurrently devised. Clearly, the first steps should have been a new passenger act based on the findings of the executive officers, which would clarify their functions and create precise discretions, and the appointment of responsible superiors for the corps. Neither was provided and the latter was not even considered in 1834.

We have already pointed out that if the 'Stephen policy' had been logically extended and universally applied, emigrants would have gained little from the existence of the corps of emigration officers. But it was not extended or applied. None of the seven officers who had been appointed to other ports in the United Kingdom in the spring and summer of 1834 was informed of the decision, and they blithely continued to report successes obtained, like Low's, through 'remonstrances' or the assumption of whatever 'discretions' went unchallenged. Indeed, Low himself soon resumed reports in the same strain. The explanation of all this lies in the absence of a real superintendence. No person or department within the colonial office was directly and specifically responsible for the officers. Hay acknowledged and filed their correspondence; but otherwise, unless a scandal arose or an expenditure was proposed they were left entirely to their own devices. So far as Low was concerned this meant, in effect, that so long as he avoided very serious disputes and unauthorized expenditure, his superiors presented no obstacle to the continuance of his old policy. But it also meant that he could not hope to advance beyond the points reached in 1833. Indeed, the Froste and Walkinshaw cases and their greater experience of the 1828 act so emboldened brokers that he found it increasingly difficult even to maintain the line which he had pushed forward in his first campaign. New legislation now presented the only prospect of improvement and throughout the remainder of 1834 he redoubled his demands for an immediate revision of the passenger act and for a definition and enlargement of his powers. In the closing months of the year he reported constantly that despite the great improvement which he himself had wrought and despite his unremitting hostility towards the 'unscrupulous' brokers, frauds abounded and the conditions of passage remained disgraceful: he could hold out no hope

of further amelioration until he was armed with certain and appropriate powers and provided with an assistant to take some of the
burden of inspections and court appearances off his shoulders.[1]

From the standpoint of the executive corps, the passenger act of
1835 was, as we have seen, a wasted opportunity. In both the numbers and the foodstuffs requirements—the cornerstone of emigrant
protection—the new statute fell short of their 'minimum' requests.
The problem of enforcing legislation was passed over altogether:
indeed, after a year's experience, the Liverpool magistrates observed
that the 1835 act had not been 'framed to be acted on'. Worst of all
the act ignored even the existence of the officers, and left them without any certain status. Small wonder that Low greeted the new legislation with the cry that the corps was still powerless to provide 'the
humane protection which the public naturally expects'. Indeed, the
1835 act changed little at Liverpool and that little not altogether for
the better. The shippers and brokers of the port (unlike their Irish
counterparts) were quick to take advantage of the exemption from
the act of vessels carrying less than one passenger per registered five
tons; and passengers on these 'short ships' were exposed to all the
miseries of detention, overcrowding and bad and insufficient water
and provisions which had characterized the former 'lawless' days.
As soon as he realized the disastrous consequences of this legislative
amendment, Low pressed vigorously for its repeal; and despite a
rebuff from the colonial office, he very properly continued his agitation. But, inexcusably, the error remained uncorrected for seven
seasons, just as, inexcusably, the patent errors of the 1828 act had
survived for as long a period. In these circumstances, Low fell back
upon the old course of 'remonstrance' and 'intimidation'. He
staunchly refused to clear 'short ships' which were, in his view, putting to sea in a dangerous state. It was true that a high proportion of
the 'short ships' took numbers of passengers aboard surreptitiously
after they had been cleared. But even this was no justification for
refusing clearances before the law had been broken, and the Liverpool magistrates and customs officers were undoubtedly right in their
private view that Low's conduct was illegal. 'Intimidation' in the
case of 'short ships' had the usual results of partial success in

---

[1] The remainder of this chapter, except where other evidence is cited, is based
on Low's occasional reports for the period September 1834 to the end of 1839,
contained in the series, C.O. 384/35–384/60.

preventing very great evils, but also of wrangling, bad relations with the trade, and abuse of office.

In general terms, as well, Low's reports for the period 1835-40 show that the 1835 act neither strengthened his hand nor improved his conduct. In the second half of the 1830s as in the first, vessels were all too often unseaworthy (a considerable number being wrecked, dismasted or otherwise forced to put back to port each season), and passengers all too often robbed in lodging houses or cheated over contract tickets or sailing dates or foodstuffs. 'Unscrupulous' owners and brokers still inflicted many and grave wrongs with impunity. Even the case of the *Cumberland* was virtually paralleled in 1835, when Robinson Brothers dispatched the *Henry* in a dreadful state of disrepair despite Low's threats and entreaties. In due course the *Henry* foundered, and when the wretched survivors (having spent thirty-one days in open boats with little food and water) were returned to Liverpool, Robinsons absolutely refused to accept responsibility or furnish fresh passages or assistance of any kind. Similarly, when in 1836 the passengers for the *Phoebe* suffered a very long detention beyond their sailing date, Low failed altogether to obtain redress, the broker in question having framed the contract tickets so ingeniously that he was freed from all liability. Indeed, in 1840, after Low had laboured for seven seasons and an assistant had been appointed three years before to share his work, the recorder of Liverpool reported that systematic fraud on passengers was still growing up on a 'frightening scale'.[1] He added that the inhabitants of the city were complaining loudly—as indeed might well have been expected, since (sympathy for the sufferings of the emigrants quite apart) it was they who had to bear most of the financial burden, either directly through the public subscriptions which Low opened in the most pitiful cases, or, if these failed, by supporting the emigrants in workhouses or by paying their return steamer fares to Ireland. The recorder specifically absolved the emigration officers from all blame, stating that they were already over-

---

[1] C.O. 384/62, 760 Emigration, 13 Apr. 1840; C.O. 386/140, pp. 21, 23, 16 and 25 Apr. 1840. Three years previously the common council was so disturbed by the growth of abuses in Liverpool that it set up a committee to investigate the local trade and make recommendations for its improvement, *Annual rep. agent-general emigration Canada*, 6, H.C. 1837-8 (389), xl. In 1841, a Liverpool magistrate, Rushton, complained of the continued growth of abuses in the port, C.O. 386/27, pp. 155-7, 24 May 1841.

worked and that the eradication of large-scale corruption was beyond their powers. This last was undoubtedly true. Low had almost four thousand complaints to investigate in the single year, 1837, and the volume of emigration from Liverpool was increasing more or less steadily throughout the period.

Conversely, Low was still condemned, or believed himself to be condemned, to pursue the lines of conduct which had been forced upon him at the start. He still concentrated attention upon the Robinsons, O'Becketts and Sherlocks of the trade, with whom he had clashed before. He still relied heavily upon municipal support: we find him asking anxiously in 1836 for an introduction to the newly elected mayor so that he might enlist his assistance in stamping out abuses. And despite the rebukes of 1834, Low's methods did not change. After his failure in the *Phoebe* case, for instance, he sought to punish the ingenious broker by prosecuting him on an altogether different charge. In fact, the prosecution was successful, but the *Phoebe* passengers gained nothing and this was precisely the sort of manœuvre which bred ill-feeling and counter 'sharpness'. Again, when in 1837 he was involved in a very trivial dispute over the removal of posters, Low threatened the brokers, Sherlock & Co., that they would be refused a licence when a new licensing system for shipping agents was introduced. When Sherlock's complained to the colonial office, Low was warned against disputatiousness and boasting of the use he would make of legislation before his superiors had so much as given an opinion upon his proposal. But like the earlier rebukes this caution had virtually no effect upon Low's subsequent behaviour.

Finally, a pamphlet issued in 1838 by a group of malcontent brokers both raises some points of interest and clearly demonstrates the unhappy character of the later as well as the first years of Low's régime. It began by asserting, perhaps justly, that Stanley had lacked authority to make the original appointment. Next it protested —again with reason—of Low's authoritarianism and of his 'despotic' and 'un-British' practice of recommending passengers to deal only with his 'favoured' houses. Thirdly, the multiplication of legislation was condemned as self-defeating: 'It will be in vain to have one Act of Parliament after another, creating fresh changes, and throwing obstacles not only in our way, but actually injuring the very people for whom you profess so parental a regard. If the trade be shackled the consequence is that it falls upon the poor emigrant who is thereby compelled to pay a higher price for his passage'. The pamphlet then went on to complain that the relationship between shipping broker and emigrant was not being treated as an ordinary commercial dealing, and that it was not recognized that the broker's interest in his own good name would suffice to protect his client. How would it be in any other trade, it was demanded, if the merchant were constantly summoned to a 'supervisor's' office, forever hauled before the magistrates, his character blackened and his time and money lost? The Liverpool brokers had been vilified by the press, magistrates and emigration office until 'the town teems with the idea that we are all a pack of swindlers for whom Botany Bay is too good an asylum', whereas in fact the so-called 'defenceless emigrants [are] robbers, runaways, villains of all sorts and descriptions . . . the offscourings of the human race'. As things stood, there was a furore if a vessel were delayed a week, yet what redress was open to a broker if he lost £100 through cargo not being delivered in time? Finally, the pamphlet attacked official inaccessibility. Though the brokers wanted full and open inquiry, the emigration officer's reports were 'secret' and his superiors evasive. 'Oh! it is excellent to have a giant's strength, but it is tyrannous to use it like a giant'.[1]

The last three charges, being new, merit some attention. Doubtless, the pamphleteers were disingenuous in objecting to the multiplication of legislation as self-defeating: what they really wanted was no legislation at all or as little restraint as possible. Doubtless, a very large number if not an actual majority of the Liverpool brokers did constitute 'a pack of swindlers'.[2] Doubtless, official correspondence should not have been published at every angry and ignorant

[1] *Letter to Lieutenant Low, R.N, . . . by a Passage Broker* (Liverpool, 1838). Despite this title, the pamphlet was a composite work.

[2] One of the pamphlet's authors, a runner, Salmon, who was also an ordnance out-pensioner, certainly belonged to the pack: on more than one occasion he was convicted of frauds on emigrants during Low's first year of office. Low asked the ordnance to deprive him of his pension on account of his 'impertinent interference', but the departmental inquiry found that although Salmon had been disrespectful 'nothing detrimental to his character emerged'. Stanley, the colonial secretary, satirically observed that he was glad at least that the inquiry admitted that Low's appointment had 'contributed to check' the sort of imposition of which Salmon had been guilty. An account of the inquiry written by Low's enemy, Walkinshaw, has the true note of Dickensian farce and rings authentic. One passage runs as follows:

demand. Yet there was a certain substance in each complaint. Legislative requirements did raise the price of passages; and—except independently by Low in making recommendations which were ignored —no attempt at 'costing' had been made before the 1835 bill was prepared, although this was an elementary precaution and one which could easily have been taken by gathering estimates from the various emigration officers. Correspondingly, it was quite true that the relationship between broker and emigrant was not being treated as an ordinary commercial dealing. There were very good reasons for not so doing, but there was no reason in logic why parliament and the colonial office should not have recognized the fact and taken steps to explain and allow for the differentiation. Again, the pamphlet's final complaint was an anticipation (almost a century beforehand)[1] of the charge of 'new despotism' in bureaucracy; and while the charge, in the extreme form in which Lord Hewart made it, was not sustained,[2] few would dispute the existence of a great and perhaps intractable problem in this relationship of government and law. Nor would many dispute the maxim that not only must justice be done, but that it must also be seen to have been done.[3] Generally, then, the pamphlet re-emphasizes the slovenliness, confusion and

'Lieut. Low—What! Did I not state to the fellow that unless he would obey me I should write up and have his pension stopped?

This question was not answered—Mr Salmon at this moment ventured to take a snuff, when Lieut. Low (turning to Capt. Henderson, the worthy officer who presided) exclaimed—See the impudence of the fellow now!

Capt. H.—What? Why?

Lieut. Low—Is it becoming for him to take snuff in *our* presence, and sit in that manner?

Capt. H.—Considering that the livelihood of his large family of twelve children is at stake, it would be cruel to refuse him the comfort of a pinch, and, for myself, I should consider it no degradation to furnish any man in his circumstances with a pinch out of my own box'.

Walkinshaw, op. cit. See also C.O. 384/33, 4449 and 5406 Emigration, 3 Sept. and 8 Nov. 1833; 384/36, 137 Emigration, 6 Jan. 1834.

[1] The first warning was sounded by A. V. Dicey in 1915 in an article entitled, 'The development of administrative law in England', *Law Quart. Rev.*, xxxi. The climax was reached with the publication of *The new despotism* by Lord Chief Justice Hewart in 1929.

[2] *Report of committee on ministers' powers* (Donoughmore Report), Cmd. 4060, 1932, p. 7.

[3] 'A long line of cases shows that it is not merely of some importance but is of fundamental importance that justice should not only be done, but should manifestly and undoubtedly be seen to be done', *per* Hewart, L.C.J., in R. v. *Sussex Justices ex p. McCarthy* [1924], 1 K.B. 256, 259.

want of both principle and perception which marked the first wave of legislation and regulation after 1825. Indeed, we find a group of humble passage-brokers pointing out (albeit obliquely and from self-interest) more of the revolutionary implications of emigrant protection than the whole body of politicians and public servants, Stephen excepted, had understood. In these circumstances it was perhaps ironical that the colonial office should have decided that the pamphlet be ignored 'considering the source from which it emanates'. Within two years, however, the Low régime at Liverpool had ended. In the spring of 1840 Low died in office, the victim, friends and enemies agreed, of overwork, of endless and largely gratuitous exertions. He was an unwise and possibly an unpleasant gentleman, but a very gallant and true-hearted officer.

THE GROWTH OF THE EXECUTIVE CORPS
1834–40

FORTUNATELY for the future of the corps of emigration officers, a decision on the success of the Liverpool experiment was taken before the more serious disputes in which Low was involved had come to a head. By the end of 1833 no less than 15,000 emigrants and more than 100 vessels had passed through Low's hands; and at that stage it was generally agreed that, as Stanley told the house of commons, Low had 'by his exertions succeeded in putting an end to a long train of abuses, and in putting the trade on a more respectable footing than it had ever stood before'. Lord Sandon, the local member, fully corroborated the 'most gratifying testimonies . . . from the people of Liverpool, and from the emigrants themselves'; and even Hume, the diehard opponent of the passenger bill of 1828, blessed Low's work.[1] Accordingly, early in 1834, the colonial secretary informed the main emigration ports that he would provide them with officers if they would afford the same facilities as Liverpool. To the six ports which accepted the offer, half-pay naval lieutenants were posted in time for the new season. Hodder was sent to Dublin, Friend to Cork, Miller to Belfast, Lynch to Limerick, Hemmans to Glasgow and Starke to Bristol. A seventh new officer, Forrest, was appointed to Leith later in the year; and offices were opened at Sligo, Londonderry and London, and Low furnished with an assistant, in the course of the next three seasons.

Like Low's original appointment, the formation of the executive corps belonged in spirit to the 'eighteenth-century' rather than the 'nineteenth-century' mode of government. Once again, there was no clear definition of either duties or status. Stanley's latest description of the functions—'to receive applications from emigrants, to give them advice as to the course which they should pursue, to see that no frauds were practised on them'[2]—was as dangerously unspecific

[1] *Hans.*, 3rd, xxii, 963–5, 18 Apr. 1834.
[2] Ibid., 964.

as before; and there was still no notion of giving the emigration officer a statutory authority. Again, the unprofessional and 'gentle-man-like' character of the office was emphasized by recruiting only naval lieutenants on reserve and by paying them as their basic stipend the difference between half and full naval pay. In fact, so vague was the concept of duties and so large the expectations from rank that in 1837 the southern English ports were refused an officer upon the extraordinary ground that 'the absence of one is less likely to be felt on this coast, where the large naval establishments in the principal harbours, as well as the constant resort of officers of the navy, afford a security which does not exist elsewhere against the growth of abuses in passenger ships'.[1] Other evidence of the survival of older administrative notions and practices is provided by the curious relationship between central and local authority in this matter, and by the method of recruitment. It was the mayor of Liverpool who had pressed for Low's appointment; and to the end of his days at Liverpool, Low was furnished with an office and a supplementary emolument by the city council.[2] The mayor of Cork gave Friend an office, and promised him 'every countenance and assistance'; and Limerick corporation presented Lynch with £25 for an outfit, and asked that he be subject to its own directions.[3] Correspondingly, the circumstances surrounding several of the new appointments were redolent of the ancien régime. Sligo, for example, appears to have been given an officer mainly because a 'suitable' candidate was available, Lieut. Shuttleworth being proposed, partly because he was a native of the town, and partly 'out of compliment to Mr Martin' to whom the government owed much.[4] The same air of patronage enveloped the Londonderry appointment, although here there were two candidates in the field and

[1] *Rep. agent-general emigration U.K.*, 13, H.C. 1837–8 (388), xl.

[2] This last was, in Low's final years of office, the subject of some dispute. In the end, it was left an open question whether the payment was *ex gratia* for Low's public services or in fulfilment of a promise made by the mayor. It was not continued for Low's successor; nor so far as can be discovered did any other officer receive an additional salary, C.O. 384/47, 1373 Emigration, 6 June 1838; C.O. 384/52, 474 Emigration, 8 Mar. 1838; C.O. 386/23, pp. 5–7, 203–4, 23 Apr. and 7 July 1839.

[3] C.O. 384/35, 1895 Emigration, 6 May 1834; C.O. 384/36, 2791 Emigration, 5 July 1834. Only in Dublin, where the appointment of an officer was strongly resisted by the shipping merchants, did the local authorities fail to provide accommodation and refuse to undertake any expense.

[4] C.O. 384/39, 124 Emigration, 4 Apr. 1835. Shuttleworth was appointed.

Dublin Castle was heavily involved. The merchants and ship-owners, backed by Sir Robert Ferguson, M.P., asked for a Lieut. Ramsay, who commanded a river steamer at the port, while the mayor and Dawson, the secretary to the admiralty, pressed the claims of Frederick Hamilton, 'who has been most serviceable in supporting the constitutional cause'.[1] Conversely, we find the mayor of Waterford refusing to accept an officer lest the appointment might seem to imply criticism of the customs authorities, whom he regarded as 'active', or of the shipping houses, which were 'resident and long-established'. And when at a later date the shipping mer-chants of the city, supported by Sir Thomas Wyse, M.P., them-selves petitioned for an officer, they seem to have been moved not so much by the merit of their case as by the desire to assert their commercial equality with Cork and Limerick.[2]

Thus the beginnings of the executive corps show clearly that although it was contemporaneous with Chadwick's inspectorates and assistant commissioners it had, initially, little in common with the new order. Even in intention it was very far from being a pro-fessional bureaucracy, let alone one subject to independent central control. Rather did the corps belong to the old world of personal connexion and local *amour propre*, of improvement commissions, turnpike trusts and co-ordinate jurisdictions. Its setting is one in which reform consisted, not of a 'rational' eradication and replace-ment of the inefficient, but of an endless addition of ad hoc and quasi-amateur instruments of government to supply the gross deficiencies of the moribund but still surviving forms. The very men selected in such a personal, informal way had no particular training for the task, except presumably a knowledge of ships and a habit of com-mand. They were set free to work with very imprecise directions, no supervision and a vague half-discretion to fulfil the politico-economic policies of assisting estate clearances and directing the emigrants towards British possessions. In some places they were regarded for a time more as state auxiliaries called in to assist in a local difficulty than as state officials proper. It is true that all this

[1] The colonial secretary observed that he himself had no candidate and in the end it was Ramsay who was selected, C.O. 384/36, 2107 and 4475 Emigration, 13 May and 15 Nov. 1834; C.O. 384/39, 5 and 183 Emigration, 20 Mar. and 15 Apr. 1835; C.O. 386/20, pp. 79-82, 135-6, 22 Sept. and 2 Oct. 1837.
[2] C.O. 384/52, 1419 and 1472 Emigration, 16 and 24 July 1839.

was soon changed by the rub and wear of experience. As the regulation of emigration was found to involve great trouble and expense,
the local authority insisted that such business belonged exclusively
to the central power, despite the intermittent efforts of the latter
to recreate a sense of local responsibility. As the officers discovered
the extent and urgency of the problem of protecting emigrants, this
absorbed almost all their energies. Willy-nilly, they became professionals—professional executors of increasingly technical legislation—and, as we shall see, the idea that they should help landlords or attempt to influence the destination of the emigrants quickly
died away. As the evils of informality and want of direction were
exposed, it became more and more clear that some body of responsible superiors should be established. But all this represents the
revolution wrought by the pressures of work and the findings of the
executive. In its origin, the corps of emigration officers bore little
resemblance to 'modern' forms of government.

The Scottish and Bristol officers discovered that the passenger
trades of their respective ports were reasonably well conducted. But
the first reports from Ireland made it clear that the same type of
problem and abuses existed in the Irish ports as at Liverpool,
although they were, of course, upon a very much smaller scale. The
chief surgeon and the local Emigration Society of Limerick informed Lynch that the passenger act was continually evaded, and
that the hardships of the emigrants were beyond description.[1] Miller
found that for years the Belfast emigrants had suffered from the most
shameless impositions, being in many cases 'left literally to starve
on the quays'. The frauds consisted principally in brokers 'detain-
ing the emigrants unnecessarily, engaging passengers without
having vessels on the spot to receive them, and refusing to abide by
the acts of their sub-agents in the country, who use gross deception
to entangle the unsuspecting countrymen, a system most injurious
in its consequences and perfectly understood between the agents
and their principals'. From the start, he encountered innumerable
breaches of contract; and reported that although he settled many by
'remonstrance or intimidation', scoundrels could still flourish in the
Belfast trade. Miller's main complaints were of his own want of
powers—he had had, for instance, to stand by and allow a notorious drunkard to take command of a vessel—and of the invariable

[1] C.O. 384/35, 1985 Emigration, 6 May 1834.

decision of the Belfast magistrates that breaches of the passenger acts did not come within their jurisdiction. The attitude of the magistrates greatly undermined his position, and he attributed all his early success to the belief current in the city that he himself had, or soon would have, the widest summary powers to check malpractices.[1]

Hodder and Friend had much the same story to tell. The former reported that an 'inferior description of bankrupt speculator . . . with few exceptions constitutes the ship agent and broker of this port [Dublin]'. Finding that 'peremptory' behaviour alone answered with the Dublin brokers, he insisted on systematic quayside examinations of the vessels and devised his own rules for conducting them. One captain who was detained threatened an action for demurrage, but Hodder masterfully and correctly dismissed this as 'idle talk'.[2] The Cork trade was equally corrupt. Friend discovered that deceptions as to the size and nature of the vessels were common, that sailing dates and other conditions of the contracts were constantly violated, and that lodging-keepers and brokers coerced the emigrants by seizing their baggage and by other methods of intimidation.[3] The worst abuse of all derived from the practice of booking passages on Liverpool vessels by placing a deposit with a Cork sub-agent. 'On their arrival they [the passengers] find that the ship has sailed, or has no room for them or from some excuse or other cannot obtain their passage'. All too often the result was vagrancy or pauperdom in a strange city.[4] These impositions were encouraged by a fatal decision of the Cork magistrates that they had no powers to grant summary relief to emigrants. As a result, Friend had only his own 'remonstrances' to rely upon; and though he found that these were effective in most cases (to the extent of recovering money obtained under false pretences at least), he asked for permission to wear his undress naval uniform so that 'greater attention' might be paid to his 'recommendations'.[5] Miller of Belfast made the same application; and it is interesting to note the similarity between these early requests from Ireland and Low's

[1] C.O. 384/35, 1818, 1841, 2151 and 2690 Emigration, 22 Mar., 14 Apr., 19 May and 30 June 1834.
[2] Ibid., 2241, 3200 and 3608 Emigration, 24 May, 5 Aug. and 8 Sept. 1834.
[3] Ibid., 1626, 1931 and 2000 Emigration, 12 Apr. and 4 and 9 May 1834.
[4] C.O. 384/41, 629 Emigration, 20 Apr. 1836.
[5] C.O. 384/35, 2689 Emigration, 30 June 1834. The permission was granted.

early demand for a 'King's boat' to secure 'respect'. Again like Low, Friend observed that the most urgent need of all was for wide and certain discretions for the emigration officer so that he might ensure that contracts were fulfilled and possess 'that control over the fittings of vessels so essential for the comfort, safety and health of the emigrant'.

Once more following in Low's path, the Irish officers soon concluded that an immediate amendment of the passenger act was the first requisite for reform. Both Friend and Hodder proposed that the numbers aboard be reduced to one for every two tons burthen or even less, and between them they directed attention besides to problems which Low had tended to neglect—water containers, clearance certificates and diet, berthing and mortality at sea. Friend believed that the prime causes of epidemics were the dirty habits and living conditions of the emigrants and their poor provisions, the latter being, moreover, altogether unsuitable for a people like the Irish who were accustomed to a vegetable diet. He also complained of the berthing on Cork vessels, where the current practice was to crowd no less than four adults into a bunk six feet long by four and a half feet wide, and of the absence of even the most rudimentary medicines and medical attention for those who fell ill upon the voyage.[1] To counter these abuses, he proposed various new statutory requirements and, with the assistance of a Cork shipping agent, drew up lists of the necessary and desirable provisions.[2] Hodder evidently shared these views for he recommended a 'jury', composed of passengers and ship's officers, to maintain health and discipline at sea, considerable improvements in the supply of water and an increase of, and greater variation in the diet.[3]

Broadly speaking, the Irish officers found themselves in much the same situation as Low and reacted in much the same manner. But there were differences between the two. In some respects, the Irish officers stood on weaker ground. No one had requested their appointment; most had been thrust unbidden and unknown upon their port; and each had considerable difficulty in advertising and

[1] C.O. 384/38, 56 Emigration, 1 January 1835.
[2] The necessary provisions were potatoes, biscuit, oatmeal and dried fish. Sugar, coffee, butter, eggs, whisky and bacon were also recommended, ibid., 1626 Emigration, 12 April 1834.
[3] C.O. 384/38, 57 Emigration, 6 April 1835. Miller of Belfast also made similar recommendations.

explaining his office to the public.[1] They received, moreover, no support from that necessary ally, the magistracy, though this was due not to ill-will but to the justices' ignorance or narrow interpretation of the law. Nor were they, as was Low at Liverpool, actively encouraged by the local authorities and a 'reforming' section of local opinion. Finally, they do not appear to have had Low's good understanding with the customs officers. This was important, at least at ports like Cork and Limerick, where vessels were sometimes cleared by customs officers before they had received the emigration officer's certificate. On the other hand, the brokers with whom the Irish officers had to deal were neither as well-informed nor as influential as the members of the Liverpool trade. They did not know, and never really discovered, the weakness of the officer's position and the strength of their own at law; and by and large the 'remonstrances' of the Irish officers achieved their ends without recriminations. There was none of that semi-organized defiance which Low was then encountering at Liverpool. In fact, one consequence of the appointment of officers to five of the six main Irish ports during 1834–5 was that the sixth, Londonderry, soon acquired 'the worst passenger trade in Ireland', brokers having 'come thither from remote places' to take advantage of the situation there.[2] In turn, the absence of complaints and protests meant that the Irish officers were given a completely free hand by the colonial office. Miller could openly report that he was trading on the ignorance of the Belfast brokers, and Hodder that he dealt roughly with all opposition, without either being in any way rebuked or cautioned. Again, it was natural that in small shipping communities an officer would attain in time a knowledge of the local trade and an influence over its members, which could not be hoped for in a vast cosmopolitan *entrepôt* like Liverpool. After a tour of the Irish offices in 1837, T. F. Elliot observed, 'I am persuaded that both as centres of information, and also as the instruments of a standing and systematic resistance against imposition, this class of officers have [sic] been most useful. . . . I found everywhere the indications of their

[1] C.O. 384/35, 1841 Emigration, Miller to Hay, 14 Apr. 1834; 2241 Emigration, Hodder to Hay, 24 May 1834. Friend reported a year after his appointment that brokers could still conceal the fact of his existence from some of the emigrants, C.O. 384/38, 56 Emigration, 1 Jan. 1835.

[2] C.O. 386/20, pp. 78–82, 135–6, 22 Sept. and 2 Oct. 1837; *Rep. U.K. agent-general emigration*, 14, H.C. 1837–8 (388), xl.

presence being valued, and of its having conduced to the repression of evil'.[1] Significantly, the Irish recommendations for new passenger legislation concentrated almost exclusively upon improvement in conditions during the passage. As to the pre-embarkation difficulties, the officer evidently believed that, with sure discretions, they could manage these comfortably by themselves.

Thus we find that, generally speaking, the emigration officers throughout the United Kingdom reached a certain level of achievement very quickly, but were then halted by the defectiveness and inadequacy of the passenger act, by their own uncertain standing and by the absence of an active, co-ordinating and responsible superior. The first infantry rush gained ground everywhere. But without legislative artillery, without staffwork or generalship, the officers could do no more than cling precariously to the early gains. As Miller of Belfast observed after his first twelve months of office, 'my arrival has been attended with much benefit, at the same time, my usefulness has been curtailed from want of sufficient power'. Before he came detentions of five or six weeks were common; now vessels were rarely more than a fortnight late in sailing. He had no real power over provisioning, but usually succeeded in 'sending back' the emigrants who were inadequately supplied. The Belfast magistrates refused to deal with breaches of passage contracts, but 'a strong remonstrance to the charterers' was occasionally effective.[2] In short, Miller's success was remarkable but also insufficient and insecure; and every other officer had the same tale to tell. The essential remedy was good legislation, but the statutory barrage of 1835 was, as we have seen, though long and loud, extremely ill-directed; and only one of the many serious defects in the passenger laws to which the officers' reports continuously drew attention was remedied during the course of the subsequent seven years.[3] Such was the measure of the incoherence of this branch of government. In the meantime, such advances as were made took place in the fields of 'generalship' and 'staffwork'. Perhaps this was inevitable. It may

---

[1] *Rep. U.K. agent-general emigration*, 9, H.C. 1837–8 (388), xl.

[2] *1st rep. poor inquiry commissioners Ire.*, Appendix C, part I, 18–19, H.C. 1836, xxx.

[3] This was the inapplicability of the passenger act to foreign vessels sailing from United Kingdom ports. It was remedied by a clause in a customs act of 1837, 1 & 2 *Vic.*, c. 113, sec. 26. Cf. C.O. 384/41, 715 and 756 Emigration, 13 & 30 May 1836; C.O. 386/19, pp. 44–45, 25 May 1837.

well have been that really satisfactory legislation had to await the appointment of a powerful superior.

In 1837, the causes of emigrant protection and systematic colonization became closely, if temporarily, intertwined. They had never been entirely separate. So far as Liverpool was concerned, the original purpose of helping 'gentlemen', poor law authorities and the clergy in promoting emigration was stillborn. Low's hands were full of much more urgent tasks. But the Irish officers were naturally drawn into this field of work. Irish government inevitably tended towards paternalism. The Irish environment rendered administrators and even 'thinking men' more or less immune to the fevers of political economy, and Irish over-population was so palpable that the desirability of emigration was scarcely open to discussion. It so happened, moreover, that state-assisted emigration to Australia[1] was being launched when the Irish officers were first appointed. In a vague and informal fashion they became involved in the business of furnishing and selecting emigrants. Each attempted, almost immediately, to set up a local emigration committee after the type which had been recently constituted at London for this purpose. We need not follow out the fortunes of these ventures here. Suffice it to say that only the Cork and Limerick officers had any success in the early years, and that even in these cases there was much mismanagement and conflict.[2]

But Australian 'colonization' is not altogether irrelevant to our subject. In the first place, it usually, and usefully, put the emigration officers in touch with influential people in their localities. Next, it may have kept alive the idea of a quasi-political function. At any rate, the Cork officer, who was much the most concerned with the Australian emigration, was also much the most eager in persuading voluntary emigrants to make for British North America rather than the United States. Again, the additional responsibilities involved in a state-managed emigration directed the officers' (and particularly the Cork officer's) attention to aspects of between-decks life which had hitherto been neglected.[3] Quite apart from its direct

[1] For an excellent and full discussion of this subject, see R. B. Madgwick, *Immigration into Eastern Australia* (London, 1937).

[2] C.O. 384/35, 2803, 3125, 3863 and 4050 Emigration, 8 and 31 July, 28 Sept. and 12 Oct. 1834; C.O. 384/38, 654 and 2026 Emigration, 21 and 30 Oct. 1835; C.O. 384/41, 2054 Australian 26 Nov. 1836.

[3] Such matters as ventilation, sanitation and sexual misconduct.

influence upon the Irish officers,[1] the Australian project was also responsible, in part, for the all-important step of appointing a United Kingdom agent-general for emigration. The second great wave of Wakefieldian agitation reached its climax in the celebrated select committee on waste lands in 1836, which advocated the immediate adoption of 'systematic colonization' and the immediate establishment of a powerful central board to put this into effect.[2] In the same year the Irish poor inquiry commissioners at last reported, boldly rejecting the plan of translating the English poor law system across the Irish Sea, and recommending in its place very large-scale government assistance for, and management of, Irish emigration.[3] Meanwhile, the scandalous inefficiency of the current state-assisted emigration to Australia was becoming, almost daily, more apparent. Partly as a sop to the clamour for a central board, partly to prepare for the possible adoption of even portions of the Irish scheme, and partly for 'domestic' colonial office reasons, T. F. Elliot was appointed agent-general for emigration in February 1837. It was a step of great consequence for our subject, and indeed for imperial history generally, for the appointment of an agent-general led on more or less directly to the establishment of the colonial land and emigration commission three years later.

T. F. Elliot was a nephew of the second earl of Minto, a Scottish nobleman who so aggrandized the public service on behalf of his relations as to have been notorious even in the great days of the 'Whig Cousinhoods'. Presumably through his uncle's influence, Elliot was, as a very young man, appointed secretary to the first emigration commission of 1831–2; and thereafter he was destined to travel permanently in the first-class compartment of the colonial office train.[4] Despite his aristocratic *entrée* and connexions—he was

[1] The Plymouth officer, Hemmans, was most involved in Australian emigration, Plymouth being the embarkation port. But Hemmans was an inefficient officer, who was eventually discharged for drunkenness, C.O. 384/80, 306 and 1136 Emigration, 27 Feb. and 1 July 1847, commissioners: Stephen and endorsements.

[2] F. H. Hitchens, *The colonial land and emigration commission* (Philadelphia, 1931), pp. 20–22. Hitchens' book is a pioneer work, of great importance and merit, in this field.

[3] Cf. MacDonagh, 'The poor law, emigration and the Irish question, 1830–55', op. cit.

[4] Elliot remained in charge of the correspondence &c. of Australian emigration after the dismissal of the commission. The emigration was actually managed, and the selections made, by voluntary committees. In 1835, Elliot went out with Lord Gosford on the Canada commission.

even first cousin by marriage to Lord John Russell—Elliot was no
Undy Scott. Nor was he Raffle Buffle or Mr Oldeschole. If he must
be categorized, he might best be placed amongst that neglected
species, the 'philosophical whigs'. 'He will go far', noted Greville
in his journal in 1835, 'he has admirable talent for business, a clear
head, liberal and unprejudiced opinions, and he writes remarkably
well'.[1] All this was true enough. Elliot was an intelligent and conscientious man, crisp and penetrating in mind and style alike. But
he was also, in part, the prisoner of his own time and circle,[2] and of
his early profession, law. In some respects, including his freedom
from cant and his fine and telling prose, he resembled James
Stephen remarkably. One of his very first minutes as agent-general
went unerringly, Stephen-like, to the heart of the very tangled
problem of the state's relationship to emigration: the ultimate question and the one which has never been resolved, he wrote, 'is whether
emigration should be made an object of national encouragement,
fostered by national funds'.[3] To a group of Irish protestants who
pleaded that Dublin Castle could no longer afford them security, he
replied, 'To assist people on the plea that the administration is
such as to render it unsafe for them to remain at home, is one of the
most singular proceedings that could be asked of any government';[4]
and in a humdrum application for assistance from the Cork board of
guardians, he at once discerned that a very great principle was at
stake, namely, whether a *local* need should be relieved from *general*
revenue.[5] Again, could Stephen himself have improved upon Elliot's
rejoinder to one of Low's complaints that the Liverpool customs
officers did not support his extra-legal practices concerning foreign
vessels, 'I am surprised that it should be left to me to suggest the obvious answer, that the commissioners of customs do not make the law,
but only instruct their officers what the law is'?[6] Correspondingly,

---

[1] C. C. F. Greville, *The Greville memoirs: first part* (London, 1887), vol. iii, p. 325.
[2] We know that as a young man he mixed with Charles Villiers, Charles
Greville, and Henry Taylor, and was at any rate on the fringe of London's
aristocracy of talent, ibid., vol. ii, pp. 58-59, 325.
[3] C.O. 384/46, 316 Emigration, 2 Feb. 1838.
[4] C.O. 386/19, pp. 289-303, 8 Nov. 1837.
[5] C.O. 384/62, 1946 Emigration, 23 Nov. 1840.
[6] C.O. 386/19, pp. 44-45, 25 May 1837. Elliot's letter concluded, 'It would
not be right that any public officer should be directed to do acts, which the
highest authorities that could be consulted on the subject have declared not to
be justified by the law'.

Elliot was just as bedevilled as Stephen by fears of 'that irritable and sensitive abstraction "the Public" ', and quite as conscious of the exposed and dangerous situation of public servants. He constantly asked the question, 'what would happen should this be made public?'[1]—constantly glanced over his shoulder lest a Horsman or a Molesworth or (perhaps worst of all) John Walter might have an opportunity of creeping up.

But Elliot was not only an analytical and exact man. He was also active and humane. In the case of the exempted foreign vessels, which we have just noticed, the matter did not end when he had acquainted Low with 'the obvious answer'. Elliot stated at the same time that 'the law' must be corrected; and despite the fact that it proved impossible to secure time for a passenger bill during the session in question,[2] he managed to tack on the necessary amendment to a rag-bag customs bill. Again, the Irish officers had reported, from their first appointment, numerous cases of vessels putting into the southern ports in distress, in several of which the unfortunate emigrants had found themselves stranded without food, money or the prospect of another passage. The law had offered no remedy, and Stephen's only contribution was to point out that the travelling expenses of the officers who attended distressed vessels were a grave matter, which must be cleared with the treasury and subject to some uniform rule.[3] When these cases reached Elliot's attention, he at once attempted to devise a compulsory insurance scheme to indemnify all emigrants against these unforeseeable disasters.[4] Elliot had perhaps a more than wholesome fear of public outcry, the treasury and exorbitant executive behaviour. He was inhibited (like most Victorians) by the notional 'maxima' with which he surrounded the field of possible action and legislation. He assumed in his heart that all government intervention and expenditure was at best the lesser of two evils, and he was never over-sanguine as to its power. 'There will always be', ran a typical minute, 'some sorts of deception which no law or administrative efforts will check, but of which the defeat must mainly depend on the good sense of

[1] E.g. C.O. 384/42, 1198 Emigration, 19 July 1837; C.O. 384/55, 2307 Emigration, 14 Oct. 1839.

[2] C.O. 386/19, pp. 38–39, 24 May 1837.

[3] C.O. 384/42, 833 Emigration, Stephen's endorsement, 24 May 1937.

[4] C.O. 384/47, 1562 Emigration, 30 June 1838. See also C.O. 386/19, pp. 285–8, 325–6, 13 and 20 July 1837.

individuals'.[1] But for all that he lived up fairly to his own maxim, 'My office might be considered to be in a great measure for the protection of the poor'.[2] He never acquiesced in what he conceived to be a remediable injustice.[3]

Certainly, the establishment of the agency-general marked the third decisive stage in the development of our story. Elliot at once provided some measure of discipline and of regular superintendence for the officers. Low, Lynch and Friend soon knew the rough edge of his pen.[4] He attempted to secure uniformity in the officers' interpretation and application of the passenger act, particularly in the measurement of surface and cubic space.[5] He set afoot inquiries, as a matter of course, into the various complaints either of abuses in the trade, or of official negligence, which came to his attention.[6] On the other hand, he defended his officers *contra mundum*. Of course, the two, discipline and defence, were intimately connected. It is a commonplace (though one which the doctrinaire administrators, to their cost, did not learn soon enough) that in a political system in which powers are concentrated, the absence of a determinate and authoritative superior, linked constitutionally with parliament, breeds weakness rather than strength in government. Corresponding improvements may be discerned in the more positive aspect of Elliot's work. He quickly determined that the passenger act of 1835 needed drastic amendment and (what was not so obvious but more important) that new legislation should be based upon the findings of the executive officers, and subject to their criticism during the course of its preparation.[7] He frankly asked his officers for advice when he was confronted with technical and practical questions.[8] He supported prosecutions wherever possible, arguing very justly that

[1] C.O. 384/62, 760 Emigration Australia, 13 Apr. 1840.

[2] C.O. 386/19, pp. 289-303, 8 Nov. 1837.

[3] E.g. C.O. 384/55, 2146 Emigration Australia, 28 Sept. 1839.

[4] C.O. 384/46, 490 Emigration, undated Mar. 1838; C.O. 384/47, 1373 Emigration, 6 June 1838; 1257 Emigration Australia, 20 June 1838. See also *Limerick Chronicle*, 9 June 1838.

[5] C.O. 386/19, pp. 308-9, 17 July 1837.

[6] E.g. C.O. 386/20, pp. 5-6, 11 Aug. 1837; C.O. 384/46, 637 Miscellaneous, 9 Mar. 1838; C.O. 386/23, pp. 137-8, 11 June 1838.

[7] C.O. 386/19, pp. 38-39, 24 May 1837.

[8] Particularly Hodder, the Dublin officer, of whom he had a very high opinion, C.O. 386/20, pp. 332-3, 21 Nov. 1837; C.O. 386/21, 30 Nov. 1837.

the delinquent 'may not cease for the mere sound of the powder, unless we can follow it up with a shot'. Most useful of all perhaps, he took the sensible course, when first appointed, of visiting Liverpool and Plymouth, and conducting a three-weeks tour of all the Irish stations, during which he gathered a great deal of information upon the various local officers and trades, and arranged for an exchange of knowledge and recommendations.[1]

All this may read like the substitution of a Napoleon for a Directory. But it was not, unfortunately, the whole story. In terms of concrete achievement, Elliot accomplished little during the three years of the agency-general. True, he pointed the way in each of the various directions in which improvement lay. But he did not travel far on any road. The fundamental explanation of his failure lies in the fact that the 1835 act still stood, barring the way to any material advance. Elliot can scarcely be blamed for the postponement of the necessary change. The more knowledge of emigration he acquired, the more the almost infinite difficulties of effective amendment became apparent. Moreover, his prime concern, as agent-general, was state-assisted emigration to New South Wales. Willy-nilly, the Atlantic passage and the corps of executive officers absorbed a small and steadily diminishing part of his attention. In 1837, he trebled the annual average dispatch to New South Wales; in 1838 he increased the total even further. Almost single-handed, he tackled the problems of discipline and mortality upon the government vessels. All through, he was involved in conflicts with his rivals, the South Australian commissioners.[2] He was, besides, grossly overworked, lacking even an adequate staff of clerks; and his status was, at first, ludicrously variegated.[3] In these circumstances, time slipped quietly by without the great matter of legislative amendment ever coming to an issue. In the one field, all was feverish activity. It was natural that, the other being obscure and quiet, Elliot should have drifted there towards complacency or at least postponement, and that he should have gradually come to view the corps and its achievements

[1] C.O. 384/45, unmarked, 22 Nov. 1837.
[2] Hitchens, op. cit., pp. 22–26.
[3] Elliot was originally permitted to communicate directly with the treasury, the customs board and the poor law commission, but not with the admiralty or the colonial governors! Cf. P. Knaplund, *The British Empire* (New York, 1941), pp. 44–45.

somewhat *couleur de rose*.[1] But from this incipient reverie—if such it was—he was roughly and suddenly aroused.

It was the publication of the Durham report in 1839 which set the cat among the pigeons. The Canadian witnesses were extremely hostile to the United Kingdom officers, and implied, if they did not directly state, that it was they who were primarily to blame for the shameful conditions of the Atlantic trade. The report arranged the selected evidence so that it constituted an attack on the existing system, developed stage by stage. Dr Morrin, a commissioner of the Quebec Emigrant Hospital, described vessels arriving at the port in the years 1826-32 in memorable and often-repeated words, 'with a few exceptions, the state of the ships was quite abominable; so much so, that the harbour-master's boatmen had no difficulty at the distance of a gun shot, either when the wind was favourable or in a dead calm, in distinguishing by the odour alone a crowded emigrant ship'. He went on to speak of mortalities of nearly 10 per cent at sea, of hundreds of passengers requiring immediate nursing, of the wretched orphans surviving their parents' deaths and of the penury and destitution of the emigrants generally. This picture drawn, Dr Skey, the president of the Quebec Emigrant Society, began the formulation of an accusation, 'A regular importation of contagious disease into this country has annually taken place: that disease originated on board ship, and was occasioned, I should say, in consequence of the ships being ill-found, ill-provisioned, overcrowded and ill-ventilated'. The evidence of Jessop, the collector of customs at Quebec, advanced the issue further. He observed three very common and grave deficiencies in the passenger trade: too little food, which caused poor emigrants the most dreadful sufferings, gross overcrowding and faulty passenger lists, all three of which the United Kingdom inspections should have been capable of preventing.[2] Finally, the evidence of Dr Poole, who had been quarantine physician on Grosse Isle since 1832, provided several specific charges. He testified that excess in numbers 'is very common . . . and it arises manifestly from want of inspection at home'. Moreover,

---

[1] This is certainly the impression conveyed by Elliot's report of 28 April 1838 upon the corps, see *Rep. U.K. agent-general emigration*, 9, H.C. 1837-8 (388-), xl.

[2] He added that Irish vessels were much the worst offenders in all these respects (with, presumably, the corollary that Irish inspections were most inefficient), and that Irish masters traded on swindling and on breaches of the passenger acts.

the poor Irish often arrived starving and, short of that, many others were on short rations—coupled with the invariable dirt and bad ventilation, this hunger produced 'fevers', often to the extent of up to ninety sick passengers upon disembarkation: 'I attribute the whole evil to defective arrangements'. Worst still was the 'system of extortion carried on by masters of vessels, chiefly from Ireland': they told emigrants that they need only lay in three or four weeks' provisions, and when the sea-stock was exhausted sold food from their own stores at prices 400 per cent of the true value. Once again, slovenly inspections were to blame. 'The captains have in many instances told me, that the agents only muster the passengers on deck, inquire into the quantity of provisions, and, in some cases require them to be produced, when, occasionally, the same bag of meal or other provisions was shown as belonging to several persons in succession. . . . The mere mustering of passengers on deck, without going below where the provisions are kept, is really no inspection at all; and it frequently happens that passengers are smuggled aboard without any provisions'.[1] Poole had a similar complaint to make of the berthing and between-decks generally: 'It is quite impossible that such fittings should escape observation in the port of departure, if that part of the vessel intended for emigrants be visited'. Finally, the incompetence of both the masters and the ship-surgeons was condemned. Poole instanced a vessel in the preceding season on which (despite the assurance of the captain and surgeon that there was no serious sickness aboard) he had found forty cases of typhus, nine of them actually in bed, the others propped up with bread in their hands to make a show of health. The so-called 'surgeons' were for the most part 'unlicensed students and apprentices, or apothecaries' shopmen', without knowledge of either prevention or cure.[2]

√   From a display of the evidence in this sequence, the Durham report passed on to a wholesale indictment of the existing system of emigrant protection. While it was granted that 'the utterly lawless and unobserved practices of former times' had been to some extent restrained, the current emigration was denounced as still shamefully

---

[1] Poole also observed that 'Very few of these vessels have on board a sufficient quantity of water', and that very many of the casks used as water containers were old and rotting.

[2] *The report and despatches of the earl of Durham* (London, 1839), pp. 177–85.

mismanaged and neglected. T. F. Elliot's observations in the preceding year that the United Kingdom officers 'constitute, as it were, the appointed poor man's friend' and that 'every effort is made for the ease and safety of their [the emigrants'] safety' were ridiculed. 'It would indeed be very mischievous', the report continued, 'if the Government were to deprive emigrants of self-reliance by doing everything for them: but when the State leads great numbers of people into a situation in which it is impossible that they should do well without assistance, then the obligation to assist them begins'. How little this was fulfilled in Canada might be judged from the fact that the agent-general for emigration at Quebec had no powers and scarcely any duties to perform, and that he had never yet received instructions or even communications from Elliot.[1] Meanwhile, Durham wrote on 20 October 1838 to the colonial secretary, Glenelg, demanding a thorough and immediate reform of the United Kingdom system, so that the great sufferings of the ignorant and the unprotected might be at once reduced. From the evidence before him, Durham said, it appeared that the emigration officers of the United Kingdom 'exercise no effective supervision over the arrangements for the passage of emigrants, and that all the old evils of filth, inadequate accommodation, inferior and insufficient food', which the passenger acts were meant to have remedied and which Elliot mistakenly believed to have been remedied, flourished still like weeds, save in so far as the colonies themselves restrained them.[2]

In some respects, the Durham report was an unprincipled indictment. It belonged to a grand but odious tradition of nineteenth-century investigations, that of public-spirited partiality, of the high-purposed manipulation of evidence to antecedently determined ends, to which so many of the great administrators and reformers of the age subscribed. And by the same token, one or two of the physicians whom the Durham commissioners interrogated appear to have belonged to another deplorable nineteenth-century line, that of the medical man whose violence of opinion outran both his exact knowledge and his capacity for a scientific appraisal of a group of facts. Generally speaking the Durham report worked towards pre-ordained Wakefieldian conclusions. To elaborate the

[1] Ibid., pp. 181-6.
[2] Ibid., pp. 404-5.

dreadful consequences of 'unsystematic' emigration was, of course, congenial to such a task; nor was the opportunity to settle old scores against the colonial office, through scarifying its subordinate officers, unwelcome. The collection, presentation and interpretation of evidence in our field was unfair. The questions were so framed and confined as to encourage but one line of evidence. The fact that most witnesses testified to the decided improvement in recent years was suppressed or muted in the report: Skey's reservation in this sense was relegated to an appendix.[1] The Canadian agent-general for emigration was examined, but not as to the state of the passenger trade or the efficiency of emigrant protection, subjects on which, *prima facie*, he was the expert. Possibly the old rivalry between the agent-general and the Quebec Emigrant Society was exploited, Morrin and Skey being officers of the latter. The abundant evidence of the two Buchanans,[2] which was contained in the parliamentary papers from 1833 onwards, was ignored; and on the whole this evidence, although acutely critical of the passenger acts, the passenger trade and the customs authorities, was decidedly favourable to the emigration officers. The senior Buchanan's annual report for 1834 had observed that 'fewer causes of dissatisfaction, from the conduct of shipbrokers, have occurred this year; and no serious inconvenience has been reported to me to have arisen from a scanty supply of provisions. This improved state of things may be attributed in a great measure, to the appointment of emigrant agents at the principal ports of the United Kingdom';[3] and although this and all the other reports[4] described and deplored numerous abuses and

[1] Ibid., appendix B, pp. 82–83. Q.571–4.

[2] A. C. Buchanan, junior, the nephew of the Quebec agent-general for emigration of the same name, virtually took over the office from his uncle in 1835: his uncle fell ill in that year. But although the younger Buchanan managed the business and wrote the reports during 1835 and the subsequent seasons, he was not appointed formally to the office until April 1838. The experience of four years, however, should have sufficed to render him a valuable, and indeed the most important, witness on the subjects referred to above. But the only questions which he was asked referred to his office, its duties and his relations with the colonial office, ibid., appendix B, pp. 80–81, Q.541–51.

[3] *Corres. with governors of colonies*, 5, H.C. 1835 (87), xxxix. See also C.O. 384/35, 1823 Lower Canada, Buchanan: Hay, 30 May 1834.

[4] *Corres. with governors of colonies*, 6–22, H.C. 1833 (141), xxvi; *Corres. with governors of colonies*, 5–23, H.C. 1837, xlii.
Annual rep. agent-general emigration Canada, 1836, 4–24, H.C. 1836–7 (132), xlii;
Annual rep. agent-general emigration Canada, 1837, 5–7, 14, H.C. 1837–8, (389), xl.

dreadful sufferings amongst the emigrants, they also showed a proper sense of the difficulties which confronted the United Kingdom officers, and of their want of powers.[1] But the worst instance of tendentiousness in the Durham report was its observations on T. F. Elliot. Not only were his remarks on the United Kingdom officers torn from a context which rendered them moderate and relative, and presented as foolish and absolute opinions. But the implied condemnation for not instructing or communicating with the Quebec agent-general ignored the facts, first, that it was not his duty to do so, secondly, that he scarcely had had time to do so—Buchanan having been appointed but shortly before—and thirdly, that the proper and established channel of communication was between the colonial office and the governor-general—all of which facts the authors of the report should surely have known.

More generally, the main misconception of the report and of Durham's letter was that Elliot and the United Kingdom officers were responsible, more or less, for the great body of evils which oppressed the emigrants. No attempt was made to distinguish what was due to the poverty and dirt of the emigrants, to the inescapable dangers and agonies of an Atlantic passage in small, overcrowded vessels, to the defectiveness of legislation and the parsimony of the exchequer—no attempt was made to distinguish all this from what was caused by individual officers failing in their specific obligations. As the emigration commissioners noted some time later, 'while on the one hand, the very nature of passages by sea must, at the best, involve a risk of casualties for which, when they happen, the agent at the port of departure must be expected to be called to account, with a view to show that his duties had not been neglected; on the other hand, the title of these officers is apt to suggest the idea of more authority than they have hitherto possessed, and they are liable to fall under blame for cases in which they might very well have foreseen the danger of misfortune, but had no power to enforce any better arrangements'.[2] Elliot's very just reply to the Durham report was that men like Poole—he might well have specified Durham and Charles Buller into the bargain—totally misunderstood the

---

[1] Only in one instance, in fact, that of Lynch of Limerick, did the agent-general ask that an emigration officer be censured, *Corres. with governors of colonies*, 23, H.C. 1837, xlii.

[2] *General rep. C.L.E.C.*, 16, H.C. 1842 (567), xxv.

nature of the responsibility which had so far been assumed. If—but only if—'sufficient public funds be granted for the conveyance and maintenance during the voyage, of a large body of emigrants, and the agents at the outports were entrusted with the engagement of the necessary accommodation, there would be every reason to complain of such evils, as, I fear, must be, in a greater or lesser degree, inseparable from the independent and unassisted emigration of persons in indigent circumstances, with probably a deficient supply of clothing, a want of cleanly habits, and no responsible superintendence over them during the voyage'.[1] Poole had named specifically only two of the many vessels of which he had complained.[2] In each case investigation showed that although the privations during the voyage had indeed been terrible as Poole had claimed, Low, the officer concerned, was free from blame:[3] in fact, he had been a warm advocate of the statutory regulation of water casks (whose deficiencies had been largely responsible for the disasters) from his first days at Liverpool. Moreover, Poole's observations on ship-surgeons were irrelevant:[4] none were required for passages to North America. This also applied to his strictures on berthing: the passenger acts were silent on the subject. As to the mustering of passengers, this was by statute the customs, and not the emigration officer's responsibility.[5]

It would not be difficult to continue this correction down to minutiae, so that it might finally seem that the Durham report contained no evidence of substance and was of small significance to our subject. But this would avoid one mistake, only to pitch headlong into a worse. Undoubtedly, the testimony of the physician-witnesses leant towards the sensational in its phrasing. But it was, for all that, first-hand testimony of the state in which passengers and vessels actually arrived in North America, and good second-hand testimony of conditions during the voyage. It was never challenged—on the contrary, it was corroborated over and over again in later years —on the facts of emigrant suffering; and with due allowance for high colouring, we may accept it on these topics without reserve. It is only the gross over-simplification of the issues involved, and the

[1] C.O. 384/52, 47 Canada, Elliot: Stephen, 5 Jan. 1839.
[2] *Durham rep.*, op. cit., pp. 407–8.
[3] C.O. 384/52, 47 Canada, Elliot: Stephen, 5 Jan. 1839.
[4] Ibid., 778 Emigration, Elliot: Stephen, 20 Apr. 1839.
[5] Ibid., 47 Canada, Elliot: Stephen, 5 Jan. 1839.

inferences as to the responsibility for these evils and the pre-embark-ation happenings, which stand condemned. In fact, the Durham report evidence of the passenger trade was important in several respects. In the first place, it reached a much wider public than any previous observations on the conditions of emigration; and the dramatic form in which the evidence was cast assisted greatly in the 'disclosure'. Secondly, the witnesses supplied much new and telling information. Never before was such copious, elaborate and compelling evidence available, let alone gathered into a single source. This was especially significant because of the general ignorance even amongst the United Kingdom emigration officers of the conditions of the voyage. Post-embarkation difficulties were little canvassed: those which preceded sailing naturally engrossed the officers, and information about the actual crossing was very meagre.[1]

To move back on to more familiar ground, the Durham report also administered a very healthy jolt to Elliot and his subordinates. The domestic inquiries which followed its publication revealed several unsuspected weaknesses and illuminated the old afresh. Let us take as examples the very important inspections of provisions and of numbers. As to the first, it is quite true that the weakness of the current system had been made known in the very early days of the executive corps,[2] and that, by and large, the officers did the best they could with the weapons at their command. But it is also true that without the Durham report the dust which had settled on the first revelations might not have been disturbed for a considerable time, and that the fact that the inspections were in a large measure ineffective might have dropped further and further out of mind. For fact it was. As a later and far from hostile report observed, 'It is enough to reflect upon the condition of a vessel into which 200 or 300 people are crowding together, each one carrying his own box or bag of provisions, in order to feel how impossible it must be to exercise an effectual superintendence under this head'.[3] As to the inspection of numbers, the reports of the customs officers revealed an extraordinary variety and confusion in the relations between

[1] No systematic first-hand account of a between-decks passage was in fact composed before 1847.
[2] *1st rep. poor inquiry commissioners Ire.*, Appendix C, part I, 18, H.C. 1836, xxx.
[3] *Rep. C.L.E.C. on necessity of amending passenger act*, 4 [355], H.C. 1842, xxv.

customs and emigration officers in the different ports: every pair appears to have had its own peculiar understanding or rivalry. The reports also established that the passenger lists were most inaccurate. At Liverpool, Londonderry, Waterford and Dublin even the pretence that accuracy might be attainable had been abandoned. At Liverpool, the great number of sailings, combined with eleventh-hour embarkations rendered this inevitable; and most of the Irish customs officers admitted that stowaways and post-clearance embarkations were very common.[1] For almost every Irish port stood at the head of a long estuary, the shores of which could not possibly be guarded by the current staff. Even in the exceptions, Cork[2] and Dublin, the emigration officers could not prevent illegal embarkations when the vessels lay off Kinsale and Kingstown respectively. In short, the investigation made it clear that, under the existing regulations and penalties, the United Kingdom inspections of numbers (and for that matter the United Kingdom lists of names and ages) were most imperfect. Meanwhile, Low, who had also been consulted, seized the chance to return to his old and noble charge with the words, 'the poor are still unprotected'; and he powerfully rehearsed all his usual complaints.[3]

Finally, the Durham report was at least partially responsible for the formation of the colonial land and emigration commission. The agitation for systematic colonization and the attacks upon the current Atlantic practices, which it had detonated, were continued throughout 1839, especially by Buller and the colonial radicals in the house of commons. Meanwhile, the tottering whig government embarked upon one of its periodic flirtations with the notion of resolving the terrible Irish question by settling British North America with the 'surplus' Irish. The ground was thus ready when the South Australian commissioners precipitated a crisis in December 1839, by demanding payment for their service. On the happy plea of economy, Stephen proposed the substitution of a permanent commission of three for both the agent-general and the numerous South Australian commission. On 10 January 1840, T. F. Elliot, E. E. Villiers, a whig 'younger son' and Col. Robert Torrens, the political economist,

---

[1] The Belfast customs authorities alone denied knowledge of this practice.

[2] Though Cork itself lay fifteen miles up-river, it formed an exception because the mustering took place at Cove, as the harbour was then called.

[3] C.O. 384/52, 509 Canada Emigration, reports of various dates between 30 January and 2 February 1839.

were so commissioned, with very wide authority over both state-assisted and voluntary emigration, and over passenger legislation and the executive corps.[1] In the course of his charge to the new commissioners, Lord John Russell wrote: 'The [passenger] act frequently proves much less effective than could be desired. The difficulty of dealing with this subject is to determine the line between, on the one hand, unduly encroaching upon the liberty of individual action in persons desiring to emigrate, and also exacting so much as to raise the cost of passage to a prohibiting price, or, on the other hand, failing that general protection which is on every account proper. . . . An extensive body of notes for the amendment of the present statute has been collected in the office of the agent-general, and will of course receive your consideration'.[2]

[1] Hitchens, op. cit., pp. 30–58.
[2] *Copies commissions appointing C.L.E.C.*, 8–9, H.C. 1840 (113), xxxiii.

THE FIRST PLATEAU

1840-5

THE appointment of the colonial land and emigration commission led to immediate improvements in the field of emigrant protection. In the first place, the commissioners undertook to investigate all complaints of breaches of the passenger acts, and to inquire into their officers' performance of their duties.[1] This produced no scandals and little evidence of previous neglect. But it did yield much useful information, and it tightened or rather re-created discipline, for Elliot had not been able to maintain control alone. Next, the commissioners began the 'education' of their officers, and the standardization of the interpretation and application of the passenger acts.[2] On 16 October 1840 the first circular was issued. It ordered all officers personally to inspect the supplies and count the passengers. It also recommended that the officers should warn masters of the penalties for the various misdemeanours, and that they should require a list of provisions prices to be posted up on every vessel.[3] Thirdly, the commissioners drew up 'returns' to be completed by the colonial immigration agents, setting out a variety of facts concerning the vessels and crews, the duration of the voyage, the number and the composition of the passengers and their health and complaints.[4] Thus began the store of comparatively full and accurate information on the passage and the operation of the law which formed the basis of the several subsequent improvements. At the same time, another vital step was taken when the United Kingdom officers were instructed 'to transmit through the post, by the earliest mail steamers leaving the country after every passenger vessel has

---

[1] C.O. 384/140, pp. 3–18, 20 Jan.–23 Mar. 1840.

[2] These innovations are described in detail in Hitchens, op. cit., pp. 123–7. Hitchens draws largely upon series G in the Public Archives of Canada, at Ottawa.

[3] Strictly speaking, all of these practices were, at this stage, *ultra vires* the emigration officers.

[4] C.O. 384/68, commissioners: Stephen, 11 Jan. 1841.

cleared for sea at their respective ports, a duplicate list of her passengers, addressed to the immigration agent of the colony to which the ship is bound'. This would enable the colonial officers 'to make timely provision for the reception and disposal [of the passengers] and . . . to exercise a check on the list furnished by the master, and more immediately to detect any improper addition to the number on board'.[1] This innovation meant that, for the first time, overcrowding might be dealt with effectively so far as British North America was concerned. Finally and not least important, the commissioners began the steady, systematic preparation of a new passenger bill, ✓ gathering and collecting evidence and recommendations from their home officers. Thus were many of the former deficiencies supplied, and thus did a new energy and direction infuse the service. As agent-general, Elliot had made small advances in each of the fields which we have enumerated. But he had not the time, administrative resources or status and authority to do much more than open up these questions. Now at last the emigration corps had a really powerful and effective superior and passenger legislation an informed and active master.

Meanwhile, the pressures which had been built up in Canada by the Durham investigations and report were renewed by the appointment of the emigration commission and by the definite prospect of an overhaul of the legislation and executive corps. This is clearly indicated by the reports of the Canadian officers for 1840 and the accompanying comments of Sydenham, the new lord lieutenant. Buchanan's report proposed five important additions to the passenger code:[2] that the vessels be made responsible for supplying the basic food requirements for the voyage;[3] that all passenger brokers and agents be licensed; that the use of spirits on emigrant ships—'the frightful source of disease and want' and shipwrecks—be forbidden; that colonial magistrates be given extraordinary and summary

[1] Ibid., commissioners: Stephen, 27 Jan. 1841. Cf. *Rep. select comm. colonization Ire.*, 16, 18–19, Q.122, 140–57 [737], H.C. 1847, vi.

[2] *Corres. rel. emigration Canada*, 77–79, 96–98 [298], H.C. 1841, xv; *Papers rel. emigration B.N.A.*, 28–9 [373], H.C. 1842, xxxi. Buchanan made a number of other proposals, some of which were adopted; but the five described above were the most significant and novel.

[3] Buchanan estimated that this would cost only 7s. 6d. per adult, and argued that passengers would cheerfully pay this amount, knowing that they would save its equivalent in sea-stock.

powers to enforce passenger legislation;[1] and that masters be rendered liable for all contracts entered into by agents or brokers with the emigrants. The report of Douglas, the quarantine physician, opened up attack upon a different front, that of illness, mortality and the sea-voyage—continuing, though in a more informed and serious fashion, the criticisms of the Durham report. Douglas began by observing that Liverpool vessels were invariably the most unhealthy—there had been deaths at sea on 10 per cent of them in the current season—and suggested that the foul and undrained cellars in which the emigrants lodged while waiting at that port were the seed-beds of contagious disease.[2] He went on to consider the consequences of the Irish emigrants' ignorance of what was needed for an Atlantic crossing, and of the inadequacy of their food, clothes and bedding. Even in the comparatively rare cases in which they had not been misled as to the length of the voyage, and in which they did take aboard sufficient sea-stock, their supply was not rationed daily, and in the extravagance of the reaction to the initial bouts of seasickness, they consumed all they had before British North America was even sighted. When the chill and fog of the north-west Atlantic struck suddenly, the ill-clad, half-starving emigrants huddled in the hold fell easy victims to the 'febrile miasma' which had been engendered by the dirt and fastened hatches. Once fever struck, despair and lassitude set in; people refused even to 'relieve' themselves elsewhere, and thus the familiar vicious circle of filth and contagion got under way. Finally, the crew was infected until at last an evil-smelling, 'floating pesthouse' arrived, with perhaps twenty persons dead or dying and a further fifty seriously ill.

Sydenham warmly approved Buchanan's recommended legislation, and conjured startling new proposals out of Douglas's

[1] Buchanan very shrewdly observed that the new act should define the proceedings exactly and in the most minute detail, because colonial J.P.s could not be relied upon to act unless they were precisely instructed and supported by the statute, *Papers rel. emigration B.N.A.* 29 [373], H.C. 1842, xxxi.

[2] Douglas referred to a recent paper by Dr M. C. Taylor on the subject of the Liverpool 'lodging cellar, the underground cave, in which drainage, light and ventilation were utterly unattainable . . . where every exhalation . . . rolled in volumes of pestilential mist round the apology for a ceiling'. Douglas added, 'From these places the emigrants embark on board of the vessels bringing with them in their foul clothes and bedding the seeds of disease', *Corres. rel. emigration Canada*, 58 [298] H.C. 1841, xv.

description of the passage. He argued first for an increase in the number and efficiency of the emigration officers to put down 'kidnapping' and frauds in the ports of embarkation, and (in the light of the habitual, 'notorious' and 'uncensured' neglect of the customs officers) he also asked that an *emigration officer's* certificate of due performance of the act be made compulsory. He then broke new ground in proposing that the emigration officers should inspect and regulate emigrant lodgings; that so far as Liverpool was concerned the central government, solely or in conjunction with the municipal authorities, should provide some at least of the accommodation; and that the sufficiency of the passengers' clothing and the cleanliness of their bedding should also be matters on which the emigration officer must be satisfied before permitting them to embark. 'But', Sydenham continued, 'no law will be effectual to protect the emigrant during the voyage, unless some person clothed with sufficient authority, be placed by Her Majesty's Government on board the emigrant vessels. . . . Once at sea the emigrants are necessarily in the hands of the captain. Whatever extortion or oppression he may exercise towards them they have no power to resist, and from the difficulties of enforcing the penalties when they arrive at their destination, and from their ignorance of their own rights, he may be tolerably confident of escaping with impunity. A Government agent on board, who might very properly combine in his person the duties of medical attendant, would prevent these evils, and he might also be charged with the custody of the emigrants' own provisions, so as to prevent the waste which is said now to prevail; and be armed with authority to enforce personal cleanliness among them'.[1]

Generally speaking, the Canadian proposals were well grounded and intelligent. Both Buchanan and Douglas could appeal to the experience of five or six years in office. Certainly, Buchanan knew

[1] Ibid., 27–32. Dr Ralph, who was Sydenham's agent in the United Kingdom at this time, described Sydenham's proposals as follows: 'that a medical attendant should go out, armed with the authority of an agent, to see that the ship was properly provisioned; that no want of provisions should take place and the emigrants should be protected from fraud and imposition, to which they have been exposed by the inefficiency of the Passengers' Act; that they should be supplied with medical assistance if sick on their arrival; and that other portions of the fund should be laid out in carrying on public works in Canada', *2nd rep. select comm. emigration Scot.*, 29, Q.3360, H.C. 1841 (333), vi.

at first hand the consequences of under-nourishment[1] and drunkenness at sea, of the non-liability of masters for brokers' contracts, and of the ineffectiveness of the Canadian court of vice-admiralty[2] in enforcing law. It is true that Douglas's account of illness and mortality at sea was at second-hand and more or less imaginative, while his 'atmospheric' diagnosis of the infectious diseases was, of course, mistaken. But evidence of conditions during the voyage which was accumulated later substantially confirmed Douglas's description—at any rate for a very considerable number of the vessels; and his condemnation of dirty lodgings and holds, and of the living habits of the emigrants was also, however unwittingly, a condemnation of some of the true pre-conditions of contagions. Buchanan's proposals as to foodstuffs and the licensing of brokers were most perceptive. Low had suggested both several years before, but he had not singled them out for particular emphasis or recommended them in so precise a form. Most remarkable of all was Sydenham's bold and logical argument from the facts of Douglas's report to the implicit and necessary remedies. Simply, he proposed to overcome the evils of dirt and inadequate bedding and clothing by new powers for, and a greater number of, emigration officers; to avoid disease by making the central government responsible for pre-embarkation accommodation; and to defeat the miseries of the voyage by subjecting the between-decks to constant surveillance by an officer armed with arbitrary powers.

Apart from their individual merits, the Canadian proposals present two very striking features. The first is the easy, inevitable-seeming passage from the evil, once apprehended and analysed, to its legislative and executive remedy. The second is the fact that the accepted contemporary doctrines of state functions and individual rights, of private enterprise and public business, were not considered at all. Rearguard actions of a sort had been fought in 1828 and 1835. But now it was being airily proposed that merchants be

---

[1] Buchanan referred to two cases which had come to his notice and in which affidavits of evidence had been prepared during the 1840 season. In one instance, an emigrant was kept at Liverpool without compensation for twenty-five days after his contracted sailing date. In the second, a family of thirteen had their passage postponed for three weeks, again without compensation, ibid., 18, 78.

[2] This was the only Canadian court in which proceedings under clause 18 of the 1835 act could be taken, and it was too slow and expensive a court for immigrants to use in most cases, *Papers rel. emigration B.N.A.*, 29 [373], H.C. 1842, xxxi.

licensed, that statutory obligations be inserted in contracts, and even that the clothing and living habits of individuals be subjected to official scrutiny, without one thought being given to the 'principles' which were at stake. To appreciate the *débâcle* to the full we must recollect that the Sydenham who crowded on every inch of regulative canvas was the same Poullett Thomson who had argued a dozen years before that emigrants as 'free agents' did not require the same protection which the law allowed to slaves. Within our own subject, this tergiversation can be capped only by Nassau Senior, whose iron orthodoxy led him to reject poor law assistance for emigration in any form in 1836, but who was moved by the Irish crisis in 1848 to propose that the state should *compel* tenants to emigrate from the more congested districts, and then force their landlords to meet the cost of the emigration as if it were a poor rate![1] So much for the ultimate resistant-force or stability of political economy.

But if economic doctrine might melt or change its very shape in the blaze of ascertained abuses, there were other clogs on action which would not. In their several ways, public opinion, parliament and the treasury presented very formidable obstacles. Elliot was by temperament and contiguity to Westminster very sensitive to these difficulties; and in the commissioners' various replies to Sydenham's letter and the Canadian proposals[2] five types of objection were put forward. The first was that of money. Even an increase in the size of the emigration corps might not go unresisted. But the provision of pre-embarkation accommodation at Liverpool and the supply of superintendents for the voyage conjured up visions of such great expenditure as to place them beyond the bounds of serious discussion. Next came the awful and never-ending responsibilities with

---

[1] *Letter from N. W. Senior on 3rd poor inquiry rep. Ire.*, 9–12, H.C. 1837 (376), li; *Hans.*, 3rd, civ. 504, 10 Apr. 1849.

[2] C.O. 384/67, 1359 Canada, commissioners: Stephen, 17 Aug. 1841; C.O. 384/64, 1653 Emigration, undated; *Rep. C.L.E.C.*, 3–7 [355], H.C. 1842, xxxv. We may take it that Elliot was the main author of these replies. The sentiments and often the very phrasing of the letters were identical with those of his earlier writings. It was only natural that this should have been so. Elliot had had four seasons' experience of emigration and its problems: the other two commissioners had none. Moreover, Torrens, who was a man of very decided opinions and who might possibly have differed with Elliot, had resigned his commissionership before these letters were written. He was succeeded by J. G. Shaw-Lefevre who was little more than a sleeping partner in the commission. Lefevre belonged to one of the 'cousinhoods'.

which the emigration commissioners would be saddled if government took over the direct management of an unsavoury private business, that of lodging emigrants. Third was the corresponding fear of the attacks of 'freedom-loving' people if their officers were called on to adjudicate such delicate personal concerns as clothing, bedding and states of cleanliness. Fourthly, emigration was a matter of public policy; and on this policy London and Quebec were not altogether in accord. The imperial government regarded the current voluntary emigration as the only gleam of light in the quickly-darkening Irish skies, and it clearly intimated that it must be encouraged in every possible way—short, at any rate, of calling on the treasury for money.[1] Hence all restrictive legislation had to clear the objection that it would reduce the volume of Irish emigration. Canada might propose, but in the last resort it was Westminster which disposed the passenger law. Finally, there were the awkward facts. It was, to use a familiar example, one thing to project medical superintendents for the Atlantic passage; it was another to find ten qualified physicians who would accept such posts, not to say the sixty who would be needed for the St Lawrence trade alone. It was easy to ask that the efficiency of the emigration officers be increased but quite beside the point to do so before an amended passenger act gave them effective powers.[2] 'When', as Elliot tartly observed some years later, 'a projector gets a plausible notion into his head and can continue to hitch in the government as an agent into his plot, he seems to think himself exempted from computing the power of his machinery—ships, money and men being all forthwith ready at his bidding, to any extent'.[3]

Like the Canadian proposals, the commissioners' replies show clearly that passenger legislation was being considered in a much more informed and realistic fashion than had been the case in 1835. Shadow and substance were at last distinguished. The well-disposed ignorance of the amateurs was yielding to the relevant cut-and-thrust of the instructed professionals. The exposure of abuses had

---

[1] Until mid-1840 it seemed likely that the government would make some considerable *direct* contribution towards promoting emigration, C.O. 384/61, 795 Canada, commissioners: Stephen, 21 Apr. 1840, C.O. 386/140, pp. 16–20. But by November 1840, this project had definitely been abandoned, C.O. 384/62, 1946 Emigration, commissioners: Stephen, 23 Nov. 1840.

[2] C.O. 384, 67, 1359 Emigration, commissioners: Stephen, 17 Aug. 1841.

[3] C.O. 384/80, 199 Emigration, 10 Feb. 1847.

by now so deeply penetrated and the consequent proposals for reform raised such genuine problems of expense and government,
that the story henceforth unrolls against a very different setting. The
five difficulties which emerged in the course of the correspondence
of 1840-1 were all, by and large, striking the surface for the first
time. But they were to be, in one form or another, the governing
factors of the situation from this date onwards. The Canadian proposals were the first to recommend in definite form direct government management of a branch of the passenger trade; the first to
recommend measures which would have involved a regular state
expenditure well above the humdrum £3,000-£5,000 per annum
level; and the first to recommend arbitrary powers, and professional
skills beyond those of the ordinary naval man, for the executive
officers. These were doubtless logical and even obvious answers to
the problems which had been set out. But they at once encountered
the obstacles of state parsimony, of official fear of embarrassing
responsibilities, and of the very limited executive resources at the
command of early Victorian administration. These obstacles
appeared clearly only in 1841 because the reform movement had not
hitherto advanced sufficiently to strike against them. The two other
difficulties, those concerned with political and parliamentary
opinion, were largely illusory. In the event, there was no public
opposition whatsoever to the very severe passenger bill of 1842, and
the increasingly restrictive measures of subsequent years provoked
relatively few protests upon the grounds of private freedom or of
Irish policy. In fact, with the exception of the two whigs in Lord
John Russell's first administration, Earl Grey[1] and Benjamin Hawes,
no secretary or parliamentary under-secretary appears to have been
in the least concerned about possible unpopularity or house of
commons 'rows'. So far as our subject goes, it was not the ministers
who told the civil servants, but rather the civil servants who told the
ministers 'what the public would not stand'. This was due possibly
to the long reigns of Stephen and Elliot, both of whom were prone
to anticipate the worst and to prize correctness. It must be confessed,
moreover, that fear of exposing a flank to criticism was a not un-
natural feeling amongst public servants in the ferocious 1830s and
1840s; and if, in the present instance, the fears of the public servants

[1] As Lord Howick he had served as parliamentary under-secretary at the
colonial office, 1830-3, during his father's administration.

were exaggerated, this did not diminish their significance as a depressing influence upon the growth of state power.

We must, however, distinguish clearly between Elliot's and Stephen's attitudes, despite the several resemblances between the two. As we have seen, Elliot (and the point applies equally to the commissioners as a body during his masterful régime) hastened slowly, where Stephen would not move at all. This was well and pertinently illustrated by the commissioners' report of 1842 on the passenger act of 1835, a document which also throws interesting light upon the early Victorian philosophy of government. The report began by asserting that, however inequitable it might be, poverty inevitably carried its own penalties, and the law's capacity to relieve them was limited. 'It is no necessary proof of a defect in the laws, or of remissness on the part of public officers', one passage ran, 'that persons who are about to leave the country suffer themselves to be misled by deceptions. Each person's best security must consist in his own good sense; nor can any enactments, or any activity of administration, supply the want of proper discretion in individuals'. Another section of the report began, 'With every rule that can reasonably be enacted by parliament, many inconveniences must, we fear, remain inseparable from the passage by sea, at their own cost, of large bodies of people in indigent circumstances. Induced to emigrate principally by want, it is not to be expected that these poor people can have the same habits, or command the same means as persons more favourably situated; they can neither have the same opportunities of knowing beforehand, or of providing against, if they know them, the exigencies of a long voyage'. The report also recognized the objections that regulation 'tended to enhance the cost of conveyance', 'interfered with the freedom of trade' and gave 'large powers' over brokers and other persons.

But having stated the case against regulation very frankly, the commissioners proceeded to counter it point by point. They argued that if the 'humble stations', the 'limited means of information', the unfamiliarity with ships and business—in a word, the vulnerability —of the emigrants meant that they would always be unfavourably situated, it also meant that 'emigration is a matter in which the law may with propriety interfere much further with individual action, than in most other subjects of legislation'. To the objection of interference with trade and merchants, they rejoined, 'on the other hand we would point to the cruel injuries upon poor and comparatively helpless emigrants, and also to the public importance of keeping as open as possible, and as free from hindrances and discouragements, the channels of emigration'. Even praise of self-help and 'initiative' were enlisted to support 'an earnest endeavour to protect the poor people who display this spirit of enterprise'. All this was, however, but the parrying of possible thrusts. The commissioners made it quite clear that the main and essential ground for further legislative action was the experience of the executive officers. The mass of inquiries, reports and recommendations, accumulated over almost a decade, had demonstrated beyond any doubt that passengers still suffered 'fearful privation' and mortality and 'intolerable' abuses, and that the only and necessary remedy was a new and much more restrictive passenger act. On the central issues there could be no argument.[1]

In some ways this piece of internal dialectic—though it was but shadow-boxing on the part of the commissioners—recalls the parliamentary debate which preceded the original act of 1828. But the differences between the two show the length of the road which had been travelled in thirteen years. The abstract arguments against regulation, or further regulation, had become merely formal. They were now easily checkmated by counter-balancing abstractions or even by turning the weapons of the bill's hypothetical opponents against themselves. What had been a matter of real passion and principle in 1828 was scarcely more than an intellectual quadrille in 1842. What counted now was the fruit of expert, official observation. This had established a vast corpus of *facts*, which in turn led irresistibly to two incontrovertible general propositions, that the current state of the passenger trade was 'intolerable' and that the necessary mode of improvement was further state intervention and control.

The contrast between 1828 and 1842 is still more remarkable if we consider the prospective statutes as instruments of remedy and control. The passenger act of 1842[2] was, for its day, a superlative piece of social legislation. Its centrepiece—the commissioners observed that 'more certain good may be hoped for [from section 6] than

[1] *Rep. C.L.E.C. on necessity of amending passenger act*, 3-6 [355], H.C. 1842, xxv.
[2] 6 & 7 Vic., c. 107.

from any other change proposed in the law"[1]—was the requirement that vessels supply each passenger weekly with 7 lb. of bread, biscuit, flour, oatmeal or rice, or the equivalent in potatoes.[2] Both the history and justification of this clause are instructive. It had been originally proposed in a general form by Low and at least two other United Kingdom officers. Later Buchanan had asked specifically for a weekly ration of 5 lb. of biscuit.[3] This was deemed to be insufficient both in quantity and variety by the United Kingdom officers; and eventually the commissioners worked on the principle of, and decided on the advice of their staff, the minimum necessary to preserve life and health. Anything more might raise fares unduly, but anything less was 'unthinkable'.[4] As to the purpose of the clause, it is interesting to note that it was recommended as much on administrative as on humanitarian grounds. So long as emigrants supplied their own food, effective examination of the quantities aboard was 'next to impossible'.[5] But the ship's stores might be judged with tolerable accuracy. Moreover the interconnexions between food, health and various other difficulties in the trade were well understood. The commissioners justly observed that the problems of extortionate food charges on the voyage, of waste, of debility and consequent infection and of putting into ports other than those contracted for,[6] would be partially resolved by the new section.

The second important innovation, that concerning abuses in the embarkation ports, bears the same mark of professional competence and forethought. The reports of the executive officers had established

---

[1] *Rep. C.L.E.C. on necessity of amending passenger act*, 17 [355], H.C. 1842, xxv.

[2] At least one-half of the foodstuffs had to consist of bread or biscuit; 5 lb. of potatoes was adjudged the equivalent of 1 lb. of bread, the amount being put so high because potatoes often went bad or were damaged on the voyage. Potatoes were allowed to suit Irish emigrants used to this diet.

[3] *Papers rel. emigration B.N.A.*, 28 [373], H.C. 1842, xxxi.

[4] The emigration officers were instructed to warn emigrants that it was most desirable, if not actually necessary to survival, to take aboard their own sea-stock in addition, especially meat or fish, sugar and tea, *Rep. C.L.E.C. on necessity of amending passenger act*, 4, 17 [355], H.C. 1842, xxv.

[5] The phrase was Buchanan's, *Papers rel. emigration B.N.A.*, 28 [373], H.C. 1842, xxxi.

[6] It was not uncommon for vessels bound for the northern ports of the United States to put into St John, New Brunswick, because there was insufficient food left aboard to supply the remainder of the journey to Boston or New York. The passengers were, of course, then left stranded hundreds of miles from their destination.

that the subsistence clause of the 1835 act was ineffective, partly because the act had so far held to the notion of free contract as to permit emigrants to 'opt out' of the arrangement if they so desired,[1] and partly because 'the time [of sailing] has commonly not been fixed with sufficient exactness to meet the objects of the law, or to be a matter of legal evidence'. It had moreover proved extremely difficult to 'bring responsibility home to the only parties within reach at the time when the evil occurs': threatened with actions, Liverpool principals simply repudiated their Irish agents.[2] For all this, the commissioners proposed three interlocking remedies: first, that subsistence be furnished from the appointed sailing-date without regard to 'wind or weather' or to any other bargain which an emigrant might make; secondly, that all agreements concerning passages be made in a prescribed form, a copy of which was set out in the act; and thirdly, that all passenger brokers and agents be licensed, and that these licences be withdrawn for proved misconduct.[3] The commissioners recognized that even these three clauses did not provide a full security. But a written contract in a set and legally impregnable form at least ensured irrefutable evidence of the sailing-date and of the ship contracted for. Doubtless, it could not *per se* afford proof of agency. But together with the licensing system and heavy penalties for conviction, it certainly acted as a general deterrent even here. The clause governing the licensing of brokers by justices of the peace, which involved several technical legal difficulties, was also most carefully framed.[4] Due notice to the emigration commissioners was required before a licence could be awarded in order that they might instruct their officers as to the attitude which they should take; and prescribed

---

[1] Under the 1835 act passengers might contract to be victualled, and the more ignorant were easily persuaded to do so. If they did they were not entitled to subsistence money but only to be kept aboard; and in fact passengers in this class generally received neither food nor compensation, because of certain technical difficulties of enforcement, C.O. 384/64, 1637 Emigration, undated.

[2] *Rep. C.L.E.C. on necessity of amending passenger act*, 21 [355], H.C. 1842, xxv.

[3] Ibid., 21-22.

[4] But it does not appear to have considered that the commissioners themselves should grant and revoke licences, as the commissioners were empowered to do eleven years later in the case of London hackney carriages by 16 & 17 *Vic.*, c. 33. I am indebted to Professor Burn for drawing my attention to this last measure.

forms and exact rules were laid down in the statute itself so that even the most timid and unlearned justices might act with confidence. Throughout this section we are struck again by the dovetailing of remedy and enforcement.

The other main features of the 1842 act were as follows. The passenger-tonnage ratio remained 3 : 5 and the surface space allowance between decks was still ten square feet, but 'short ships' were no longer exempted from the law; a fine of £5 *per capita* for excess passengers replaced the former, inadequate maximum of £20; and all children under fourteen years were henceforth to count as half-passengers.[1] These new requirements were unquestionably more useful in the prevention of overcrowding than any mere reduction in the numbers ratio would have been. They were supported by a new clause prescribing a set form of passenger list to be completed by the master and counter-signed at the last customs post to be cleared, and a secondary list on which the master had to enter the names of any passengers taken aboard after that stage. Together with the new practice of sending passenger lists ahead by steamer, this clause made it possible at last to establish the facts of culpable excess and of the master's responsibility.

As to the enforcement of the act generally, the emigration officers were at last nominated as its executors,[2] and summary processes at last provided for at both the ports of departure and disembarkation. All penalties and monies recoverable under the act were recoverable before two justices of the peace; one justice might issue a summons upon information or complaint; and two might issue a warrant for arrest if the summons were unanswered. A number of corresponding and supporting clauses supplied other deficiencies of jurisdiction, and Buchanan's recommendation that justices be given a simple procedure, clearly prescribed in the act itself, was carried out. The penalties for breaches of the act were increased considerably in all cases. 'Seeing', the commissioners observed, 'the importance to human life of many of the regulations . . . and the profit that may

---

[1] Infants under one year were, as usual, excepted. The former calculation that two children under fourteen years, or three under seven years, equalled one statute adult was the source of much confusion and deceit on the ground of ages.

[2] The emigration officer was specifically charged with surveying the provisions, water and casks, with acting on behalf of emigrants for all breaches of contract and of the act, and with adjudging seaworthiness. Only in his absence was the customs officer to take on these duties.

occasionally attend a disregard of them, it seems not too much to impose a penalty as high as £50'.[1] As to the actual sea-passage, there were three new clauses of some importance. The first regulated the size and structure of the berths, the second required water to be stored in 'sweetened' containers of specified dimensions,[2] and the third laid down the number of the lifeboats which must be carried, scaled according to the vessel's size.[3] Moreover, the drinking or sale of spirits was altogether forbidden under the very heavy penalty of £100; the regulation height between decks was increased to six feet; and there were various additional requirements as to the thickness and security of the decks. All other clauses of the 1835 act were either left untouched or but slightly altered.

It may well be thought that the 1842 act has been analysed in tedious and excessive detail. But the charge of excess, at least, may be refuted. Although the statute introduced several novelties (two of them truly revolutionary), it is not these which set the act apart as great legislation. Indeed in some respects it was, in content, a moderate and even cautious measure. All the emigration officers agreed that the 3 : 5 numbers ratio meant overcrowding; the food allowance was cut to the very bone; and the berthing space was only nine square feet per adult. The essential merit of the act lay rather in its confident selection of the significant, in its comprehension of the relationship of the various parts to the whole, and above all in its enforceability. All three characteristics, but especially the last, can only be appreciated by an exhaustive analysis of details. It was the obscure minutiae of execution, the prescribed schedules, the patient forestalling of the multitudinous evasions, which really

[1] C.O. 384/64, 1637 Emigration, undated.

[2] The maximum size of casks was 300 gallon capacity. The daily ration of water was three quarts per passenger. This was ample if the water were pure and if the containers did not leak so badly that the water went short in mid-voyage. But the water was usually brackish or foul, and the casks (especially those with pine heads) were often so leaky that the water was totally exhausted several days before arrival, *Annual rep. agent-general emigration Canada*, 24, H.C. 1836-7 (132), xlii. Hodder, the Dublin emigration officer, had asked for legislation on these points eight years before.

[3] Vessels of less than 250 tons were required to carry two lifeboats; vessels under 500 tons were required to carry three; and those above 500 tons were required to carry four. A vessel of 400 tons might well have carried, quite legally, more than 300 souls aboard, allowing for children and the crew; a vessel of 490 tons might well have carried more than 400. Thus the clause was undoubtedly inadequate, though certainly an advance upon no regulation at all.

signified. Prohibitory enactments might have been framed in ten minutes of generous emotion, but to carry a single one, such as the passage contract clause, thoroughly into effect and to anticipate its every ramification and repercussion might cost days upon days of labour. The 1842 act was not a perfect measure, even technically. But taking it all round, and in its time and circumstances, it was a pioneer and *beau idéal* of the new sort of regulative legislation. It was the fruit of almost a decade of direct observation, and of twelve months of continuous drafting and review. Every clause other than the purely legal had been originally proposed by an executive officer working in the field. Every clause had been submitted to several executive officers for criticism. The London, Liverpool and Dublin officers, Lean, Henry and Hodder, were constantly consulted by the commissioners;[1] Buchanan and Wedderburn, the emigration agent for New Brunswick, proffered advice at different stages.[2] Outside interests and persons had made proposals,[3] but none was adopted or (for that matter) important. The protests of the shipowners and the shipping agents[4] may possibly have had some restraining influence. But even this is unlikely. No one could have been more thoroughly imbued with the notion that fares must be held as low as possible than Elliot, the chief and dominant commissioner; and no other or theoretical deterrent appears to have the least effect. In short, the passenger bill of 1842 was almost exclusively the work of a professional inspectorate and their professional superiors, an 'administrative' not a 'political' venture.

It was clearly presented as such by Stanley, who was once again colonial secretary, this time as a conservative under Peel. In introducing the measure to the house of commons, Stanley stated that it had been built upon the experience of the executive officers over several seasons, and derived immediately from the reports which all these officers had furnished during the previous year upon the 'defects' of the 1835 act and 'the principal modes by which their utmost diligence was evaded'. The officers' subsequent recommendations

[1] *Rep. C.L.E.C. on necessity of amending passenger act*, 6 [355], H.C. 1842, xxv; C.O. 386/140, p. 18; C.O. 384/62, 541, 648, 1018 and 1344 Emigration, 1 Mar.–20 June 1840.

[2] E.g. C.O. 386/27, pp. 147–8, 19 May 1841; C.O. 386/28, pp. 20–21, 21 Sept. 1841.

[3] E.g. C.O. 384/27, pp. 155–7, 24 May 1841.

[4] E.g. C.O. 384/73, 324 and 341 Emigration, 25 and 28 Feb. 1842.

formed the basis of the new proposal, which was, Stanley concluded, quite uncontroversial.[1] Lord John Russell, who had
preceded Stanley at the colonial office, agreed that the bill should
arouse no conflict, and added, generously, that the officers' reports
established that there had been gross abuses in Irish emigration
during his secretaryship, and that the new measure must be 'welcomed'.[2] The bill passed almost unscathed and commentless   ✓
through parliament.[3] A few changes were made in committee. The
commissioners had proposed a 1 : 2 numbers ratio in place of 3: 5,[4]
but this was disallowed. They had proposed the savage penalty of
£200 for the sale or use of spirits at sea, but this was halved. Finally,
their proposal that the 'wind and weather permitting' qualification
be dropped from the requirement to supply subsistence from the
sailing-date[5] was rejected. Only the last alteration was a material
loss. Generally speaking, the bill was passed in virtually the same
form as it had left the hands of the commissioners. In certain respects, therefore, it was a prime example of 'expert government'.   ✓
What could better have fulfilled the Benthamite ideal of a continuous process of rule from investigation and calculation down to
legislation and concrete execution? Yet it is quite likely that the
naval lieutenants and colonials who proposed these things had not
so much as heard the name 'utility'. They did what they did because little or no other course seemed open, if the evils which
appalled humanity were to be overcome. Lastly, we may profitably
recall that the majority of the new restrictions in the passenger act
of 1842, and some even of its technical devices, had been proposed,
in general terms at least, by Low more than nine years before. 'By
such slow degrees do the most useful and seemingly the most
obvious arts make their way among mankind'.

The bill as it passed through parliament had a mixed reception

[1] *Hans.*, 3rd, lx, 76–79, 4 Feb. 1842.
[2] Ibid., 85.
[3] Ibid., lxi, 419–20, lxv, 644–67. The only point of controversy was the extent
and consequences of 'coolie' emigration, a subject only incidentally involved in
the bill.
[4] *Rep. C.L.E.C. on necessity of amending passenger act*, 15 [355], H.C. 1842,
xxv. Buchanan had recommended, in addition to a 1 : 2 ratio, that all children
count as full passengers, *Papers rel. emigration B.N.A.*, 28 [373], H.C. 1842,
xxxi. But the commissioners rejected this last as too drastic a change.
[5] This qualification opened the door, of course, to many evasions of the
clause.

from the trade.[1] Naturally, brokers and agents were agitated by the prospect of being licensed. But the many nervous letters which reached the commissioners during the spring of 1842 were met with the doubtless reassuring answer that 'fitness' to engage in the business was a matter for the local magistrates to decide. Equal consternation was caused by the clauses concerning height between decks and 'permanent' beams. Most of the Irish vessels were Clyde or Cumberland built, and lacked the requisite six feet in height. A Limerick ship-owner, Spaight, complained that he had had several vessels made for him in the previous three years in conformity with the requirements of the 1835 act, and that none of them could now be used for passengers.[2] Martin & Co. of Belfast declared that 50 per cent of the vessels currently employed in the emigrant trade would henceforth be excluded. Again, many protested against the new 'children's clause' (Spaight prophesied that Irish families would abandon all those below the age of seven in the workhouses), and against the reduction in the numbers ratio. It was commonly said that these two, together with the foodstuffs clause, would so increase fares as to bring Irish emigration to a standstill. The new detentions clause was also criticized, partly upon the ground that several days were needed for embarkations at the Irish ports and partly because the time of sailing was always contingent upon the uncertain wind and weather. As we have seen, concessions were made on this last point and also on the numbers ratio. But otherwise the government stood firm against all protests.

Other members of the trade, however, welcomed the bill and even asked for further and more stringent regulation. The Sligo owners and brokers (who according to their usual practice spoke in concert) condemned the provisions clause as insufficient and, by its emphasis on cereal foods, ill-suited to Irish habits. Sligo put forward three new suggestions of considerable merit—that the surveys for seaworthiness be conducted by the customs officers and not by the emigration officer, 'as the former are more competent to give it immediate attention and prevent delay, being more experienced in shipping than the latter'; that Liverpool brokers be compelled to name

---

[1] This paragraph and the next are based upon the large collection of letters from shipowners, brokers, agents and others contained in C.O. 384/73. See also C.O. 384/69, 380 Emigration, 8 Mar. 1842 and C.O. 386/31, pp. 188, 246.

[2] Spaight's complaint need not be taken too seriously. He remained the leader of the Limerick passenger trade for many seasons after 1842.

all their authorized sub-agents in the shipping register and on their handbills and tickets; and that the numbers aboard be limited according to the amount of cargo carried as well as according to the tonnage.[1] More was to be heard in later years of each of these matters. Brown, a magistrate and a partner in one of the best Liverpool houses, Brown, Shipley & Co., asked for very strong measures against runners, and argued that summary jurisdiction, without right of appeal, was needed for all cases which involved not only agents, but also runners, emigrant-lodgings or 'slops' or 'jerry' stores. Justice, if not immediately and informally done, could not be done at all. Brown also suggested, among other things, further precautions in the prescribed form of contract and the close regulation of berthing. The commissioners, however, refused to adopt any of the new proposals, although they did, after heavy pressure from several members of the trade, slightly improve the clauses concerning ship's boats and water-casks by amendments in the house of lords. Thus, for worse as well as better, the reaction of the trade played a very small part in shaping the passenger act of 1842.

The act was the culmination of several years of hard endeavour. But it was also—far from the commissioners' expectations—the beginning of a fresh activity. In the course of their efforts to enforce the statute, the commissioners were led on gradually to project further legislation, to act quasi-judicially in deciding the criteria which their officers should use and to move towards further centralization and autonomy. A few cases may serve to illustrate these tendencies. The first resistance to the 1842 act centred round the foodstuffs clause, and was especially marked in Ireland. Two ingenious evasions were observed immediately. Steerage passengers were represented as 'cabin'—the latter being exempt from the act because they dined with the master—and emigrants were induced to 'lend' their provisions temporarily to the master so that they might be passed off as the ship's stock at the inspection. Although the commissioners ordered their officers to use common-sense tests and to act with confidence, the difficulty of conducting satisfactory inspections remained; and three months after the act came into

---

[1] The London ship-owners also acted in common, and sent a deputation to discuss the act with the commissioners. They, too, approved of the bill substantially, and they had only a few minor and more or less technical amendments to propose.

operation they asked for powers to compel owners and charterers to prepare their stores in such a way that they could be properly inspected, stowed and issued. Stephen at once objected to the further network of regulations which he saw developing, and Stanley rejected out of hand the notion of a legislative amendment hard upon the heels of a consolidating statute: he added, characteristically, that the 1842 act would fulfil the commissioners' objects if 'sufficiently' enforced.[1]

Immediately after this rebuff, the problem re-presented itself in another form. Buchanan discovered that several Cork vessels had taken aboard foul breadstuffs as well as good, and shown only the latter for inspection. Having been reprimanded for his negligence, the Cork officer instituted a prosecution in the first case of this abuse which he discovered. But the Cork magistrates, while protesting the warmest indignation at the cruel deception, decided that they had no powers to convict as the vessel had not actually sailed. Meanwhile, the Quebec magistrates had interpreted the clause as meaning that the master was not liable to supply food until the passengers themselves requested it! Patiently the commissioners obtained crown lawyers' opinions to confute both sets of magistrates; they insisted that prosecutions be pressed vigorously on either side of the Atlantic; and they laid down a minimum standard for emigrant provisions—'navy bread'—and a standard procedure for inspections. At least one food package in every ten and one water cask in every five was to be opened and examined thoroughly, and it was expected that each inspection would last three to four hours.[2] These developments show clearly how legislation might breed the impulse to further legislation, and to quasi-legislation in the form of departmental glosses and instructions. To view the matter in another light, the commissioners' reactions were thoroughly sensible, and though their counter-measures were by no means as successful as they at first supposed, they were not altogether ineffective.

The history of the clause governing the licensing of brokers also

[1] C.O. 386/33, pp. 94–9, 3 May 1843; C.O. 384/74, 336 Emigration and endorsements, 29 Mar. 1843.
[2] C.O. 386/33, pp. 158–9, 176–7, 18 and 24 May 1843; C.O. 386/34, pp. 85–6, 2 Sept. 1843; C.O. 384/74, 607, 781 and 838 Emigration, 9 June, 27 July and 11 Aug. 1843; *Southern Reporter*, 16 May 1843. It was Lieut. Lean of London who advised the commissioners on the standard inspection.

provides an interesting example of the difficulties of predicting practice. Here the commissioners were themselves partly to blame. They do not appear to have considered fully the implications of 'receiving due notice' of every application; more especially, they had not considered on what grounds, if any, they should instruct their officers to oppose an application. A test-case arose immediately.[1] The Belfast magistrates asked the commissioners for their recommendation concerning a broker of doubtful repute. After some hesitation, the commissioners replied that as there was no *proved* misconduct they would not oppose him. This seemed to imply that only a conviction under the passenger act would disqualify a broker; and as it worked in practice, this was further contracted to only recent or even current convictions. After the experience of three seasons the commissioners complained that magistrates usually insisted, before they would refuse a licence, upon such actual proofs of fraud that even men of known 'improper character' were commonly accepted. On the other hand, it was clearly difficult for the commissioners to weed out the trade without exercising an arbitrary veto and superseding the ordinary law. To escape the dilemma, they proposed embarking upon another tack—annual payments for licences (£10 at Liverpool and £5 at other ports) as was the practice in the trades of pawnbroking and game-dealing. 'The necessity', they declared, 'of stringent laws to check frauds [is] apparent'.[2] Stephen's comment was that the 'discrimination' against Liverpool would be hard to defend,[3] while Gladstone, who had recently been appointed colonial secretary, rather fatuously asked for information 'as to the frequency of the cases of fraud and hardship upon emigrants through want of respectability in the brokers'. The commissioners readily supplied him with heart-rending cases, but added that they grounded their request rather upon the 'general opinion entertained by the most experienced of our officers'. The distinction between Liverpool and the other ports was drawn because the

[1] C.O. 386/33, pp. 13-14, 4 Apr. 1833.
[2] C.O. 384/78, 182 North America and endorsements, 26 Feb. 1846.
[3] It is true that the local patriotism of the Liverpool passenger trade was intense, cf. C.O. 384/68, 2419 Emigration, 10 Nov. 1841; C.O. 384/30, p. 267, 20 May 1842. But its leaders and spokesmen were by this time the 'respectable' agents who were loudest of all in complaining of the abuses in Liverpool. It is very unlikely that they would have objected to a £10 stamp duty, the intention of which would have been to exclude the 'disreputable'.

Liverpool trade was both much worse and much more prosperous than any other.[1] But Gladstone and Stephen were still unconvinced. When, a year later, the commissioners repeated this project in their heads for an amendment bill, Stephen roundly condemned the proposed burden on the brokers. 'No class of men', he wrote, 'have a more lively or a more just dread of the intervention of the legislature in their affairs; and although necessity may occasionally justify it, the necessity should be at once urgent and evident'.[2] The clause was dropped and the licensing system remained in its very imperfect state for some further seasons.

The history of the survey clause throws another and rather different light upon administrative development. At first, the commissioners, though reluctantly, accepted Lloyd's survey as evidence of seaworthiness, with the tacit understanding that their officers should judge for themselves in cases where Lloyd's had not pronounced.[3] But it eventually appeared, through a chance calamity, that this optimistic procedure was very dangerous. When, at the end of 1845, an American vessel, the *Robert Isaacs*, put back in great distress, it was clear that the Liverpool emigration officer should have called for a survey for seaworthiness: like most foreign vessels the *Robert Isaacs* was not registered at Lloyds. After a great deal of uncertainty, the commissioners decided that in future all foreign emigrant ships should be surveyed by Lloyds. But new difficulties sprang up at once. Lloyd's surveyors refused to depart from their ordinary practice and to survey merely for seaworthiness for the voyage in prospect;[4] while the American masters, supported by their consul at Liverpool, protested vigorously against the new delays and standards. The commissioners hastily abandoned the Lloyd's survey. Instead they instructed their officers to accept A2 and better categories where a vessel was registered at Lloyd's and in all other cases to conduct their own surveys. This was followed by another stream of complaints against the new surveys; and finally in the spring of 1847 the commissioners secured the appointment of a permanent professional as government surveyor at Liverpool. In other ports, the emigration officers began to call on experienced shipwrights to

[1] C.O. 384/78, 222 North America, 11 Mar. 1846.
[2] C.O. 384/80, 58 Miscellaneous, 15 Jan. 1847.
[3] C.O. 384/68, 2419 Emigration, 10 Nov. 1841.
[4] This last was all that the 1842 act demanded.

make the surveys, when such men were available.[1] The episode is not only an interesting case of the post-legislative growth of government. It is also the first instance in our subject of regulation reaching beyond the competence of the 'general practitioner' executive officer.

Finally, a glance at a number of the other difficulties which arose may indicate the extent as well as the complexity and intractability of the problems of enforcement. It was soon discovered that the 1842 act was not always effective against the abuse of a wrong destination being advertised, and the commissioners instructed their officers to announce the true destination at the time of muster to the assembled emigrants.[2] Again, although the 1842 act gave them no direct powers over cooking between-decks the commissioners, after complaints, instructed the officers to insist on at least one cooking grate for every hundred souls aboard.[3] Difficulties over the measurement of space and over co-ordinate authority led to a *démarche* with the board of customs, which firmly established the superior powers of the commissioners and incidentally produced the elaboration of a considerable body of departmental instructions. As to measurement, the commissioners had to lay down much more exact and comprehensive rules,[4] and to secure the customs board's agreement to instruct their own officers to follow the same procedure.[5] The commissioners also defeated the board's attempt to exercise dispensing powers over penalties under the passenger act,[6] and vehemently opposed a customs proposal that the foodstuffs clause of the 1842 act be repealed.[7] With the growth of remittance trade came an outcrop of new frauds; and when one of their officers brought this to

---

[1] The whole of the voluminous correspondence upon the subject of surveys is contained in C.O. 384/77 and C.O. 386/40, 27 Apr.–7 July 1846. See also *7th rep. C.L.E.C.*, 41 [809], H.C. 1847, xxxiii.

[2] C.O. 384/74, 207 Canada, 21 Jan. 1843.

[3] C.O. 384/78, 969 Canada, 9 Sept. 1845.

[4] The commissioners ordered that in computing cubic space, three measurements of width should be taken, equidistant from one another, and that the average of these measurements should be multiplied by the vessel's length; and that in computing surface space, the actual floor of the passenger deck should be measured. Whichever of these two measures allowed the lesser number of passengers was to be adopted. There were various other minute regulations, *6th rep. C.L.E.C.*, 52–3 [706], H.C. 1846, xxiv.

[5] C.O. 386/39, p. 47, 5 Jan. 1846.

[6] C.O. 384/75, 852 and 965 Canada, 6 Aug. and 6 Sept. 1844.

[7] C.O. 384/80, 1069 Emigration, 19 June 1847.

the commissioners' attention, they ordered the corps to do everything possible—but what *was* possible?—to safeguard the recipients.[1] Again, the commissioners received repeated requests from
British North America for medical inspections and the rejection
of infected persons at the embarkation ports—especially at Liverpool whose vessels sometimes suffered dreadful outbreaks of typhus
and smallpox. The Liverpool officer responded to these complaints
by sending all persons whom he suspected of disease to a nearby
hospital to be examined. It was clearly a haphazard, amateur procedure, but as the commissioners themselves remarked, they were
'embarrassed by many difficulties in attempting to find any effectual
security': there was no money to pay physicians or to support the
rejected; there was not even power to detain people against their will.[2]
And when in 1843 they tentatively suggested further legislation to
overcome these evils, Stanley rejected the proposal as firmly as he
had done the inspections project: it was still too soon for an amending statute.[3] As a final example, it is interesting to note that when,
with the return of relatively large-scale emigration in 1845, small
'casual' vessels crept back into the trade and the commissioners declared that such ships were 'inconsistent with the intentions of the
powers of the 3rd and 4th clauses of the passenger act',[4] they none
the less found it virtually impossible to expel them. The crown
lawyers ruled that the requirement that the beams of the passenger
deck be part of the 'permanent' structure was very different from
requiring them to be part of the 'original' structure.[5] Thus did experience mark out weak places in the 1842 act and thus did the act
itself open out like a paper flower in water, into unforeseen practices
and rules.

This emphasis upon the imperfections of the 1842 act should not
be taken to mean that that measure was, substantially, a failure. On
the contrary, it was relatively successful. In fact, the first three
seasons of its operation seemed like a golden age after the hardships

[1] C.O. 386/140, 16 June 1846.
[2] C.O. 384/78, 1039 Canada, 19 Sept. 1845.
[3] C.O. 384/74, 327 Emigration, 24 Mar. 1843.
[4] These clauses dealt with the height between decks and the security of the
beams enclosing the passenger room.
[5] C.O. 384/77, 507 and 630 Emigration, 30 Apr. and 30 May 1845. For glosses
on other uncertain clauses, see 329 Emigration and 1594 Miscellaneous in the
same volume.

and scandals of the preceding decade. Even before the act came into
force there was a decided improvement in the Atlantic trade, due
mainly to the commissioners' superintendence over and support of
the executive officers, and to the rapid forwarding of intelligence
concerning the vessels which had been cleared.[1] None the less the
trade was disgraceful even in 1841–2. A very large number of vessels,
perhaps a majority, were still within the 150–200 tons range and
thoroughly unsuitable. The beams for the passenger deck were
usually but temporary and uncaulked boards. There were rarely
any, and never satisfactory, kitchens or lavatories. The customs
officers habitually measured incorrectly, often allowing up to twenty-
five passengers over the statutory complement.[2] Vessels were still
commonly mismanaged and in disrepair.[3] The *Mersey* from Liverpool put back twice in 1842, after voyages of seven and five weeks,
before it reached New York eventually.[4] The *Countess of Arran*, a
new and well-appointed vessel, returned to Belfast after seven
weeks at sea because of the incompetence of a master who was not
even a professional seaman.[5] In each of these cases, hundreds of
emigrants eventually lost their passages and were left destitute at
the home ports, without redress. As to the operation of the 1835
act, a glance at the Canadian trade in 1841 well confirms the contemporary comment that it was 'continually infringed upon'.[6] Even
the commissioners admitted that although the season had been
marked by great improvements due to the increased vigilance of
their officers, the usual abuses of insufficient foodstuffs and want,
and terrible overcrowding abounded.[7] No less than twenty-five of
the vessels arriving at Quebec had excess passengers aboard.
Among them, the *Lord Cochrane* from Tralee carried sixty in excess;
the *Pomona* from Sligo carried twenty-seven and a Robinson

---

[1] *2nd rep. C.L.E.C.*, 19, H.C. 1842 (567), xxv; *3rd rep. C.L.E.C.*, 26, H.C.
1843 (261), xxix.
[2] C.O. 384/62, 1018 Emigration, 14 May 1840; C.O. 384/73, 767 Emigration,
7 Apr. 1842.
[3] C.O. 386/30, pp. 358, 374–6, 16 and 18 June 1842.
[4] C.O. 384/69, 767, 1472 and 1591 Emigration, 13 May, 28 June and 30 Aug.
1842; C.O. 386/30, p. 358, 16 June 1842.
[5] C.O. 384/69, 574 and 865 Emigration, 23 Mar. and 22 Apr. 1842.
[6] C.O. 384/63, 870 Emigration, 24 Mar. 1841. This observation was made by
the shipping firm, Carter & Bonus, who dominated the London passenger
trade.
[7] C.O. 384/69, 748 Emigration, 7 May 1842.

6

Brothers' vessel, the *Grace*, twenty-nine. On the *Hope* from Dublin, the emigrants' provisions were exhausted half-way through the voyage, and for three weeks the master supplied them at exorbitant prices and ran them hopelessly into debt.[1] In all these cases, crime paid £50–£100 net profit, even where the maximum fine of £20 was rendered. The brig *Lively* from Galway sailed four weeks after her appointed departure date. Though advertised for New Brunswick, she turned up at Quebec; and there were fourteen passengers in excess. The attempt to prosecute her master failed.[2]

It is against this background that the 1842 act must be judged. Whatever its authors' expectations, it was a small first step and not a final measure. But it did end, virtually overnight, some of the worst evils of the old order. The decline in mortality in the Canadian emigration after 1840 was most remarkable. From 1·02 per cent in 1840, it fell to ·82 per cent in 1841, to ·73 per cent in 1842 and to ·38 per cent in 1843.[3] Even the figures for 1844, ·48 per cent, might be regarded as an improvement, as the extraordinarily bad weather of that season had led to an increase of more than one week in the average length of voyages.[4] The colonial officers attributed the general downward trend to the good management of the commissioners, and the sharp fall in 1843 and 1844 to the new food and space requirements. Douglas's annual report for 1843 spoke with delight of the absence of the usual cases of acute privation, and the consequent general level of good health. Buchanan noted in his report, 'The care with which the act has been framed seems to have secured a provision against all attempts to impose on the emigrants, and there can arise few cases in which the recourse provided by it will prove insufficient';[5] and in the following year he testified to the continuing benefits of the new legislation which ensured ample supplies and tolerable treatment for emigrants during the voyage.[6]

[1] *Annual rep. agents for emigration Canada*, 15–18 [373], H.C. 1842, xxxi. See also C.O. 384/67, 1282, 1635 and 1636 Canada, 3 Aug. and 14 Oct. 1841.

[2] C.O. 386/31, pp. 148–50, 27 Aug. 1842; C.O. 384/69, 1721 Emigration, 19 Nov. 1842; C.O. 386/32, p. 47, 19 Nov. 1842.

[3] *4th rep. C.L.E.C.*, 10, H.C. 1844 (178), xxxi. There are no full statistics for the years before 1840, but the fragmentary evidence of the agent-general's reports suggests that the mortality must have averaged 2 per cent, at least, and possibly as much as 3 per cent.

[4] *5th rep. C.L.E.C.*, 10–11 [617], H.C. 1845, xxvii.

[5] *4th rep. C.L.E.C.*, 10, H.C. 1844 (178), xxxi.

[6] *5th rep. C.L.E.C.*, 12–13 [617], H.C. 1845, xxvii.

Buchanan's comments were, in fact, wildly over-optimistic, but at least they mark the sharp and very real contrast between the pre- and post-1842 régimes.

The number of prosecutions under the 1842 act was, initially, small, averaging less than twenty in the years 1843-5. But this may have been a measure of success rather than failure in enforcement. As the commissioners observed in their report for 1843, masters and brokers knew well by then that the passenger acts would be rigorously enforced in every case, and with fines now running into very considerable sums, they behaved well in consequence.[1] Herein lay the importance of handling the first cases of evasion firmly, and of the keen pursuit of every difficulty in applying the law. Herein lay the significance of the commissioners' instructions to the United Kingdom and colonial officers to press for the utmost penalties, both for the sake of the victims concerned and *pour encourager les autres*. In 1843 and 1844, they themselves fought a case against a Glasgow broker, Somerville, who had acted as a sub-agent without written authority and in the process defrauded several emigrants, right up to the Scottish court of sessions. They justified the heavy expense of the prosecution upon the grounds that the passenger act must be upheld upon this vital point and that Somerville's term of imprisonment would have a very wholesome effect upon the trade.[2] It was certainly true that a heavy and well-publicized punishment deterred many potential offenders for a time. When, a few years later, two brothers were sentenced to seven years' transportation each, others hastily and voluntarily disgorged illegal gains.[3] During the years 1843-5, moreover, the United Kingdom officers recovered some £1,500 annually for emigrants without actual recourse to law. As the commissioners said at the end of 1844, the most satisfactory aspect of the 1842 act was that so very stringent a measure was being put into operation with extraordinarily little need to call upon its penal clauses.[4] The commissioners were surely right if they saw their task (like that of every good police force) as being primarily the prevention of crime and only if that failed, the successful prosecution of malefactors.

---

[1] *4th rep. C.L.E.C.*, 10, H.C. 1844 (178), xxxi.
[2] Ibid.; *5th rep. C.L.E.C.*, 13 [617], H.C. 1845, xxvii.
[3] *8th rep. C.L.E.C.*, 17 [961], H.C. 1847-8, xxvi.
[4] *5th rep. C.L.E.C.*, 13 [617], H.C. 1845, xxvii.

Thus, the passenger trade seemed, in the first flush of achievement, to have been substantially righted at last. Doubtless, loopholes in the legislation remained to be closed, but by and large the brokers and agents appeared to have been cowed, the vessels to be increasingly appropriate to their business, the passage and its problems to be better understood,[1] and *mirabile dictu* masters to have undergone a Scrooge-like transformation.[2] There was even an instance of a group of Irish emigrants refusing to present the testimony necessary to convict a master at Quebec because he had treated them so kindly during the voyage![3] And much of the evidence for this impression was provided by Buchanan and Douglas, the men who had denounced the former evils so furiously five years before. Looking back in 1847 upon the decade which has passed since the agency-general was first established, the emigration commissioners proudly reviewed the manifold advances, and quoted it as the general Canadian opinion that 'the passage across the Atlantic [has] quite changed its character'.[4] And it was true that a plateau of achievement had been reached. Agents and masters had been educated into new standards of conduct and new modes of viewing every feature of their business from passage-contracts to provisioning. The long struggle begun by Low in 1833 had issued in a new sort of trade in which the emigrants had to be regarded not as inconvenient, though tolerably remunerative, ballast for the outward voyage, but as persons with legal rights and members of a regular movement indispensable to transatlantic commerce.

But though the gains had indeed been considerable, the years 1843–5 represented a false dawn. In the first place the emigrations of 1843 and 1844 had been for various reasons[5] extraordinarily small—the combined totals of the two seasons only equalled that of the single year 1842. Few vessels had carried full complements of

---

[1] In 1843 the commissioners drew up regulations for life between-decks on the voyage, and sent copies to their officers for distribution amongst the masters. The officers reported that there was a general disposition amongst the masters to follow and profit by this advice, *3rd rep. C.L.E.C.* 27, H.C. 1843 (261), xxix.

[2] *4th rep. C.L.E.C.*, 12–13, H.C. 1844 (178), xxxi.

[3] Ibid., 13.

[4] *7th rep. C.L.E.C.*, 3 [809], H.C. 1847, xxxiii.

[5] It must not be supposed that the increase in fares occasioned by the passenger act of 1842 was the sole or even the main reason for the fall in emigration. The political excitement centred around the repeal agitation in Ireland and the current depression in the United States and Canada were generally blamed.

passengers during these years: 40 per cent carried less than thirty statute adults. This provided the most favourable conditions in which to introduce the new act. As the commissioners had observed in 1840, the best results were always to be hoped for in years of small emigration, with least overcrowding and least liability to infection.[1] It was natural that the commissioners in their pride and relief should have forgotten their own excellent dictum, and attributed to law and rule much that properly belonged to fortune. Secondly, the commissioners did not know—and never elaborated a machinery for discovering—exactly how legislation was interpreted by their executive officers and how far and to what effect it was applied. To take but one instance, it was the fortuitous scandal of the *Robert Isaacs* which led to the disclosure that the law with respect to surveys was most variously and imperfectly enforced. There were, as we have seen, several other rude awakenings before 1846, and scores of similar disclosures lay ahead. Compared with the former days of total neglect, the measure of co-ordination, knowledge, control and uniformity secured by the commissioners *vis-à-vis* their officers and the trade was very large. But judged by what was absolutely required, it was still grossly deficient. The consequence was successive evictions from fools' paradises, as issue after issue came, from one accident or another, to be scrutinized. Finally, there was, for reasons which we shall discuss later, a natural momentum towards improvement in these affairs. What once seemed, in contrast to the recent past, a thorough-paced reform might well appear, even five years later, altogether inadequate and faulty. The accepted standards of emigrant 'comfort' and of effective enforcement rose imperceptibly but ceaselessly; and there were always, to the very end, new tracts of the subject to be opened. By 1846 the commissioners already showed signs of dissatisfaction with the level reached in 1842. But by 1846 the general situation also was changing rapidly. There was a sharp increase in mortality in 1845, due partly to the return of Irish emigration to the relatively high level of 75,000, but more particularly to the first terrible effects of the potato blight observable in the late sailings of that season. And from that time onwards, the clouds gathered fast.

---

[1] C.O. 384/61, 1273 Canada, 2 July 1840.

CATASTROPHE

1845-7

THE great Irish famine affected passenger legislation and its execution profoundly. It is important to realize that the famine was not the outcome of one year's blight or its terrible effects concentrated into one season. It was rather a succession of great blows, two of them particularly devastating, delivered over seven years. In every year between 1845 and 1851 the Irish potato crop—the mainstay of the entire economy—failed in a greater or less degree. In 1846 and 1848 the failure was virtually complete. So far as emigration was concerned it was these two hammer-strokes which really told. But the disintegration of Irish society would not have been so quick or general had these catastrophes not belonged to a seemingly endless series, and been accompanied by mounting and interacting burdens and disheartening influences of every kind: ruinous rates and vanishing capital, the collapse of commerce, the continued scarcity and high cost of food, the common spectacle of death, and political humiliation. The terrified mass-flight of 1847 was followed by an almost mechanical exodus of despair in 1849, 1850 and 1851. By then, the great famine and its concomitants had broken the stubborn back of Irish agriculture. In massive waves, Irish emigration swept through the old psychological and material restraints. From 54,000 in 1844, it rose to 75,000 in 1845, to 106,000 in 1846, and, the first crescendo, 215,000 in 1847. The partial success of the harvest of 1847, combined with the ghastly fate of the 1847 emigrants, produced a sharp decline in the first half of 1848. But the potato failure of 1848 released so enormous an autumn and winter outflow that the total for the year was nearly 180,000 in the end. In 1849 the terrible level of 1847 was equalled, and in 1850, with an emigration of 209,000 nearly reached. Then came two seasons of almost unbelievable magnitude during which nearly one-half a million persons emigrated. In 1853 the total fell to 193,000, in 1854 to 150,000. The climax had been passed. 'Here then', wrote James Stephen a decade later, 'you have a measure by which to

judge the sufferings of the people of Ireland during the eight years
of which 1847 was the first. The number of Irish emigrants in those
years is estimated by the emigration commissioners to have exceeded 1,700,000—an estimate which they consider as far below the
truth. Those figures, well weighed and meditated, will reveal a
tragedy which no mere words could disclose.'[1]

The sudden change in the scale and pace of Irish emigration
intensified the old problems. The vast numbers, the high incidence
of extreme poverty and debility, the haste and the want of preparation[2]—often the example of neighbours led to a lightning decision
to be off—threw unfamiliar strains upon the trade, the executive
corps and the existing legislation. 1847 was the supreme season of
disaster. But there were lesser crises in the autumn of 1846, the
winter of 1848, the spring of 1849 and the spring of 1851, as the
volume of emigration for the season in question reached unprecedented heights and was touched, more or less, by panic. We
have already noted that this was manifested by periodic shortages
of shipping, especially in the Dunkirk-like year of 1847 when even
coasting schooners were pressed into service. But shipping was only
the final region of difficulty. At every stage in their journey, emigrants suffered from inadequate forethought, means of carriage and
accommodation. Organized transport in Ireland was still primitive
in 1847. Only 120 miles of railway, some of it suburban, were in
operation. Mail-coach travelling was extremely expensive and negligible in capacity. Bianconi's long-cars and caravans in the south
could handle only a few thousand persons in the year. Even the
canals, which connected the midlands and the Shannon and Barrow
basins with Dublin, could not have carried more than 10 per cent
of the emigrants of 1847 to the capital. As it was, there were continuous reports of emigrants being disappointed of passages at the
canal termini. The overwhelming majority of the emigrants walked
to the ports, with children and baggage riding in their little carts.
There are many pitiful descriptions of the country roads choked with
long, slow trains of people winding their way towards the sea, having
first undergone the piercing experience of parting: 'some of the

[1] *Trans. Soc. Science Assoc. 1858.*, pp. 103-4.
[2] In 1848 and subsequent years, large numbers left hurriedly after harvesting
and selling their crops. The haste was due to their efforts to avoid paying arrears
of rent.

women would fall fainting when they saw any person going, others would hang out of the car to keep back the departing one; but when it would go, the whole lot, men and women, would raise a cry of grief that would wrest an echo from the peaks'. All this was but the first ordeal. Lodgings in the home port, space on the cross-channel steamers, lodgings in Liverpool—these, too, were overtaxed, sometimes with terrible consequences. By 1853, vessels were plentiful and incomparably superior to their pre-famine counterparts; Galway, Limerick, Waterford and Belfast were connected by rail with Dublin; and in all its other aspects the resilient emigrant business had adjusted itself to the new demands. But it was the famine emigrants who bore the brunt of the painful transformation; and it is against a background of precipitate departure, acute privation and overcrowding that the actions of government must be viewed and judged.

The first danger signs appeared in the autumn of 1845 with a marked increase in emigrant mortality and a great difficulty in provisioning the Irish vessels, which largely relied upon oatmeal and potatoes for their sea-stock. At the close of the year, the commissioners were so far apprehensive as to contemplate extensive new legislation, and to devise new regulations to ensure that the provisions of the 1842 act were thoroughly understood, and uniformly enforced, by customs and emigration officers alike. As we have seen, Stephen and Gladstone gave a preliminary proposal concerning brokers' licences short shrift; and the notion of new legislation withered there and then. The commissioners also considered two other courses of action, which might have done more to secure the enforcement of the 1842 act than any body of regulations or instructions: to increase the number of the executive corps, and to restrict emigration to the ten or twelve leading ports in the United Kingdom. But on reflection they decided that there was no hope of money for the first, and that the latter would meet with 'insuperable objections'.[1]

It may appear extraordinary that the corps was not increased. Even twenty additional officers, quite sufficient to perfect the protective system up to the limit of its statutory capacity, would have cost only £4,000 per annum. But the treasury of the 1840s strove not only to control public spending but also to prevent, so far as possible, every new expenditure. From the outset, the commissioners

[1] C.O. 386/37, pp. 205–6, 16 Apr. 1845.

—we should perhaps singularize Elliot—were oppressed by a sense of general treasury disapproval. One of their earliest actions was to withdraw an officer from Waterford to compensate for improvements in the Liverpool office.[1] Down to 1842, the executive officers had even to meet many official expenses from their own pockets. Henry at Liverpool was so overwhelmed by inspections and court appearances that he employed a clerk privately to keep his returns and statistics. Friend also employed his own assistant to maintain the Cork office while he visited the outport. Even such items as postage, the printing of handbills and (despite many years of agitation) travelling expenses to meet vessels in distress were not regularly defrayed by the treasury.[2] The crowning absurdity came in 1845 when in order to secure a badly needed assistant at Liverpool the commissioners had to reduce the salary of one of their existing officers from £208 to £120. A species of musical chairs then developed, at the end of which it was the unfortunate Lieut. Shuttleworth of Sligo, possibly the most overworked of all the Irish officers, who was the victim.[3] All of which makes it clear why the climate was unfavourable to any, let alone a sufficient, increase of staff.[4]

But the commissioners did take one step, early in 1846, to mitigate the effects of the Irish blight. Much of the potato crop having perished, there were many requests from Ireland for permission to use Indian meal (which had been imported in great quantities by the government) in making up ships' provisions. Indian meal was not amongst the scheduled foods in the 1842 act, and the commissioners replied that they had no power to deviate from the statute. But when it became clear that other foods were virtually unobtainable in Ireland, they changed their minds and instructed the officers to 'take no steps for preventing' the substitution of meal for potatoes.[5] The argument they now used was that it must 'have been the intention of the legislature to invest the government with

[1] C.O. 384/62, 541 and 648 Emigration, Mar. 1840.
[2] C.O. 384/73, 1945 Emigration, 29 Aug. 1842. For the corresponding difficulties of the first factory inspectors, see Thomas, op. cit., p. 100.
[3] C.O. 384/77, 89, 105 and 253 Emigration, 25 Jan. and 7 Mar. 1845.
[4] Requests for the appointment of an officer to Waterford, which then ranked fifth in importance amongst Irish ports, were refused in 1846, ibid., 499 and 568 Emigration, 23 Apr. and 4 May 1846.
[5] In the first draft, the word 'permit' was used, but in the second the more anodyne form was preferred. The officers were also instructed to do everything possible to prevent potatoes being put aboard.

some discretion respecting the enforcement of the passenger acts'.[1] In fact, Indian meal proved worthless as a sea-stock—it deteriorated rapidly—and the tacit permission was subsequently withdrawn.[2] But meanwhile, in the spring of 1846, it was discovered that the only Indian meal available in Ireland was in government stores, and various Irish owners and charterers begged permission to buy this for their waiting passengers. The treasury brusquely refused upon the ground that 'it would be very objectionable for the government to interfere with the provision market to a greater extent, or in any other manner that is required for the purpose [of relieving desti- tution]'.[3] The whole episode, though unimportant in itself, was sinister. It foreshadowed both the later crises and the ineptitude of the state's reactions. It also showed the commissioners, for the first time, sanctioning an action whose consequences they could not foretell, and stepping outside the pale of constitutional orthodoxy in presuming to read the minds of the legislators. This too was a har- binger of things to come.

As 1846 wore on, the situation grew more threatening. It soon became apparent that the year's emigration would be the largest on record. It also became clear that the mortality rate would be the highest since the catastrophes of the 1830s: in the end, it reached 2 per cent. Many very small vessels were employed; there were numerous sailings from ports not normally used for emigration; and the colonial prosecutions for breaches of the passenger act rose alarmingly. Worst of all perhaps, matters deteriorated rapidly in the last two months of the season. Emigrants were unusually destitute; their departure had been very ill-prepared; and a large number went down with typhus.[4] The year even yielded a scandal which recalled the worst of the old lawless days. The *Sarah and Elizabeth*[5]

---

[1] C.O. 386/39, pp. 148-9, 363-4, 13 Feb. and 31 Mar. 1846; C.O. 384/77, 239 and 323 Emigration, 27 Feb. and 13 Mar. 1846; C.O. 384/78, 61 Emigra- tion, 27 Feb. 1846.

[2] C.O. 384/80, 61 and 500 Emigration, 14 Jan. and 27 Mar. 1847; Papers *rel. emigration B.N.A.*, 24 [777], H.C. 1847, xxxix. See also *Cork Constitution*, 23 Feb. 1847.

[3] C.O. 384/77, 371 and 410 Emigration, 21 and 31 Mar. 1846. It is possible that biscuit and flour were eventually obtained from Liverpool.

[4] *7th rep. C.L.E.C.*, 32-36 [609], H.C. 1847, xxxiii; *Papers rel. emigration B.N.A.* 9, 39 [777], H.C. 1847, xxxix.

[5] The *Sarah and Elizabeth* was a small vessel built eighty-four years previously and thoroughly unsuitable for passengers.

cleared from Killala a month after her appointed sailing-date with eighty-six and a half excess passengers. By the time she left the emigrants had exhausted most of their sea-stock. But their miseries were only beginning when they sailed. Thirty-six berths had been provided for 260 persons. The master was a drunken brute who issued no provisions and only a little putrid water. Conditions in the hold, wrote Buchanan, 'fully realized the worst state of a slaver'. When want led to fever, the master, too, fell a victim and his body and the bodies of the many passengers who had died already were left to putrefy on deck. Had not Buchanan on his own initiative, and at a cost of £200, hired a steamer to tow the *Sarah and Elizabeth* to Quebec, the entire complement of emigrants might have perished.[1] Although the case was most exceptional, it pointed to the writing on the wall. With shipping short and the need for passages desperate, it was inevitable that ramshackle vessels and reckless masters would enter the trade, and sail from ports which lacked emigration, or even experienced customs, officers. The total failure of the potato crop in 1846 made it certain that these pressures would increase prodigiously in the coming season.

All the colonial emigration officers' reports for 1846, moreover, looked forward with the deepest apprehension. With labour scarce and wages high in Canada, the season had not been altogether unsuccessful.[2] But the extraordinary rise in disease and debility amongst the autumn emigrants could be attributed only to the distress in Ireland.[3] Buchanan warned the commissioners that Canada could not handle more than 35,000 immigrants in a season, and complained that he held only a miserable balance of relief money to deal with what threatened to be an emigration of 'unequalled destitution'. His fellow officer in Upper Canada wrote that he would need a very large grant to prevent a fatal concentration of the Irish in the inland cities, and Douglas reported, 'The partial failure of the potato crop in 1845 caused much sickness; its almost total failure this year . . . will have the effect of pouring on our shores thousands of debilitated and sickly emigrants'.[4] If the Canadians were

[1] *Papers rel. emigration B.N.A.*, 9–10, 26–7 [777], H.C. 1847, xxxix; C.O. 384/78, 1181 Canada, 3 Oct. 1846. See also *Nation*, 5 Sept. 1846.
[2] Canada smoothly absorbed a large Irish emigration of 25,000, *Papers rel. emigration B.N.A.*, 26–8 [777], H.C. 1847, xxxix.
[3] *The Elgin-Grey papers* (Ottawa, 1937), vol. iii, p. 1093.
[4] *Papers rel. emigration B.N.A.*, 14–16, 29–31 [777], H.C. 1847, xxxix; *Further*

nervous, the Americans were thoroughly alarmed. The mortality upon vessels arriving at United States ports during the summer and autumn of 1846 had been extraordinarily high, New York, Boston and Philadelphia suffering particularly;[1] and the agitation against 'importing contagion' was loud and sustained. Both congress and the state legislatures promised the most severe restrictive legislation to guard the American shores against the coming year. Even in Ireland some alarm as to the inadequacy of the 1842 act was expressed.[2] Such was the situation in the winter of 1846 when the commissioners came to consider what steps they should take in the emergency.   •

Meanwhile, the colonial office had changed hands. Gladstone, who had had little time and perhaps no inclination to consider the problems of emigration during his six months as colonial secretary, went out with Peel in June 1846. There were great expectations of his successor, the third Earl Grey. Grey had long 'specialized' in overseas empire. If not a thorough-paced Wakefieldian, he was a fellow-traveller;[3] and when he appointed the like-minded Benjamin Hawes as his under-secretary and persuaded Charles Buller to accept the sinecure office of judge-advocate upon the understanding that they should work together in colonial affairs,[4] the radical position seemed secure. Moreover, Grey's brother-in-law, Charles Wood, held the exchequer, and his cousin, Sir George Grey, the home office: and this was generally supposed to give him a strong hand in the cabinet. Prince Albert noted on 6 July 1846, 'There is the *Grey Party*, consisting of Lord Grey, Lord Clarendon, Sir George Grey and Mr Wood; they are against Lord Lansdowne, Lord Minto, Lord Auckland and Sir John Hobhouse, stigmatizing them as old women'.[5]

These appearances were deceptive and, so far as our subject at

---

papers rel. emigration B.N.A., 5 [985], H.C. 1847–8, xlvii. See also *Rep. select comm. colonization Ire.*, appendix 5, 33–4 [737], H.C. 1847, vi.

[1] *2nd rep. select comm. colonization Ire.*, 333, H.C. 1847–8 (593), xvii (evidence of R. B. Minturn, a New York commissioner of emigration); *Freeman's Journal*, 18 July 1846; *Nation*, 6 June and 25 July 1846.

[2] In the last months of 1846, the *Nation* published a series of remarkably able letters from William Power reviewing and criticizing the existing passenger code.

[3] Cf. Morrell, op. cit., p. 202.

[4] E. M. Wrong, *Charles Buller and responsible government* (Oxford, 1926), pp. 56–8.

[5] *The Letters of Queen Victoria* (London, 1908), vol. ii, p. 86, 6 July 1846.

least is concerned, Grey's appointment may even have been unfortunate. He has commonly been depicted as a stern realist, and a species of imperial ironside.[1] But his work on emigrant protection gives a very different impression. Here he was both ignorant and obstinate and forever reaching after grand but impracticable designs but neglecting to learn the small, necessary details of his business. Nor did he enter into the feelings, or understand the situation, of the emigrant. As the *Economist* shrewdly observed at a later date, 'Grey's tone of thought and speech had always the cold impartial ring of an aristocratic statesman passing judgement on things in which he would feel little direct concern'.[2] Worst of all, perhaps, he clung to the last to what Disraeli called his 'visionary projects'.[3] Like Lord John Russell (although the two did not co-operate but rather presented rival schemes), Grey toyed repeatedly with 'masterstrokes' which would simultaneously resolve Irish and colonial difficulties by a simple translation of hundreds of thousands from one side of the Atlantic to the other.[4] So far as Ireland at least was concerned—and it was Ireland which most concerned men in the late 1840s—a systematic colonization was a dangerous delusion. For several obvious and overwhelming reasons,[5] it was inconceivable that the government should even attempt it upon a significant scale. Yet Grey and Russell returned endlessly to the charge, the one

[1] E.g. Morrell, op. cit., pp. 201–3; K. N. Bell and W. P. Morrell, *Select documents on British colonial policy, 1830–1860* (Oxford, 1928), p. xxxiii; Madgwick, op. cit., pp. 196–7.

[2] *Economist*, 13 Nov. 1858.

[3] W. P. Monypenny and G. E. Buckle, *The life of Benjamin Disraeli*, vol. i, p. 1052, Disraeli: Stanley, 28 Dec. 1849.

[4] MacDonagh, op. cit., in *The Great Famine*, sec. 3.

[5] The Irish people were already transferring themselves in such vast numbers annually that any state-fomented augmentation was otiose; and it was plausibly argued that even a hint of government assistance would bring the current movement to a standstill. Money was also a stumbling-block. Grey did secure a promise of £50,000 from Charles Wood early in 1847. But this would have paid for the removal of only one thousand people, a drop in the Irish ocean. The £50,000 was never used, Grey's scheme being altogether impracticable; and Wood fiercely and successfully resisted all further efforts to obtain money for colonization. Again, it was quite clear that by the 1840s the colonies possessed an effective veto on all such schemes; and it was equally clear that they would one and all refuse to accept a large Irish settlement. Moreover, the commissioners were well aware (and so informed Grey) of the almost insuperable mechanical difficulties in organizing a planned emigration from first to last—to say nothing of the intimidating responsibility for the welfare of the emigrants which the state would be forced to assume.

impelled by ambition and 'imperial faith' (which, however, without good public works was lost), the other by the successive failure of alternative Irish nostrums and by his own incurable impulsiveness. All this represented a large diversion of interest from the sort of work which the state might usefully have done. It also bred in Grey an undiscriminating resistance to improvements in the passenger acts. Although he never ceased to deplore the wasteful, higgledy-piggledy character of the voluntary movement, he crudely equated new legislation with increased fares, increased fares with reduced emigration and reduced emigration with the worst of all possible conclusions.

When the commissioners considered the protective system again in the winter of 1846–7, they distinguished three possible lines of improvement: increasing the grants for immigrant relief in the colonies; increasing the number and the efficiency of the United Kingdom executive corps; and amending the passenger act of 1842. As to the first, the treasury was always hostile to this expenditure,[1] and the Canadian, much the largest grant, was occasionally as low as £1,500 for the season.[2] Grey did secure £10,000 for Canada for 1847. But he made it clear that he did not expect all or even most of this sum to be spent. It was a comprehensive insurance against the worst that could possibly befall, and the utmost economy was to be observed in its expenditure.[3] 'All that is necessary to do', Grey told Elgin, the new governor-general, 'in order to provide for the un-usually large emigration, which may be expected this year, is to persevere in the system which has now for some years been acted upon with such advantage . . . extending the means employed in proportion to the expected increase in the number'.[4] As to the execu-tive corps, the commissioners (with, to his credit, the full support of Grey) pressed strongly for some increases, but only as a stop-gap policy. They merely asked for five temporary appointments for Irish ports which lacked officers, and for a professional surveyor for Liverpool.[5] Clearly the requests were inspired by the cases of the

---

[1] See, for example, C.O. 384/43, 1066 Lower Canada, 29 June 1837.

[2] The commissioners scaled the sum up or down according to the anticipated magnitude of a season's immigration.

[3] *Papers rel. emigration B.N.A.*, 35–7 [777], H.C. 1847, xxxix; *Papers rel. emigration B.N.A.*, 15, H.C. 1847–8 (50), xlvii.

[4] *Papers rel. emigration B.N.A.*, 35 [777], H.C. 1847, xxxix.

[5] *7th rep. C.L.E.C.*, 21 [809], H.C. 1847, xxxiii.

Sarah and Elizabeth and *Robert Isaacs* respectively, and only calculated to supply the particular deficiencies revealed in these
scandals. Not that the commissioners did not fully realize their weakness on this front. As they observed, an officer at every embarkation
point was the only sure security; vigilance at some ports drove inferior vessels to sail from others; and an emigration officer's work,
to be properly performed, required permanent residence. But to
multiply the corps sufficiently to provide officers for every port
was 'impossible'. Even the proposed increases, which were 'temporary' and would in any event have cost less than £1,000 per annum,
would not be easy to obtain.[1] In these circumstances, they concluded, the old scheme of limiting emigration to particular ports
deserved consideration. Hawes and Grey, however, ignored this
feeler. The latter's severe but inconsequential comment was that the
1842 act must be rigorously enforced, even in the most minor ports,
in 1847. He added that much might be achieved if prosecutions
were undertaken in the colonies. After four months in office, to say
nothing of twenty years' interest in emigration, he was apparently
still unaware that this was the standard and indispensable procedure.[2]

A new passenger bill remained. The commissioners had slowly
moved from regarding the 1842 act as a final measure to, first, an
awareness of its various imperfections in drafting and confusions in
intent, and subsequently, a belief that the general level of regulation must be deepened. By 1846 they had come to conceive of their
task as the gradual but constant improvement of the trade,[3] rather
than a single adjustment followed by the maintenance of the equilibrium. Naturally, in the winter of 1846, the time seemed ripe for
a further large-scale advance, and accordingly they determined not
only to close the gaps which had appeared in the existing legislation,
but also to open up new ground. Stephen denounced the proposal
as most untimely. 'The months that are approaching', he wrote, 'will
have so many sources of panic' that nothing could be more foolish
than to add to them by fresh restraints. A new passenger bill would
merely set up more obstacles to emigration 'when the sufferings
of the voyage, be they what they may, will be as nothing compared

---

[1] Nor were they easy to obtain. The 1847 season had actually begun to run its
disastrous course before treasury consent was won.
[2] C.O. 384/78, 1181 Canada and endorsements, 3-12, Oct. 1846.
[3] Cf. *Rep. select comm. colonization Ire.*, 17-18, Q.130-8 [737], H.C. 1847, vi
(evidence of T. F. Elliot).

to the miseries of not undertaking it'. Grey was torn between sympathy with Stephen's fears and a desire to appease colonial opinion lest it be altogether soured with emigration. Finally he agreed to a new bill, but only if its requirements were pared to the bone. No defective clauses should be retained but no 'unnecessary obstacles' were to be thrown in the way of the Irish exodus. No 'serious abuses' were to go unchecked, but nothing new was to be enacted.[1] All this was, of course, to beg the question, and the commissioners made no attempt to hide their dissatisfaction. Not only did they reiterate the need for a major consolidating measure,[2] but they also exposed their differences with Grey quite publicly in their annual printed report for 1847.[3] For the moment, however, they had no alternative but to submit. The emasculated bill which eventually reached the statute book in July 1847 contained a few useful clauses, mostly of the loophole-closing kind. But generally speaking it was unimportant, while its preparation had been so delayed that it could not, in any event, have affected the great body of the 1847 emigration.

Meanwhile, distress signals had gone up from Ireland in January and February 1847, when Liverpool vessels put into Cove with sickness aboard. Private charity and gifts from the Cove relief committee enabled the first stricken emigrants to renew their voyages, but clearly both the patience and the means of the local inhabitants were running short.[4] Soon after came the terrible news that typhus had broken out at sea. Vessels returning in distress to the Irish ports in March and April had been ravaged by the disease. In the same months the commissioners learned of desperate shortages of shipping in Liverpool, Cork, Limerick and Sligo, of great sufferings and mortality amongst those awaiting passages in the fever-ridden slums, and of the overwhelming exodus which was proceeding none the less.[5] The emigration for the first quarter of 1846, 15,000, had seemed at the time immense. But that for the first quarter of

[1] C.O. 384/80, 58 Miscellaneous, 15 Jan. 1847; *7th rep. C.L.E.C.*, 20 [809], H.C. 1847, xxxiii.
[2] C.O. 384/80, 162 Emigration, 5 Feb. 1847.
[3] *7th rep. C.L.E.C.*, 20–1 [809], H.C. 1847, xxxiii.
[4] C.O. 384/79, 241 Emigration, 15 Feb. 1847.
[5] Ibid., 588 and 709 Emigration, 12 and 28 Apr. 1847; C.O. 384/80, 651 and 652 Emigration, 19 Apr. 1847. The files of the *Cork Constitution, Northern Whig* and *Limerick Chronicle* for the months March–May 1847 supply many details of vessels returning in distress to port, and of the difficulties in the embarkation ports

1847 was almost 40,000. In a single day 3,000, and in one three-day period 5,000, embarked at Liverpool alone.[1] By mid-April the commissioners were clutching at the straw that the large increase in fares and the great volume of German immigration into the United States might serve to restrain the Irish outflow.[2] But the flood continued unabated; and during June the worst fears of all were exceeded when news of the calamities at sea and in North America began to arrive.[3] By then it was quite certain that 1847 would be a year of unparalleled disasters.

Not only did the commissioners receive ever more depressing tidings almost daily, but they, and the law which they administered, were subjected to unusual scrutiny and criticism.[4] The lay reaction to the news of disasters was (as ever) to demand stronger remedies than the acts allowed and much more activity than the commissioners could provide. The Belfast customs office roundly declared that 'government is bound to take into its own hands the whole business of conveying all steerage passengers whatever to North America'.[5] 'To avoid detention to the ship and worse consequences to the emigrants', wrote an angry vice-admiral from Cove, 'I would rather pay the expenses myself of this charitable supply'.[6] Similar outraged sentiments were expressed in the house of commons during the early summer, especially by the protectionists, Lord George Bentinck and Lord John Manners, who continuously agitated for the provision of physicians for all vessels, and other large measures of relief.[7] Hawes complained to Lord John Russell of his invidious rôle as the opponent of humanitarian demands: 'as Lord George Bentinck based his amendments on the score of humanity to the Irish emigrants, I ought not to have been placed in the position of resisting alone amendments on such a ground.'[8]

[1] 7th rep. C.L.E.C., 6 [809], H.C. 1847, xxxiii.

[2] C.O. 384/80, 651 Emigration, 19 Apr. 1847; Papers rel. emigration B.N.A., 168, H.C. 1847-8 (50), xlvii.

[3] C.O. 384/80, 997 Emigration, 11 June 1847; Papers rel. emigration B.N.A., 171, H.C. 1847-8 (50), xlvii; Rep. select comm. colonization Ire., 9, Q.50 [737], H.C. 1847, vi.

[4] E.g. Vernon Smith's speech in the house of commons on 4 March 1847, Hans., 3rd, xc, 838-46.

[5] C.O. 384/79, 709 Emigration, 28 Apr. 1847.

[6] Ibid., 241 Emigration, 15 Feb. 1847.

[7] Hans., 3rd, xciii, 1164-5, 1237-41, 20 and 21 May 1847; xciv, 276-8, 589, 13 and 20 July 1847.

[8] Russell papers, P.R.O., box 6, Hawes: Russell, 22 May 1847.

The commissioners naturally resented such wild demands, fired often by emotional reflexes to visible suffering, and they dismissed the more extreme calls for state control as 'impracticable and unnecessary'.[1] If reform 'were pushed to any immoderate length', they reported on 30th April, 'the only effect would be not that the poor would be carried across the sea in better circumstances, but that they would be prevented from going at all. . . . These are occurrences for which no law or administrative powers alone can provide, but by the zealous and humane exertions of the officers on the spot, supported by private charity, it has been endeavoured to meet each of the cases as well as circumstances would admit'.[2] But beneath this appearance of *sang froid* the commissioners were badly shaken —and several of their reactions were as impulsive and ill-considered as their critics'. When, for example, they were informed of the wholesale flouting of contracts which followed the huge demand for passages, they instructed their officers to enforce the acts ruthlessly. A moment's reflection would have told them that 'ruthless enforcement' was nonsense in the bedlam at Liverpool, Cork and Limerick during the spring of 1847. When they learned of the suffering between-decks on the first vessels which put back, they asked for powers to issue stringent regulations governing discipline at sea. Yet it was they themselves who had observed only four years before that state possessed no power to enforce such regulations on the high seas, or to punish masters subsequently for their disobedience. When the news of the great mortality arrived, they tried to add a new clause to the amendment bill requiring every Atlantic vessel with more than 150 passengers aboard to carry a physician. Yet they must have known that such a requirement would have called for at least 300 physicians in 1847; and as they themselves had asked the Canadians a little earlier, where were any good physicians, let alone such great numbers, to be found? In short, the commissioners lost their heads in the emergency, and lapsed into the weakness of wishful government.[3]

---

[1] As to the shipping shortage, the commissioners observed that 'it is better not to attempt any interference by government', C.O. 384/79, 660 Emigration 22 Apr. 1847.

[2] *7th rep. C.L.E.C.*, 3, 6 [809], H.C. 1847, xxxiii.

[3] Ibid., 20–1, 62; C.O. 384/80, 650 Emigration and endorsements, 17 Apr. 1847. The commissioners were in a position to estimate the number of surgeons who would be required under their proposed new clause, because they had analysed the complements of passengers on the various Atlantic vessels in the 1846 season.

It is true that they did take some effective steps to mitigate the consequences of the disasters. As the pressure mounted at Liverpool, they secured the appointment of an additional assistant officer and a second clerk.[1] Even this small increase in numbers was difficult to obtain—the parliamentary estimate had already been well exceeded[2] —and in June 1847 Elliot frankly admitted the inadequacy of protective system in the United Kingdom, blaming it all upon the lack of money.[3] The commissioners also supported their officers bravely in the assumption of arbitrary powers. They sanctioned retrospectively the compulsory landing of passengers suspected of infection, and approved efforts to compel owners to pay the cost of medical inspections. 'We do not know', they wrote, 'how far there may be any strict legal power for these steps but all parties appear to acquiesce from obvious necessity'.[4] When the news of the Canadian calamities arrived, a newly invented disinfecting fluid was rushed out to Grosse Isle, and the inventors, Calvert and Ledoyen, packed off hastily to superintend 'experiments' at the quarantine.[5] Grey rather wildly proposed that all emigrant vessels be supplied with the disinfectant (as yet quite untested and probably quite worthless), and authorized a further Canadian relief expenditure of £20,000.[6] But these distracted gestures of the early summer could not seriously affect the issue. By April 1847, when the commissioners really awoke to the situation, it was much too late for turning back, or even for palliative measures. The die had been cast several months before. At every important port the congestion was having deadly consequences,[7] both for the thousands who were disappointed of

[1] C.O. 384/80, 652 Emigration, 19 Apr. 1847.
[2] *Papers rel. emigration B.N.A.*, 35, H.C. 1847-8 (50), xlvii.
[3] *Rep. select comm. colonization Ire.*, 482, Q.4504-6 [737], H.C. 1847, vi. Eventually the emigration vote was more than doubled, from £10,364 in 1846-7 to £23,815 for 1847-8.
[4] C.O. 384/80, 651 Emigration, 19 Apr. 1847.
[5] C.O. 384/79, 1225 Emigration, 17-31 July 1847; *Papers rel. emigration B.N.A.*, 35-6, H.C. 1847-8 (50), xlvii; *8th rep. C.L.E.C.*, 15 [961], H.C. 1847-8, xxvi. Calvert later died of fever at Grosse Isle. A different fluid, Sir W. Burnett's, was supplied to the last vessels of the season. Neither appears to have been at all effective; and indeed the commissioners themselves appear to have known very little about Calvert's and Ledoyen's at the time they sent it out.
[6] *Papers rel. emigration B.N.A.*, 35-6, H.C. 1847-8 (50), xlvii.
[7] *Cork Examiner*, 5 Apr. 1847; *Northern Whig*, 27 Apr. 1847; *Nation*, 1 May 1847; *Limerick Chronicle*, 8, 19 and 22 May 1847; etc.

passage and forced to linger in miserable lodgings, and for the scarcely more fortunate who departed in ill-found, ill-checked and overloaded vessels. Almost from the commencement of the season the United Kingdom corps had lost control over the trade.[1] Despite the heroic exertions of the executive officers (and especially of Hodder, Starke, Friend and Lynch),[2] who threatened, cajoled, coerced and laboured to enlist whatever support they could to restrain abuses, and relieve the worst destitution, the protective system collapsed. In the whole of this great and terrible season there were but seven prosecutions in the United Kingdom, and none whatever in Canada,[3] where even the pretence of punishing offences was given up.[4] Vessels departed freely without the statutory requirements of food or water or berths; many even sailed without a clearance. The plea that passengers would probably starve and certainly contract fever, if detained,[5] could not well be controverted.

The departing emigrants came fleetingly into view, were packed off with much haste and little ceremony, and then passed over the horizon to unseen trials and terrors. The immediate responsibility of the state at the ports of embarkation was necessarily limited and brief. It was otherwise in British North America. There, willy-nilly, the state's responsibility was endless and inescapable. The colonists justly protested that they had neither desired nor encouraged the immigration, whereas the imperial government had striven might and main to keep the Irish sluice-gates open. In any event, the stricken multitudes presented themselves 'in crowds, almost without forewarning'[6] at Grosse Isle and Partridge Island.[7] Some relief had to be attempted and, in the absence of any other responsible persons, attempted by the emigration and medical officers on the spot. The colonies had made no useful preparation for the emergency. New Brunswick had done nothing whatsoever, and the

[1] *Papers rel. emigration B.N.A.*, 103, H.C. 1847–8 (50), xlvii.

[2] Hodder had become chief officer at Liverpool in 1845 in place of Lieut. Henry, who asked to be transferred to a less heavy office, and was in fact sent to Hodder's old station, Dublin. Starke was the Belfast officer: he replaced Lieut. Miller.

[3] *8th rep. C.L.E.C.*, 14 [961], H.C. 1847–8, xxvi.

[4] *Papers rel. emigration B.N.A.*, 132, H.C. 1847–8 (50), xlvii; *Further papers rel. emigration B.N.A.*, 15 [964], H.C. 1847–8, xlvii.

[5] *Papers rel. emigration B.N.A.*, 44–5, H.C. 1847–8 (50), xlvii.

[6] *Further papers rel. emigration B.N.A.*, 19 [964], H.C. 1847–8, xlvii.

[7] Partridge Island was the quarantine station at St John, New Brunswick.

Canadian officers had assumed that the coming difficulties might be overcome by a rapid dispersal of the immigrants to prevent concentrations of disease. For this money was the main, almost the sole, requirement—to pay for the St Lawrence steamer passages and for food for the immigrants while they were on the move. But Grey's grant had been £10,000 and the immigrant tax of 5s. *per capita*[1] would of course mount proportionally with the increased numbers: surely these resources would suffice. None of the Canadian officers foresaw that the initial and essential crux would arise in quarantine,[2] although as things turned out, the problem of quarantine was so large and intractable that no other problem could, so to speak, emerge except as a direct consequence of the first calamity. Thus, no steps had been taken to improve the food or water supplies at the stations, or to increase their staffs; and the only shelter which awaited the miserable hordes from Ireland was old and rotting hospital sheds, relics of the cholera epidemics of the 1830s, and capable of holding a few hundred persons at the most.

The storm broke in mid-May 1847.[3] Every vessel arriving at Grosse Isle in May had lost passengers at sea through typhus, dysentery or 'ship-fever', and landed others in sickness and distress. The sheds were filled within the first few days, and before the season was three weeks old there were 12,000 immigrants on the island, the great majority lying roofless on the open ground. Food and water were running low and the dreaded warm season was at hand. Both Buchanan and Douglas acted boldly. Buchanan sent several tons of foodstuffs to the island with orders that it was to be distributed free to the impoverished. He chartered a steamer to land the sick and collect supplies; procured sufficient canvas to cover more than 3,000 persons; and forced every servant on the island to remain at

[1] After various changes in the 1830s, the immigrant tax was fixed at this level in 1840 and the money used, in conjunction with the imperial grant, to pay the salaries of the emigration and quarantine officers and to furnish relief to destitute immigrants, mainly in the form of transport allowances. The tax was scaled downwards, according to age, for children.

[2] Douglas had observed in his annual report for 1846 that he doubted whether his staff could cope with the coming season, but he made no clear and specific requests.

[3] The parliamentary papers relating to emigration to British North America in 1847 (50), [932], [964] and [985], (all of which are contained in volume xlvii of 1847–8) are almost exclusively devoted to the 1847 crisis, and unless otherwise stated, all references for the remainder of the chapter are drawn from this source.

his post unless he could provide a substitute.[1] Douglas acted with equal dispatch and authority. On his own initiative he bought large quantities of medical supplies and recruited, so far as he could, additional nurses and physicians; and early in June he took the momentous step of ordering 5,000 of the least infected immigrants to the interior, so that the quarantine station might be relieved. Douglas was well aware that most of these immigrants would subsequently fall ill, and spread typhus and other diseases far inland. But it was a choice of evils, and he chose the more remote, if greater. Despite these measures, the situation on Grosse Isle deteriorated during June, as stricken vessels continued to arrive, and the sun to burn more terribly. The death-rate mounted and contagion spread, when families refused to desert members who had fallen ill, and those who had disembarked free from fever fell victims in their turn. So it continued during July and August. A man who worked on the island spoke of the immigrants as 'ghosts, not men'.[2] The quarantine chaplain described them as dying like stranded fish amongst the mud and stones, with thousands prostrate on the open fields and beaches.[3] A midshipman whose vessel was anchored in the St Lawrence wrote to his father that his blood ran cold when he saw the mounds of bodies heaped by the shallow burial holes, and the sick almost naked and uncovered on the earth; 'such a sight I think no man before ever witnessed'.[4] Scarcely a person on the island escaped infection for longer than three weeks. Twenty-three of the twenty-six doctors who worked there, and nineteen of the priests, contracted fever. Forty of the combined staffs died, and Buchanan himself was at death's door. The exact total of the mortality on Grosse Isle is not known.[5] In the early panic and confusion medical records were neglected. But when the death-rate fell to 100 weekly in September, the colonial officers told themselves that the corner had been turned at last.

Meanwhile, clearing the island periodically of the least distressed immigrants had meant that the inland towns and cities,

[1] C.O. 384/81, 1518 Canada, 4 Aug. 1848.
[2] N. F. Davin, *The Irishman in Canada* (Toronto, 1877), p. 541.
[3] Maguire, op. cit., pp. 136–7. See also *Morning Chronicle*, 24 June 1847.
[4] *Cork Constitution*, 5 Aug. 1847.
[5] Some years later Douglas estimated the 1847 mortality at the quarantine station alone at 5,300, *1st rep. select comm. emigrant ships*, 152, Q.2791–2, H.C. 1854 (163), xiii.

from Quebec to Montreal and farther west, were successively visited by pestilence. On the St Lawrence steamers the immigrants were 'packed like pigs on the deck of a Cork and Bristol packet',[1] and large numbers died during the voyage. As news of the approach of the Irish reached the river towns, hundreds fled in terror to the countryside. Lazarettos were hastily set up, and local boards of health collected; but, as the archbishop of Quebec observed, the new relief systems were organized too late and too hurriedly to save the situation.[2] Every St Lawrence city had its own Grosse Isle, but Montreal, where over 6,000 immigrants perished,[3] was worst of all. An eye-witness described the endless rows of immigrants lying in its makeshift hospitals 'as if they were in their coffins';[4] while the hospitals themselves were so under-staffed that the test of fever was to require the immigrants to crawl under a cord three feet high, declaring all who stumbled to be infected, and all who did not fall to be well.[5] An entire community of nursing nuns died of typhus at Montreal; and only one of the local priests survived at Point St Charles, where the bishop himself fell a victim.[6] Although some 30,000 of the Irish had crossed the border to the United States before the year's end, Canada still groaned under appalling burdens in the winter of 1847.[7] Relief depots were further extended, the emigrant hospitals at Quebec and Montreal enlarged to hold 14,000 persons, and every almshouse and refuge thronged with orphans. In all, it was estimated that 20,000 of the 70,000 Irish who had taken ship for Canada in 1847 died during the year; and that at least 25,000 of the remainder either had been, or still were, patients in Canadian hospitals. Amongst the great Victorian mortalities only the Crimea and the Irish famine exceeded this calamity in magnitude. Perhaps

[1] The description was that of an eye-witness, Stephen de Vere. It had been suggested in 1841 that the numbers aboard these steamers should be regulated by law, but this was not done until the end of 1847.

[2] *Tipperary Vindicator*, 3 July 1847.

[3] There is a great mound in Montreal to this day bearing the inscription, 'To preserve the remains of six thousand immigrants who died of ship-fever'.

[4] Maguire, op. cit., pp. 144-5.

[5] *Ami de la Religion*, quoted by *Tipperary Vindicator*, 25 Aug. 1847; *Waterford Mail*, 18 Aug. 1847.

[6] Maguire, op. cit., pp. 136-7, 145-8. See also G. R. C. Keep, 'The Irish congregations in nineteenth-century Montreal', *Irish Ecclesiastical Record*, Dec. 1950, pp. 503-6.

[7] Fortunately the Canadian harvest of 1847 was very good, and food was cheap in consequence.

neither exceeded it in horror, so concentrated in time and space were the terrible events of Grosse Isle and Montreal.

Much the same disasters, although upon a lesser scale, befell the New Brunswick immigration of 1847. Whereas the Canadian death-rate for Irish immigrants was two in seven, the New Brunswick was one in seven, and this fairly represents the proportionate miseries of the two colonies. For various reasons both Partridge Island and the New Brunwick towns escaped more lightly than their Canadian counterparts. The main (though but partially realized) object of the chief immigration officer, Moses Perley, was to prevent over-crowding at the quarantine. He persuaded the council of St John to erect temporary shelters on the mainland to house immigrants in transit; and whenever the island was extraordinarily pressed for space, he compelled the passengers on newly arrived vessels to re-main aboard. This last was, of course, harsh treatment for the immi-grants concerned, but considering the problem as a whole a wise course of action. Again, about half-way through the season Perley called upon the army to take charge of the commissariat, rationing and supplies, which produced an immediate improvement in both health and the working of the station. Most important of all per-haps was the relatively small number of the immigrants, 16,000, and the proximity of the United States border. For generally speak-ing the difficulties grew in geometric ratio according to the numbers involved; and the New Brunswickers were naturally anxious to trans-fer—in some cases to return—as much as possible of their burden to their republican neighbours. None the less, New Brunswick suffered grievously. Almost every detail of the Canadian *débâcle* was repeated from the sick lying unattended on the open ground or in filthy, airless tents to the spread of typhus in the interior once the immigrants were dispersed. Indeed there were two aggravating factors in New Brunswick. First, several vessels which had been rejected by Boston or New York because of their degree of sickness turned northwards for refuge to St John. The effect of this, psycho-logically as well as substantially, upon the New Brunswickers was very bad. Secondly, New Brunswick was by no means as assured as Canada that the imperial treasury would meet the costs of its relief schemes. Grey made no promises whatever during the season; and unfortunately New Brunswick had hitherto treated the immigrant tax as a part of general revenue, not as a trust for the immigrants themselves, and there was now a danger that the executive council might be told that they must take the losses with the gains.[1] This uncertainty as to who would ultimately pay the bill naturally inhibited the New Brunswickers in their undertakings.

When the costs of 1847 in British North America were counted, they were found to amount to almost £200,000. Grey had, in two stages, authorized an expenditure of £30,000 in Canada, and the colonial immigrant taxes had raised another £19,000. But who was to pay the enormous deficit? The colonists, at least, were in no doubt: the smallest recompense which the United Kingdom might make was to defray the relief expenses. Feeling against emigration in general and against the imperial government in particular was running high, all the more so as the colonists could not in decency condemn the unfortunate immigrants themselves but must find some other outlet for their indignation. Elgin, no alarmist, was greatly perturbed by his tour of the provinces in the autumn. He told Grey bluntly, 'that section of the French who dislike British emigration at all times find, as might well be expected, in the circumstances of this year, a theme for copious declamation. Persons who cherish republican sympathies ascribe these evils to our dependent condition as colonists'. The plain facts were that British North America had spent more than five times as much as the United States upon relief; that much of this expenditure had been incurred because British North America did not, and could not, erect the same barriers against immigration as had the individual American states; and that the Canadians and New Brunswickers were now in an ugly and uncompromising mood. Grey had originally encouraged Elgin to do whatever he considered necessary in the emergency. But when the large extent of the relief became apparent, he had tried to hedge. In July 1847, he informed the Canadians that he would not discuss the total debt at all until he had exact details of the expenditure. But Elgin had only to point out the fearful suffering which would follow cheese-paring at that juncture, to silence Grey's admonitions, if not to win his formal assent. We may well suppose that Grey's negotiations with his cabinet colleagues were not pleasant. But in the end even the chancellor, Charles Wood, a fanatical economizer, submitted. 'I have read', he wrote on

[1] T. Walrond, *Letters and Journals of . . . [Lord] Elgin* (London, 1872), pp. 43-5.

5 September 1847, 'Elgin's letter on the disease of the Canadian immigration, and I really think that *we* ought to pay the bill for the effects'.[1] But a condition precedent of this indemnity was that the colonies would henceforward assume all responsibility for immigration. The imperial treasury would grant Canada £1,500 annually, and, *ruat coelum*, not a penny more. Grey proposed that the colonies should raise their immigrant tax to enable them to shoulder the new burdens. But here he preached to the converted. No one was more determined than the colonists both to procure more money for relief, and to diminish the necessity for spending it.

Meanwhile, the United States had to a considerable degree avoided the misfortunes of British North America. The Americans had been disquieted by the high death-rate of 1846 and the destitution of the last immigrants of that season, and they were very well informed of the progress of distress in Ireland. Accordingly, they took strong precautionary measures in the spring of 1847. First, the federal legislation was tightened up. Henceforth, every passenger, regardless of his age, was entitled to at least fourteen square feet of surface deck space, and the penalties for overcrowding were increased: masters might be fined £150 for each passenger whom they carried above the statutory number.[2] On paper, at any rate, this represented a considerable advance upon the British numbers ratio; and although the federal machinery of enforcement was inadequate, the new act achieved its immediate purpose. The harsh penalties and evident determination of the Americans frightened shipping agents into raising United States fares so high that the poorest and most debilitated of the 1847 emigrants were diverted, almost without exception, to British North America. The states themselves formed the second line of defence. The New York legislature established an emigration commission in May 1847, directing the commissioners to provide, from the proceeds of a head-tax of $1·50 on each emigrant, a quarantine hospital, an emigration staff and transport assistance for the distressed. The new commission was reasonably successful in its first and very difficult year. Out of the 7,000 patients admitted to the quarantine hospital during the latter half of 1847 only 850 died; and the emergency procedures adopted by the com-

[1] Russell papers, box 6, Wood: Russell, 5 Sept. 1847.
[2] *Rep. select comm. colonization Ire.*, 261–2, appendix 28 [737], H.C. 1847, vi.

missioners aroused few complaints.[1] None the less, neither New York nor the other Atlantic ports escaped the effects of 1847 altogether. Temporary 'hospitals' had to be set up on Long and Staten Islands, and there were also outbreaks of typhus at Philadelphia and Baltimore.[2] Some of the river towns, like Albany, refused to allow the west-bound immigrants to leave their steamers; and there were scenes reminiscent of the panic in the St Lawrence towns in several places. Boston was worst hit of all during the spring, and the Massachusetts legislature rushed through a bill requiring masters to enter bonds of $1,000, indemnifying the state against all expenses incurred on the head of any of their passengers.[3] This outrageous demand virtually prohibited emigration to Boston during the second half of 1847. Vessels apprised of the new demands on their arrival turned northwards to the misfortunate New Brunswick.[4] Eventually, the Massachusetts act was held by the supreme court, in the celebrated 'passenger cases', to have been unconstitutional.[5] But by the time this judgment was delivered, the damage was done so far as British North America was concerned. The cumulative effect of federal and state legislation during the spring of 1847 was to deflect the worst of the emigration from the shores of the United States. Although the mortality amongst Irish emigrants bound for the United States may have been as high as 8,000 or 9,000 persons, and although the season was amongst the worst which the United States ever experienced, New York and Boston were spared the horrors of Quebec and Montreal.

1847 was a very extraordinary year. Not only was the volume of emigration more than twice as large as that of any earlier season, but the death-rate was at least twenty times higher than the annual average of the preceding half decade. Of the 215,000 Irish who sought to settle overseas in 1847, some 25,000 to 30,000 perished in the attempt.[6] Where is 'the reason why' of this gigantic tragedy? It

[1] *3rd rep. select comm. colonization Ire.*, appendix Q.86-7, H.C. 1849 (86), xi; *State of New York in assembly, document no. 46, 1848*, 81-2.
[2] *Morning Chronicle*, 15 and 29 June 1847; *Limerick Chronicle*, 17 and 27 July 1847; *Waterford Mail*, 26 May 1847.
[3] *2nd rep. select comm. colonization Ire.*, 286, H.C. 1847-8 (593), xvii.
[4] C.O. 384/79, 1079 Emigration, 16 Aug. 1847.
[5] Because it interfered with foreign commerce which was the province of the federal government.
[6] The death-rate for the years 1842-6 averaged only ·63 per cent annually on a total emigration of 173,000 persons, *8th rep. C.L.E.C.*, 14 [961], H.C. 1847-8,

was generally agreed that the great mortality was caused by 'ship-fever', a form of typhus, and dysentery, a deficiency disease. But to locate and deal with the sources of infection was another matter. Here there was much disagreement. Some blamed the dirt and foulness of the holds; some, the want of ventilation; some the absence of kitchens and orderly cooking; some, the fact that peasants accustomed all their lives to a vegetable diet were forced to eat altogether different food aboard.[1] But none of these explanations met the facts completely. Former emigrations had been subject, without such ill-effects, to much the same disadvantages; and during 1847 itself ship-fever had ravaged vessels with 'good' living conditions quite as severely as those with 'bad'. Clearly, then, the distress and under-nourishment in Ireland were contributory factors. But still less did they afford a total explanation. Most of the emigrants were of the same social standing and had undergone much the same hardship and privation before they embarked, yet typhus by no means attacked particular groups with equal force. Two large parties of assisted emigrants from a co. Kilkenny estate sailed at the same time, under identical conditions, on similar vessels, but the death-rate of one was three times higher than the other; and there were very many cases of this kind.

To contemporaries, therefore, the medical problem was baffling, whichever direction they might turn. The real solution, that typhus was spread by lice either directly or in faeces, was not finally estab-lished until the present century, and was not even canvassed in 1847. Yet much could have been discovered by observation. Douglas found confirmation of his earlier diagnosis of the lodging-house as the seat of disease in the events of 1847. He noted that one factor, the high mortality on vessels sailing from the larger city ports, was constant throughout the season, and discovered that wherever ship-fever had broken out the infection had been carried from the shore. The first victim was found, almost invariably, to have been suffering

---

xxvi. According to United States statistics, 17 per cent of the total Irish emigra-tion of 1847 perished during the year, *1st rep. select comm. emigrant ships*, 100, H.C. 1854 (161), xiii. Other estimates of the mortality varied between 15 per cent and 22 per cent. While certainty is impossible because of incomplete records, we may safely take it that at least 25,000 and possibly as many as 30,000 died.

[1] *2nd rep. select comm. colonization Ire.*, 344–5, Q.3302–13, H.C. 1847–8 (593), xvii. Other suggested causes were the long passages, the smallness of the vessels, and the fact that many of them carried freight.

from the disease when he came aboard. Douglas thereupon concluded that he had been right in regarding the filthy and overcrowded lodging-houses of the embarkation ports as the true seed-
beds of infection.[1] So far as it went, this was a useful diagnosis,
whatever its underlying medical theory. Had Douglas's proposal
been taken up and the lodging systems thoroughly reformed, there
is no doubt that the danger of typhus and cholera epidemics would
have been reduced. Yet is is difficult to condemn anyone for failing
to act upon Douglas's advice, either when it was first delivered in
1841, or in 1847. We can appreciate the merits of Douglas's scheme
because we know the certain answer to the problem. To contemporaries, it was at most but one of a dozen theories none of which was
proved or disproved by experiment. And even if the true cause of
typhus were known in 1846, could the disasters of 1847 have been
prevented? Only if we also suppose that the commissioners, or
whoever was in charge, had unlimited resources, boundless coercive
powers and a large body of competent professionals to call upon, can
we confidently answer 'yes'.

This brings us to the critical question—though one which English
contemporaries in their charity or want of interest forebore to ask—
to what extent was the government, through its neglect, responsible
for the calamities? What steps, which might have reduced the suffering, did Grey and the commissioners fail to take? Clearly, they
cannot be blamed for the state of medical knowledge or the manifold
difficulties which derived from this groping in the dark. It is equally
certain that new legislation was virtually irrelevant. Even the 1842
act was largely unenforced; still less would any additional restraints
have been effective.[2] None the less much that was practicable and
potentially beneficial was omitted. It would not have been difficult

---

[1] Emigrants who subsequently contracted fever had often complained of feeling bilious and depressed after leaving their lodging-house.
[2] To the degree to which the commissioners pinned their hopes on statutory
amendments they were mistaken; and Grey's refusal to entertain their large
proposals did nothing to increase the miseries of 1847. On the other hand, Grey's
reasoning was false. Fares did increase prodigiously—by up to 120 per cent
at times—without affecting the demand for passages; and the small additional
costs which new legislation might involve would not have materially reduced
the emigration. Taking the long view, a consolidating measure in the spring
would have accelerated the progress of improvement in the passenger trade,
though it would not have influenced emigrant protection in the slightest during
the first season of its operation.

to recruit twenty or thirty additional executive officers. True that the newly appointed officers, where they were not posted as assistants in the larger ports, would have been uncertain and overwhelmed in their first months of office. True also that the executive's range of choice was much reduced in 1847; it was always a question whether a detention or a premature clearance was the worse. Yet every additional officer would have increased in some degree the executive's control over the trade, and in many informal ways have kept down profiteering, breaches of contract and reckless preparations for the voyage. Again, the type of emergency measures which were adopted in British North America might well, and much more profitably, have been carried out in the United Kingdom. To provide medical inspections at the outports, hospital hulks or shore lazarettos, and relief for the distressed and convalescent, was certainly within the power and capacity of the government. Without attempting any new techniques or legislation the emigration commissioners might have substantially reduced the death-rate at sea and the post-disembarkation epidemics.

We cannot condemn the commissioners out of hand for their inaction. It is at least arguable that the real villain was the treasury and the attitude towards public expenditure which (with the hearty endorsement of 'public' and politicians alike) it tended to engender. £25,000 would have sufficed for most of the work which the commissioners might usefully have undertaken. But when one had to struggle to establish the necessity of an assistant clerk, what hope was there for large and (the real crux) *anticipatory* measures? Yet, even for public servants in the 1840s, official parsimony scarcely provides an automatic and general absolution. All the happenings of 1847, both in Ireland and British North America, showed that where human lives were at stake and administrators acted boldly, the imperial treasury ultimately, however reluctantly, met the bill. Should not the commissioners have done likewise? In their defence, it might be pleaded that unauthorized expenditure might be very well if an officer were hundreds or perhaps thousands of miles from Whitehall; if he had no delicate balance of policies to hold; and if he were suddenly confronted with crowds of sufferers who, come what might, could not be ignored; but that the commissioners' situation was very different. They could not say that there had been no time to obtain the treasury's consent. They were committed

ex officio to promote emigration; and their political superiors had
laid it down that the prime consideration of the year was the encouragement of the Irish outflow. They never, so far as we can tell,
encountered an emigrant of 1847 face to face, let alone the inert and
piteous masses which drove Buchanan and Douglas and their
counterparts in Mayo, Kerry and West Cork, to take such audacious
steps. Finally, we must take into account the argument which they
used on their own behalf in their annual report for 1847, that the
evils of the year altogether exceeded the worst forebodings.[1]

Does this provide a complete defence? Not quite: two stubborn
points persist. It is still a question whether the commissioners
should not have foreseen more clearly, and provided better against,
the numbers and epidemics of 1847; and whether, once the blow had
fallen, they acted with reasonable promptitude and resolution. On
each count, the case against them is very strong. As to the first, both
the Americans and Canadians, at the end of 1846, clearly expected
a season of unparalleled sickness and distress. The sad progress of
the Irish harvest and its aftermath was described almost daily in
the London press. Even Irish provincial newspapers prognosticated
fairly accurately the march of disease and the huge numbers who
would seek passage in the spring. It is true that the commissioners
showed some concern in December 1846, when they proposed new
legislation and additions to their executive staff. But there was little
sense of urgency behind, and little appropriateness and realism in,
their proposed precautions. The problem of typhus, which then
raged in Ireland, was scarcely mentioned; the question of the overseas quarantines, or hospitals in the home ports, was never raised.
No one could have anticipated altogether the calamities of 1847. But
any person of intelligence who considered the matter seriously
during the last months of 1846 would have known that the wave of
typhus and deficiency diseases then sweeping eastwards across
Ireland would appear in due course, and terrible strength, at the
ports of embarkation. In short, even when every allowance is made
for the natural reluctance to spend or demand public money for a
future contingency, and for the sharpened perception of the Americans where their self-interest was involved, the commissioners must
still stand condemned for want of forethought and perhaps also
courage.

[1] *8th rep. C.L.E.C.*, 14 [961], H.C. 1847-8, xxvi.

Nor can we regard the commissioners' reactions, when they were fully alive to the disasters, as either energetic or well-considered. We have already shown the ineffectiveness of several of the steps they took. We must also consider the steps which they omitted. However late in the day they were established, medical inspections and hospitals at the embarkation ports might have saved something from the wreck, and however late in the day it was begun, the systematic collection of information about the passage and North American events would have been of importance for the future; but nothing was done in either of these directions. In fact, crucial though the American state and federal legislation was to the happenings of 1847, the season had almost ended before the commissioners so much as attempted to discover the provisions of the American enactments.[1] One or two actions of the commissioners, such as their bold support of their officers, were admirable. But regarding their conduct as a whole, we cannot but characterize it as feeble and passive. As for Grey, the ineptitude of his comments and projects in the winter of 1846–7 was excelled by his later effrontery in claiming credit for holding down the volume of the 1847 emigration.[2] Despite his efforts to launch a scheme of systematic colonization, and despite a bland assurance which he gave the house of lords as late as 15 March 1847 that the current emigration promised to be the largest and perhaps the most successful ever,[3] he congratulated himself at the season's close upon his wise refusal to stimulate artificially a natural movement. But this patrician calm and the cool fatalism of the commissioners' report for 1847 were but the public face. In reality, the permanent officials, at least, were shocked by the earthquake force of the catastrophe. As Tolstoi has observed, 'In calm and untroubled times it seems to every administrator that it is only by his efforts that the whole population under his control is kept going. . . . But when a storm arises and the sea begins to heave and the ship to move, such a delusion is no longer possible.'

---

[1] C.O. 384/79, 1728 Emigration and endorsements, 27 Oct. 1847.
[2] Grey, op. cit., i, pp. 239–40.
[3] *Hans.*, 3rd, xc, 1330–1, 15 Mar. 1847.

RECONSTRUCTION

1847–51

THROUGHOUT the greater part of 1847 Grey and the commissioners maintained that the year was wholly exceptional, and that the disasters should not be allowed to weigh against the accumulated experience of the preceding decade.[1] The calamities were presented as an act of God; and when in August 1847, the Canadian legislative assembly asked for a thorough revision of the passenger acts, and suggested a number of amendments, the commissioners brusquely replied that they could not afford to lose sight of the liberty of the person, or to countenance irresponsible tinkering with the permanent body of law.[2] But when the season drew to its close and the costs and the dead were counted, a cooler judgment on the protective system might prevail. Elliot, who had been a thorough-paced 'exceptionalist' for the greater part of the year, certainly changed his attitude. Broadly speaking, he now said, there were two common and erroneous approaches. One was that the whole pre-1847 experience went to prove that the existing code was sufficient in ordinary times; the other, recoiling from the horrors of 1847, demanded a security against their repetition at whatever cost. A middle course must be steered. The total collapse of the current system, even if only in a year of extraordinary strain, could not be ignored; yet one must not force men to starve at home when they might instead reach a land of plenty. In short, an overhaul of the passenger acts was imperative but great care must be taken to keep 1847 in perspective.[3] Elliot's change of mind was significant. He had been promoted to the assistant under-secretaryship of the colonial office in December 1847, when Stephen left the scene.[4] But for some time still Elliot was

[1] *7th rep. C.L.E.C.*, 3 [809], H.C. 1847, xxxiii; *Papers rel. emigration B.N.A.*, 27–8, H.C. 1847–8 (50), xlvii.

[2] *Papers rel. emigration B.N.A.*, 175–6, H.C. 1847–8 (50), xlvii. It is interesting to note that the commissioners subsequently adopted almost all the Canadian proposals.

[3] *1st rep. select comm. colonization Ire.*, 49, H.C. 1847–8 (415), xvii.

[4] On his retirement from the colonial office, Stephen became Regius Professor of History at Cambridge.

scarcely less important in the field of emigrant protection than he had been as chief commissioner. His successor, T. W. C. Murdoch, a career civil servant, was quite as dominant amongst his colleagues —the 'player' amongst the 'gentlemen' again—as Elliot had been during 1840-7. But Elliot's thorough knowledge of the legislation and the corps, combined with his legal and constitutional understanding, ensured his continued influence in the department.

Certainly Elliot and the commissioners did not lack advice. A torrent of proposals poured in upon them in the winter of 1847. Most were ignored or curtly rejected, but two groups of suggestions did influence the shaping of new legislation. The first concerned the health of the emigrants. Between them, Douglas, the Canadian executive council and the New Brunswick board of physicians made a number of recommendations for regular medical inspections and tests for contagious disease in the embarkation ports, and proposed a number of sensible precautions against dirt during the passage.[1] A naval officer, Budd, put forward some complementary measures, amongst them, the compulsory bathing of all Liverpool emigrants before their embarkation, and the compulsory cleansing of emigrant vessels with chloride of lime or vitriol before they sailed.[2] The second and much the more important source of new legislation was a letter written by Stephen de Vere to his uncle, Lord Monteagle. De Vere was a recent convert to Rome and a man of great charity and courage. He undertook a steerage passage to Quebec in 1847 so 'that he might speak as a witness respecting the sufferings of emigrants', and do something to improve their lot.[3] Upon his arrival in Canada, de Vere wrote, at Elliot's suggestion, a full account of the voyage and proposed various measures which might remedy the evils. Grey was so impressed that he obtained Monteagle's permission to make the letter public.[4]

De Vere painted a terrifying picture of life between-decks, all the more so as he insisted that the vessel on which he had sailed was

[1] *Papers rel. emigration B.N.A.*, 128, H.C. 1847-8 (50), xlvii; *Further papers rel. emigration B.N.A.*, 3-7 [932], H.C. 1847-8, xlvii. A typical recommendation was that the space between berth and deck be boarded up so that filth and effluvium might not be allowed to gather there.

[2] C.O. 384/81, 749 North America, 5 Apr. 1848.

[3] W. F. Ward, *Aubrey de Vere* (London, 1904), p. 184. Stephen de Vere was a younger brother of Aubrey de Vere, and a very young man at this time.

[4] *Monteagle Papers*, N.L.I., Grey: Monteagle, 21 Jan. 1848; Monteagle: Grey, 23 Jan. 1848.

better, not worse, than the average. The food and water were issued irregularly and in quantities well below the statutory requirements. Emigrants sank listlessly into disease, disregarding all precautions, and exerting themselves only to repel every effort to bring them or their bedding up on deck. Hundreds lay huddled together in the dark and stifling hold. Those with fever, 'without food or medicine other than casual charity', had hardly room to turn in their narrow bunks. The passengers who were not yet infected were haunted by the ravings of the sufferers. Demoralization led to drunkenness and drunkenness to debasement. The ship's officers sold liquor freely and at a large profit to themselves, despite the statutory prohibition. The worst consequence of the weeks of filth and degradation, wrote de Vere, was not sickness or death, but the total loss of self-respect and elasticity of spirit. The provincial emigration officer's inspection for 'complaints' was a 'mere farce'. The master would prevent any emigrant with a grievance from approaching him; and in any event, the ignorant and penniless emigrants, dejected and anxious to proceed, would never prosecute. Reviewing his experiences as a whole, de Vere observed that the main deficiencies of the trade were in food, space, discipline and morale. He recommended, among other things, a large increase in the food allowance; a reduction in the numbers ratio; separate quarters for single men and women; the employment of a surgeon and a chaplain for each vessel; the provision of kitchens and ovens; hospital wards for the sick; and ventilation mechanisms for the passenger decks.[1]

De Vere's letter did much to reveal the actual conditions which prevailed at sea—or to regard it in its most favourable light, the conditions which might prevail at sea in especially unfortunate circumstances—to those who administered from their desks. Douglas had speculated on the subject in former years, but this was the first occasion on which an educated observer had made the Atlantic voyage between-decks, and described exactly what he saw. The letter made a profound impression on the commissioners.[2] It is scarcely too much to regard it as the basis of most of their future legislation for ship life. Attempts were made sooner or later to achieve every one of de Vere's projected reforms except for the provision of chaplains,

[1] *Papers rel. emigration B.N.A.*, 12–16, H.C. 1847–8 (50), xlvii.
[2] C.O. 384/79, 535 Canada, S. de Vere: Monteagle, marginal comments; *1st rep. select comm. colonization Ire.*, 44, H.C. 1847–8 (415), xvii.

and even this subject was to some extent explored.[1] Elliot pointed out, of course, that all could not be accomplished at one stroke. The opposition from the trade, which such sweeping amendments, all together, would provoke, might prevent any improvement whatsoever in the critical season that lay ahead.[2] Nevertheless, the commissioners went far towards meeting de Vere's suggestions. First, they proposed that the general consolidation of the passenger acts, for which they had pressed a year before, be carried out at the beginning of 1848. And secondly, amongst the specific changes which they recommended were five of prime importance: (1) to reduce the number of passengers from one for every ten square feet of surface deck to one for every twelve; (2) to require every emigrant vessel whatsoever to carry a physician; (3) to compel ships to supply *all* the food for, and assume complete responsibility for the maintenance of, the passengers; (4) to restrict emigration to a small number of specified ports in the United Kingdom so that adequate inspections and control might be established; and (5) to issue an order-in-council laying down minute regulations for ship-life, *to be enforced under pain of fine or imprisonment.*

The first of these schemes was an extension of an existing line of regulation, but the second, fourth and fifth were startling proposals, and even the third represented a very radical change. It was one thing to require vessels to hand over sufficient breadstuffs to the passengers to safeguard them against starvation, another to charge vessels with the entire maintenance of their passengers from first to last. True, all these measures had formerly been considered, in one form or another, by the commissioners. But consideration and definite recommendation were very different things; and the firm proposal of these revolutionary changes at the beginning of 1848 is most revealing. In the first place, it shows that, under the pressure of sudden distress, the theoretical limits to state action simply disintegrated. The third, fourth and fifth recommendations absolutely contradicted the common conceptions of the liberty of trade and of individual responsibility and choice. If outer walls had long before been breached, the inmost citadel was now threatened. Even the 1842 act might have been represented as merely imposing, so to

---

[1] C.O. 384/81, 752 Emigration, 18 Apr. 1848. Archbishop Murray informed the commissioners that he had no priests available for the work.

[2] *1st rep. select comm. colonization Ire.*, 49–50, H.C. 1847–8 (415), xvii.

speak, 'exterior' restrictions. But the new demands leapt forward to the notion that government must exercise a positive control over the inner workings of the trade, must largely direct the conduct of the merchant in his business and the master in the management of his ship, in order to secure its objects. Secondly, the fourth proposal illuminates some of the important consequences for government of the impecuniosity of the state. Clearly the key to the problem was the staff of executive officers, and equally clearly the commissioners were well aware that this was inadequate. Yet they made no attempt to increase it in 1848, and but faint efforts to do so in later seasons. The proposal to restrict emigration to particular ports was the logical alternative. Now this is the first of several illustrations within our subject of the manner in which the very poverty of the adminis-trators might *accelerate* advances in state power. The fanatical economy of mid-nineteenth-century England was the hinge on which the very mode of its government might turn. By a supreme irony, a penny off the income tax might be the price of 'liberty'. Thirdly, the commissioners' proposals show them abandoning their policy of gradual and careful change in an emergency. Instead, they rushed recklessly into measures which they should have known they could not possibly fulfil. Here we may take the physician require-ment, once more, as an example. An agitation for some such regula-tion had been aroused during the year by an American social reformer, Mrs Morley,[1] and, as we have seen, by the protectionists in parliament; and once the season ended, both Canada and New Brunswick pressed the matter very keenly.[2] But when the com-missioners consulted the various medical schools of the United Kingdom they were informed that nothing like the 600 or so who would be required to supply the emigrant vessels would be avail-able.[3] The president of the royal college of surgeons at Dublin declared that only if the physicians were employed as permanent *state* servants would any be forthcoming, and that the only effect of the clause in contemplation would be to 'interfere with emigration' which was so essential to Ireland.[4] Yet in the teeth of these replies the commissioners recommended that a physician be required

[1] Albion, op. cit., p. 348.

[2] *Papers rel. emigration B.N.A.*, 124, 176, H.C. 1847-8 (50), xlvii.

[3] Ibid., 41-4. The presidents of the five main medical schools in the United Kingdom (in London, Dublin and Edinburgh) were consulted.

[4] C.O. 384/79, 1770 North America, 2 Nov. 1847.

for every vessel. To some extent this may have been a concession
to public agitation. As Hawes, the parliamentary under-secretary,
observed, 'It is not easy to defend the sending out of 300 or 400
emigrants in a ship—especially the emigrants of late, without some
medical aid'.[1] But there is no positive evidence that it was this
alone, or even this mainly, which weighed with the commissioners.
Undoubtedly, they were moved as well, like the general public, by
the feeling that since common humanity seemed to demand such a
measure it must be so decreed, whatever the actualities of the
situation.

To conclude our drawing of lessons, the proposals, though unimportant in themselves, demonstrate two large truths about the
governmental revolution as a whole. First, that many of the improvements in legislation came from the publicizing of abuses which
appeared 'intolerable' once they were exposed. Then, it was not at
all a question of the state's functions or even of the state's capacity
for the business, but simply that some action must be taken—and
by government, in default of any other remedial agency. Second,
that the state's consequent, if reluctant, efforts at reform often outran the instruments and techniques at its disposal. Immediately,
this issued in what might be termed 'wishful' legislation or projected
legislation, and a refusal to face up to the implications of what had
been enacted. But in the long run it proved a most profound source
of social reform. Given time, a mechanical age and a public opinion
sensitive to inhumanity, the legislative demand tended ultimately to
create its own supply.[2]

Only the first and last of the commissioners' proposals were
accepted in their original form. The second and third were watered
down almost to nothing, and the fourth was dropped completely.
These rejections are not surprising. The impracticality of the surgeon requirement needs no further demonstration; and the political
opposition of the ports which would have been deprived of a portion
of their trade had the fourth clause been enacted, or of the shippers
were they suddenly called on to maintain their passengers, would
have been very formidable. Immediately, it was Grey who was
responsible for the defeat of the majority of the commissioners'
proposals. But it was not an awareness of the practical difficulties or

[1] Ibid., 1473 Canada, minute dated 31 Aug. 1847.
[2] *Papers rel. emigration B.N.A.*, 28–38, H.C. 1847–8 (50), xlvii.

of the ideological offences which inspired him, but rather his old hostility to increasing the exactions of the law. Having had to surrender all control over colonial immigrant legislation in return for escaping financial responsibility, Grey tried to make a virtue of necessity and argued that the colonial amendments would render any improvements in the imperial code superfluous. And although he failed to hold back in 1848 every change which threatened an increase in fares, he did succeed in postponing the promised consolidation for yet another season, upon the familiar ground that fresh impositions would check the Irish outflow.

Having set out their backgrounds, we may now consider the 1847 and 1848 amendment acts[1] as they were eventually passed. Although confessedly stop-gap and minor legislation, each was, in its own way, a significant measure. The 1847 act contained five useful clauses. The operation of the passenger acts was extended to all vessels carrying more than one passenger for every twenty-five registered tons;[2] inducing passengers to part with their contract tickets or receipts was declared a punishable offence; owners or charterers, as the case might be, were rendered clearly and specifically responsible for the embarking of sufficient food and water; ships putting back in distress were to be re-furnished with sea-stock if they sailed again—if they did not, the emigrants were to receive their passage money and compensation for their inconvenience; and all passenger vessels were to be surveyed for seaworthiness by two or more professional surveyors appointed by the emigration commissioners.[3] So far as it went, this was good legislation. Each of the five clauses met a widespread and thoroughly authenticated abuse or deficiency, and was readily enforceable.[4] If the line of legislation did not advance, a number of weak points were successfully reinforced. So far, the

[1] 10 & 11 Vic., c. 103 and 11 & 12 Vic., c. 6.
[2] The former restriction of the operation of the passenger acts to vessels carrying thirty or more passengers had proved insufficient, and some vessels which cleared with twenty-nine or less took on additional passengers later, occasionally to the extent of having forty or fifty as their final complement, C.O. 384/80, 939 and 997 Emigration, 2 and 11 June 1847. The 1847 act also ordained that all passengers whatsoever might claim the protection of the pre-embarkation clauses of the 1842 act.
[3] Secs. 1, 3, 6, 9, 10 and 13.
[4] All these clauses were drafted with the problems of enforcement very much in mind. As an example, we may take the recovery of passage money and compensation, if a vessel putting back in distress did not sail again. A special provision for a rapid and informal summary process was included.

amendments accorded with the then accepted principle of careful,
gradual change. But the 1847 act also contained three clauses which,
although generally regarded perhaps as mere formalities or window-
dressing,[1] none the less mark significant stages on the road of regulation. The commissioners were granted powers to alter the food
schedule as they thought desirable, and the emigration officers were
charged with two new duties, that of judging the sufficiency and
competence of crews, and that of securing 'the natural supply of
light and air' by means of the hatchways leading to the passengers'
quarters or, if these were 'unduly impeded', by some alternative
device.[2] The grant of powers to vary the food schedule was the first
open and indisputable instance of delegated legislation within our
subject. Correspondingly, the other clauses constituted the first
open and indisputable grant of discretionary powers to the executive. Earlier statutes may possibly be construed as implying the
delegation of some quasi-legislative and quasi-judicial powers: it
may even be that such powers are implicit in all social legislation of
this type. But though the two are connected, a great gulf, both constitutional and substantial, divides implicit from explicit delegation;
and no grants could have been more explicit than those which the
1847 act contained. The 'light and air' clause, for example, instructed the emigration officer to direct such 'provision to be made
for affording light and air to the between decks as the circumstances of the case may, *in the judgment of such officer*, appear
to require, which directions shall be duly carried out *to his satisfaction*'.[3] A larger or more secure award of powers can scarcely be
conceived.

We may also discern in the 1847 act some interesting patterns, or
portions of the basic patterns, of governmental growth. One is the
manner in which executive actions thrown up in the course of

[1] The clause concerning ship's crew was included as a sop to Manners,
whose demands for a physician clause had been refused, *Hans.*, 3rd, xciv, 276–8.
[2] Secs. 2, 5 and 7.
[3] The phrase, 'to his satisfaction', is repeated in the clause awarding the
emigration officer discretions over the manning of emigrant vessels. (The italics
in the short passage quoted above are mine.) Cf. The equivalent of this phrase,
i.e. 'is satisfied', was held to be unconstitutional in an Irish case, *Pigs Marketing
Board* v. *Donnelly* (1939) I.R. 413 (Hanna J.), upon the ground that it conveyed
a judicial power to the executive. Such a finding was, of course, only possible
because reference was made to a written constitution, which laid down a
separation of powers.

ordinary administration, and deriving but imprecisely and indirectly from existing legislation, became enshrined in statute. The commissioners' last decision on ship surveys in 1846; their varying of the food schedule in the same year; and their choice of 'navy bread' as the minimum of quality, were all simply translated into formal law. Secondly, we can see how a known defect or inadequacy in an existing measure might be remedied by a clause which, because its framing must be general, enlarged the field of regulation disproportionately. We may take as an example the 'distressed vessels' clause. The difficulty of relieving and re-equipping the emigrants who were returned to Cove in January 1847, had re-emphasized the failure of the existing legislation to insure passengers against the deficiencies or misfortunes of their vessels. But when the remedial clause was framed not merely did it require that the ship's stock of water and provisions be renewed: it also required that the passengers be compensated for all their losses, and (to secure this last) provided still more informal and expeditious procedures for recovery. Thus, two important precedents were established without either having been advocated in its own right. The decision to remedy the abuse led on naturally to a consideration of its larger implications and of the legal processes which the circumstances of the case seemed to require. A third noteworthy development was the abandonment, in some technical matters, of the attempt to anticipate all contingencies or comprehend all relevant details, in favour of relying upon the individual judgment of the executive officers. Very possibly, the new subjects of ships' crews and ventilation were dealt with in this new way because of previous experience of the weakness of would-be comprehensive clauses or because of the inherent difficulty of laying down detailed regulations to govern such complex and variable affairs. But it was inevitable that passenger legislation would turn sooner or later in this direction; and, in fact, the practice of cutting the Gordian knot by an award of administrative discretions was very freely followed in later statutes. Finally, the history of the survey clause provides a microcosm of one of the regular movements of governmental growth. The first step was the general discretion as to seaworthiness; the second rendered this precise by requiring the formal examination of the 'survey' in doubtful cases; the next rendered it universal and compulsory by requiring surveys of all vessels; and the last removed the examination

7*

from the hands of the 'general practitioner' executive officer and placed it in those of the specialist shipwright, even to the extent of employing such a specialist as a public servant in the largest port. Each step was prompted by revealed necessity. It may not be too bold to say that no small part of the development of the modern state is here summarized.

The 1848 act was also an interesting measure. Again, there were five main clauses. First, the surface space allowance was, as the commissioners had proposed, increased from ten to twelve square feet for every adult passenger. Secondly, every vessel with 100 or more passengers[1] aboard was now required to carry a physician,[2] or, alternatively, allow fourteen instead of twelve square feet of space. Thus, it was hoped, the difficulty of securing surgeons had been overcome. If none could be found, the emigrants would at least be compensated by more room between-decks. Thirdly, each vessel with 100 or more passengers had to provide a cook, cooking apparatus and cooking places—all 'to the satisfaction' of the emigration officer. Fourthly, each emigrant had to be certified as free from infectious diseases by a medical officer before he might embark. And, finally, the commissioners were empowered to issue orders-in-council governing life at sea. Quite apart from the substance of the major clauses, the devices for enforcing them are of considerable interest. Further discretionary powers were heaped upon the executive officer. He was to be the sole judge of both the professional qualifications and the personal suitability of ship physicians. It was he who would fix the fee to be paid by the owner or charterer to the medical officer who inspected the emigrants. He was even empowered to permit a vessel to sail without any medical inspection if, in his opinion, no suitable inspector were available. Again, we may note some astonishing departures in the devices for enforcing discipline at sea. It was the traditional villains of the piece, the master and the ship's physician, who were charged with maintaining order during the voyage; while the colonial justices of the peace might fine or *imprison* recalcitrant passengers after their disembarkation. A final point of interest is the transference of the burden of

[1] In calculating 100 passengers for the purposes of the physician and cooking clauses, children counted as one each.

[2] The 'physician' had to be qualified to practise as a physician or a surgeon or an apothecary in the United Kingdom. It was also required that he 'shall not be objected to by the said emigration officer'.

proof from the crown to the defendant in all cases where exemption from the operation of the acts was claimed. Thus, the escape from the entanglement of common law and conventional constitutional assumptions gathered pace. 'Principles' went down like ninepins in 1848.

The 1847 act had been very sharply criticized by the humanitarians as inadequate. But the trade had not protested, for the very good reason that it was not seriously threatened by any of the new requirements except that concerning ships' crews, and even this last clause produced few novelties in practice. The 1848 act was, however, caught between two fires. Several members declared that it had not gone far enough; others pointed out defects in particular clauses.[1] But Liverpool and the Irish ports were also up in arms against the statute as a whole.[2] The shippers argued that it contradicted the previous policy of the commissioners; that it was impracticable; and that it would destroy the British transatlantic trade. If the last argument was groundless and the second only partly true, the first was incontrovertible. J. & W. Robinson used extracts from the parliamentary papers, written as late as December 1847, to show that the commissioners were then determined that that most exceptional season should not form the basis for permanent legislation. Yet two months later 'government proposes to assume the responsibility of now arresting the progress of the vast multitudes who have been for months preparing. . . . Out of their mouths they are condemned'. The commissioners could only reply, somewhat disingenuously, that since the papers had been written 'the tidings of disaster have become . . . much fuller, and the call for measures of protection much stronger',[3] for, as we have seen, they were proposing still more severe measures than those made public before the ink of their deprecating annual report was dry. The truth was that their whole attitude towards regulation had been unsettled, and that they were now in much confusion and subject to contrary impulses. The act itself reflected their dilemmas. The space requirement was the only one which could be thoroughly enforced. It

[1] See the debate upon the passenger bill on 21 February 1848, *Hans.*, 3rd, xcvi, 1024–35.

[2] *Northern Whig*, 24 Feb. 1848.

[3] C.O. 384/41, 421 Emigration, printed circular of J. & W. Robinson, 25 Feb. 1848, and endorsements, 26 Feb. 1848. J. & W. Robinson may have been the infamous Robinson Brothers, under a new title.

was often violated, but retribution followed certainly.[1] The clauses concerning cooking were a dead-letter from the outset, and the medical inspections—at any rate, at Liverpool—a mere matter of form.[2] As for the carrying of surgeons, this involved the commissioners in immediate difficulties. Some vessels sailed illegally without them,[3] others took them aboard to pass the customs and then re-landed them along the coast.[4] The shippers pleaded that it was impossible to persuade qualified and competent men to make the crossing;[5] and they did not exaggerate. The employment was irregular, and the salary necessarily small. Hawes proposed, in fact, that medical students be accepted.[6] In these circumstances, appeals to exercise moderation in enforcing so harsh a rule were only to be expected. To such appeals Elliot replied that 'if we had once begun to deviate, there was not likely to be any want of manœuvres in Ireland to evade the law generally'.[7] But in practice, the commissioners did accept men without the professional qualifications which the act required, and,[8] generally, had to be content with a very partial enforcement of the clause, for neither the United Kingdom nor the colonial officers pressed hard upon offending masters. After 1848 owners almost always chose to allow the additional space rather than employ physicians, so that the general consequence of the clause was the happy one of reducing the numbers ratio on vessels with large complements of passengers.

Broadly speaking, the 1847–8 legislation presents two main points of contrast to that of 1842. It was much less effective and appropriate, and it was much less careful of the conventions and proprieties of trade and law. Both qualities appear in their most extravagant form in the order-in-council on discipline at sea which was issued by the commissioners in April 1848.[9] The order laid

[1] *Further papers rel. emigration B.N.A.*, 11–12 [964], H.C. 1847–8, xlvii; *Papers rel. emigration B.N.A.*, 27 [1025], H.C. 1849, xxxviii.

[2] *Treatment of passengers on board* Washington, 2, H.C. 1851 (198), xl.

[3] E.g., C.O. 384/81, 1405 Emigration, 18 July 1848.

[4] E.g., C.O. 384/84, 3155 Emigration, 27 Mar. 1849.

[5] E.g., ibid., 1202 Emigration, 17 June 1848.

[6] C.O. 384/79, 1640 North America and endorsement, 10 Oct. 1847. This proposal was, of course, rejected. Grey's only comment on the problem of securing surgeons was that 'the question of what ought to be done is a very difficult one'.

[7] C.O. 384/81, 1405 Emigration, 19 June 1848.

[8] E.g., C.O. 384/83, 3980 North America, 2 May 1849.

[9] *8th rep. C.L.E.C.*, 58 [961], H.C. 1847–8, xxvi.

down precise times for rising and retiring, for taking meals and turns at cooking, for opening and shutting portholes, and the rest. It ordered passengers to roll up their beds, sweep the decks, scour and holystone the beams and remove all dirt between 7 a.m. and 8 a.m. each morning, and to appear on deck in 'clean and decent' dress at 10 a.m. each Sunday, which day was 'to be observed as religiously as the circumstances will permit'. Amongst a large number of other rules and prohibitions, smoking, drinking and gambling were forbidden. To appreciate this extraordinary manifesto to the full, we must recollect that the penalty for disobedience might be as high as two months' imprisonment, and that its subjects were not the inmates of a workhouse or of a convict hulk or of a military transport, but civilians freely undertaking a journey for which they had paid themselves. Elliot was greatly troubled about the reaction of the trade. 'I hope', he wrote, 'that we may infer from their indifference that there is nothing in the order to excite much opposition'.[1] His concern was unnecessary. Not the slightest attempt was ever made to put it into practice.[2] Indeed it is difficult to believe that anyone could seriously have expected it to be enforced in the absence of an independent authority and supervisor on board ship. Yet we can scarcely suppose that Elliot and Murdoch were altogether disingenuous, that the order was a brazen and empty show. How is the discrepancy to be explained? The genesis of the order is clear enough. It was an amalgam of the commissioners' earlier advice to the North Atlantic masters, and of their instructions to the surgeon-superintendents of the state-managed Australian emigration, tailored and extended to meet, point by point, the evils described by Stephen de Vere. But how did the commissioners, realists and professionals as they were supposed to be, come to multiply a paper regimentation with as little relation to the world of facts as the decrees of the Emperor Seth? There is no certain answer, but the explanation is very probably, as we have said before, that the commissioners reacted to shocking disclosures such as de Vere's in the same generous but unthinking way as the impulsive public at large. Come hell or high water, the infamy must be erased; and the first and natural impulse was to identify erasure and legislative prohibition.

[1] C.O. 384/81, 670 Emigration, 3 Apr. 1848.
[2] C.O. 384/94, 11088 Miscellaneous, 30 Nov. 1855.

The second major reaction to the 1847 disasters concerned Liverpool alone. Originating in the demands of various independent persons[1] and Canadian authorities[2] that the seat of disease and misery, the lodging-house, should be reformed and that passengers should be cleansed and subjected to rigorous medical inspection before being permitted to embark, a vast scheme of total centralization was evolved. The scheme was first drawn up, probably jointly, by the senior Liverpool emigration officers, who communicated it to C. A. Wood, one of the commissioners, when he visited Liverpool in August 1848.[3] Briefly, what was proposed was nothing less than bringing the entire Liverpool emigration under official surveillance from the moment of the emigrant's arrival at the port to the moment of his embarkation. This was to be done by means of a central depot complete with wharves, refectories, dormitories, baths, retail shops and brokers' offices.[4] Such an undertaking might defeat every evil in the port. The runner (who was to be excluded from the depot and its grounds and would in any event become economically superfluous) and the lodging-house would disappear. Fraud would become much more difficult when an official money exchange was established and brokers carried on their business under immediate observation. The emigrant would be kept from drunkenness by living within bounds, and from infection by clean food and beds, and bathing. Medical inspection could be organized efficiently, and might at last become a genuine precaution against epidemics; and the emigration officer's duties would at least come within the range of possible performance.[5] The whole was a dazzling prospect, and indeed much of it might have been accomplished. It was small wonder that the commissioners (now that Elliot had been replaced by the less reflective and inhibited Murdoch) should have taken up the project eagerly, or that Grey, with his usual weakness for the

[1] C.O. 384/81, 536 Canada and 749 North America, 18 Mar. and 5 Apr. 1848.
[2] See above, p. 194.
[3] Wood had been sent to Liverpool to investigate the lodgings problem. It is clear from the report that the depot project had been prepared, in general terms, some time before his visit and that the mayor and some of the magistrates (all of whom warmly approved) had been consulted. C.O. 384/81, 1694 Emigration. 30 August 1848.
[4] Hitchens, op. cit., pp. 148–50, confuses this project with the embarkation depots for assisted emigration to Australia, and wrongly attributes the init i tive in the matter to Grey.
[5] See below, pp. 216–18.

grand design, should have endorsed it, 'a most excellent arrangement'.[1]

Curiously enough, the scheme was not pared down even after the commissioners had sifted the details of sites, finance and management. On the contrary, the need for absolute state control was more clearly asserted. The half-way house of farming out the depot to various shipping firms was rejected—'the Government would virtually establish a monopoly in a business which is every day expanding'—and the commissioners also insisted that the scheme be universal and compulsory. They confessed frankly that, if it were not, very few emigrants would enter the depot voluntarily, while the lodging-keepers and the runners would do their utmost to destroy it. The commissioners proposed to use a building large enough to house 3,000 persons at a time. A tax of 1s. was to be imposed on every Liverpool emigrant, in return for which he was to be entitled to two nights' lodging at the depot.[2] In addition to the existing emigration staff, the establishment was to be composed of twelve policemen, two managers, two medical officers, two ship surveyors and a large body of porters and other servants. The commissioners anticipated that the annual cost would be £6,500, about half of which would be spent on rent and maintenance and half on salaries and wages. Against this, they estimated that the emigrant tax would raise at least £5,000 annually, and the surpluses upon the medical examinations and surveys at least £1,000 each.[3] Finally, the commissioners fairly set out the probable arguments against the scheme: first, that the Liverpool emigration might suddenly decline and the government be left with a white elephant upon its hands; second, that if a calamity such as 1847 recurred the government would be much more directly responsible and vulnerable to attacks than it had been before; and third, that emigration did in fact take place from Liverpool without 'undue' sickness—in 1848, the largest

[1] C.O. 384/81, 1694 Emigration, 30 Aug. 1848.

[2] Two nights was the usual stay of an emigrant at Liverpool: he might stay longer at a charge of 6d. per night. Meals were to be paid for separately.

[3] Even on this estimate there would have been a surplus of £500 annually. But the calculation of £5,000 from the emigrant tax was based upon an emigration of only 100,000 persons each year, which was far below the annual average of the next decade. In fact, the emigrant tax would have brought in between £7,000 and £8,000 annually during the early 1850s. But the commissioners (doubtless properly) argued that 'in a service so novel and extensive' large margins should be left for the inevitable unforeseen.

season Liverpool had ever known, the mortality upon its vessels had been only 1 per cent. But to counter these arguments they stressed the terrible hardships—short of death or beggary—to which the Liverpool emigrants were subjected, and the fact that, considering Irish circumstances and the growth of Irish remittances and the huge sums which the Americans were just then sinking in the Liverpool passenger trade, the danger of the outflow falling below 100,000 annually was negligible.[1]

The commissioners, then, ultimately decided in favour of the depot project and were ready to undertake both the responsibility and the control. It was Elliot who brought forward the fatal objections. The 1842 act had represented, more or less, the limit to which he was prepared to push state intervention. He was increasingly unhappy about the trend of legislation in 1847–9;[2] and this last proposal both frightened him as a public servant and shocked his sense of constitutional propriety. He first complained of the 'discrimination' against Liverpool which a compulsory tax upon its emigrants alone would constitute; and although the commissioners assured him that the leading merchants and the city fathers were amongst its warmest supporters, he was not reconciled to the 'injustice'. Next, he observed that the depot would 'involve the Government in responsibilities of an unusual kind. It will in fact be in the position of a great Lodging House Keeper paid by money received from the poor people for which they would be entitled to demand that they receive full value'—and correspondingly the criticisms would be at once more numerous and more unscrupulous than if mere private persons were the targets. The climax of Elliot's report was reminiscent of Mr. Podsnip's 'I see what you are driving at. I knew it from the first. Centralization. No. Never with my consent. Not English!' 'The whole spirit of administration in England', wrote Elliot, 'is that such Establishments should be managed by persons of importance resident on the spot. They are able by periodic meetings to check the subordinate officers, and their character lends weight to the decisions of such officers when right. They are also much less inviting objects for attack than the Government of the Country, and are not liable to be assailed for political purposes.'

[1] C.O. 384/84, 4584 Emigration, 22 May 1849.
[2] He was particularly concerned about the danger of offending the trade, and the probable increase in fares.

Logically enough perhaps, Elliot's conclusion was that the formation and management of the depot should be the business of the
corporation of Liverpool, not the state.[1]

Doubtless with some relief, the politicians followed the nice tack
which Elliot had steered between the Scylla of the 'intolerability' of
the Liverpool trade and the Charybdis of the omni-responsible
department. Hawes, the parliamentary under-secretary, endorsed
the commissioners' report, 'Depot would involve too much responsibility and future expense, as to be undesirable'; although he did
allow that the government might make an annual donation, if it
were clearly understood that it was not liable for any mismanagement or misfortune.[2] Grey substantially agreed. He still believed,
he wrote, that the depot was a splendid proposal;[3] he promised
government support for a private bill to enable the Liverpool corporation to levy the tax; he would throw open the treasury of
colonial office counsel to the depot managers; but—the all-important
but—he had now come to realize that the state should not intervene
directly.[4] It would be a misleading flippancy to say that the mayor of
Liverpool refused to accept the buck. His plea that the central
power extend 'its paternal care' of the unfortunate does not seem
disingenuous. First, he made it clear that the evil was indeed real
and widespread. Despite his and the magistrates' best efforts, almost
all the Irish were more or less imposed upon and some reduced to
the greatest distress. When brokers and runners were fined to the
limit of the law, they paid 'cheerfully' as they could 'well afford' to
do. But 'the Corporation', he continued, 'could not in my opinion
undertake with advantage the charge of a large emigrant depot for
reasons of a local nature—which I need not particularize'. As it later
transpired that many of the members of the corporation and common council of Liverpool were financially interested in both the
lodging and provisions houses,[5] the force of the mayor's argument
is obvious. He ended by pointing out the national character of the

[1] C.O. 384/84, 4584 Emigration, minute of 25 May 1849.
[2] Ibid., Hawes's endorsement, 25 May 1849.
[3] Characteristically, however, Grey started a new hare by suggesting that the
depot might contain a workhouse ward for distressed strangers, even though
they were not contemplating emigration at all. This would of course have
altered the whole basis of the proposal, and Grey's new notion received no
support.
[4] C.O. 384/84, 4584 Emigration, Grey's endorsement, 26 May 1849.
[5] C.O. 384/85, 7384 Emigration, 4 Sept. 1850.

problem and the psychological advantages of state control, which 'gives the depot a prestige and stamps it at once with a character in the eyes of the ignorant emigrant which would only otherwise be attained through a long course of time in other hands'.[1] Hope for the depot temporarily revived when Grey misread the mayor's letter as guaranteeing that the corporation would indemnify the government if emigration did fall off and the depot was left useless upon their hands. But when it became clear that nothing new had been proposed, the original decision was confirmed[2] and the scheme dropped for the moment out of sight.

There can be few more interesting or revealing episodes than this in the history of government in the United Kingdom in the mid-nineteenth century. The more we reflect upon the constitutional and political implications of the scheme, the age in which it was born and the fact that it came reasonably close to being adopted, the more curious does it all appear. Two features stand out immediately: one, that the proposal was a perfectly completed essay in collectivism, as centralized, comprehensive and compulsory, as large an invasion of the field of private business, as direct and politically dangerous a responsibility for government to assume as any measure which the state has subsequently adopted; the other, that nothing could have been more 'tutelary', 'bureaucratic' and apparently doctrinaire in concept than the concentration of the entire traffic into a single isolated depot under a central expert rule. Yet the date of the project was 1848–9; its authors humdrum civil servants-cum-naval officers; and its aptness for its purpose so indisputable that it was immediately and universally recognized as the only really satisfactory solution.[3] Common necessity then might be the mother of even the most intricate and seemingly national inventions of government.

But the matter is still more complicated. We must also recall the delicate convolution of the issues and the ultimate failure of the

[1] C.O. 384/84, 9485 Emigration, 31 October 1849.
[2] Ibid., 10656 and 10665 Emigration and endorsements, 13 Dec. 1849 and 14 Jan. 1850.
[3] This is further borne out by the fact that the New York emigration commissioners were driven along a very similar path. Their efforts to stamp out fraud in that city culminated in the establishment of Castle Garden in 1855; and the new immigrant station resembled the model for Liverpool to a remarkable degree. See below, pp. 315–16.

project to carry the day. For example, our picture of emergent collectivism is deepened when we realize that, and understand why, at a moment remarkable for the resistance of local authorities to centralization,[1] there should also have been local authorities begging for its extension. Nor can we dismiss out of hand the argument of Elliot in favour of the local tradition of English government. Again, an analysis of the reasons for the project's failure reveals the range of half-hidden obstacles to governmental growth. Fear was the fatal force—fear of responsibility, fear of the untried. Well, it may be said, *que voulez vous*: is it not in the nature of the *routinier* and the second-rank politician, in the mid-eighteenth or mid-twentieth no less than the mid-nineteenth century, to evade labours, dangers and difficulties where he can? Such an observation grates on the historian. Century by century, men and circumstances are never quite the same; nor is a decision often reducible to so simple a motivation. Of course, there was 'no saint, no spartan, no reformer' amongst our actors. But none was, on the evidence before us, inhumane, none unmoved by the sufferings which so many eye-witnesses described. Not the least interesting aspect of the whole affair is that neither the magnitude of the evil nor the merit of the proposed remedy was at any stage disputed; that is to say, a very fair cross section of the middle and upper classes was unanimous as to both the desirability of the end and the probable efficacy of the means. Why then did the project fail? In the general complex of fears three seem to predominate: the fear of state expenditure; the fear of public and political attack; and the fear of violating 'principle'. It is true that the probable loss on the depot, should the worst come to the worst, was never placed above £2,500.[2] The most savage criticism might have been deflected at least by pointing out that the government acted from pure humanity and upon the advice of the most knowledgeable, respectable and disinterested persons in the community concerned. As for 'principle', what lines had not, in one place or another, been trampled and obliterated by 1849? Yet these are undoubtedly the reasons why the project failed. The plain fact is that

[1] Cf. Halévy, op. cit., p. 227; J. L. and B. Hammond, *The age of the chartists* (London, 1938), pp. 308–9.
[2] It was generally supposed that the buildings would be converted into warehouses at a relatively small cost, and readily sold, cf. C.O. 384/84, 9485 Emigration, 31 Oct. 1849.

certain marks of the middle decades of the nineteenth century—the fever of economy; the ferocity with which administrators were assailed; the clarity of the images of 'fields', 'spheres' and 'limits' dividing the personal and the private, the national and the local, the individual and the communal—have no true counterpart in either the earlier or the later years. These extraordinary passions contribute essentially to the special quality of our period, to the peculiar texture of government in the early and mid-Victorian age. Nor does the fact that they constituted an immaterial barrier to collectivism mean that they were altogether ineffective.

We have not yet exhausted the reactions to the disaster of 1847. One in particular should be noted; the thorough-going reform of the British North American protective systems. Originally, Grey's programme for 1848 envisaged no change in the passenger code or arrangements beyond an increase in the provincial immigrant tax to provide more effective relief in the colonies and a substitute for the lost imperial grant. But while, on the one hand, de Vere's letter and pressure from the Canadian executive council forced him to accept the amendment act and order-in-council of 1848, on the other, the colonists proceeded to out-Herod Herod in imposing new restrictions on immigration. In every British North American province the basic immigrant tax was doubled, further increased by half-a-crown *per cap.* for each day spent in quarantine, and still further increased for those arriving in the last weeks of the season; masters were required to enter heavy indemnifying bonds for every passenger whom the quarantine officers adjudged a likely public burden; and the various minor regulations were equally severe.[1] Grey's protest that the colonial trade would be destroyed went unheeded.[2] Having cut the provinces adrift, he could no longer direct their legislation: and the burnt child feared the fire.[3] Certainly, the new provincial measures proved a deterrent. Masters and owners regularly engaged in the St Lawrence or St John runs were outraged. Some withdrew altogether from the passenger trade; others changed

---

[1] *Papers rel. emigration B.N.A.*, 23–7 [932], H.C. 1847–8, xlvii; *Further papers rel. emigration B.N.A.*, 39–40, 52 [964], H.C. 1847–8, xlvii.

[2] *Papers rel. emigration B.N.A.*, 27–9 [932], H.C. 1847–8, xlvii.

[3] Elgin and Colebrooke both told Grey that nothing could be done until the colonies were nursed back into confidence, ibid., 49; *Further papers rel. emigration B.N.A.*, 35, 58 [964], H.C. 1847–8, xlvii.

the destinations of their vessels to New York or Boston.[1] In the event, the total emigration to British North America fell from 109,000 in 1847 to 31,000 in 1848, and the Irish emigration from 97,000 to 23,000. There were, of course, some compensations. The mortality rate was reduced to 1·5 per cent. Elliot observed that whatever the decline in the volume of emigration, it was better 'than to send them forth, as happened last year, merely to be thrown overboard into the sea or die in the first hospital they reach after landing'.[2] Elliot's reasoning may have been unsound—most of the emigrants who would normally have sailed for British North America must have embarked for the United States instead, and the American mortality was no larger than the Canadian[3]—but his relief was very natural. A more substantial compensation was the opportunity to reorganize the quarantine systems which the small numbers to be handled, and the surplus revenue of the heavy immigrant tax, provided. Permanent cookhouses and convalescent sheds were built on Grosse Isle and Partridge Island; an army officer was placed in charge of the commissariat and domestic organization of each of the stations; and internal transportation was cheapened.[4] Once again, de Vere's observations formed the basis of the reforms.[5] But on this occasion they came to a more successful issue. Immigrant protection in British North America was henceforth really effective, at any rate so far as immigrants who had sailed from ports in the United Kingdom were concerned.[6]

In 1849 the commissioners at last fulfilled their promise of a consolidating statute.[7] For the fruit of (to use Grey's words) at least two years of 'revision and consultation' the measure was modest enough. Only four major changes were proposed. First, the act forbade the berthing together of single men and women. This practice had long disgraced the passenger trade, and considering that it was

---

[1] *2nd rep. select. comm. colonization Ire.*, 271, 285–94, H.C. 1847–8 (593), xvii; C.O. 384/81, 438, 734 and 820 Canada, 25 Feb., 7 and 20 Apr. 1848.

[2] C.O. 384/82, 976 Emigration, 17 May 1848. See also C.O. 384/83, 1848 British North America, 2 Feb. 1849.

[3] *9th rep. C.L.E.C.*, 2 [1082], H.C. 1849, xxii.

[4] Further papers rel. emigration B.N.A., 1–9 [985], H.C. 1847–8, xlvii. See also *Cork Examiner*, 8 May 1848.

[5] *1st rep. sel. comm. colonization Ire.*, 51–2, H.C. 1847–8 (415), xvii.

[6] Scandinavian immigrants caused considerable trouble in the middle and late 1850s, because of the inadequacy of the Scandinavian passenger codes.

[7] 12 & 13 Vic., c. 33.

in some respects less difficult to secure reform upon the ground of sexual morality than of humanity,[1] it is perhaps curious that the prohibition should have come so late.[2] Secondly, the food scale was very largely increased and changed. No longer were breadstuffs to be the sole commodity furnished by the ships: oatmeal, tea, rice, sugar and molasses were also to be issued—and (an important change) to be issued twice weekly in advance.[3] This was in intention, at least, a great reform. Henceforward, emigrants were not only ensured against actual want but also promised a reasonably varied and more balanced diet. It is true that the new clause fell short of the commissioners' ideal, which was to compel the vessels to furnish all the food for their passengers. It also fell short of their 'second choice', a larger and more complicated diet which included meat and vegetables. Having in mind the fate of the Irish in 1847, the commissioners held out strongly for one or other of these measures.[4] But finally they were induced to modify their demands upon the old ground that fares should be kept as low as possible.[5] Even the compromise clause raised the cost of the foodstuffs supplied by the vessel from 8s. 9d. to 17s. per cap. as against the 13s. 8d. of the latest congressional scale. Naturally it was argued, on the one hand, that Irish emigration would be retarded by the increased fares and, on the other, that the faltering St Lawrence trade would suffer the *coup de grâce* if it had no advantage to offset the superior appointments and speed of the American vessels[6]—and these were

[1] Cf. Halévy, op. cit., p. 20.

[2] The commissioners had also proposed that the berths, which commonly held four or more people, should be divided, and that the statutory berthing space of nine square feet per adult should be increased. But when the shipping merchants explained that it was the custom of Irish families to economize by using the same berth for all during the voyage, and argued that these additions to the berthing clause would cause great hardships, they were withdrawn; C.O. 384/184, 3155 Emigration, 13 Apr. 1849.

[3] The actual weekly ration was to be two and a half pounds of bread or biscuit, one pound of flour, five pounds of oatmeal, one pound of rice, one pound of sugar and molasses and two ounces of tea.

[4] C.O. 384/84, 361 Miscellaneous, 13 Jan. 1849.

[5] C.O. 384/88, 1293 North America, 16 Feb. 1850.

[6] It was also argued that 'passengers would rather lay in their own provisions than have the ship do it and be charged', C.O. 384/84, 3155 Emigration, 27 Mar. 1849. The commissioners replied that the emigrants would actually save money as the provisions which they bought were often putrid and always exorbitant in price.

arguments to which both Grey and Elliot[1] were susceptible. The third major reform concerned shipping brokers and their agents. Four years after it had first been proposed, a new licensing system was introduced. Moreover, brokers were now required to enter bonds of £200 to guarantee their good behaviour, and to furnish two sureties resident in the port town. They were also required to post up lists of their authorized runners and to supply signed copies of these lists to the emigration officer at least once a month; and no broker's agent might act in the passenger trade unless he carried a written authority from his principal. The last significant change wrought by the 1849 act was the reduction of the number required to bring the 'physician or additional space' clause into operation from one hundred to fifty persons. Since scarcely any vessels now carried less than fifty passengers, this meant that the overwhelming majority of emigrants would henceforth benefit from the clause; and since the shippers almost invariably chose to allow 14 square feet of space rather than engage a surgeon—as one group observed, 'no respectable doctor will go aboard for what we can afford to pay him'—its general effect was to increase the room between-decks.

Much the same sort of intensification of existing lines of regulation took place in the field of enforcement. The number of prescribed schedules of contract tickets, bonds, licences and the like was increased to seven. The summary processes were consolidated and further simplified. A *minimum* penalty for breaches of the passenger act, £5, was, for the first time, pronounced. The burden of proof was transferred *in every case* to those claiming exemption from the act; and suing passengers were declared to be competent witnesses. Again, the award of discretionary powers to the executive officers was continued. Thus, for example, even such a matter as the worth of the two sureties now required for a passenger broker's bond was left to the emigration officer to adjudge. The commissioners' powers were similarly enlarged. An attempt to give the treasury a right to mitigate penalties imposed for breaches of the act was successfully resisted upon the ground that the commissioners, through their agents on the spot, could do this more effectively and informally;[2]

---

[1] Six months before Elliot had argued against any concessions to the American trade in view of the Canadian difficulties, C.O. 384/81, 1293 Emigration, 4 July 1848.

[2] Ibid., 5069 Emigration, 7 June 1849.

and the commissioners were permitted to centralize and control medical inspections and found emigrant depots in the embarkation ports should these steps prove feasible.[1] Finally, we may note that the J.P.s were given a lead at last in the matter of brokers' licences. Any two of them might cancel a licence for any breach whatever of the act.

Generally speaking, the 1849 act was a conventional measure. It resembled the first consolidation act of 1842 rather than the panic legislation of 1847–8, and it extended earlier controls and methods rather than invented new ones. Yet the accumulated advances since 1842 were very considerable on any count. Each of the three basic problems of the trade, space, food and fraud, was tackled boldly in 1849. In part obliquely, the space allowance had been increased by 40 per cent for the great majority of passengers. The quantity of provisions had been almost doubled, and the first step taken towards furnishing the emigrants with a full diet as against the barest minimum of bread and water. As for the runners and brokers, their business had been subjected to the most minute and overbearing regulations, from the requirement that runners carry written authorities in their pockets, or that brokers send signed lists of their agents monthly to the emigration officer, to the extraordinarily severe demands of annual licences, and bonds of £200 guaranteed by two sureties of substance. Yet the act must not be accepted at its face value. Certainly, both in itself and as a stage in the gradual process of improvement it did raise the standards in the trade. But the actual advances fell far short of the expectations. The new numbers clause was the only one which was fully enforced. The success of the foodstuffs clause—involving as it did many new difficulties of enforcement because of the number of the commodities and the relative smallness of the quantities—was but partial; and both the berthing and the brokers and runners clauses were ineffective. The first was generally ignored; and an attempt to put the most crucial elements of the second into practice at Liverpool in the spring of 1850 failed altogether.[2]

The comparative failure of the 1849 act to achieve its objects is revealing. The fundamental reason for this failure was the intolerable burden which was being placed already upon the executive

[1] Ibid., 361 Miscellaneous, 13 Jan. 1849.
[2] See above, p. 36.

officers. The pressure upon the executive had increased by leaps
and bounds since 1845, and it was to increase still further in the
1850s. This raised new problems in the field of emigrant protection,
problems which, by and large, were never solved, except in part by
extraneous and accidental forces. The mere physical load of inspections and other work was growing inordinately. Whereas the volume
of emigration increased fourfold during the 1840s, the executive ✓
corps was not even doubled in size. Moreover, the disproportion
was worst precisely where additional officers were needed most, at
ports like Cork and Liverpool. This undermanning was further and
very greatly aggravated by the rapid multiplication of the officer's
duties and the increasing complexity of his tasks. Each new piece of
legislation increased the load. Let us take some of the new features
of the 1849 act as an example. To arrange the berthing so that the
sexes were separated, to check all brokers' lists of agents and runners'
letters of authority, to test and count the tea and sugar, molasses and
rice—to perform even these few new duties thoroughly would have
added hours to a day which was already much too short. Finally, the
advancing regulation carried (or should have carried) with it more
statistics to be collected, more returns to be furnished, more negotiations with brokers, more court appearances. Nor was the physical
the only pressure upon the officer. There were also new technical
and psychological burdens. The discretionary powers which the
legislation of 1847-9 had heaped upon him formed, to say the least,
an *embarras de richesse*. Could the officer really adjudicate the
mechanics of ventilation devices or the professional qualifications of
physicians? Was it fair or even sensible to expect him (living and
working amongst the people whom he did) to disallow sureties, to
reject ship surgeons or medical officers upon the grounds of personal unfitness, to lay down the rate of payment for his medical
colleagues, to specify the number of the crew or the type of ovens
and utensils to be employed in the passengers' galley, and so on? A
man like Low might have welcomed the opportunity to play the
despot. But most of the officers did not, and these duties were almost
universally neglected. Clearly the corollary of the 1847-9 legislation
should have been a large increase in the number of, and a considerable degree of specialization in, the corps. But neither came about.
Only two additional appointments were made in the years 1848-50.
A second assistant was sent to Liverpool in 1849, and a temporary

officer was stationed at Scattery Roads at the mouth of the Shannon in 1850. Both appointments were long overdue. Hodder and his staff at Liverpool had been overwhelmed with work for several years,[1] and the Limerick officer had never succeeded in checking illegal embarkations along the sixty miles of shore-line between that port and the sea.[2] But there were all the usual difficulties of finance,[3] and even these desperately needed posts had been hardly won. The commissioners did not so much as seek any greater enlargement.[4]

Thus the chasm between law and practice widened almost year by year, and the flaw in the protective system grew. But it must be repeated that this failure was but comparative, a failure in relation to what was aimed at and proclaimed, not a failure absolute. In absolute terms there could be no question but that the trade was steadily improving, and that the 1849 act contributed something to this upward trend. All the colonial emigration agents testified to the act's good effects. Certainly, the passenger space[5] was substantially increased. The old difficulties of enforcement—the perennial problems of stowaways and unwatched headlands, of measuring unencumbered surfaces and determining ages—did persist.[6] But relatively speaking their effect was small. In few cases would the evasions have added more than 5 per cent to the legal complements. Again, although there can be little doubt that the provisions actually issued fell below what the law demanded both in quantity and whole-

---

[1] C.O. 384/84, 2663 and 2888 Emigration, 29 Mar. and 4 Apr. 1849.

[2] Cf. *Papers rel. emigration B.N.A.*, 4–5, H.C. 1849 (593–II), xxxviii; *Copies despatches rel. emigration B.N.A*, 14–15, H.C. 1850 (384), xl.

[3] The manœuvres preceding the Limerick appointment were extraordinary. The commissioners still believed that the customs officers were quite unreliable for emigration work, and all references to them had to be suppressed in the application to the treasury lest the new task be handed over to them to save the £100 p.a. at stake. The Scattery Roads assistant had to provide his own boat out of his salary, C.O. 384/81, 918 and 1250 Emigration, 3 May and 22 June 1848; C.O. 384/84, 369 Emigration, 13 Jan. 1849; C.O. 384/85, 3111 Emigration and endorsements, 17 Apr. 1850; 3885 Emigration, 13 May 1850 and 6434 North America.

[4] On the contrary, they provided 'compensations' to the treasury by withdrawing some of the Irish assistant officers appointed in 1847. This had particularly bad effects at Galway, C.O. 384/86, 9462 North America, 13 Nov. 1851; *1st rep. select comm. emigrant ships*, 35, H.C. 1854 (163), xiii.

[5] *Copies despatches rel. emigration B.N.A.*, 4–5, 40, 46, H.C. 1850 (348), xl. See also *Hans.*, 3rd, cxiv, 1164, 10 Mar. 1851 (speech of Grey).

[6] On the problem of stowaways, see C.O. 384/84, 10688 Emigration, 14 Dec. 1849.

someness, they were still immeasurably superior to the former daily wedge of navy bread. And there were even some indications that fraud and impositions were being dealt with more effectively. Twenty-eight successful prosecutions were undertaken during 1849 and—most telling of all—no less than five Liverpool brokers were deprived of their licences.[1] It is true that the death rate for 1849 itself, almost 3 per cent, was the second highest during the 1840s. But, as the commissioners very forcibly argued, when the extent of cholera in the United Kingdom in 1849 was considered, and a comparison made with its effects upon the emigrations of 1832–4, there was much reason to be thankful. 'We trust it is not presumptuous', they wrote, 'to attribute this result, under Providence, to the greater care now observed in the medical inspection of emigrants before they are allowed to embark—to the better regulations on board—and to the limitation of the numbers in proportion to space and tonnage'.[2]

But the argument must shift ground yet again. While it is true that the improvement in the trade was steady, substantial and absolute, it is also true that the trade was still, in many of its aspects, quite disgraceful. This was but gradually revealed. The administrator's inherent bias towards complacency and accepting the familiar as immutable (all the more powerful in this instance because he could point to considerable achievements) worked as ever below the surface. There was moreover the dreadful memory of 1847, in contrast with which nothing seemed disturbing. The first awakening came with C. A. Wood's visit to Liverpool to discuss the lodging-house problem at that port. On the basis of his observations, and of his conversations with the emigration officers, magistrates and city councillors on the spot, the commissioners produced a report on fraud in Liverpool which might almost have been extracted from one of Low's earlier accounts. The runners, crimps and lodging-keepers who systematically defrauded the emigrants; the cheating in the money exchange and retail shops attached to lodgings and brokers' offices; the broken contracts and delays arising from the Irish practices of pre-paying passages or booking them through sub-agents; and the general dangers of disease and destitution to which

[1] *10th rep. C.L.E.C.*, 12 [1204], H.C. 1850, xxiii. Ten of the cases were settled out of court.
[2] Ibid., 23.

the lodging-houses and the runners exposed the Irish were all once more described.[1] The commissioners appear to have reacted strongly to Wood's revelations. The severity of the brokers and runners clauses in the 1849 act, Hodder's determined effort to eradicate unauthorized runners from the trade, and the five Liverpool brokers who lost their licences in 1849, are all evidence of a considerable attempt to stamp out these abuses. But it is unlikely that the commissioners were under any illusions as to the very limited achievements of the 1849 offensive. Indeed, at the year's end they qualified their hopes for the success of the brokers and runners clauses by the careful phrase, 'so far as these objects are capable of being effected by legislation'.[2] In fact, they were never seriously concerned about their relative failure in this field. They always took the view that short of a central depot being established their liability for the pre-embarkation happenings was, in the nature of things, extremely limited; that it was confined, in fact, to ensuring that properly completed contracts were fulfilled. Any further success was a windfall, a supererogation. 'The emigrants', said Murdoch in 1854, 'do not come within our view until they are almost on the point of embarking'; and he refused point blank to entertain a suggestion that the emigration officers should direct emigrants to respectable lodgings and regulate their fares and contracts.[3] The embarkation, the mustering on deck and the voyage were very different matters. Here the commissioners accepted a full responsibility, and harboured many more delusions. Three events in 1851 were to reveal, suddenly and to their vast embarrassment and surprise, that these affairs were little better managed than the others.

The first premonitory shock was felt in the course of a commons debate upon a new amendment bill in February 1851.[4] This was a routine measure designed to supply deficiencies which had appeared in the existing legislation. One clause empowered the commissioners to alter the diet scale and various other requirements in the case of steam vessels, whose passages would, of course, be much shorter than the average. A second required foreign masters to enter special

---

[1] C.O. 384/84, 4584 Emigration, 22 May, 1849.
[2] *10th rep. C.L.E.C.*, 11–12 [1204], H.C. 1850, xxiii.
[3] *2nd rep. select comm. emigrant ships*, 45–48, H.C. 1854 (349), xiii. Murdoch added, 'there is nothing would justify such an interference as that'.
[4] *Hans.*, 3rd, cxiv, 769–71, 16 Feb. 1851.

bonds for due performance of the passenger acts, and a third required a certificate of fitness before re-sailing for all vessels which had put back to port in a damaged state. No doubt it was expected that the bill would pass smoothly and unchallenged into law. But not merely were the particular clauses criticized, upon technical grounds, as insufficient or ill-drawn; there was also a demand from Sidney Herbert that the whole bill be postponed pending a parliamentary inquiry (for which he gave due notice of motion) into the operation of the passenger acts.[1] 'The evils of [the Irish] emigration', said Herbert, 'arise through the absence of all precautions as to health, cleanliness, or the separation of the sexes in the emigrant vessels. Indeed, the state of these vessels is such as to generate disease and immorality of every description'. The bill was not withdrawn.[2] But neither was Herbert's motion. At last the passenger acts were to be exposed to the (occasionally, at least) fearless and favourless Star Chamber of the Victorian age, the parliamentary select committee. It was the beginning of the end of the self-satisfaction with which the commissioners had regarded the progress of emigration since the great catastrophe.

[1] It is not clear what prompted Herbert to ask for an inquiry. Grey and the commissioners had been heavily assailed during 1850, mainly by Lord Mountcashell, on account of the alleged abuses in Australian emigration which they managed. But Herbert specifically excluded the Australian emigration from his terms of reference.

[2] It became law, in time to be operative for the new emigration season, as 14 & 15 Vic. c. 1.

10

THE FIFTH REFORM

1851-2

THE first revelation of 1851 came from Vere Foster, a social reformer like de Vere, who had made the Atlantic crossing as a steerage passenger in an American vessel at the end of 1850. Foster's report of his experiences aroused considerable interest in both the United Kingdom and the United States.[1] The commissioners, stung perhaps by the unusual publicity, took up Foster's complaints immediately[2] and published his account of the treatment of passengers on the *Washington* in the parliamentary papers. Although the *Washington* was a large new liner built especially for passengers and one of the best-known vessels of the powerful Black Star company, Foster exposed a dreadful system of imposition and intimidation on the part of the ship's officers—even the physician was described as a foul-mouthed bully who touted for money amongst the emigrants— and many flagrant breaches of the passengers acts, so far as they concerned the voyage. Nor were the scandals confined to events at sea. Both directly and indirectly, Foster impugned the emigration and medical officer's inspections at Liverpool. In fact, the latter was described in these words, 'I passed before him [the physician] . . . which occupied only one or two seconds. He said without drawing his breath, "What's your name? Are you well? Hold out your tongue: all right," and then passed on'.[3]

Foster being a witness of unquestionable probity, the commissioners were naturally perturbed by his report. But when, eager to make an example where the climate of opinion seemed so favourable and the testimony so sound, they sought to institute a prosecution for the impudent flouting of the passenger acts at sea, a fatal flaw in the protective system was disclosed. This was the impossibility of enforcing United Kingdom law upon foreign vessels *after* they had

[1] C.O. 384/88, 9428 North America, 12 Nov. 1851.
[2] Ibid., 518 North America, 17 Jan. 1851.
[3] *Treatment of passengers on board* Washington, 1–6, H.C. 1851 (198), xl.

sailed. 'There is', as the commissioners later put it, 'no power of enforcing . . . upon Foreign Ships, as soon as they are clear of the Land'.[1] Before 1848 this would have mattered relatively little. American vessels bound for the United States (which constituted more than 90 per cent of the class concerned) were subject to congressional enactments when at sea, and in one of the most important relevant requirements, the numbers ratio, American legislation was considerably ahead of British.[2] As to pre-embarkation and embarkation matters, these could of course be dealt with by the United Kingdom officer before or at the mustering. But from 1848 onwards the situation was very different. The imperial legislation of 1848–9 attempted to secure life, decency and comfort on the voyage to an extent which congress did not essay;[3] and one clear lesson of Foster's report was that more rather than less regulation of the between-decks was required. Again, the Americans were capturing an ever-larger proportion of the Atlantic passenger trade. Were the commissioners, then, to be permanently frustrated in their efforts to improve conditions during the voyage so far as fully two-thirds of their charges were concerned? An attempt was made to close the gap when a clause was tacked on to the amendment bill of 1851 requiring foreign masters to enter bonds for faithful performance of the requirements of the imperial code.[4] But for technical reasons which we shall discuss below the clause proved a dead-letter from the outset for the great majority of offences. It is, of course, easy to exaggerate the importance of the new issue. Whatever

[1] C.O. 384/92, 449 North America, 10 Jan. 1854.

[2] The congressional act of 1819, which remained unchanged until 1847, limited the numbers aboard to two passengers for every five tons (custom-house measurement) and required vessels to carry 60 gallons of water and 200 lb. of foodstuffs for every adult passenger. This last was a precaution against starvation: the vessels were not required to *issue* the 200 lb. But the penalties for overcrowding were severe; if more than twenty above the complement were carried, the vessel might be forfeited, *An act regulating passenger ships and vessels*, 2 Mar. 1819. The congressional amendment act of 1847 increased the severity of these requirements, but otherwise added no new burdens, *An act, to regulate the carriage of passengers* . . . 22 Feb. 1847.

[3] The only features of between-decks life which congress even attempted to regulate were ventilation and cooking places, *An act to provide for the ventilation of passenger vessels, and for other purposes*, 17 May 1848, and *An act to extend the provisions of all laws now in force relating to the carriage of passengers* . . . 3 Mar. 1849. See also C.O. 384/88, 6313 Emigration, 29 July 1850.

[4] American masters had entered bonds before 1851, but these had never been put to the test and were in fact worthless.

their deficiencies, American vessels were still generally and rightly regarded as superior to the British, and the commissioners' control over even the British vessels, when at sea, was slight.[1] None the less, the Vere Foster episode did expose, clearly and for the first time, both the relative ineffectiveness of all passenger legislation so far as the voyage was concerned, and the total want of power over foreign ships.

The second revelation of 1851 was the accidental discovery that the chief emigration officer at Liverpool had solved the problem of enforcing the passenger acts by the simple neglect of many of his duties.[2] An investigation into Hodder's procedure, which followed an angry complaint from the port officer at New Orleans, disclosed several omissions; and the report of his successor at Liverpool, Commander Patey, revealed a most shocking state of things. During Hodder's six years in office, no ships bound for the United States were ever measured; he had accepted without question the master's own estimate of the passenger space. Nor had there been any attempt to test the water-casks, or any proper mustering of passengers. The officer had merely checked the passenger list, supplied to him by the broker, to see that the number did not exceed the maximum, calculated from the master's estimate. Thus, there was no official guarantee of either the legal or actual complement of any American vessel between 1846 and 1851. Finally, wrote Patey, ships were often passed before any emigrants had come aboard, and even before the cargo had been stowed. The clearance was 'a matter of form', often taking place while the vessel left the dock, in the midst of the most dreadful confusion, with passengers and luggage being thrown aboard at the eleventh hour.[3] Such was the reality of the Liverpool inspection in the famine years.

No less interesting than this disclosure of neglect is the fact that the commissioners fought hard to prevent Hodder's dismissal. They were unsuccessful.[4] As Elliot wrote, whatever Hodder's merits the government could not 'overlook a systematic omission for one year after another to perform one of the leading functions imposed

---

[1] C.O. 384/92, 449 North America, 10 Jan. 1854.

[2] C.O. 384/86, 5705 North America, 1 July 1851.

[3] C.O. 384/86, 6983 North America Emigration, 30 July 1851. See also *Morning Chronicle*, 15 July 1850, p. 6.

[4] Three years later, a Lieut. Hodder was employed by the commissioners to select assisted emigrants for Australia. It may have been the same man.

on the Emigration Officers, without a hint that from the extent of the business or any other cause, it was so omitted': this was a 'Public Question'.[1] But the commissioners had good reason for their disquietude. It was not merely that Hodder's response to the famine crisis as a whole had been magnificent, or that the Liverpool magistrates and merchants alike paid tribute to his tact and energy.[2] It was not even (as was now generally acknowledged) that it was physically impossible for the Liverpool officers to perform all their tasks. What really touched the commissioners to the quick was Hodder's defence against the charge that he should have demanded more assistance, namely, 'the extreme *reluctance* which was shewn whenever I spoke [of increases in the Liverpool establishment]'.[3] This—for the 'reluctance' was never denied—was the root of the matter. The commissioners were surely guilty of contributory negligence or cowardice. A very little reflection would have told them that three men could not thoroughly inspect thirty vessels in a day, when the ships often lay four miles apart along the docks,[4] and each inspection —to say nothing of all the other duties—should have occupied at least four hours. Hodder was in fact the unlucky victim of the collision between the impulse to reform, born of compassion and expert knowledge, and the mania for governmental economy.

Belatedly, the commissioners tried to save the situation at Liverpool. Patey proposed a large number of reforms including the measurement afresh of all vessels; the filling of the water-casks at least a day before the examination;[5] the stowage of all cargo, luggage and provisions before the inspection; the rejection of all contract tickets which were not fully and accurately completed;[6] and the postponement of the final inspection until the vessel was actually ready to sail, even if this meant boarding her in mid-river. He also poured scorn upon the current medical examinations, which, he wrote, were often evaded, or took place many days before the sailing;

[1] C.O. 384/86, 5705 North America, 1 July 1851. Grey concurred, see his endorsement, 2 July 1851.

[2] Ibid., 6897 North America, undated. See also C.O. 384/80, 651 and 652 Emigration, 19 Apr. 1847; A Mills, *Systematic colonization* (London, 1847), p. 24.

[3] 384/86, 5705 North America, 1 July 1851.

[4] C.O. 384/84, 2663 Emigration, 29 Mar. 1849.

[5] So that leaks &c., might be discovered. Patey also proposed as a further check that no casks be put aboard until after they had been inspected.

[6] Patey reported that these were often either incomplete or fraudulently filled out.

8

and he suggested instead that two inspections be held, one upon the emigrant's arrival at Liverpool, the other at the time of the last muster aboard ship.[1] Patey's final requests were for more assistants, wider summary powers and a cutter for mid-river examinations.[2] The commissioners accepted these recommendations *en bloc* and assured Patey that his powers would be extended as he wished when the next passenger bill was being prepared.[3] They admitted that the neglect at Liverpool had been disgraceful, attributing it, quite rightly, to the vast increase in the Liverpool emigration, and still more to the numerous additions to the emigration officer's duties since 1842.[4] They even overcame the reluctance of Herman Marivale (Stephen's successor as permanent under-secretary) to ask the treasury for money, and eventually secured the additional assistants and the cutter for which Patey asked.[5] They were also called on to help Patey in another way. One consequence of his efforts at reform was that war was declared between the American masters and the new officer at Liverpool. Supported by the United States consul at the port, the Americans sailed their ships away without complying with the imperial legislation, which they dismissed as 'too troublesome' and 'an annoyance'.[6] The pirate flag of free enterprise was soon run up. One captain proclaimed, 'if I am not Capable of Judging what is proper for the Stowage and Management of any Ship after twenty-one years, Masters of American Ships leaving this Port may hereafter know that the Confidence hitherto reposed in them has been misplaced'.[7] The commissioners stood firm. They insisted that their officer continue to exercise his powers to the full, and that bonds be enforced to make

[1] Patey asserted that many passengers slipped by without any medical certificate, and that in other cases healthy persons were substituted for sickly in order to get the tickets 'stamped'. The second check aboard ship would prevent fraud and also, it was hoped, weed out those who had become infected in the interval.

[2] C.O. 384/86, 6983 North America, 30 July 1851.

[3] Ibid., 6983 North America, endorsements of 9 and 13 Aug. 1851.

[4] Ibid., 10445 North America, 17 Dec. 1851. This, we may note, was the first reference ever made in the official papers to the immense widening in the scope and nature of the officer's work from 1842 onwards.

[5] They might have been hard put to it to redeem their first generous promise had not the select committee on the passenger acts reported in the meantime, and in doing so denounced with equal indignation the evils of the Liverpool trade and the insufficiency of the number of government officers.

[6] C.O. 384/88, 9669 and 10116 North America, 15 and 20 Nov. 1851.

[7] C.O. 384/88, 7161 Emigration, commissioners: Stanley, 20 Aug. 1851.

an example of the recalcitrant.[1] But the large extent of these reforms is also a measure of the previous deficiencies; and with it
all neither the commissioners nor Patey were now sanguine as to
their ultimate success.

The third and most comprehensive and dispiriting of the revelations of 1851, was the report of the select committee upon the
operation of the passenger acts. The report, which also summarized
the evidence, made melancholy reading, the committee's general
conclusions being that the existing legislation did not give adequate
guarantees of safety, decency or health. Liverpool was the first subject of complaint. We have already described sufficiently the systematic fraud which marked the Liverpool trade, and the ineffectiveness of the earlier efforts at improvement. But the committee, learn-
ing of the true state of things at first hand and for the first time, was
profoundly shocked. Murdoch recounted the sad story of the central
depot project, and went on to describe how Liverpool's mercantile
interests had subsequently succeeded in getting the powers of the
Liverpool dock committee, in a private bill currently before parliament, watered down from those of establishing such a depot to a
mere right to lease buildings to individuals for this purpose.[2] Two
men who had already set up emigrants' homes under the encouragement of the dock committee were then examined.[3] The first,
Frederick Sabell, reported that financially his venture was not unsuccessful: more than 4,000 emigrants had lodged at his home during
1850. But he had been thoroughly discouraged by the 'unscrupulous combinations' of runners who had actually entered his house
and laid hands upon the emigrants in their efforts to wreck the
project. He was no better pleased with the emigrants themselves.
Many were, he said, filthy in their habits; his attempts to segregate
the sexes were repeatedly broken down; and nothing short of policing
the entire building would adequately protect single women. The
other hostel-keeper, Frederick Marshall, did guard unaccom-
panied women by providing a completely separate apartment for

---

[1] C.O. 384/88, 9286 Emigration, 7 Nov. 1851. This last was not an empty
threat in these cases where there was no difficulty of jurisdiction or of furnishing
evidence to secure a conviction.

[2] *Rep. select comm. passenger acts*, 754–64, H.C. 1851 (632), xix. See also ibid.,
ix–xi.

[3] For an earlier attempt to establish a home of this type for Munster emigrants,
see *Tipperary Vindicator*, 3 Mar. 1849.

them. But he, too, testified to the fierce resistance of the bands of runners, who assaulted and 'dragged away' the emigrants, seized their luggage and demonstrated and hooted constantly in front of the house.[1] Several reputable witnesses, either despairing of any lesser remedy, or inspired by the recent success of the shipping offices established under the mercantile marine act in protecting sailors, begged the state to reconsider its decision on the central depot.[2] One of these witnesses, a Liverpool barrister, Sir George Stephen, went so far as to advocate in addition the compulsory allotment of emigrants to particular vessels.[3]

To these appeals the select committee replied that other means should be tried 'before so great a departure from principle should be sanctioned as the undertaking by the state of functions which are legitimately within the province of private enterprise'.[4] But it did admit that a comprehensive government depot might in the end prove necessary; and it also proposed that all runners, porters and lodging-keepers should be badged and licensed, and that the police, armed with wider powers, should exercise a much more strict surveillance.[5]

The committee next found that the emigration officers' examinations at Liverpool and some of the Irish ports were scamped and insufficient, and recommended an increase in staff.[6] But it was the

[1] *Rep. select comm. passenger acts*, 132, 427-9, 436-9, H.C. 1851 (632), xix (evidence of Lieut. Hodder, F. Sabell and F. Marshall). Both Sabell and Marshall appear to have been 'respectable'; certainly they were warmly supported by both the local and emigration authorities. Sabell was a German, and many of his clients were his own countrymen emigrating via Liverpool, although he also catered for the Irish. Marshall's home was almost exclusively used by the Irish. A chaplain was attached, and the home was warmly recommended to their flocks by the Irish catholic clergy. *2nd rep. Emigrant Society* (Dublin, 1851).

[2] *Rep. select comm., passenger acts*, 157-9, 222-3, 318-19, H.C. 1851 (632), xix (evidence of G. Hadfield, Lieut. Prior and Sir G. Stephen). Hadfield and Stephen were 'social reformers', and Prior the senior assistant emigration officer at Liverpool. Stephen was also a cousin of James Stephen, and a *bête noire* of Elliot's.

[3] Ibid., 316-17.

[4] Ibid., xi-xii.

[5] Ibid., xii-xiii.

[6] The committee was almost as shocked to learn of the plight of the Cork and Limerick officers, who had to deal with 10,000 persons annually unaided and cover several outports into the bargain, as to hear that three men had to cope with more than 150,000 emigrants each year at Liverpool. The committee, however, recognized that the United Kingdom inspections could never furnish a complete security, but must always depend more or less upon the supplementary American examinations upon disembarkation.

medical inspections which aroused most wrath. It was discovered that as the emigrants passed through the surgery in a line the doctor merely looked at their tongues, and if satisfied with this stamped their contract tickets. With up to a thousand persons jostling in and out of the 'doctor's shop' each day, the inspection was, in Sabell's words, 'a regular farce . . . two doctors employed in looking at the people's tongues and stamping tickets as fast as they can; that is no inspection'.[1] There was moreover no means of checking whether the person who owned the ticket was the person who had passed the test; and in any event the emigrant returned to his lodging after the examination, so that, for all practical purposes, its object was defeated.[2]

The findings of the select committee confirmed, and even exceeded in horror, Vere Foster's report on life at sea. It was established that, the 1849 act notwithstanding, berthing was still commonly arranged in a numerical sequence without regard to the sex or age of passengers. Men, women and children, crowded into a single steerage deck, had to undress and sleep together without a pretence of decency. The berths, which were insecurely divided, held four persons each, usually covered by a single blanket. 'I have known', said the port chaplain at Liverpool, 'cases of females who have had to sit up all night on their boxes because they could not think of going to bed with strange men'.[3] The emigration officer at Londonderry admitted that, even after the passage of the 1849 act, indiscriminate berthing had led to a great deal of immorality upon the Irish vessels; he added that before 1849 conditions had been really 'dreadful': girls had often come to him in an hysterical state when they learned how the berthing had been arranged.[4] The picture of sanitation at sea was just as black. In the few cases where water-closets were provided, they were said to have been altogether inadequate in number and so insubstantial that the first heavy sea

[1] Ibid., 409–11. In defence of the physicians it must be said that there were never more than three employed, that they worked all day long, and that their remuneration was less than $2\frac{1}{2}d.$ per cap.

[2] Ibid., xvi, 104–6.

[3] Ibid., 195–6 (evidence of Rev. J. Welch).

[4] Ibid., 629–32 (evidence of Lieut. Smith). Lieut. Friend testified that the Cork vessels were relatively free from these abuses. This he attributed to the almost universal Cork practice of providing a 'protector' for a girl travelling outside a family, ibid., 489–90, 493–4.

swept them overboard.[1] Both Lieut. Friend and Sabell were very doubtful whether, even had the privies been sufficient and effective, passengers would have used them properly: the emigrants were often content to 'live like pigs' between decks, where filth and effluvium were recklessly allowed to accumulate.[2] Again, it was discovered that the clause in the 1848 act governing cooking and cooking places was ineffective. Where stoves had been introduced they had worked badly; there was no order or regularity in the service; the weak went to the wall, and were often reduced to eating raw flour and water.[3] Nor had the new foodstuffs clause of the 1849 act lived up to even the most modest expectations at the time of its passage. Apart from the difficulties of ensuring wholesome provisions and full measures, the clause had one unforeseen but unfortunate consequence. Owners supplied less of the bulky and perishable oatmeal and potatoes to which the Irish were accustomed. But the foods which were convenient for the owners were also unfamiliar to the Irish, who often attempted to eat rice, molasses and the rest uncooked[4].

Finally the committee dealt with omissions and imperfections in the acts themselves[5]. The current system of surveying was condemned, the report pointing out that, in estimating space, British surveyors included parts of the vessel which could not be occupied, whereas the Americans sensibly based their calculations upon the living quarters only. Again it was found that the lifeboats provided under the acts were altogether insufficient—a very simple exercise in arithmetic established this—and that the cargo was often stowed unsafely. Further, it reported several loopholes in the statutes of which the unscrupulous might take advantage. Thus, for example, passengers whose vessel was wrecked—and not merely damaged— might still receive no compensation whatsoever;[6] or a master might take bad provisions on board as well as good and then issue only the

---

[1] Ibid., 486 (evidence of Lieut. Friend).

[2] Ibid., 416–30, 491–2.

[3] Most emigrants were sea-sick for the first three or four days; little cooking was done; the ship's officers and crew had no time to spare; and disorder was consequently established from the start, ibid., 417–20.

[4] It was not uncommon for the Irish passengers to attempt to smoke tea in their pipes, *Morning Chronicle*, 15 July 1850.

[5] *Rep. select comm. passenger acts*, xviii–xxi, H.C. 1851 (632), xix.

[6] The existing legislation demanded compensation only if a vessel were *damaged* and put back into port, not if it were actually wrecked.

former when he was out of port; or owners or charterers might supply only unwholesome provisions in the first instance, knowing that even were the fraud detected they would go scot-free, as penalties were imposed only if the vessel had actually *cleared* without sound foodstuffs.[1] Nor did the want of power over American vessels at sea escape attention. The committee recommended that all these weaknesses in drafting and otherwise be immediately corrected. As for the American vessels, they shrewdly noted that the only satisfactory solution was a close agreement between the United States and British governments and suggested that negotiations be at once commenced. We have already mentioned their proposals for Liverpool which were also to apply in so far as appropriate to the Irish ports. Their recommendations for life at sea were equally bold. The centrepiece of their scheme was the compulsory employment, at least on the larger vessels, of passenger stewards whose sole business would be the promotion of the welfare of the emigrants.[2] The steward was to superintend the berthing, messing and cooking, to maintain order and cleanliness in the steerage, and generally to promote health and decency. As to the rest, the committee recommended that sanitation be no longer left to the discretion of the emigration officers but subjected to minute regulations; that all food be served to the passengers in a cooked state; that ship-owners be compelled to supply beds, and sufficient cooking and other utensils for the passengers; that no more than two persons be permitted to occupy the same berth; and that all single men be cut off by a bulkhead from the remainder of the passengers.[3]

[1] If the unwholesomeness of the provisions were detected by the emigration officer, they might be withdrawn and good provisions substituted. There is no evidence that owners and masters were in fact aware of these various loopholes in the statutes, or that they took advantage of them. On several occasions owners or masters were fined by magistrates for merely *embarking* unwholesome provisions.

[2] The masters of a few of the larger Liverpool vessels had adopted the practice of selecting five or six of the most respectable passengers to act as monitors, or else allowing the passengers to choose their own leaders, *Morning Chronicle*, 15 July 1850. Apart from the practice being confined to a handful of vessels, it was obviously open to abuse in various ways.

[3] *Rep. select comm. passenger acts*, xx–xxx, H.C. 1851 (632), xix. A proposal that all single women be also placed in a separate compartment divided by a bulkhead was rejected upon the ground that most parents would prefer to protect their daughters themselves, and not to expose them to bad companions in the 'female quarters'.

The report then mercilessly stripped away any remaining illusions about the success of the legislation of the 1840s and the general condition of the trade. It may also appear to have exposed the commissioners, by implication at least, as supine and ineffectual.[1] Such an inference would not have been altogether unjust. The commissioners had not, of course, the committee's capacity to call for evidence, nor could they shroud large demands with the same air of impartiality and authority. But it was, after all, the emigration officers themselves who had supplied most of the evidence to the committee; and the commissioners had certainly proposed some very bold expedients in former years. In fact, it cannot be denied that the commissioners' approach to their task was passive and desk-bound. They did not search out evils or check systematically the effectiveness of the measures, which, under one exterior pressure or another, they had launched. They rarely journeyed to the ports or summoned their officers to London. In short, they did not make trouble for themselves. None the less, upon a more general plane, a very fair defence may be made out. The report of the committee had many merits. It was fair, conscientiously drawing attention to all reports of improvements, even in matters such as the lodging-house in Liverpool or sexual morality at sea, where the general picture was so black; it was ingenious, as the exposure of so many obscure flaws in the existing legislation will indicate; it was shrewd and unsentimental, eschewing the easy road of recommending a larger diet in favour of the better course of ensuring that the passengers received their current due; it argued logically and firmly, as in its conclusions upon the problem of foreign vessels, or the necessity for an emigrants' champion and tutor in the between-decks. But for all its merits the report dealt only, however well, with the surfaces of things. The committee did not appreciate the fundamental difficulties—the narrow limits of the staff and monies at the commissioners' disposal; the fact that in both its quantity and nature the work which was being laid upon the executive officers outstripped their capacities; the limitations of parliamentary enactments in themselves; and the government's reliance upon emigration as the only hopeful prospect in the Irish murk, with the corollary

[1] The fact that the report ended with a conventional tribute to the commissioners' endeavours does not, of course, automatically exclude such a gloss upon the main body of the observations.

that 'no unnecessary obstacles' be erected. Nor was it understood that the problems were partly new, some of them dating from 1846 at earliest; or that the standards to be expected from the trade had risen out of recognition both because of the sudden publicity which the famine emigration had received and because of the gradual shift in perspective which the passage of time always brought about. Nor was it realized that the commissioners' most heartfelt complaint might well have been directed against the very public on whose behalf the committee admonished and enjoined.

The last point deserves some consideration. Passenger legislation was now entering a more hostile atmosphere than any it had encountered since the 1820s. It was caught between a crossfire of intellectuals and practical men. Their larger victories won, some radicals, philosophical and free trade alike, began to notice this little canker in the rose; and as emigration mounted to the level of a great and steady business, richer and more influential shippers moved in to reap the profits and resent the bureaucrats. The state was equally assailed by the intellectuals for the inefficiency and the impropriety of its interference. 'Until spontaneously fulfilled a public want should not be fulfilled at all', declared an article in the *Westminster*, 'Side by side with the Emigration Board under whose management hundreds die of fever, from close packing, and under whose licence sail vessels which, like the *Washington*, are homes of fraud, brutality, tyranny and obscenity, stands Mrs Chisholm's Family Colonization Loan Society,[1] which does not provide worse accommodation than before but much better; which does not demoralize by promiscuous crowding; which does not pauperize by charity but encourages providence; which does not increase our taxes but is self-supporting . . . Social vitality may be trusted to by-and-by fulfill each much exaggerated requirement in some quiet spontaneous way'.[2] 'Shipping', wrote the *Economist*, 'is one of the ordinary businesses of individuals, and if Governments are to prevent negligence in carrying it out, it ought to have boards to watch over the business habits and conduct of all tailors, shoemakers and

---

[1] The contrast was most misleading. Mrs Chisholm's society was, in fact, financed to a considerable extent by aristocratic philanthropists, and many of the loans were never repaid; while Mrs Chisholm herself was a very warm advocate of the extension of passenger legislation, M. Kiddle, *Caroline Chisholm* (Melbourne, 1948), Chaps. iv–vi.

[2] 'Over-legislation' by 'J. Chapman' in *Westminster Review*, lx, pp. 70, 74–75.
8*

234 A PATTERN OF GOVERNMENT GROWTH

merchants in the kingdom'; what would happen 'if, wholly forgetful
of sound principle, it continues to give effect by law to all the temporary alarms of ignorance and the crochets of sentiment?'[1] Surely
the heedless extension of state action introduced dangerous novelties: if emigrants were to be pampered, why not other classes in the
community? Stephen had been disturbed by this very problem as
early as 1835 when he rejected a new proposal for combating fraud
upon the ground that 'you introduce a new principle into the law of
England, the benefit of which might be claimed with equal justice
by any other helpless and ignorant class of persons'.[2]

And then there was the trade itself to be considered. The
passenger business of Liverpool alone was worth over a million
pounds a year and employed more than half a million tons of shipping: 'the folly', as the Liverpool chamber of commerce grandly
observed, 'of throwing needless obstacles in the way of such a
trade is very obvious'.[3] The commissioners were well aware that
business counted for much in England of the 1850s. 'It is extremely
difficult', Murdoch admitted in 1854, 'for any government board to
interfere with matters connected with the regulation of the commerce of the country'.[4] 'These are not the days', wrote Elliot ner-
vously in the same year, 'in which trade is willing to be interfered
with more than can possibly be helped'.[5] Not that we should consider the officials as implacable, if covert, enemies of private enterprise. On the contrary, their inclination (as especially Elliot's) was
naturally towards the shibboleths of the day. One commonly finds
generalities of this kind amongst the office endorsements: 'Goods
and passengers find out the best channels—the first by the alertness
and intelligence of merchants, the second by self-interest enlightened
by the copious information afforded by competitors for custom' or

[1] *Economist*, 4 Apr. 1857, p. 365. See also *Illustrated London News*, 26 Apr.
1854, p. 178.
[2] C.O. 384/38, 63 Emigration, 15 Apr. 1835.
[3] C.O. 384/89, 3302 Emigration, 19 Apr. 1852. See also *The Times*, 10 Feb.
1859.
[4] *2nd rep. select comm. emigrant ships*, 50, H.C. 1854 (349), xiii.
[5] C.O. 384/92, 449 Emigration and endorsements, 10 Jan. 1854. The pugnacity of the trade was much accentuated by the feeling amongst British shippers that they were being steadily betrayed by parliament through such measures
as the repeal of the navigation acts, Lord Campbell's act and the mercantile
marine act; and passenger legislation was all the more resented because it inevitably bore more heavily upon British than upon foreign vessels, *Hans.*, 3rd,
cxxii, 69–70, 4 June 1852 (W. Brown).

'questions of private interest and convenience are much best weighed by private judgement'.[1] This acceptance of the current orthodoxy did not positively prevent the civil servants from extending the scope of their legislation. They were, rather, Occamists in the matter, keeping their faith in the 'broad principles' of laissez-faire apart from their consideration of the acts. None the less, this various outside pressure against the interference of the state must have confused the issues, tied down the imagination and narrowed the field of seeming possibilities.

But the period was also one in which public opinion was coming to demand—at least by implication—more state action instead of less. We have already seen that whenever the true condition of the passenger trade was revealed, and especially in times of calamity at sea, the cry went up for remedies at any price. At these junctures people who ordinarily denounced the improper interference of the state would complain of the ineffectiveness and timidity of the legislation.[2] As a superb instance of the professional's irritation at sentimental criticism, we may take Elliot's glittering reply to a demand by Palmerston for a ship surgeon for every vessel, which arose from a complaint from Limerick during an epidemic. The passenger code, wrote Elliot, 'has been cautiously and with peculiar pains compiled over many years'; it was the fruit of vast experience and of the careful consideration of a multitude of interests, 'which would not so much as enter the head of anyone who may write off on half a sheet of paper at the Home Office the first crude suggestion which may offer itself upon receiving a letter from the mayor of Limerick'.[3] We cannot but sympathize with Elliot's resentment of what he termed the 'meddling' of 'men of good intentions but no knowledge'. But neither should we forget that it was just this unreasonable humanitarianism which was the ultimate source of many of the reforms. However much the commissioners repudiated absolute responsibility in times of stress, the public—outrageously yet fruitfully—insisted that they should bear it. When, for example, Queenstown demanded a hulk for stricken passengers during the cholera outbreak, and the commissioners replied that the emigrants

[1] C.O. 384/88, 158 Canada and endorsements, 9 Jan. 1850.
[2] E.g., *The Times*, 27 Dec. 1853.
[3] C.O. 384/92, 851 North America, 18 Mar. 1854.

themselves should bear the expense since they derived the benefit, the town bluntly stated: 'the responsibility for providing for the health, and preserving the lives of the emigrants rests on the government of the country'. In similar circumstances, the mayor of Liverpool told the colonial secretary that emigrants had a positive right to 'that assistance, which a state is bound, and in this country always disposed, to afford a class peculiarly in need of protection'.[1] For 'responsibility' must lie somewhere, and faced with the realities of suffering and abuse, the ordinary man saw no alternative but to call upon the central power for action. Nor did his normal objections to regulation count for much in such a situation. It was not difficult after all—as Stanley had shown so many years before—to find reasons for treating passenger legislation as exceptional. One might base one's case (as one 'reformer' did) upon the fact that none of the usual restraints upon the merchant operated in this instance: 'The law will not practically touch them;[2] there is no public opinion; and their self-interest is not strongly acted on, because they will never see their customers again . . . emigrants are not to be compared to other persons; they are an exception; they are the most helpless people in the world'.[3] Or one might simply take the issue on its merits as did a Mr Bolton when he set aside the 'old dogma that government has no right to intervene in . . . the enterprise and speculation of the subject' in favour of twenty years' experience of an emigration which 'disgraced a Christian country. . . . Who can contend that there is not a full cause here for interference of government?'[4] The select committees of 1851 and 1854 followed, although tacitly and more soberly, Bolton's line of argument. The first was inclined to reserve the issue of the state-managed depot;[5] but

[1] C.O. 384/41, 612 Emigration, 16 Apr. 1836. See also 384/84, 9485 Emigration, 31 Oct. 1849.

[2] He may have meant the common law, which, theoretically, governed many of the relationships in the passenger trade.

[3] *2nd rep. select comm. emigrant ships*, 62, 64, H.C. 1854 (349), xiii. These were the observations of a social worker, S. Sidney.

[4] *The Health of Towns Journal*, 2 Dec. 1848.

[5] This 'reservation' may be explained perhaps by Benjamin Hawes's memberships of the committee. Not only would he have represented the colonial office view on this question; we must also remember that he was a strong opponent of the scheme from the very outset. Moreover, the fact that the report allowed that the central power might have to be called upon in the end suggests that there may have been some opposition to Hawes's line amongst the other members of the committee.

otherwise no consideration of 'principle' or precedent or even policy towards Ireland restrained its recommendations. The second was still more radical and downright.[1] Yet both committees were composed of the very type of men who might well have denounced excessive legislation had they learnt nothing at first hand of the miseries to be endured at sea. The members of each formed a very fair cross-section of the house of commons, or at any rate of the run-of-the-mill M.P.s—whigs and protectionists, Peelites and Irish, oligarchs, bankers, lawyers, admirals and squires. The most distinguished of the sixty-odd were perhaps the respective chairmen of the committees, Sidney Herbert and John O'Connell, and those perpetual under-secretaries, Hawes and Vernon Smith. None of these was a firebrand or an intellectual, to say the least; and the same is true *a fortiori* of the still more mediocre men. In short, the unleavened lump of the educated mid-Victorian public was thoroughly represented; and the reports are telling evidence of both the ultimate, crushing power of facts and the volatility of men's opinions. Together with the other parts of the survey they provide the setting for passenger legislation and executive practice in the last phase of our subject, of which we may, broadly speaking, say that in the actual formulation of the statutes the evidence before the select committees was such as to preclude all possible resistance by either doctrine or the trade; but that in the intervals between the statutes, and in the application of the new legislation, these forces were by no means powerless.

The consolidation act of 1852[2] was a most ambitious measure. To appreciate its scope and severity we must at least enumerate the manifold changes which it wrought. Vessels sailing without a clearance might now be declared forfeit. It was forbidden to use any but the main decks for passenger accommodation.[3] Stowaways and their abettors were rendered liable to three months' imprisonment. The number who might occupy the same berth was reduced from four to two,[4] and all single men above the age of fourteen years were to be placed in a completely separate compartment. Vessels

---

[1] *2nd rep. select comm. emigrant ships*, iv-v, H.C. 1854 (349), xiii.

[2] 15 & 16 Vic., c. 44.

[3] The worst vessels still accommodated passengers occasionally on the orlop deck down to 1852.

[4] But more than two members of the same family might still sleep together.

were required to provide sick bays, four to twelve privies,[1] two to six lifeboats, ventilation apparatus, life-buoys, night-signals and fire-engines, the size or number of all these varying according to the complement of passengers. Certain specifications were laid down in the act, but in general the emigration officer was to be the sole judge of the effectiveness of the mechanisms and arrangements. He was also empowered to reject absolutely any cargo or ballast which he 'deemed likely to endanger the health or lives of the passengers or the safety of the ship'; to pronounce upon the 'sweet or good condition' of all water and provisions and the charring and soundness of the casks; and compulsorily to re-land all or any of the passengers.[2] Finally, he was permitted to nominate the ship surveyors, although in this case the owner or charterer had certain rights of appeal against the surveyors' decision.[3]

To turn now to the actual passage, the act laid down that provisions were to be issued *daily* and *in a cooked state*. Every vessel with more than one hundred passengers aboard was required to employ a passenger steward whose sole business was to be the supervision of berthing and meals,[4] and a passenger cook whose sole business was to be the preparation of the food for passengers;[5] and irrespective of the amount of deck space which each passenger was allowed, every vessel with more than five hundred passengers aboard had now to employ a physician. Once again, it was the emigration officer who was to adjudicate the fitness of the stewards, cooks and physicians, and the suitability of the kitchens, ovens and medical supplies; and he might also require vessels with foreign passengers to employ an interpreter. As to the delays and disasters,

---

[1] The privies were required to be placed in different and specified parts of the vessel.

[2] He might also refuse to allow them to re-embark; and to encourage him to use his power where necessary it was provided that their fares were to be refunded to such passengers. The purpose of providing for the re-landing of all the passengers was to allow for the fumigation &c. of a vessel, in the case of infection.

[3] The owner or charterer might nominate three experienced shipwrights himself to act as a court of appeal. But only if their decision *unanimously* reversed that of the first surveyors would the vessel be permitted to sail. Thus, the chances of a successful appeal were small.

[4] The stewards were required to be 'sea-faring persons'.

[5] If the number of passengers exceeded four hundred, two cooks were to be provided.

if a vessel were wrecked or put back in a damaged state, the passengers were to receive appropriate compensation and another passage (or their original fares in lieu); and the colonial office or the
local British minister might return them to their port of departure
or forward them to their destination (as might be more convenient)
and recover the cost and all the expense of maintenance and re-
equipping from the owner or master as a crown debt; and vessels
which put back from sea or which were delayed for more than a
week before sailing were required to be completely replenished, re-
examined and re-cleared. Next, the commissioners were empowered
to draw up alternative food scales, to make regulations by order-in-
council 'for preserving order, for promoting health, and for securing
cleanliness and ventilation', and to prepare abstracts of passenger
legislation which masters were required to post in conspicuous
places on their vessels and produce upon request for any passenger's
perusal. Correspondingly, all port authorities were empowered to
make bye-laws governing entry to passenger docks, embarkation,
and the licensing of porters, and to attach penalties of up to £5 for
the breach of such bye-laws, and cause the offenders to be arrested
if necessary. Again, the bonds required of masters and brokers were
raised to £2,000 and £1,000 respectively. As to procedure, it was
enacted that all penalties and monies were recoverable before two
J.P.s; that two J.P.s might try a case in the absence of the defendant
if a summons were not answered; that one J.P. might issue a warrant,
without any preliminary summons, if he believed that the party
concerned was likely to abscond; that if the moneys or costs were
not immediately forthcoming two J.P.s might directly commit the
defendant to gaol for three months; that no objection be allowed or
conviction quashed 'for Want of Form'; and that no action might be
taken against an emigration officer without ten days' clear notice, or
after three months had elapsed, and that in any such action the
officer might 'plead General Issue and give the act and any Special
Matter in evidence'. Finally, the number of prescribed schedules
was increased to twelve, and included forms of summons, conviction
and order of adjudication for the benefit of J.P.s, although, as has
been indicated above, the J.P.'s decision would not fail if he did not
use, or used incorrectly, such a form.

As we said of the earlier consolidation act of 1842, however
tedious the enumeration of a long catalogue of provisions may be,

it is necessary if the character of the new legislation is to be understood. It was the mass and the interlocking of the detail which really told. Only when the vast, articulated accumulation is perceived and weighed, and it is remembered that the requirements of the 1852 act which we have listed were all additional burdens laid atop of the incubi of 1842–9, can the truly awful comprehension of the passenger code be grasped. There is no need to expatiate upon the regulatory, collectivist and bureaucratic nature of the statutes of 1842–52, and especially of the last: this is plainly apparent. But the manner in which these characteristics were developed in 1852 deserves some drawing out. The first of the main features of the act was the vastly increased responsibility of 'the vessels'. They were now called upon to provide a multitude of new mechanical and material contrivances and comforts; to employ a number of professionals charged with promoting the interests of the passenger rather than, or against, those of the owner and the master; to insure the passenger against the consequences of all maritime misfortunes, whether fortuitous or culpable; and (in effect) to feed and bed and guard the passenger instead of giving him raw food and space and curses. This was the culmination of the process, begun in 1842, whereby the role of the vessels was changed from that of the simple carrier to that of the almost universal provider and compensator. It was also a large step forward from the state's first major interference in 1848 in what we have termed the interior workings of the trade. The second striking feature of the 1852 act was the compulsory isolation of all single men under lock and key at night. However sensible the precaution, its singularity, considering the voluntary nature of the passage contract, is very plain. The third was the free extension of the executive officer's arbitrary powers step by step, with all these new demands, and the corresponding enlargement of the commissioners' powers of delegated legislation. This vital, though now familar, development will be considered later. Next, we should notice the curious sub-delegation of comparatively wide legislative and executive powers to port authorities to deal with certain portions of the problem of pre-embarkation and embarkation abuses. The state having shrunk from the responsibility and possible expense of the central depot project, it had been hoped that the local authority would take over the scheme in its entirety. When this failed in turn at the crucial point of Liverpool, the Liverpool dock act[1] and the passenger act of 1852 provided between them for the possible elaboration of every feature of the central depot project with the exception of official management of the lodging. But as was so commonly the case when spending money, doing rather than checking, or exposing a flank to criticism was concerned, the statutes were permissive not compulsory; and the permissive was, as usual, construed as permission to do nothing. It is quite as instructive to observe this pocket left behind as to follow the grand advance of the passenger code on all other fronts. The fifth peculiar development of the 1852 act was the increased scale of penalties. The general minimum penalty of £5 was scarcely less of a deterrent for the runner or master (when multiplied by the number of persons defrauded or above the quota) than the horrific bonds of one and two thousand pounds which the brokers and masters respectively were now required to enter and to inveigle sureties to sign, or than the seizure of a recalcitrant vessel; and at the end of every vista, more or less distantly, a gaol might clearly be discerned. Considering the resources of many of the men involved these punishments were of Star Chamber dimensions; and doubtless the purpose was admonitory and dramatic no less than practical. Finally, we should note the further subversion of the principles of common law, and the baleful oncoming shadow of le droit administratif. To an extraordinary degree the presumption of guilt was being substituted for the presumption of innocence; and no less remarkable was the first, but firm, step towards affording immunity to the official for his official acts. Those with a taste for irony may also note that the year in which these last clauses were enacted was also the year in which Albert Venn Dicey first went to school.[2]

Through all the particular features ran the old pattern of the revealed abuse determining, almost without let, the attempted remedy; and the movement of recommendation into law was all the more effortless in 1852 because of the preliminary inquiry. The great majority of the proposals of the select committee were embodied in the original bill,[3] and the majority of the new clauses

[1] 14 & 15 Vic., c. lxiv (Local and Private).
[2] It must be confessed, however, that because of his infirmities, Dicey began school late!
[3] The main omission was the committee's recommendations for the regulation of runners, lodging-keepers and porters. But the powers granted to port authorities covered some at least of these matters.

derived from the select committee.[1] In fact, had the new colonial
secretary, Sir John Pakington,[2] not been able to call upon the oracu-
lar support of the committee, it is most unlikely that so severe a bill
would have been presented, or that whatever bill had been presented would have passed unscathed through parliament. For the
proposed measure naturally enraged the trade. The battle with the
American masters at Liverpool had continued in the winter of 1851–2,
being marked, even, by the 'curious piece of effrontery' whereby a
substantial fine in the United States was preferred to being 'subjected' to a United Kingdom inspection;[3] and the British shippers
were not the less dissatisfied for their inability to imitate their
rivals. Moreover, upon Patey's transference as a new broom to
Liverpool, he had been succeeded at Glasgow by a Capt. Brownrigg,
who had attempted some sweeping on his own account, and caused
a furore amongst the local trade.[4] Thus, the new bill was salt in
open wounds. It was the Liverpool chamber of commerce which led
the charge. The chamber resolved that only if the entire bill were
withdrawn would it be fully satisfied. But failing this, it demanded,
as a minimum, a right of appeal against the emigration officer's decision in all cases (together with a provision for compensation where
that power had been frivolously exercised); a reduction, rather than
an increase, in the amount of the owner's, master's and broker's
bonds; the removal of the 'arbitrary and objectionable' discretions
of the commissioners; and the striking out—as altogether dis-
proportionate—of the new penalty of confiscation of the vessel for
sailing without a clearance.[5] Both the Liverpool and Glasgow ship-
owners' associations concentrated their fire upon the 'arbitrariness'
of the emigration officer's powers, and demanded an easy and

[1] A few of the new clauses had been prepared some time before by the commissioners or been promised by them, as in the case of Patey's proposals; and
the independent suggestions of an Irishman, Russell, who had thirty years'
experience of the passenger trade, may also have had some influence, especially
on the privies and cooking clauses. Russell also criticized the Liverpool inspections severely: 'I have always observed that the government officials are
above paying attention to their official duties', C.O. 384/88, 71 Emigration and
1828 North America, 27 May and 2 Nov. 1850; C.O. 384/89, 3365 Emigration,
14 Apr. 1852.
[2] Pakington had come in as a colonial secretary upon the formation of Derby's
first administration in February 1852.
[3] C.O. 384/88, 9669 and 10116 North America, 15 and 20 Nov. 1851.
[4] Hans., 3rd, cxii, 68–69 (4 June 1852).
[5] C.O. 384/89, 3302 Emigration, 19 Apr. 1852.

summary right of appeal.[1] The Glasgow ship-owners also attacked
the new provisions clause, while the steamship proprietors asked for
exemption from some at least of the clearance requirements upon
the ground that a steamship should depart with the dispatch and
punctuality of a railway train.[2] The commissioners duly promised
to 'consider' all these objections and indeed went through the
motions of 'consulting' the trade in London.

Meanwhile, the shippers campaigned in parliament. When the
bill was in committee, Cardwell, one of the Liverpool members,[3]
asked for a right of appeal from the emigration officer's decisions.
To Pakington's observation that 'practically speaking, a sufficient
court of appeal existed in the emigration commissioners', Cardwell
rejoined that even at best this would be so costly and dilatory a
process as to provide no real remedy. Pakington next argued that the
officers, being naval men, were 'very competent and . . . acquainted with nautical matters; and the appeal would probably be to
persons less competent to decide and having no knowledge at all'.
But he, too, promised to consider the matter.[4] 'Consideration'
however, failed to change the mind of the government; and at the
eleventh hour, W. Brown, one of the members for South Lan-
cashire, moved as an amendment to the passenger bill that a right of
appeal from the emigration officer's decision be granted in all cases;
that the appeal be heard by two J.P.s; that one of the two J.P.s
appoint 'two competent disinterested persons as adjudicators'; and
that both J.P.s make a final and absolute order upon the adjudicators'
report. 'Was it right', Brown asked, 'to entrust to any individual,
without appeal to some competent tribunal, a power which might
be abused from caprice, ignorance or vindictiveness?'; and he went
on to ridicule 'the universality of talent' which the bill demanded
of the officers, and to observe that the commissioners would naturally tend to favour their own subordinates if appealed to. Brown
was supported by some seaport members, one of whom claimed

---

[1] Ibid., 3379, 4336 and 4537 North America, 23 Apr. and 17 and 22 May 1852.
[2] Ibid., 2568 North America, 27 Mar. 1852.
[3] M.P. for Liverpool since 1847, Edward Cardwell was himself the son of a
Liverpool merchant, and may well have had a very genuine sympathy with the
shippers' standpoint. He was created viscount in 1874, after he had held the
secretaryship for war in Gladstone's first administration, in the course of which
he introduced his celebrated army reforms.
[4] *Hans.*, 3rd, cxx, 869-71 (19 Apr. 1852).

that petty persecution by the officers had been rife since 1849, while another asked the very awkward question, 'on what ground the power of appeal could be refused'? The only member of the select committee who spoke in the debate was Henley, a crabbed but clever protectionist from Oxfordshire.[1] His speech, though very short, was interesting. He argued, first, that a government officer was quite as likely to be impartial as a justice of the peace, and secondly, that the amendment would injure the shipping interest: the only effect would be 'that both the justices and the shipmasters would be landed in the Queen's Bench upon such a simple question as whether a cask of biscuits was good or bad'. Pakington, relying solely upon the fact that neither the findings nor the report of the select committee had suggested that there was any need or demand for independent adjudication, announced that he would rather abandon the entire bill than accept Brown's amendment. Brown's motion was lost by twenty-five votes to seventy-three.[2]

One noteworthy feature of the contest was the supremacy of the select committee. Possibly Sir John (one of the 'who-whos', no doubt, of this very inexperienced ministry) decided that in the strange waters upon which he had so recently embarked, his best security lay in a blind adherence to the latest and highest judgment. Certainly, he dealt equally with pressure to extend, as well as contract, the bill. When, for example, Sidney Herbert appealed for more generous provision for ship's hospitals, Pakington replied that they must follow the recommendations of the committee.[3] But whatever the colonial secretary's reasons, it is clear that the parliamentary inquiry proved the most efficient instrument for translating plain deductions from the evidence into law. It could gather better testimony, reason more boldly and speak with higher authority and less of an appearance of partiality than any permanent agency of state. Whereas each of the four earlier attempts at large reform, those of 1828, 1835, 1842 and 1849, had been marked, in some degree, by compromise and concession, the consolidation act of 1852 was intact from first to last. No less interesting is the tussle

[1] Henley was included in Disraeli's famous roll of honour of the loyal, large-acred county families who had resisted the betrayal of 1846. In fact, his father, a city merchant, had purchased his estate early in the nineteenth century.

[2] Ibid., cxxii, 67–72 (4 June 1852).

[3] Ibid., cxx, 871–2.

over bureaucracy. The fact that those who spoke against the emigration officer's discretions belonged to the liberal side, and that those who favoured them belonged to the protectionists, is probably of no significance. It was not a party matter; the supporters of the amendment were obviously under pressure from their constituents; and no politician or intelligence of the first rank (unless Henley be accounted either) was engaged. None the less, the course and conclusion of this, perhaps the first presentation of the problem of *quis custodiet ipsos custodes* in its modern form, are revealing. Particularly remarkable are the arguments of the two conservative gentlemen who contended that responsible official superiors constituted a sufficient court of appeal; that the officers being the experts, independent adjudicators would know less and judge worse; that the officers were just as likely to be impartial as the J.P.s; and that the net result of constitutional nicety would be the ludicrous spectacle of the vast machinery of the law bearing upon the most trifling and obvious matters of fact. And in so far as arguments were decisive, it was these which carried the day. It would be otiose to rehearse the various criticisms which latter-day opponents of 'despotism', from Dicey onwards, might level against each of these contentions. But it may not be unprofitable to observe that the contentions tell us something of the perennial (or at least the nineteenth century) character of English government, of the essentially practical reaction, of the simple appraisal of the means to hand, and of the unspoken reliance upon the integrity, moderation and common sense of the humble public servants upon whom powers were lavished. Not the least striking resemblance between the politics of fifth-century Athens and nineteenth-century England is the common presumption that the character of government is determined ultimately by the character of the governors.

11

THE MOVING FRONTIER

1852–6

WE have already shown in the case of the 1842 and other acts, that the growth of government was not halted by the passage of even a major statute. The lines of development continued despite—and also *because* of—the definitive legislation. But in addition to the usual extra-statutory growths, the early 1850s saw considerable enlargements of the field of state action which derived from new sources, from the increasing mechanization of the shipping industry; from scientific inquiry; from the use of delegated legislation and executive discretions; and from the ever-greater responsibilities thrust upon the central government, in contra-distinction to local or private authorities. The boundary of regulation now advanced as rapidly, and was as fluid at its extremities, as the great American frontier of the day. How and why this was so may best be illustrated by examining in detail certain of the new developments, in the years between the consolidation act of 1852 and the final consolidation act of 1855.

Diet and ventilation are simple but interesting cases. From 1848 onwards the commissioners had power to vary the first by order-in-council;[1] and—in effect—power to vary the requirements for the second by issuing instructions to, and lay down specifications for, their officers, who had been granted full discretion in the matter. The commissioners' direct management of the assisted emigration to Australia meant that they were intimately concerned with these subjects, and especially so when scientific inquiry into shipping affairs gathered pace in the late 1840s. Thus, we find Elliot discussing ventilation appliances in an informed fashion, and corresponding with Dr Arnott and Sir James Clarke on the subject, as early as 1848; and it is doubtless to Elliot's credit that at this stage he rejected both Arnott's pump and a new admiralty device, a funnel

---

[1] They might not, however, increase the quantities, but only vary the specified foodstuffs and the number of alternatives or substitutes.

system, because they introduced excessive cold air to the passenger deck.[1] During the early 1850s the commissioners themselves took up and experimented with various shafts, fans and screws which were proposed from time to time,[2] until in 1856 a really satisfactory mechanism, Watson's, was found. Diet followed a similar course. The commissioners steadfastly pursued two lines of inquiry. First they periodically consulted the 'best' medical opinion upon the nutritional value of the different foods—especially for children;[3] and secondly they experimented upon their vessels with various forms of preserved vegetables, milk and eggs, and with methods of distilling and purifying water.[4] Again, it was only in 1856 that they considered that firm and satisfactory conclusions had been reached. In each of these fields, when the commissioners decided that appropriate findings were scientifically established, no legislative amendment was needed to enforce what they desired. Orders-in-council concerning diet and water-distillation, and an instruction to their officers as to the type of ventilation mechanism to insist upon, sufficed.[5] Although this was not a formal, it was certainly a material enlargement of regulation, and one which involved government in a new type of experimental and creative activity. And whether they were impelled by the censorious undertone of the report of the select committee of 1851, or by a simple Victorian passion for gadgetry, or some other cause, the commissioners certainly made the pace in these subjects, in contra-distinction to their usual habit of waiting on events.

These were straightforward and legitimate, if unexpected, developments. Stowage and cargoes presented more complex and

[1] C.O. 384/82, 129 Emigration and endorsements, 17 Jan. 1848; 1094 Emigration and endorsements, 30 May 1848.

[2] C.O. 384/90, 5003 Emigration, 10 May 1853.

[3] C.O. 384/94, 2968 Emigration, 29 Mar. 1855; C.O. 384/96, 3362 Emigration 12 Apr. 1856.

[4] The commissioners obtained powers to issue orders-in-council permitting the use of water-distilling and similar machines, and varying the water requirements of the passenger acts accordingly, in 1855, 18 & 19 Vic., c. cxix, sec. 59. But it is interesting to note that the commissioners 'allowed' their use only on steam, and not on sailing, vessels, presumably because of the absence of engineers on the latter. Experiments made during the Crimean War assisted the commissioners in their work on water purification, C.O. 384/98, 2624, 4900 and 5062 Emigration, 25 Mar. and 20 and 29 May 1857.

[5] C.O. 384/96, 3362 and 5073 Emigration, 12 Apr. and 7 June 1856.

uncertain issues.[1] Down to the late 1840s the emigration officers had virtually ignored these matters. But from 1849 onwards large quantities of pig and bar iron were exported in emigrant vessels to the United States, mainly from Liverpool and Glasgow;[2] and it soon became apparent that the carriage of iron was dangerous. It needed very careful stowage if the vessel were not to become top-heavy or too low in the water, and it caused serious inaccuracies in the ordinary compasses. Two or three of the emigration officers attempted to devise and apply special regulations for vessels carrying iron; and one of them, Patey of Glasgow, 'invented' a rule-of-thumb which limited the weight of the iron cargo to two-thirds of the registered tonnage.[3] Part of the furore amongst the Glasgow and Liverpool shippers in 1851 was caused by the efforts to enforce 'Patey's rule'. Not only was the professional *amour propre* of shippers and masters wounded by so crude and amateur a regulation.[4] The authority of the emigration officers in this matter was also doubtful. All that they could call on to justify their interference were the vague discretions concerning 'seaworthiness' and 'the health and safety of passengers' which the current passenger acts afforded. The protests of the shippers, however, merely emboldened the commissioners; and (as we have seen) the passenger act of 1852 awarded the officers discretionary powers over both the *quantity* and the *nature* of the cargoes.

The next development came in 1853 when a number of shipwrecks amongst passenger vessels with iron cargoes aroused considerable attention, and were the subject of a board of trade inquiry. The inquiry decided that the probable cause of some at least of the wrecks was bad stowage; while the evidence before the inquiry seemed to show that the two-thirds rule-of-thumb was insufficient, and that the actual stowage of cargo should be superintended.[5]

[1] For a fuller discussion of the subject, see O. MacDonagh, 'Delegated legislation and administrative discretions in the 1850s: a particular study', *Victorian Studies*, vol. ii, no. 1, pp. 29–44.

[2] The main reason for the increase in exports was the sudden expansion in railroad building in the United States, but a secondary cause was the rise of steam vessels, which often captured the light cargoes hitherto carried by the emigrant ships, and thus forced them to turn to the iron trade. A little of the iron was exported from Derry and Sligo, after trans-shipment from Great Britain, *2nd rep. Select comm. emigrant ships*, 139, Q.5563–72, H.C. 1854 (349), xiii.

[3] C.O. 384/92, 2188 Emigration, 8 Mar. 1854; *1st rep. select comm. emigrant ships*, 14, Q.198, H.C. 1854 (163), xiii.

[4] C.O. 384/88, 7161 Emigration, 20 Aug. 1851.

[5] C.O. 384/91, 10416 Emigration. See also *Liverpool Times*, 6 Oct. 1853.

Murdoch himself attended the inquiry, and the commissioners (Murdoch being the chief and decisive member throughout the 1850s) took immediate steps to meet the difficulties which had been revealed. First, they sent a circular to all officers warning them that Patey's rule should not be blindly followed: even a small quantity of iron if stowed solidly on the ship's bottom might make her unseaworthy. They themselves laid down no precise direction except that the weight should be distributed as much as possible. Secondly, they proposed to appoint a special officer at Liverpool to superintend the stowage of cargo. He was to supply the emigration officer with the facts and the latter would then take whatever action was required.[1] Elliot objected strongly to all this. Though laws such as the passenger acts, he wrote, did tend to supersede private responsibility, 'for that very reason they ought not to be carried farther than absolutely necessary'. Ordinarily, executive officers performed only those duties which were expressly laid upon them, to which category discretion over the 'nature' and 'quantity' of the cargo now belonged. But the *manner* of stowage could not be so regarded except by 'rather a circuitous mode of acquiring so large a power'. The new political chiefs, Sir Frederic Peel and the duke of Newcastle,[2] however, backed the commissioners, the latter observing that 'the whole spirit of the acts demands this extension'.[3] Accordingly, the circular was not withdrawn, and a special officer was appointed at Liverpool in 1854, albeit 'experimentally'.[4]

The commissioners soon reaped the harvest of their circular. The chief emigration officer at Liverpool was faced with an action for £3,000 damages for refusing to clear a vessel which he considered 'too low in the water', the owner contending that the officer had no power over the mode of stowage.[5] This was followed by a new wave of protests from Liverpool when the special officer arrived. The

[1] Circular to emigration officers, 16 Nov. 1853. The officers were warned against (a) cargo being stowed too low in the vessel, which caused slowness; (b) cargo being stowed too high in the vessel, which caused top-heaviness; and (c) cargo being concentrated in any one place.

[2] They were, respectively, parliamentary under-secretary and secretary in Aberdeen's recently formed administration.

[3] C.O. 384/90, 10929 Emigration, 10 Nov. 1853.

[4] Ibid., 12361 Emigration, 7 Jan. 1854. The treasury strenuously resisted the appointment of a special stowage officer, on the ground of economy. Doubtless, it was for this reason that the appointment was labelled 'experimental'.

[5] Ibid., 12165 Emigration, 20 Dec. 1853.

burden of these complaints was that the shippers did not know
what they had to conform to. This was a reasonable objection, but
the commissioners pointed out that the nature of the business left
them with no alternative. Vessels varied so greatly in build and construction that the matter could not be reduced to a fixed ratio of the
registered tonnage: what really counted was the degree of immersion
in the water, which could only be decided by observation on the
spot. No doubt, the uncertainty caused inconvenience. But, the
commissioners stoutly declared, 'inconvenience is not for a moment
to be set against the risk of life of leaving the whole matter uncontrolled'.[1] In truth the problem was very difficult and complicated.
The total prohibition of iron cargoes, the only sure solution, was
impracticable.[2] But to attempt to regulate storage by statute was also
impracticable, partly because, as we have seen, no precise regulation
would have been satisfactory, and partly because the effect of iron
cargoes was still scientifically *sub judice*. So far as the officers themselves were concerned the dilemma was this: while the discretion
was general and vague, they were liable to prosecution for exorbitance, and their morale was correspondingly undermined; but to
protect them by making their duty exact and statutory was impossible from the circumstances of the case. In this very difficult situation, the commissioners eventually decided to ask for statutory
authority to regulate the matter by periodic orders-in-council which
could easily be changed if found to have been mistaken or out of
step with the latest scientific discoveries.[3]

Meanwhile similar and tangential problems had arisen. One was
coal combustion, an increasingly important issue with the coming of
steam. After a shipwreck due to fire on a steam vessel, the emigration officers began to direct the stowage of coal according to their
own opinions. Some required a platform at either end of the coal
hold to provide ventilation; some, vertical shafts leading to the
upper deck; some, water-casks to divide the mass. Certainly this regulation was haphazard and unscientific and, very probably, *ultra vires*.
To check the confusion and complaints by a standard instruction,

[1] C.O. 384/92, 2188 Emigration, 8 Mar. 1854.
[2] Iron was an important export; and its prohibition might have driven so
many vessels out of the passenger trade that fares would have become prohi-
bitive, *2nd rep. select comm. emigrant ships*, 49, Q.3861-3, H.C. 1854 (349), xiii.
[3] *2nd rep. select comm. emigrant ships*, 50, Q.387-8, H.C. 1854 (349), xiii. See
also *1st rep. select comm. emigrant ships*, 15, Q.201-10, H.C. 1854 (163), xiii.

the commissioners consulted Sir H. de la Beche and the 'scientific men' of the admiralty—much to the annoyance of Elliot who had considerable experience and a correspondingly low opinion of admiralty 'science'.[1] Again, statutory authority for regulating the matter by order-in-council was sought.

The board of trade inquiry which Murdoch attended had also raised other issues, notably the effect of iron upon compasses; and the commissioners took precautionary action by instructing all officers to require every emigrant vessel to carry an azimuth compass.[2] Once again, Elliot was frightened by their audacity in ordering 'very humble officers of the government' to act where 'parliament has either shrunk from the task, or has not thought it advisable'. But again Peel and Newcastle backed the commissioners, and told them to enforce their regulations, at any rate *pro tem*.[3] This time, however, the commissioners had acted rashly. Within a week, threatened by legal proceedings, they had to instruct the officers *not* to refuse clearance to vessels without azimuth compasses, as the law was uncertain on the point, and they feared further actions for damages for delays.[4] The general clause as to 'promoting the health and safety of passengers' might possibly cover the mode of stowage,[5] but it certainly did not cover the azimuth compass. A further difficulty soon arose. It was discovered that ordinary ship's compasses needed to be examined and 're-swung' both before an iron cargo was loaded and after one had been carried in a vessel. The emigration officers had not the requisite knowledge to do this: what was needed was a specialist, 'a scientific officer'.[6] The commissioners, now out of their depth, expressed a hope that so technical a matter would be taken up with the board of trade, a proposal which Elliot warmly endorsed, adding that the board should be responsible for

---

[1] C.O. 384/94, 362 Emigration and endorsements, 13 Jan. 1855.

[2] Circular to emigration officers, 17 Mar. 1854.

[3] C.O. 384/92, 1986 Emigration and endorsements, 3 Mar. 1854.

[4] Ibid., 2506 Emigration, 21 Mar. 1854. At the same time the commissioners instructed the officers to warn all masters of the very grave responsibility they assumed if they sailed without an azimuth compass.

[5] Murdoch himself admitted that even this was a forced and doubtful application of the clauses, *2nd rep. select comm. emigrant ships*, 48, Q.3852–3, H.C. 1854 (349), xiii.

[6] *1st rep. select comm. emigrant ships*, 23, Q.363–5, H.C. 1854 (163), xiii; *2nd rep. select comm. emigrant ships*, 15–16, Q.3435–53, H.C. 1854 (349), xiii. The term 'scientific officer' was coined by the chief emigration officer at Liverpool.

'the creation of any new powers and duties on the part of the executive government'.[1]

All these developments present points of interest. Generally, we may remind ourselves that it was but twenty years since Low was first stationed at Liverpool. But how remote seem those early days from the age of technology, which had now arrived. More particularly, it is very clear that experimental science (more or less a new factor in our field) spoke in the imperative mood, whether it spoke with certainty or not. The fact that scientific conclusions had not yet been reached did not mean the postponement of regulation. On the contrary, regulations tended to be all the wider, to be 'blanket' precautions, if the authorities did not know what precisely to guard against, or how to provide security. Thus, to the usual types of administrative momentum was added a new, and practically irresistible, stimulus to growth; the findings, or even the want of findings, of experimental science. At any rate, this was so whenever the attention of commissioners was focused upon appropriate subjects, which also included danger to human life.[2] Next, the assurance with which the commissioners acted, and their large view of their own rights (a view fully endorsed by their political chiefs), were remarkable. The commissioners' attitude towards regulation was by now very different to Elliot's. Whereas Elliot continued to interpret statutes strictly—in fact, correctly—the commissioners spoke the language of *salus populi suprema lex*, and halted only when they were threatened with suits for damages which they would almost certainly have lost. But the commissioners' attitude was not, perhaps, so indefensible as, formally and legally, it might seem. Experience had taught them that statutory powers, in this type of field, were to be had for the asking. The only reason why they did not currently possess what they required was that they had not foreseen, or properly assessed, the need. This explains the confidence with which they pressed existing permissions to the extremity, and drew upon the next statute in advance. The fact that danger to human life was involved made them impatient. Many ships might be wrecked before twelve months—the least time an amendment would require

---

[1] C.O. 384/92, 3573 Emigration and endorsements, 25 Apr. 1853.

[2] From 1854 onwards the commissioners subscribed ten guineas annually to an association for the promotion of inquiry into ships' instruments and kindred subjects.

—were up. The question, whether they were right or wrong, cannot, therefore be answered simply, and fortunately it need not be answered here. What concerns us is the subtle but definite change in the outlook of the administrators after large numbers of discretionary powers had been effortlessly obtained. For good or ill, the appetite grew with eating; the very concept of government altered; the expert regulator filled the scene.

This is confirmed by the commissioners' experience, and conduct, in other matters. They moved steadily towards autonomy and the exercise of quasi-judicial, no less than quasi-legislative and executive, powers in certain spheres. After Hodder's dismissal, their decisions in relation to their staff were always accepted by their superiors. In fact both Elliot and Newcastle, when he was colonial secretary, went out of their way to assure them that they had full discretion in selecting and managing their officers.[1] Correspondingly, their discretions in reducing fines, varying penalties and otherwise acting in a semi-judicial capacity were not only gradually extended, but also fully accepted by their superiors.[2] When in 1854 the treasury questioned their 'discretionary power of fixing the amounts of penalties',[3] and when in 1857 the board of trade threatened to supersede (under the merchant shipping act of 1854) their inquiries into misconduct on the part of masters and crews,[4] the 'rights' of the commissioners were upheld on each occasion. The commissioners in turn encouraged boldness and decision amongst their officers. After the passage of the 1852 act they were at pains to bring home to each officer the extent of his discretionary powers under the statute, and his consequent *duties* of intervention. An instruction issued in 1853 told the officers that one of the objects of passenger legislation was to provide 'a more comprehensive remedy than the ordinary rules of the law supply', and emphasized the importance of the executive discretion—down even to vetoing the ship's physician. 'But although the documents may in themselves be satisfactory, yet, if the emigration officer is aware of any circumstances which in his judgment would render it improper to commit the charge of an emigrant ship to the holder of them, it will be his

[1] C.O. 384/91, 6482 Emigration, 23 June 1853; C.O. 384/92, 11227 Emigration, 23 Dec. 1854.
[2] C.O. 384/91, 6554 North America, 25 June 1853.
[3] C.O. 384/92, 2299 Emigration, 13 Mar. 1854.
[4] C.O. 384/98, 6817 Emigration, 28 July 1857.

duty to object to him under the authority conferred by the law'.[1] As a corollary, the commissioners supported their officers to the hilt—and in the law courts, where various actions for demurrage arising not only from disputes over iron cargoes but also from delays over sickness and other causes were fought out.[2] 'The law', the commissioners wrote, 'has designedly invested the emigration officer with a very large discretion upon many points . . . it has been indispensable from the circumstances of the case'; even if they themselves wished to do so, they had no power to vary his decision;[3] he was the 'expert . . . without bias or interest'.[4] The last phrase epitomized the new claims and confidence of government in our sphere.

The next interesting developments, or potential developments, were the problems of jurisdiction raised by the entry of steam vessels into the passenger trade. Even by 1850 it was widely recognized that steam vessels would attract more and more of the emigrant traffic, and that speed would bring an easy solution to many of the old problems of the voyage. The passenger acts of 1851 and 1852 made some concessions to the new form of locomotion. Steam vessels were permitted to carry less food because their passages would be shorter, and *bona fide* steamship cabin passengers on steamships were exempted from the requirements of the acts. But these two relaxations by no means satisfied the steam shippers,[5] and after the passage of the 1852 act they continued their protests and agitation.

[1] *Return of names emigration officers; with copy instructions*, 7–22, H.C. 1854 (255), xvi.

[2] C.O. 384/92, 5502 Emigration, 28 June 1854; C.O. 384/93, 8043 Emigration, 15 Sept. 1854. The commissioners paid the cost of counsel and other legal expenses, when an emigration officer was defendant in a suit. There is no record of an officer losing one.

[3] C.O. 384/90, 5445 North America, 23 May 1853. It was not absolutely true, of course, that the emigration officer's decisions were invariable. When Capt. Keele, the officer at Glasgow, rejected some vessels in 1853, and the local trade protested that his decisions were altogether unreasonable, the commissioners sent the chief officers of Liverpool and London to investigate. The latter passed the vessels with minor alterations. The bad feeling at the port was so great that Keele had to be transferred. But the commissioners, because Keele's activity was strictly within his duty and undertaken from 'the most praiseworthy motives' and zeal, insisted, despite a protest by Elliot, that he should not lose a penny by the change, C.O. 384/92, 11227 Emigration, 23 Dec. 1854.

[4] C.O. 384/88, 7161 Emigration, 20 Aug. 1851.

[5] The shippers also asked to be allowed to carry less water, to be exempted from post-embarkation inspections, and for other concessions. The commissioners rejected these proposals, C.O. 384/89, 2568 North America, 27 Mar. 1852.

In fact throughout 1853 and 1854 there was conflict at Liverpool over steamship clearances. The principal steamship company, Richardson & Co., belied the Quaker persuasion of the owners by their extraordinary pugnacity and disobedience, which issued eventually in the supreme offence of sailing without a clearance. Richardson's were tamed by a prosecution for this misdemeanour, and by the shipwreck of one of their newest vessels, *City of Glasgow*, in 1854. But generally the steam shippers continued to obstruct the emigration officers as much as possible. Taking aboard a single sack of mail in order to qualify for exemption from the acts as a 'mail steamer' was a common subterfuge.[1]

The demands of the steam shippers were both particular and general. The particular demand was that their vessels should not be subjected to inspections by the emigration officers, which delayed the sailing. Speed and quick dispatch were everything. Passengers did not arrive until the hour of sailing, nor was the crew, who had only two days ashore, collected until the last moment. Correspondingly, most of the food for the voyage, which was fresh and kept in ice-boxes, was put aboard as late as possible. But the general demand of steam shippers—what they really wanted—was total exemption from the passenger acts, on account of the alleged probity and the comparative wealth of all the firms engaged in that particular business. Here we may note that the resistance of the steam shippers was part of the general opposition to the passenger acts which marked the 1850s and which was centred on Liverpool, where, between 1845 and 1855, the majority of the trade was captured by relatively big shipping concerns which could afford to specialize in passengers. Owners and companies of the new sort felt that their capital, their large, modern vessels and their high professional standing obviated the need for regulation. They were (according to their own belief) sufficiently responsible and moneyed to foster their own good name and preserve the well-being and safety of their vessels; while their engineers and masters were more competent to judge the new technical and nautical problems than any landbound and sail-bred officials. Naturally, these sentiments were most powerful—and best grounded—amongst the steamship proprietors.

[1] C.O. 384/92, 11344 Emigration, 30 Dec. 1854. This loophole was closed by the passenger act of 1855.

Thus, beneath the occasional and specific complaints lay a fundamental issue: had the passenger acts and the protective service of the emigration officers been superseded, at any rate in the better sections of the trade; and if so, should those sections have been freed from regulation? And in turn behind this issue lurked one larger still: was government intervention to cease when, and in so far as, the conditions which had brought it into being disappeared? For their part, the commissioners had no hesitation in rejecting the steam shippers' and similar pleas. On the specific question of inspections, they observed that inspections made before the cargo was stowed, or all passengers and crew were aboard, were worthless. Doubtless, the delay was inconvenient, but 'it is not a question whether it is inconvenient but whether it is necessary'. On the major issue, they argued first that it was impossible to legislate for individual firms or groups of firms, no matter how reputable or efficient they might be; and secondly that no degree of probity or competence on the part of the private trader could relieve the state of its responsibility to the passenger. The fact that steam would soon be general in the passenger trade was not a reason for relaxing the law in favour of such vessels, but very much the contrary. Elliot was delighted with the commissioners' stand. 'The Steam Companies are powerful', he wrote, 'and for that very reason it is more incumbent on the government . . . to uphold the officers . . . When passengers are lying in a comfortable dock they fret at every delay,[1] but after they had got to sea, and storm rages or a fire breaks out, they would not feel obliged to the government officer who had violated his duty of seeing that the ship had every requirement demanded by law'.[2]

We are here concerned (however little the actors themselves may have appreciated it and however small the scale) with a general crisis. The original principle of state intervention in our field was to set wrongs to right. It was by no means clear that the intervention would be permanent. Reform was then commonly understood as a single and finite, no matter how difficult and protracted an operation. We can scarcely describe the commissioners' observations in

[1] Elliot was certainly right in saying that steamship passengers fretted at the delays while still in the comfortable dock. One of them delighted the steamship agents by threatening 'to shew up the Government Officers in the Times', C.O. 384/92, 2178 North America, 28 Mar. 1854.

[2] C.O. 384/90, 4034 Emigration and endorsements, 6 Apr. 1853; C.O. 384/91, 3105 and 4043 Emigration and endorsements, 7 Mar. and 7 Apr. 1853.

the steamship cases as a decision. It was rather an instinctive recognition and ratification of what had silently come about. In effect, however, the commissioners asserted that state regulation could not be superseded because the state's task was continuing. Social legislation was not a martial law, terminable when the initial disturbance had subsided, but a part of the permanent underpinning of organized society. Even if, as was by no means the case, the law were universally obeyed, the inspector or executive officer would not be rendered superfluous thereby, any more than the policeman whose beat was quiet or the judge who received white gloves.

Finally, the subjects of public expenditure and central, local and private responsibility are so well illuminated by the case of the emigrant hospital at Cork harbour that it deserves a detailed examination. Cork harbour lay on the main shipping route to North America, and vessels on which sickness broke out soon after sailing almost invariably put into Cove, a little town which lay at the mouth of the harbour some sixteen miles down-river from the city. Such cases were quite common even before the rise of mass emigration,[1] but it was not until the end of 1847 that complaints about the burden on the town became serious. In December of that year, six vessels put into Cove in distress. When fifty of the emigrants had been placed in the fever hospital at Cove, and maintained there at the expense of the Cork union, the Cove relief committee and the Cork emigration officer, Lieut. Friend, appealed to the admiralty for a hospital hulk. They pointed out that vessels were putting back more and more frequently, and argued that it was unfair that the town should bear the cost and the danger of infection. Moreover, they observed, a hulk would answer the growing problem of finding shore accommodation for the emigrants;[2] and if all the passengers could be removed together from their own vessel, it could be 'purified' for the continuation of the voyage.[3] Nothing came of this appeal, but the matter was raised again when cholera broke out amongst the emigrants of 1849. When the St John, bound for New York from Liverpool, put in with cholera aboard, and the epidemic

[1] C.O. 384/73, 1186 Emigration, Dr Scott (of Cove): emigration commissioners, 25 May 1842.
[2] The lodging-houses of Cove, the complainants added, were 'hardly better than stables'.
[3] C.O. 384/81, 67 Emigration, undated, December 1847.

9

spread further while the ship was in the harbour, Friend, on his own authority but at the instigation of the Cove board of health, hired a hulk, transferred the passengers, and had the vessel fumigated. Presented with a *fait accompli*, the commissioners sanctioned the expenditure of £50, which they paid from a small parliamentary grant for distressed vessels. They argued that the circumstances had demanded some extraordinary action, and that its effect had certainly been good. But, on the ground of expense, they rejected the renewed appeals from Cove and Cork union for a permanent hospital hulk.

The commissioners had merely taken the easiest course, and decided the matter by expediency: they privately admitted that a hulk might become 'inevitable' if cholera gripped the southern Irish ports and Liverpool. But, in fact, a principle of considerable importance was involved. The Cove board of health had stated bluntly that the responsibility rested upon the central government, not upon a small community which could scarcely support its own poor, and whose connexion with the emigrants was accidental. Elliot alone faced this issue squarely. 'Beneath these occasional questions', he wrote, 'lies a general one of much difficulty and importance. About two or three hundred thousand persons annually embark, who are barely able to provide for themselves. If unforeseen contingencies should occur which can neither be met from their own resources nor by charitable aid, what is to be done? The spirit of our institutions and customs is that expenses arising from such cause should be charged to the particular localities to which the people belong. But when once they are on board ship, this has ceased (at all events practically), to be the case; and I apprehend that to bring in a bill against particular unions or parishes for their disasters by wreck, fire or pestilence would be quite impossible. Are the contingent expenses of this vast body to be charged to the general revenue of the kingdom? This would be contrary to general usage, and would, I have no doubt, lead to extravagant claims and excessive expenditure. On the whole, if ever the time came that the state was obliged to undertake these duties for the moving population, I confess that I think the only fair way of meeting it would be by a tax falling on those who are to benefit by the expenditure, and accordingly that an emigration rate (which would soon become very heavy) ought to be imposed on passengers by law, but it is evident that this is very undesirable so long as it can be avoided'.[1] Neither Hawes nor Grey was pleased that matters of principle had been raised. Hawes tartly observed that Elliot's constitutional excursion did not solve the matter in hand, and that the commissioners must exercise their own discretion on every case in turn, while Grey deprecated the anticipation of a general question which he hoped would never arise—'it has been avoided for many years'. Grey added that payments should be made from the distress fund, though with the greatest economy:[2] if a still greater emergency occurred, the treasury might be approached.

When cholera returned in 1852, no accommodation could be found in Cove—or as we should now say, Queenstown[3]—and, finally, in a desperate situation the local military hospital[4] was called upon to house the sick. But the outcome was unhappy and by the end of 1852 all parties at Cork harbour had been alienated. The military hospital, the Queenstown lodging-houses and sanitary board, and the Cork local authorities refused absolutely to assist infected emigrants in future. All insisted that the responsibility was the state's, and asked, in particular, for a hospital hulk and not a land establishment, so that the infection might not reach the shore. The commissioners rejected the last request. A hulk would be more expensive, inconvenient[5] and unhealthy than a hospital on the mainland. But they did admit that some permanent solution must be found and that the state must make a contribution. The local authorities might be persuaded to meet some of the cost of establishing a hospital, and the majority of the running expenses might be met by persuading—and later compelling[6]—the owners or

[1] C.O. 384/83, 5507 Emigration, Cove board of health: commissioners, and endorsements, 22 June 1849.

[2] The distress fund for 1849 was already almost exhausted.

[3] On 6 August 1849 Queen Victoria wrote to her uncle, the King of the Belgians, 'We had previously stepped on shore at *Cove*, a small place, to enable them to call it *Queen's Town*', *Letters of Queen Victoria*, vol. ii, p. 225. The present name of the town is Cobh.

[4] The military hospital was built upon Spike Island, which was separated by a few hundred yards of water from both Queenstown and the naval establishment on Haulbowline Island.

[5] 'The proper use of a ship', as Elliot, agreeing with them, delightfully put it, 'is locomotion', in which it was 'more agreeable than the most perfect means of conveyance on land which the ingenuity of Man has devised'; but for 'all other purposes a house was to be preferred'.

[6] The commissioners proposed to insert a new clause in the next passenger bill making it compulsory for owners or charterers to meet the cost of maintaining sick emigrants.

charterers of vessels in distress to pay for the maintenance of the emigrants, as they were always impatient at the delays which led to the loss of return freights and other inconvenience.[1] But even so, the central government could not hope to avoid all expense.[2] Where was the additional money to be found? At this point, it was discovered that the medical inspectors at Liverpool, who were paid on a *per capita* basis, earned almost £600 a year each, and the commissioners proposed instead to give them a flat salary of £400, and to apply part of the surplus to an emigrant hospital for Cork.[3] The morality of the transaction was very doubtful. The tax was raised to pay for pre-embarkation inspections; and by no means all the vessels which put into Queenstown in distress even hailed from Liverpool. But with the treasury ominously hostile at the mention of possible new expenditure,[4] there was no room for niceties of conscience, and the commissioners were only too glad to have some money at their back. They began, therefore, to search for a building in Cork or Queenstown which might be converted into a hospital when the next epidemic occurred.

But the blow fell before this plan bore fruit. Early in November 1853, the *Kossuth* put into Queenstown in distress. Of her six hundred passengers, twenty-one had died of cholera already. Again on his own initiative, and regardless of cost, Friend hired a hulk for the sick;[5] and when the mayor of Cork appealed for permission to use some vacant stores on Haulbowline Island, the naval station, for a hospital, the Irish lord lieutenant decided that 'the circumstances render such a temporary appropriation urgently necessary', and ordered them to be placed at once at the disposal of the emigrants.[6] All parties could plead necessity, for the feeling in the port ran very high, and riots were threatened at every rumour that the passengers

---

[1] C.O. 384/90, 6656 Emigration; C.O. 384/92, 6386 Emigration, 25 July 1863. The commissioners were prepared to refuse sick emigrants admittance to the hulk unless the owner signed an agreement to meet the expenses. In effect, they could coerce the owner by refusing to re-clear the vessel while there were sick aboard, as there was no place but the hospital hulk which would receive the infected emigrants.

[2] Cf. C.O. 384/90, 10265 Emigration, 24 Oct. 1853.

[3] C.O. 384/90, 3589 Australia, 21 Mar. 1853.

[4] C.O. 384/91, 4112 Emigration, 9 Apr. 1853.

[5] C.O. 384/90, 10917 Emigration, Friend: commissioners and endorsements, 7 Nov. 1853. The hulk cost £6 per day.

[6] C.S.O. Registered Papers (Dublin Castle), carton 699, 10072, 11 Nov. 1853.

would be disembarked upon the mainland.[1] 'The Town', Friend reported, 'is in considerable excitement and every means will be used to prevent those poor people landing'.[2]

When the commissioners returned to their quest for a permanent solution, it was only to discover that the fear of cholera was so great that no building could be found ashore either in Cork or Queenstown. Hard on the heels of this failure came an admiralty report that to send a frigate to Queenstown to be used as a hospital ship would cost no less than £2,600.[3] At this point Elliot decided that the people of Cork had always been 'excessively timid', and that their demand for a hospital ship must once for all be refused, firstly because of the expense, and secondly because 'it would be the concession of a new, and certainly an important, principle for the imperial government to undertake to supply different towns and ports with the means of accommodating the casual sick by whom they may be visited'. He and Newcastle thereupon proceeded to the extraordinary conclusion that the infected emigrants were the exclusive responsibility of Cork union, and threatened the Queenstown sanitary board that the emigrants would be loosed upon the town '*unless* they [the board] can at once provide a suitable building'.[4] This was attempted blackmail; and to add to its force the home secretary, Palmerston, and the Irish permanent secretary, Waddington, were asked by Newcastle and Murdoch respectively to persuade the Irish lord lieutenant to bring pressure to bear upon 'the Cork local authorities'.[5] Nothing came of these machinations. Evidently the lord lieutenant was unwilling to enter a contest with a nationalist board of guardians on such a ground. When a second

[1] *Cork Constitution*, 8, 10 and 12 Nov. 1853.

[2] C.O. 384/90, 10940 Emigration, Friend: commissioners, 10 Nov. 1853; see also *1st rep. select comm. emigrant ships*, 35, Q.501, H.C. 1854 (163), xiii (evidence of T. Murdoch). In fact the good treatment accorded to the emigrants paid dividends. Within four days of their translation to the hulk, the mortality had almost ceased, C.O. 384/90, 11000 Emigration, Friend: commissioners, 10 and 11 Nov. 1853. All passengers were supplied, twice weekly, with beef and potatoes. They were also provided with boats so that they might take exercise ashore which had the dual purpose of enabling the ship to be purified and keeping up the spirits of the passengers. Later, many got lodgings ashore, the owners of the vessel granting a small lodging allowance.

[3] C.O. 384/90, 11134 Emigration and endorsements, 17 Nov. 1853.

[4] Ibid. and C.O. 384/91, 11496 Emigration and 11533 Emigration and endorsements, 29 Nov. and 1 Dec. 1853.

[5] C.O. 384/91, 11351 Emigration.

vessel, the *Preveslaw*, bound for New York from Hamburg, put into Queenstown with cholera aboard later in November, Friend hired again the hulk which he had used for the *Kossuth*. He noted the remarkable fact that no case of cholera occurred amongst the passengers of either vessel after they had been dispersed.[1] But another remarkable fact was unnoticed. This was that foreign passengers on a foreign vessel sailing from one foreign port to another were cared for, when ill, at the expense of a distress fund of the central government of the United Kingdom.

Within a few months, the question arose once more. In the spring of 1854, the *Dirigo* was driven into Queenstown with a very serious outbreak of cholera aboard, and a heavy death roll. As it happened, she was a government vessel bound for Australia, and, since money was for once no object, the ship was towed back immediately to Liverpool, where the passengers could be cared for in the depot from which they had embarked. But the mayor of Cork seized the opportunity to renew the appeal for a hospital ship, and the commissioners used his letter to secure a reversal of the previous decisions. They had by now come to agree substantially with the local authorities, who had, they reported, 'justly' pleaded, first, that Cork had no funds which could legally be applied to the support of distressed emigrants, and secondly, that there was no reason why Cork, through an accident of geography, should bear what was properly a national charge.[2] Tacitly the report admitted that the responsibility was the central government's. But what now was to be done? Clearly, neither Cork nor Queenstown could—or would—furnish a building for a hospital, and the best, and cheapest, alternative seemed to be either a portion of the half-empty military hospital or the vacant naval stores on Haulbowline Island.[3] But both the war office and the admiralty refused to yield an inch of space. A hulk it had to be. Partly in the hope of keeping down expenses, the commissioners now entered into negotiations with the admiralty for the

[1] C.O. 384/90, 11334, 11494 and 11775 Emigration, 22 and 29 Nov. and 3 Dec. 1853.

[2] See also *2nd rep. select comm. emigrant ships*, 164, Q.6007–17, H.C. 1854 (349), xiii (evidence of Lieut. de Courcy).

[3] C.O. 384/93, 7368 Emigration, mayor of Cork: commissioners and endorsements, 19 Aug. 1854. Lieut. Friend had reported in 1853 that there was ample room for an emigrant hospital in the buildings on both islands, a fact which the commissioners emphasized in their applications, and one which neither the war office nor the admiralty denied.

'loan' of a naval vessel for use as a floating hospital. The admiralty acted with precipitate dispatch. Early in September H.M.S. *Inconstant* turned up at Cork harbour, before the commissioners had made any formal application to the admiralty and before they had any notion of the cost. They accepted the *fait accompli*, however, in the belief that the costs of installation and maintenance would be small.[1]

But two blows fell soon afterwards. The first was an admiralty estimate for the cost of fitting out the *Inconstant* at £750. The second was Elliot's return to the colonial office. He had been absent for some months, which may explain why the commissioners had resurrected the hospital project. 'I do not find', wrote Elliot, 'that the Treasury concurrence had been obtained or even that . . . [of] the Colonial Office'. The admiralty had presented a staggering, but by no means complete bill: 'by and by' the full account would arrive 'of which from past experience the amount is not to be conjectured', and as yet 'the Chancellor of the Exchequer has received no hint'. The colonial secretary took all this coolly, merely observing that there was ample evidence of 'the importance, if not the necessity, of such an establishment'. But the problem of finance remained. The admiralty was importuned to reduce its bill, and in the end provided many services and fittings free of charge;[2] while the treasury finally consented to the remaining capital expenditure, the £500 surplus of Liverpool medical fees being deducted from the next estimate in lieu.[3] As to recurrent expenditure, the 1855 act contained the promised clause requiring owners or charterers to pay for the maintenance of sick emigrants and their dependants on the hulk; and the additional recurrent expenses, a small sum, were accepted at last as an annual charge upon the state.[4]

Thus deviously did the emigrant hospital at Queenstown come to be established. It had taken nearly ten years to achieve. During

[1] C.O. 384/92, 8369 Emigration, 26 Sept. 1854.
[2] C.O. 384/94, 431 Emigration, 13 Jan. 1855; C.O. 384/95, 290 Admiralty, 9 Jan. 1855.
[3] C.O. 384/94, 192 Treasury and 10126 Emigration and endorsements, 20 Nov. 1854.
[4] When it was proposed to use the surplus of Liverpool medical fees to meet the annual *Inconstant* expenses as a regular thing, the treasury refused on the ground that the Liverpool emigration might decline and the money be needed to make up the £400 p.a. salaries of the medical officers, C.O. 384/94, 10326 Emigration, 7 Nov. 1855. See also, C.O. 384/95, 1273 and 11383 Emigration, 21 Feb. and 10 Dec. 1855; C.O. 384/96, unmarked, 18 Nov. 1856.

that time, private charity, three Cork local authorities, the war office, the admiralty, the Liverpool medical officers, and numerous owners and masters impatient to set sail again, had wittingly or unwittingly met most of the cost of the relief, the remainder being paid from the distress fund. Every possible expedient was employed, to avoid new public spending, and even after the hospital ship was set up, the direct state expenditure was negligible.[1] The episode shows very clearly how crucial the 'economical' passion of the time might be to developments in administration. To appreciate this to the full, we should note the contrast between voluntary emigration, where two or three hundred pounds was a vital matter, and the assisted emigration to Australia, where the colonies met the bill. The commissioners spent nearly £10,000 upon immediate relief when *three* Australia vessels put back with cholera in 1854. Four or five medical officers were employed in each case, and a hospital was set up at Birkenhead, and a convalescent home at Liverpool.[2] Thus, it was only fear of the treasury, and behind this fear of the parliamentary watchdogs which led to the pitiful expedients and the eventual Dotheboys establishment at Queenstown. It is true that 'principle' was also involved. But apart from Elliot, whose constitutional perception was unusually nice, no one genuinely considered the question of responsibility for emigrants in transit on its merits. All were governed by expediency. But the efforts of the commissioners to shift the burden on to any party who might be induced to bear it was not buck-passing in the ordinary sense. It was not the trouble or responsibility of management which the commissioners sought to avoid; it was asking the treasury for new moneys. Finally, there is the question of 'principle' to be considered, however little it weighed with anyone but Elliot. The simple facts were that bodies of helpless people, some of them foreigners who never intended to touch the shores of the United

[1] The commissioners' applications for sanction for minor expenditure on the hospital ship were couched in the most apologetic and tentative terms, e.g. C.O. 384/94, 431 Emigration, 13 Jan. 1855.

[2] C.O. 384/94, 2776, 7146 and 7873 Emigration, 22 Mar., 30 July and 2 Nov. 1855. It is interesting to note that the alarm of the local inhabitants of Birkenhead and Greenock and their opposition to the infected emigrants being disembarked was quite as strong as the resistance in Queenstown. The emigrants had to be landed at dead of night at Birkenhead, and an 'Iron House' used for those actually in the throes of cholera; and the port medical officer at Greenock refused initially to permit the emigrants to be landed at all.

Kingdom, needed succour; that the usual local and private agencies of relief and charity either could not or would not provide it; and that in the circumstances the state had eventually, however reluctantly and economically, to fill the vacuum. There is perhaps an interesting lesson here. Men were already habituated to regard the central power as responsible for relief not merely in the midst of a calamity, but also in a continuing difficulty; not merely to prevent and deter, but also to anticipate and build. Even the strong and cunning fox, economy, could be run to ground if the chase were long enough. We may also note in the Queenstown hospital an early precedent for the most striking single feature of the national health service, namely, that care was bestowed as of right upon people in need who presented themselves, irrespective of their nationality, contribution or place of residence.

The cases which have been analysed here were petty and obscure. But they enable us, I think, to feel the very texture of day-to-day government, as it really happened, beneath our hands. This, in itself, may be a useful corrective to studying laws, or powerful individual reformers or administrators, in isolation. But, more important, we can also catch in each of these episodes a fugitive moment of decisive change. We can mark—and this may be the most significant achievement of minute analysis—clear stages in an evolutionary process. That the modern system of government evolved is perhaps well known, or well suspected. But precisely how and why it did so are still great questions. This chapter has been written in an attempt to supply a few preliminary materials for the answers.

12

THE LAST SCANDALS

1853-4

THE 1852 act was greeted by the colonial emigration officers as the final solution of all difficulties. Douglas's report of that year lauded 'the excellent regulations now enforced by the Imperial Passenger Act', and Buchanan observed that it 'provided for the protection of the emigrant to as great a degree as it is possible for legislation to provide'.[1] The commissioners and their superiors might not have gone so far. But they certainly considered that the 1852 act had wrought 'undoubted improvements upon the previous law' and 'carried Government interference in this matter as far as it could well be carried'.[2] They were, however, soon to be disabused of the last idea.

Before the act had been eighteen months in force an agitation for its revision and extension was in full spate. To some extent this was the consequence of an uncommon run of misfortunes. The last quarter of 1853 was marked by an extraordinary number of shipwrecks, which were moreover so dramatic in character as to draw public attention like a magnet. The *Annie Jane*, from Liverpool to Quebec, was lost off Barra Island in September with 340 passengers drowned; 180 perished in the wreck of the *Staffordshire*, from Liverpool to New York, in December; and more than 250 emigrants were lost when the *Tayleur* foundered off the Wicklow coast in the same month. Equally arresting was the wreck of the *California Packet* off Achill in November, although relatively few lives were lost in this calamity, The owner, master and crew of the vessel cold-bloodedly cut the passengers' boats adrift, having robbed them of their water beforehand. Seventeen passengers died before they reached the Mayo shore, and the owner and master were subsequently convicted of manslaughter.[3]

[1] *Papers rel. North American colonies*, 8, 23 [1650], H.C. 1852-3, lxviii.
[2] *Hans.*, 3rd, cxxxi, 211-12, 2 Mar. 1854.
[3] C.O. 384/90, 11571 Emigration, 1 Dec. 1853; 384/92, 1581 and 2415 Emigration, 16 Feb. and 18 Mar. 1854; and 384/93, 2602 Emigration, 22 Mar. 1854.

Both singly and cumulatively, these disasters were sufficiently sensational to win widespread publicity in even the undramatic newspapers of the 1850s. But they were only fuel added to a fire already raging. During the last quarter of 1853, the emigration bound for North America suffered a particularly severe epidemic of cholera.[1] By November the mortality was so great—almost 10 per cent—that the commissioners issued a warning against emigrating during the next few months, or at least against emigrating in vessels without surgeons, or with full complements of passengers. They admitted that this interference was 'improper', but trusted that public opinion would endorse the caution. The colonial secretary agreed: 'Any possible complaints of the ship-owners', he wrote, 'must not be considered where so many lives are at stake'.[2] In fact, the public complaints were of a very different sort. The epidemic at sea was—wrongly—reported by the newspapers as the worst mortality which had ever been experienced. The commissioners could not furnish mortality statistics at the time, and journalists supplied the deficiency with figures of 30 and even 40 per cent. From this it was a short step to condemning the commissioners for sloth and want of foresight. The crisis came at the year's end when *The Times* took up the question and in a lengthy editorial upon the epidemic insinuated that overcrowding, insufficient berth-space, bad cooking and unsuitable food, and the want of co-operation between the commissioners and their American counterparts in gathering information and combating the disease, were to blame. The numerous and laborious clauses of the 1852 act were dismissed as 'the stinted and niggardly provisions of that most narrow and paltry measure', and 'exemplary punishment . . . of those officers and owners whose negligence, callousness, brutality or avarice shall have endangered the lives of helpless fellow-creatures intrusted [*sic*] to their care' was demanded. Finally, *The Times* recommended that United States vessels be debarred from the passenger trade unless they complied with British law.[3] Tom Towers indeed!

The commissioners pointed out that most of the vessels ravaged by cholera were Liverpool–New York liners, the largest and most

[1] There had been cholera epidemics amongst emigrants in 1849 and 1851 but they were not so severe as that of 1853. For the 1849 epidemic, see C.O. 384/84, 2888 and 8397 Emigration, 4 Apr. and 2 Oct. 1849.

[2] C.O. 384/90, 10939 Emigration and Newcastle's endorsement, 10 Nov. 1853.

[3] *The Times*, 27 Dec. 1853.

spacious in the trade, and that the proposal to debar the American vessels was absurd. By now United States ships carried three-quarters of the Atlantic emigrants and their exclusion 'would throw into confusion all those extensive social improvements which are based on the assumption of a constantly flowing Emigration at the rate of Six Thousand persons every week'.[1] Nor had the commissioners been remiss in the collection of information or in co-operating with the Americans. They certainly appreciated—and in an extraordinarily acute fashion—the importance of statistics. 'There is', they had told the Northcote–Trevelyan inquiry, 'a peculiar object to be attained by their collection, which has a material bearing upon the conduct of emigration itself. . . . The proper dietary, the space to be allowed between decks, the proportion of children to adults, the exact limits as to age, and other matters of this kind can only be ascertained by experience and such experience can only be gained by a careful compilation of statistics'.[2] From 1848 onwards they had wished to set up a statistical department, or at least to employ a whole-time, trained statistician, only to be 'restrained from applying to the treasury' because of the expense involved;[3] and their first reaction to the cholera outbreak in 1853 was to seize the opportunity to secure the United States statistics of deaths and health during the voyage. 'Such returns', they added, in a private note, 'would be of paramount value in any future legislation'.[4] Nor had the subject of joint action with the Americans been neglected once the Vere Foster episode had brought it to attention. While the passenger bill of 1852 was under discussion, Pakington repeatedly impressed upon the United States minister the need to co-ordinate legislation and executive action on both sides of the Atlantic, and indeed at last persuaded him to propose such a measure to congress. And although the United States senate rejected this proposal,[5] the commissioners continued to urge, on every promising occasion, that a congressional act which conformed with British legislation, and a federal executive corps to enforce it, were indispensable to a satisfactory passenger trade.

[1] C.O. 384/90, 12223 North America, 23 Dec. 1853.
[2] *Rep. and papers relative re-organization civil service*, 268 [1870], H.C. 1854–5, xx.
[3] C.O. 384/90, 88 Emigration, 4 Jan. 1853.
[4] Ibid., 12223 North America, 23 Dec. 1853.
[5] *14th rep. C.L.E.C.*, 31 [1833], H.C. 1854, xxviii.

But despite the injustice and ignorance of many of the comments, the newspaper clamour continued, and was soon joined by Palmerston, restless as home secretary, who had already attempted once or twice to invade the commissioners' territory. He now presented the home office as the proper channel of communication between the commissioners and the public. Newcastle and Peel were complaisant. But Elliot overbore them, and insisted that Palmerston's interference be repudiated. 'It is', he wrote, 'an axiom in the conduct of administrative business that every subordinate Board should be under the orders of some one Minister of State . . . otherwise it would not be long before subordinate Officers of the Government would find themselves placed in the midst of conflicting directions and demands for explanations'.[1] Unabashed, Palmerston continued to 'intermeddle' (the word was Elliot's) and to proffer the facile suggestions of *The Times* again together with some of his own devising. He proposed that ship surgeons be required for all vessels during the epidemic; that American masters be compelled to enter bonds; and that the British consuls inspect the vessels upon their arrival at United States ports and take depositions from the disembarking passengers with a view to later prosecutions. The first was of course impracticable, and the second already law, while the crown lawyers made short work of the third by asking what value such *ex parte* testimony would possess. The commissioners for good measure pointed out that a consul had no power to detain passengers; that the New York port authorities would not allow their anchorages to be cluttered up while investigations were pending, and that the Americans would not countenance foreign tribunals, at which moreover there would be no compulsion to testify, or penalty for false testimony.[2] In short the professionals were justly irritated by the ignorant and truculent criticisms of the outside world.

But wilful and uninformed though the outside world might be, it had its uses. As occasionally in our story, the children of light required the children of passion to drive them forward. The agitation of 1853-4 in the United Kingdom and the United States did issue in closer co-operation between the two governments, and in the setting up of a select committee of the house of commons to investigate the operation of the passenger acts. As to the first, the

[1] C.O. 384/92, 449 North America and endorsements, 13 Jan. 1854.
[2] Ibid., 851 and 2760 North America, 18 and 29 Mar. 1854.

commissioners found, when they were supplied with the American statistics of emigrant mortality, that 'the most important details', age, sex and cause of death, were not recorded. Encouraged by the readiness of Crampton (the United States secretary of the treasury) 'to join hands in this work of humanity and justice towards a class of persons standing in peculiar need of protection', they then asked that the missing information be gathered and transmitted. This was eventually done. In fact, the United States treasury collected still further details of mortality and conditions during the voyage, and duly transmitted them to the British consuls.[1] Thus, before the close of 1854 the foundations of a full store of statistics on the North Atlantic passage, and a free and complete interchange of information, were laid.

Meanwhile, on 2 March 1854[2] John O'Connell[3] moved in the house of commons 'the appointment of a select committee to inquire into the recent causes of loss of life on board emigrant ships'. His motive was apparently altruistic, although he may have also felt that a predominantly Irish subject was especially his own. In introducing his motion he observed that the emigration commissioners, whom he had first consulted, had confessed that they could not furnish the mortality statistics or deal effectively with the epidemic without American co-operation; and that cholera would probably return and the problem re-present itself in the autumn of 1854. These formed, he believed, sufficient grounds for a new inquiry. The old argument that the outrush of Irish emigration should not be impeded was certainly invalid now that Irish unemployment was negligible and Irish wages were rising fast. In any event, 'human comfort, human health and human life have paramount claims'. O'Connell clearly thought that the net of the inquiry should be spread wide. Amongst the subjects which he wished to be reviewed were these: the cross-channel passage to Liverpool; the stoutness and good order of vessels; sanitation—'so cruelly are the feelings of decency of the female passengers outraged'; the enforcement of the numbers requirements; ventilation; the possibility of retaining all or part of the passage money until the voyage was successfully

[1] C.O. 384/93, 2974, 4153, 4455 and 6395 Emigration, 20 Feb., 17 Apr., 4 May and 21 June 1854.
[2] For the debate see *Hans.*, 3rd, cxxxi, 203–23, 2 Mar. 1854.
[3] The son and political heir of Daniel O'Connell.

accomplished; the merits of single- as against multiple-decked vessels; and ship's instruments.

On behalf of the government Sir Frederic Peel hotly opposed O'Connell's motion because the subject had been examined less than three years before, and the legislation which sprang from that inquiry had been only eighteen months in force. 'The large question of the passenger law, which had been so fully investigated, and was working so satisfactorily' should not be reopened. 'It was a mistake to suppose that the House could by any legislation prevent vessels from going to pieces, or from running upon the rocks'. Peel elaborated this last theme at length, arguing (in effect) that what was not an act of God—such as cholera or bad weather—was either not a fit subject for statute, or the fault of the Americans. When, however, it was apparent that O'Connell had the sympathy of the house—the seven other members who spoke all supported the motion—Peel grudgingly withdrew his opposition, provided that the inquiry was strictly limited to the 'loss of life'. Henley, the Derbyite, who made much the most effective contribution to the debate and who mercilessly exposed gross statistical errors by which Peel had minimized the mortality, 'could not see the wisdom of restricting them in their inquiries: the more information they collected, and the more extensive their inquiries, the better for the public'. Henley also contrasted the care lavished upon the state-assisted emigrants to Australia with the neglected state of the voluntary movement. 'With the unassisted, the Commissioners have no right to interfere, but of these Parliament should take care'. The most interesting feature of the debate was that most of the other speakers of whatever party repudiated Peel's doctrine of the limitations of legislation and 'his own opinion that Government interference in this matter had been carried as far as it could well be carried'. Henley's simple stand, that if further legislation promised to be effective it should be passed without more ado, was generally approved. 'It is a very dangerous principle to lay down', declared Bentinck, another Derbyite, 'that by further legislation we cannot guard ourselves more effectually'.

The select committee which inquired into the loss of life in emigrant ships provides a full and final picture of the emigrant trade, and a measure of the success of reform down to the 1850s. There were two major points of interest in the testimony. One was the demonstration of a general change in attitude to state regulation;

the other, the demonstration of further unsuspected weaknesses in the protective system. Murdoch was, of course, the main official witness. His evidence was substantially what might have been expected; that although the protective system was still defective, and perfect security could never be attained, very large improvements had been made. What was striking in his examination was that on almost every issue he appeared as the embattled conservative, ringed about by a radical committee. He was, for instance, scandalized when such proposals as these emanated from members of the committee: that the state should receive and retain all fares until the voyage was successfully concluded;[1] that the emigration officer should fix the rate of passage at his discretion after his final inspection; or that a central state office to regulate fares and issue contract tickets for the entire United Kingdom should be instituted. 'It would constitute a gross interference with the rights of buyer and seller'; 'I do not see how you could interfere in that matter'; 'There is nothing that would justify such an interference as that' were the outraged chief commissioner's replies.[2] Radical schemes are not, of course, always seriously meant at select committees; Aunt Sallies have their uses. But in this instance the framing and pursuit of the questions while Murdoch was on the stand make it clear that the members were led to project the measures by hearing from Murdoch's own lips of the relative failure of every other means of securing the emigrants. Murdoch, in fact, displayed a conventional distaste for state intervention and a particular respect for commerce which, to all appearances, the committee did not share. He was genuinely reluctant to enlarge the number of subjects under regulation. Phrases like, 'I do not think it would be desirable to do more by law than is absolutely necessary' or 'it would be a great interference with trade' or 'it would not be right to stop emigration by a side wind' can be found on almost every page of his testimony. He did not wish to go beyond the legislation of 1852. He was the

[1] Presumably the intention was that the state should redistribute the money amongst the passengers if complaints about their treatment during the voyage were substantiated.

[2] This section on Murdoch's views is based upon his evidence before the committee generally, but with special reference to these passages, *1st rep. select comm. emigrant ships*, 5-6, Q.52-63, H.C. 1854 (163), xiii; *2nd rep. select comm. emigrant ships*, 45-48, Q.3820-50, H.C. 1854 (349), xiii. For the remainder of this chapter, and in the next, these reports will be referred to simply as *1st* and *2nd*.

professional, inured to the injustice and suffering by long association, and conscious of both the practical obstacles to reform and the
opposite moods of the leviathan, opinion. But on these issues Murdoch now appeared old-fashioned and certainly stood alone. For
one general lesson of the 1854 inquiry was that the centre of the
debate had altogether shifted from the proper limits of state intervention to the most effective means of state control. Like Peel in the
commons debate, Murdoch was still engaged in combat upon the
old ground. But here the battle had really passed him by. The shipping merchants examined by the committee naturally considered
that the government had intervened sufficiently—or rather excessively—already. As Phillips, one London broker, sturdily declared,
'We have had too much legislation on the subject; if we could have
less we should do a great deal better';[1] and by 'less' Phillips meant
not only lighter burdens but simpler drafting. But no other witnesses, professional or lay, nor any of the members of the select
committee was in the least concerned about the further and indefi-
nite extension of regulation. It was merely the *mode* of the regulation
which was disputed.

Here the emigration commissioners as a body and Murdoch
especially had decided and by no means conservative views. Murdoch may have wanted no further regulation, but he also wanted
those subjects which were already regulated to be as effectively,
yet variably, controlled as possible. To this end he advocated
the order-in-council as the means of dealing with all doubtful or
inconstant matters. He wished to see large sections of the legislation
and all the emigration officer's discretions superseded by orders.
Statute was, he declared, too slow and cumbrous a procedure to
give effect to scientific discoveries or other technical advances, or
to deal with calamities and catastrophes, or to tighten particular
regulations as, gradually, it became practicable to do so. Both the
order-in-council and the executive discretion had the essential
merit of flexibility, but Murdoch preferred the first. It was, he said,
conducive to a known and uniform practice, and it should encourage
the officers to act boldly by protecting them from suits for damages.
If the officers retained any discretions at all, Murdoch concluded,
they should be 'enjoined' and not merely empowered to use them.

All the emigration officers who testified before the select

[1] *1st*, 102, Q.1784-5.

committee favoured the executive discretion as against the order-in-council, though some wanted general and undefined, and some precise discretions. Lieut. Lean of London had no scruples about penalizing the trade if it served the interests of the emigrants, and he confessed that he interpreted his discretions very freely. 'I think', he added, 'in the broad view I take of this [the 1852] act of parliament that sufficient powers are vested in me . . . I take a responsibility upon myself in so doing, but I have never hesitated to do it'.[1] On the other hand Commander Schomberg, the new chief emigration officer at Liverpool in place of Patey, found absolute but unspecific powers 'very distressing and distasteful'. He wished the officer's powers to be large but also detailed and exact: nothing less would secure him from recriminations and prosecutions.[2] Schomberg also—and a-typically—showed some understanding of the shipper's viewpoint. 'I can only believe now', he declared, 'that the point objected to is the despotic authority of one person': and to meet this feeling of insecurity and powerlessness, he suggested arbitration wherever practicable.[3] Most of the officers endorsed Lean's hearty determination to take care of the emigrants and let the trade fend for itself:[4] and two board of trade inspectors who were also examined by the select committee inclined in the same direction. Both favoured unlimited powers for the executive;[5] both testified to the great prudence and experience of the emigration officers; and one, Capt. Beechey, simply advocated the enactment of everything which promoted 'the safety of the ship and the lives of the passengers'. Shipowners, he said, had patently failed in these respects: 'the Legislature had better pass a law which will ensure [them]'.[6]

[1] *1st*, 106, 112, 116–17, Q.1844, 1950–1, 2033–56.
[2] Schomberg was at that time being prosecuted in a stowage case for the improper use of his discretionary powers.
[3] *2nd*, 14, 16, 19–21, Q.3422–4, 3437–53, 3487–511.
[4] E.g. the evidence of Lieut. de Courcy, Friend's successor at Queenstown, *2nd*, 156, Q. 5855–62.
[5] They were at pains to point out the difficulties which legislative 'rigidity' might lead to, and the merits of flexible and comprehensive authority for the executive.
[6] *1st*, 130–1, 134, Q.2425–8, 2482 (evidence of Capt. Beechey); *1st*, 141–3, Q.2604–55 (evidence of Capt. Walker). In advocating the most authoritative state regulation, Beechey was particularly concerned with stowage, instruments, crews and fittings. There were, he added, 'many other things which are desirable, but which would not be practical, or perhaps prudent'.

Two philanthropists who testified were even more radical and imperious in their proposals than the administrators. The veteran reformer Mrs Chisholm warmly applauded the practice of gradually and systematically increasing the load in the passenger acts (some of the officers also commended this sort of Fabianism).[1] She went on to praise the commissioners' concern with minutiae in the regulations. At the same time, she wanted 'something plain and simple, like the regulations for hackney coaches' in certain fields. But her 'simplification' was far from what Mr Phillips and his fellow-brokers had in mind. One of her proposals was that all vessels and masters should be licensed, the licences to be withdrawn when the vessels deteriorated or the masters misbehaved.[2] Samuel Sidney, another social reformer, who had a fair working knowledge of the trade, put forward three major principles. First, that common law notions be altogether set aside in the case of emigrants: they were inappropriate to this 'most exceptional' problem. Secondly, that the emigration officers be induced to act boldly by providing them with absolute security against prosecutions under any head. And thirdly, that the commissioners be given a large measure of autonomy, with at least the same powers of formulating regulations as, say, the board of trade possessed in the case of railways.[3] One other point of interest in this aspect of the evidence was the recommendation that specialist officers be added to the corps to deal with the new technical matters which were proliferating; and that some of the technical issues be transferred to marine departments which were engaged in the relevant research.[4]

From all this it is clear that the debate on regulation had moved to a new plane. Apart from the self-interested shippers, only Murdoch and (in a lesser degree) Schomberg paid the smallest attention to what the trade or the public might not stand. Only Murdoch —and even he but faintly—still employed the argument that fares must not be raised too high. Generally, the discussion was reduced to the bare essentials of evils and remedies; and all the complex arguments as to the mode of regulation were cast in terms of which would most surely secure the universally accepted goals. No one at

[1] E.g. *2nd*, 153, Q.5796-806.
[2] *1st*, 167, Q.3064-75.
[3] *2nd*, 64-66, Q.4168-255.
[4] *2nd*, 16, Q.3437-53. The admiralty and the board of trade were suggested.

all appears to have been concerned that the powers might be abused or operate tyrannically. Perhaps it was innocently assumed that the good sense of the officers was a sufficient bulwark against despotism. It may even be that such fears now seemed *démodé*. Certainly, the testimony as a whole was cast in a remarkable governmental idiom. Executive discretions were not new; but their nature, their critical importance in the system of controls and the difficulty of ensuring that they were exercised, had never hitherto been recognized. Delegated legislation was not new; but it had never hitherto named or advocated in its own right. The calls for government by order-in-council, for the rule of natural science, for exorcizing the lingering shades of common law, for official immunity, for overt specialization in the corps, for reservoirs of executive authority—all these spoke a language never heard before in this subject. The further developments in state power which had been gathering force since 1849 were now breaking through the surface, breaking, at any rate, into consciousness and words.

The other interesting feature of the testimony before the 1854 committee was the striking demonstration of the inefficiency of the current protective system. The evidence of the large number of lay but informed or experienced witnesses who were summoned threw a new and very cheerless light upon the scene. We shall select seven from amongst these witnesses to cover the main features of the trade. Lieut. Hutchinson, harbour-master at Kingstown, provided the severest criticism of the vessels and their fittings. He found almost all to be deficient in stoutness, equipment and the number of the crew.[1] Few would have satisfied the admiralty specification for convict ships, though this was only Æ at Lloyd's; and the same was true of the appointments. 'It should be the business of the authorities', Hutchinson declared, 'to see that the vessel is fit in every way to convey the man and his family safe. . . . An emigrant does not understand the nature of the vessel he is going in; he may go in a sieve; in fact, his whole object is cheapness'.[2] Ventilation, sanitation and berthing were also bad on most passenger ships. The statutory requirements were seldom fulfilled. Hutchinson had never

[1] Hutchinson advocated four men for every 100 tons as a minimum, instead of the two or three then generally employed. He also pressed for the improvement of navigation.

[2] *1st*, 71, Q.1116–17.

known a case in which the single men were separated from the remainder by a bulkhead. The young men and girls were usually mixed together, 'in a very indecent kind of way'. Berths for four adults, a mere six feet by six in area, were still the rule: 'they have not more room than in their coffins'.[1] The few water-closets provided were 'wretchedly unsubstantial', and temporary, uncaulked decks, sources of wet and filth, were still common, and effective ventilation shafts still rare. The general picture painted[2] was probably too black. Hutchinson did encounter some United States and Liverpool vessels at Dublin, but not the best or nearly a proportionate number. Even so, it is all too clear that some of the trade was still disgraceful, and that the passenger acts were very ill-enforced in certain fields.

The burden of the testimony of John Duross, a constable who had special charge of the emigrant docks and lodgings at Cork since 1849, was that the emigrant was imposed upon from first to last. He was seized as soon as he arrived in Cork by runners, who led him to the passage-broker, the grocer, the baker, the chandler, the bacon store and so on. Everywhere he was told that he needed a multitude of supplies. Everywhere he was overcharged, quite apart from the runner's commission of 5 to 15 per cent at all places. Duross said that he and the magistrates had been struggling for five years— and with some success—to protect the emigrants. Even when prosecutions failed, the publicity was useful: the newspaper reports of trials acted as a deterrent. But neither he nor the magistrates could do enough. No measure short of compelling the vessels to supply all the food and furnishings for passengers would stamp out these abuses; and even if this were enacted, the police would still need more power over runners, power to search houses, to demand licences, and to arrest on suspicion; while the magistrates would still need the widest jurisdiction over profiteering and 'every fraud', and the power to try issues out of hand. Like a number of other Irish witnesses,[3] Duross was also a warm advocate of a central government depot at Cork to serve as a control point for the south of Ireland. He was at pains to point out the improvements in the

[1] Hutchinson also testified that the statutory between-decks height was seldom observed. Only a five-feet clearance was usually provided.

[2] *1st*, 60-67, 71, 75-78, Q.910-1079, 1111-27, 1230-93.

[3] *1st*, 77, Q.1278-80 (evidence of Lieut. Hutchinson); *2nd*, 103, Q.4878-88 (evidence of J. Besnard); &c.

Cork trade since the late 1840's and to stress the merits of the emigration officer at Queenstown.[1] But at several points his evidence is disconcertingly reminiscent of early reports of Friend, Miller and the other first generation officers.

During the course of the examination of Sylvester Redmond, a Liverpool journalist, whose 'assignment' had included the passenger business for many years, the chairman read out a long passage from the evidence before the select committee of 1852 detailing the Liverpool abuses, and asked Redmond whether any of the abuses still survived. 'That system is still in existence', he replied. The lodgings were still filthy and overcrowded, half-drinking shops, half-cellars. A few runners were respectable, but the majority rogues. Not one in a hundred possessed the written authority from a principal which the 1852 act enjoined: they still acted as freelances, touting the emigrants from broker to broker, and merchant to merchant, in search of the best commission. The rule that the brokers post up lists of their runners in their offices was never observed, and the police regulation of the 'mancatchers' but spasmodic and ineffectual. 'I think', Redmond declared, 'that there is no provision at all which protects the emigrants from the frauds of these people'. The crux of the matter was that emigrants could not, or would not, wait for redress, and all new remedies should take this fact as their starting point. Full summary powers for the executive officers, the police and the magistrates were, he believed, the obvious conclusion. Redmond had also a wide experience of vessels and their fittings. He said that the majority still provided no segregation of the sexes, although the proportion which obeyed the law in this respect had steadily increased since 1852. By now most of the Liverpool vessels also provided enclosed privies, but almost all on deck and so far unsatisfactory.[2] Lighting, ventilation and water casks were still deplorable, although the food requirements were well observed. He knew of no case of sea-faring men being appointed as passenger stewards, as the 1852 act stipulated. 'Persons who have been in the habit of going to sea are very hard to be found for that

---

[1] 2nd, 80–81, 84, 86–90, Q.4458–93, 4548–62, 4597–645. Duross's evidence was fully corroborated by another Cork witness, J. Besnard, who had at least fifteen years' close knowledge of the passenger trade in that port. For Besnard's evidence generally, see 2nd, 90–108, Q.4651–980.

[2] Women, Redmond explained, would not go amongst the sailors, especially at night, and deck privies were, moreover, always in danger from the seas.

purpose, and therefore they are obliged to resort to passengers':
and passengers were practically worthless. Vessels which should
have employed ship's physicians often failed to do so, and some of
the 'physicians' who were employed were not merely unqualified
but totally ignorant of medicine.[1]

The main complaints of Dr O'Doherty, a physician who had
made ten crossings as a ship's surgeon between 1850 and 1854, were
of the food, water and medical attention. He said that the water
allowance was almost invariably short, with the initial deficiency
often aggravated by the bursting of bad casks. O'Doherty also deplored the quality and the cooking of the food—it 'is not what you
would give your servants'—and he described American vessels on
which the bread left over from one crossing was furnished again for
the next. But the real interest of his testimony lay in the account of
the difficulties of the ship physician, virgin soil so far as the commissioners and the officers were concerned. He pointed out that the
physician had no control over embarkation inspections or ship's
medicines; he had no coercive power at sea but must 'cajole and
persuade'; and (what was really fatal) as an employee of the master
or owner, he could not side with the passengers as he should.
O'Doherty was quite clear that the improvement since 1848—before
which all had been 'lawlessness'—was great and cumulative. But
equally the emigrants still suffered. Amongst his specific recommendations for reform were the doubling of the food and water
allowances, the search for some better means of enforcing these requirements, and (a striking proposal) that all ship's physicians be
state employees. This last, O'Doherty declared, was the only means
of ensuring discipline and justice at sea, and the necessary co-ordination of the work of the emigration officer and the physician at the
ports of embarkation.[2]

A second witness who described the passage was Delany Finch,
who had crossed the Atlantic in the *Fingal* in 1853. The *Fingal* was
a large, modern vessel but the shifting of her cargo, 780 tons of railroad iron, nearly in the ratio of 4 : 5 to the registered tonnage, caused
her to wallow and labour in mid-ocean.[3] No attempt was made to
segregate the sexes although the passengers included some sixty to

[1] *1st*, 80–81, 83–84, 86–88, 91–94, Q.1330–73, 1400–42, 1475–514, 1883–1617.
[2] *1st*, 52–58, Q. 726–889.
[3] See also ibid., 153, Q.2809.

eighty girls without 'protectors'. Sexual immorality was widespread and this, Finch added, only confirmed what was common knowledge about the trade and what several Irish masters had told him about their vessels. The ventilators were ineffective, and the stench of the between-decks almost unendurable. The closets were soon broken down or broken open, with all the concomitant embarrassments for women passengers. The kitchen was a bear-garden, with 'great fighting and mauling' around the stoves:[1] the old and the sick often waited for hours, half-starving, for a chance to cook. There was no ship's physician aboard—the passenger-tonnage ratio was such that none was compulsory—and when cholera broke out the macabre was added to the squalid. The medicines were plentiful but no one aboard understood their nature. Thirty-seven died between-decks, but it was very difficult to get the corpses moved because all feared infection. The captain denied that the passengers' health was his responsibility, but in the end administered epsom salts and castor oil to everyone.

Finch was an educated man; but the next witness to the passage was that rare prize, an ordinary emigrant. John Ryan, a Munster labourer, contracted at Limerick to sail from Liverpool to New York upon the vessel *Commerce*. When he reached Liverpool it was to discover that the *Commerce* had sailed a fortnight previously. He was directed to another vessel which proved to have no room, and finally packed off on a third, a 'short ship', the *E.Z.* Ryan had spent two nights meanwhile at the house of his broker's tout at his own expense: he had never heard of detention money. Nor had he any recollection of seeing an emigration officer before he sailed.[2] There was no segregation of the sexes on the *E.Z.* Single girls over fourteen years lived together with the remainder. The vessel carried an iron cargo and was soon in trouble. The passenger quarters were awash to knee-level, while the emigrants huddled on their boxes. Seventeen days out, a deckhouse, with all the passengers it accommodated and five or six of the crew, was washed away by heavy

[1] No passenger cook was required by law because the passenger-tonnage ratio was so low; and there was none aboard.

[2] As a 'short ship', the *E.Z.* would have been exempt from most of the requirements of the passenger act. This might explain the officer's absence. Schomberg said that the great evil of 'short ships' was that 'the poor, ignorant people' did not realize that they were in a different category to the rest. *2nd*, 11, 13–14, Q.3364–5, 3401–11.

seas; and a little later the *E.Z.* foundered. When he reached Liverpool again, Ryan received his passage money back and a few shillings 'compensation'. He had made no complaints and sought out no emigration officer. He knew nothing of his legal rights or of the possibility of redress. 'I did not care', he concluded, 'if I could come home'.[1] Ryan was, of course, extraordinarily unfortunate. But his evidence is useful none the less. It brings out clearly the depths of the possible bewilderment and ignorance of the emigrants. It shows that an emigrant might make the crossing as late as 1853 without knowing anything whatever of the protective system. Moreover, the *E.Z.* was almost certainly stowed badly; Ryan had heard the crew complaining that she was unsafe before they sailed. His contract was broken shamelessly; the ship's fittings were disgraceful; and there was doubtless much else at fault.

The last of our witnesses is Dr Douglas, who had by 1854 served nearly twenty years as chief medical officer at Grosse Isle. In more or less equal parts his evidence extolled the improvements in the passenger trade during his term of office, and deplored the evil practices which still survived. The most striking advances were in the vessels and the passengers' health. When he was first appointed the ships were small and cramped, and in almost every case typhus, dysentery or cholera broke out during the passage. Now vessels were large and heavy mortalities exceptional. The provisions were usually up to the statutory requirement, and the enforcement of the passenger act so stringent at Quebec that masters never attempted to evade them in the main items. Retribution was certain .in British North America, which was, Douglas added complacently, far from being the case in the United States.[2] But apart from the London vessels, few even yet attempted to segregate the sexes; ventilation was still poor except on the very largest and most modern vessels; the stench between-decks was sickening, especially in summer; the ship physicians were scarcely ever 'regularly educated' or even moderately competent; the cooking arrangements were generally disgraceful, with the weak suffering pitifully in the uproar in the kitchens; and the diet was still deficient, particularly in the

---

[1] Ibid., 52-7, Q.3896-4061.
[2] Douglas said that Vere Foster had consulted him about obtaining redress at New York for the illegalities on the *Washington* in 1850, but they had found that his only recourse was publication.

absence of all fish or meat.[1] This was a clear, comprehensible balance sheet, which agreed completely with the other evidence on the British North American trade at this time. The only surprising feature was the failure of the colonial emigration officers to prosecute for breaches of the requirement that single men be separated from the rest. It is impossible to say why this requirement was not taken seriously, but such was certainly the case.

We have, so to speak, summoned only witnesses for the prosecution. But there was practically no defence. Where they overlapped, the evidence of the emigration officers generally confirmed that of the laymen with experience. When specific vessels were named, the responsible officers naturally attempted to show that they had not been negligent. But the defence was very unconvincing.[2] The one subject on which there was always a direct clash of evidence was the segregation of the sexes.[3] But even here there could be no disputing the essential fact, that the sexes were not separated upon very many, and possibly the majority of the vessels. On the whole, we must accept the testimony of the seven witnesses. The main assertions were not controverted; the discrepancies were few and minor. The composite picture was convincing, and as we have said above, drawn from only a portion of the evidence. Everywhere there was support in depth.

As in Douglas's evidence, two themes predominate. One is the remarkable rise in the standards of the trade, first in the years 1849–52, and latterly since 1852. Whenever a witness could draw the comparisons this was especially, often spontaneously, noted. The other is the stubborn survival of so much abuse. Weaknesses and insufficiencies in the legislation were yet again exposed; and where the legislation was satisfactory it was often most imperfectly enforced. This last was the most interesting feature of the testimony, and the

---

[1] 1st, 154–61, Q.2830–973.

[2] See especially 2nd, 3–4, 135–9, Q.3286, 5519–62.

[3] Whenever a particular vessel was specified, the independent witness had seen no bulkheads dividing the passengers' quarters, while the responsible emigration officer asserted that bulkheads were standing when he last saw the vessel, 1st, 61, 119, 154, 156, Q.935–57, 2086–99, 2830–5, 2878–80. 2nd, 4, 135–7, Q.3287–8, 5519–50. Possibly the bulkheads were taken down after the emigration officers' inspections. But it is also possible that the officers had been negligent, but did not wish to admit it in the case of so palpable an offence and one which the select committee, so concerned with morality and decency, regarded very seriously.

conclusion is very plain. The officers were too few in number and too generalized in function to execute the law efficiently. What had been threatening throughout the history of the corps and especially from 1847 onwards was now scandalously apparent. The earlier disclosures of 1851 had galvanized the commissioners for a time. Between September 1851 and September 1852 the corps, which had been practically static since 1848, was considerably augmented.[1] First one, and then two more assistant officers were added to the Liverpool staff. The London establishment was also increased and the office at Galway reconstituted.[2] Finally, the Cork and Glasgow officers were provided with lay assistance—or rather the state tardily took over an expense which the officers themselves had had to bear for many years.[3] Moreover, the stipends of all the Liverpool and London officers were increased. But after 1852 not merely did the corps cease to expand: it actually contracted.[4] In 1854 and 1856 respectively Limerick and Liverpool lost one officer each. In 1857 the Dublin and Galway, and 1858 the Sligo and Waterford offices were closed; and this decline continued down to 1870. London alone escaped retrenchment, possibly because it was decided in 1851 to transfer some of the expense of the London station to the broad shoulders of the Australian colonies.[5]

The middle decades of the nineteenth century were, of course, remarkable for an indiscriminate hostility to the enlargement of the public service; and it is perhaps the burst of growth rather than the slow decay which calls for explanation. The last increases in the corps came in two waves, in 1846–8 and 1851–2. Both were responses to crisis and scandal. The second also derived from a

[1] A considerable part of the files C.O. 384/86 and 384/89 falling within these dates relates to these additions and changes. For the details of these appointments and stipends, see also Hitchens, op. cit., pp. 168–71.

[2] The Galway officer had been withdrawn, for reasons of economy, when emigration from that port declined in 1849. The result was a dreadful deterioration, as well as a large increase, in the Galway passenger trade, *1st*, 20, Q.301–3.

[3] At both stations, supplies were taken on at the main port, but some at least of the passengers at the outports, Greenock and Queenstown. While the officer attended the outport, he had to employ a clerk to serve in the main office.

[4] For the early reductions in staff, see C.O. 384/94, 3926 Emigration, 25 Apr. 1855; 1671 Emigration, 20 Feb. 1856.

[5] The argument was that much of the time of the London staff was taken up with assisted emigration to Australia, Hitchens, op. cit., p. 168. I do not know if the Australian governments concerned ever discovered that their money was being spent in this way.

fortunate coincidence of pressures. Not merely did the Vere Foster and Hodder disclosures and the revelations of the select committee of 1851 follow hard upon one another's heels; but the colonial secretary of the day, Pakington, was—a rarity perhaps amongst the mid-Victorian ministers—one who pressed for good conditions of service for the permanent officials.[1] When some proposed increases came up for his comment in 1852, he wrote, 'I quite concur—no public servants ought to be so worked—nor can the public service be carried on as it ought to be on such terms'.[2] And for good measure, succour came from some large, influential shipping companies, like Train's and Richardson's, who began to agitate for an increase in the corps so that the current long delays in inspections might be reduced.[3]

In 1854–5 the situation seemed ripe for another round of growth. The evidence before the select committee of 1854 was quite conclusive in establishing its need. But now everything seemed to conspire against expansion. First and perhaps foremost were the rampant principles of treasury control and reduced public spending: Trevelyanism and Gladstonian finance were just then settling in the saddle. In fact the expenditure upon emigration more or less steadily declined from 1852 to 1875.[4] A ranging shot was fired in 1851 when F. Scott objected in the house of commons to the amount of the commissioners' estimate;[5] and in 1854 the assaults of the financial reformers began in earnest. Bright demanded an all-round reduction in the commissioners' staff, and was strongly supported by other radicals and economizers.[6] These demands were repeated in 1855 and 1856, by which time Henry Labouchere, a sympathizer, had become colonial secretary. Labouchere promised that as the business of the commissioners diminished 'the Government would, of course,

[1] C.O. 384/89, 3533 North America, April 1852, Elliot's and Pakington's endorsements.

[2] Ibid., 5855 North America, commissioners: Merivale and endorsements, 3 July and 6 Aug. 1852. See also Pakington's defence of the commissioners and their officers in 1856, *Hans.* 3rd, cxli, 1010–13, 14 Apr. 1856.

[3] E.g. C.O. 384/89, 4970 and 5210 North America, commissioners: Merivale, 3 and 18 June 1852.

[4] The 1851 vote was £25,331, that of 1875, £4,176. The last occasion on which the vote exceeded £10,000 was 1865. The corps of emigration officers accounted, of course, for a relatively small part of the total expenditure.

[5] *Hans.*, 3rd, cxviii, 14 July 1851.

[6] Ibid., cxxxiv, 720–1, 26 June 1854.

feel bound at the same time to diminish, as far as possible, the expenditure'.[1] In 1857, 1859, 1860, 1862, 1863, and 1864 the attacks upon the estimates continued,[2] as did indeed the fall in the commissioners' expenditure, and the decline in the executive corps.[3] The officers were not a direct target of the reformers—in fact the most persistent assailant, C. B. Adderley, observed in 1859 that he did not object to that part of the vote which paid their salaries[4]—but they inevitably suffered from the pressure to present ever-lower totals. And when one officer was restored to the reduced Liverpool establishment in 1864, the appointment did not escape the searching eye of another economizer, W. Williams, who demanded an explanation.[5] Throughout this phase, such small gains as were achieved were usually presented as economies.[6]

Again, the commissioners were unfortunate in that when the time was ripest for an enlargement of the executive, in 1854-5, the demands of the Crimean War upon reserve naval officers were making it difficult to maintain, let alone increase the corps.[7] It was unlucky, moreover, that during the vital thirteen months from June 1854 to July 1855, no less than five new and different ministers served at the colonial office, the last three of them with a nonentity,

---

[1] Ibid., cxxxviii, 208-10, 7 May 1855; cxli, 1010-13, 14 April 1856. Labouchere was the son of a wealthy merchant, and a connexion of the Barings, who had shipping interests.

[2] Ibid., cxlvi, 909-12, 3 July 1857; clv, 529-30, 28 July 1859; clx, 1366-7, 16 Aug. 1860; clxvii, 514-16, 12 June 1862; clxxi, 1489, 25 June 1863; clxxv, 1891-6, 16 June 1864. The attacks were resumed in the late 1860s and early 1870s, but by then they were made by the imperialists as much as the economizers.

[3] The commissioners themselves were not spared. When C. A. Wood retired in 1857, he was not replaced.

[4] In the course of the 1859 debate referred to above. Adderley was later Baron Norton. Adderley had served on the passenger acts committee of 1851 which may account for his restraint towards the executive officers.

[5] In the course of the 1864 debate referred to above.

[6] E.g. C.O. 384/89, 5210 North America, 18 June 1852. When the special officer, R. W. Evatt, to supervise stowage at Liverpool was appointed in 1854, it was for twelve months only, for a stipend of £200. At the end of this time he was to report on the subject, and the ordinary emigration officers to take over, C.O. 384/90, Merivale: commissioners, 10 Jan. 1854; 384/92, commissioners: Merivale, 4 Apr. 1854; in fact, he proved indispensable and had to be retained.

[7] Quite apart from calling-up, there was a new difficulty in recruiting young and active officers because the salary was so small and the work so heavy, C.O. 384/90, 349 Australia, 13 Jan. 1853.

John Ball, as under-secretary.[1] None had time to learn the needs of the department; and none showed any sympathy with the cause of emigrant protection. On 26 June 1854 John O'Connell, fresh from the emigrant ships committee, pleaded for an increase in staff and status for the commissioners and their officers.[2] But this was the last voice ever raised in parliament in favour of enlargement; and it fell (we need hardly say) upon deaf ears. These were two strokes of ill-fortune. But the commissioners were also, in a sense, hoist with their own petard. They had based all their earlier requests for increased staff upon the increased numbers of emigrants. This was the natural, and certainly the easy course to take in presenting a case to reluctant laymen. But in the long run it proved disastrous. In 1854 the total voluntary emigration was lower than in any season since 1848, and it fell even more steeply in 1855, recovering but slightly in the next two years. Now the tables were turned: 'we are obliged', one of the commissioners told a naval captain in 1857, 'to take every opportunity which presents itself of reducing our appointments'.[3] Not merely were no increases in staff granted or even asked for, but, as posts became vacant through deaths and resignations, the pressure to contract the corps was irresistible. In fact, the number of the emigrants was only one of the factors which should have signified. The increase in the extent and difficulty of the officers' work was of much more than counterbalancing importance. In 1852 a hostile critic satirically listed the officer's duties which had accumulated even at that date as follows, 'He must be the judge of the beams, the decks and of the berths, and the best means of separating the sexes. He must be the judge of the sufficiency of the hospitals, and of the conveniences that are necessary to relieve nature, and of lights and ventilation, which men of science cannot efficiently accomplish. He is to determine what boats, life-buoys, fire-engines and night signals are necessary. The quantity and the quality of provisions and water for passengers are to be determined by him; he is to survey the crew; he is to regulate the stowage of the cargo and stores; he must have the knowledge of a cooper to judge of the sufficiency of the water casks or tanks; he is to see what stewards,

[1] The colonial secretaries were, successively, Sir George Grey, Sidney Herbert, Lord John Russell, Molesworth and Labouchere. None of these, or Ball, appears to have contributed anything to the developments in our field.
[2] *Hans.*, 3rd, cxxiv, 720–1.
[3] C.O. 386/120, p. 206.

cooks and cooking apparatus is sufficient. When foreigners embark as passengers, he must be a linguist to be able to judge whether the ships must take interpreters. He must be that judge of the qualifications of medical men, and he ought to have the knowledge of a chemist, and he decides upon the quantity and quality of the medicines, of the surgical instruments necessary, and the quantity of disinfecting fluid that passenger ships must carry. No man could possess all that knowledge however clever he might be'.[1] This was in 1852. Further tasks crept in in 1853-4 and another round of duties was, as we shall see, imposed by the passenger act of 1855. Clearly the legislation had so outgrown the capacity of the executive officers that large increases of staff were needed despite the fall in the volume of emigration. This was especially the case in the main ports, but even the others required additional assistance, particularly in the technical fields.[2]

There is no question of attaching serious blame to the officers themselves for the deficiencies exposed by the 1854 inquiry and subsequent events. It was not their fault that adequate machinery for enforcing the legislation, technical and otherwise, was not provided. Not only were they too few in number: the sort of service which they had to offer was also insufficient for and in some respects inappropriate to the demands of the regulatory state. For by the 1850s we have clearly reached a watershed. The emigration officers were amongst the best tools of the old, rough-and-ready, essentially personal type of administration.[3] Up to a point, they succeeded in applying a new sort of social control, and in smoothing the way for the great mass movement. But various forces emerging about this time made it appear necessary that they should go further than they did—or could. The growing body of exact knowledge of the actual plight of emigrants, the spreading and intensification of

---

[1] *Hans.*, 3rd, cxxii, 69, 4 June 1852 (W. Brown).

[2] Iron cargoes provide one example. There may have been only three ports, Liverpool, Glasgow and Londonderry, where they were directly shipped on emigrant vessels. But re-stowage after vessels had put back was often necessary at Belfast, Dublin and Cork, and there were similar cases from time to time in smaller ports. The instruments also required re-setting on most of these occasions.

[3] Much of the atmosphere of the 1830s survived in the Irish ports with relatively small emigration down to the 1850s. The trade was still divided into 'trustworthy' brokers, extra-legal pressure employed and 'authority' used masterfully to achieve substantial justice.

humanitarianism, the mechanical contrivances which opened up new possibilities in the trade, and many other things, were driving the state to attempt a much more positive and ambitious regulation. In its later stages at least, passenger legislation was exceeding what the emigration officers could even plausibly have been expected to accomplish. By its emphasis upon the specialist,[1] and the volume and diversity of the work which it entailed, it implied a very different type of administration, and certainly a much larger and more highly articulated executive.

We cannot absolve the commissioners from all blame for the reckless multiplication of duties, the insufficiency in staff and the failure to appoint experts to deal with experts' issues. In fact, they never took stock, never systematically investigated the cumulative effects of new enactments and changing circumstances. Had this been seriously done, they could scarcely have failed to press upon their superiors the need to increase and diversify the corps. We have stressed, rightly, the commissioners' misfortunes and miscalculations, and the deepening rigour of the economic climate. But after all the total sum required for the necessary extensions might not have exceeded £5,000 a year. It is difficult to believe that £5,000 would have been unattainable, even in the most hostile circumstances, had a brief been thoroughly prepared and tirelessly advocated. Men of higher calibre in similar situations at this time succeeded in enlarging their departments.

The loss may not have been confined to enforcement. The growth and perfection of regulation were perhaps equally involved. Generally, it was the executive which constituted the drastic element in our story; and it may be significant that those officers who supplied the select committee with fresh ideas for regulation, or admitted that they strove to secure more than the law enjoined, had all been recruited within the three preceding years.[2] If the pressure of labour had been relieved, if new officers and specialists had entered the field in strength, the corps might well have developed a new dynamic. The way was open for a further general advance in regulation and control. The emigrant ships committee clearly wished it; the

---

[1] Cf. E. W. Cohen, *The growth of the British civil service* (London, 1941), pp. 77–78; S. T. Bindoff, 'The unreformed diplomatic service', *Trans. Royal Hist. Soc.*, 4th series, xviii.

[2] Especially Cdr Schomberg and Capt. de Courcy, *1st*, 173–81; *2nd*, 1–25, 132–64. Capt. Kerr also belongs to this category.

public, so far as it spoke, agreed. But only a revivified and reinforced executive could have devised it in detail, experimented with it and carried it ultimately into effect. The lay witnesses before, and members of the 1854 committee were infinitely fertile in producing schemes of reform, from licensing masters to state control of passage rates, from saloons for exercise to oral examinations for the seamen. But this was not how practical improvement was achieved. It was built up painfully from and by professional experience, or not built at all. But the crippled executive of the 1850s and 1860s was only intermittently creative.[1]

It was in the nature of things, however, that the select committee of 1854 should not have understood this need for a re-casting of the executive. Then at least, the outside world conceived of reform in terms of legislation rather than enforcement, and generally failed to understand the necessary relationship between the two. The select committee did remark upon the inadequacy of the inspections. But it was a brief, perfunctory mention. Legislative amendment engrossed almost all attentions.

---

[1] Schomberg was, however, outstanding for energy and imagination even in this phase. Cf. *17th rep.* *C.L.E.C.*, 15 [2249], H.C. 1857, xvi.

13

THE 1855 ACT

DESPITE the presence amongst its members of stern antagonists of state power and state expenditure, such as C. B. Adderley, the legislative and executive recommendations of the emigrant ships committee of 1854 were decidedly radical and headstrong. Various arguments against state intervention, for example, the evil of 'fettering' mercantile enterprise, and the desirability of keeping fares as low as possible, were noticed in the report. But it was firmly declared that all such arguments were outweighed by 'the great counterbalancing consideration of increased security for human life'.[1] 'Inasmuch as Parliament has interfered to protect factory children, and other ignorant and helpless parties from ill-treatment',[2] the chairman had suggested during the examination, there could be no objection in principle; and on this basis, the committee proceeded to demand much greater and more severe regulation. In dealing with the pre-embarkation abuses, it advised that no improvement could be hoped for 'while the system of lodging-houses subsists' and that the long-deferred central government depot at Liverpool should be immediately established; that control over brokers should be still further extended; that the runners should be 'badged under police regulation'; and that detention money for emigrants should be increased by 50 per cent. As to the sea passage, the committee recommended, first, a drastic reduction in numbers, by imposing a ceiling of 500 passengers for all vessels, by allowing fourteen square feet of deck space for every passenger and by permitting only one portion of the vessel to be used for passenger accommodation. Secondly, it recommended that, since the current statutory diet was altogether insufficient and the Irish practice of taking supplementary rations aboard unsatisfactory and even dangerous,[3] the food-scale should be largely augmented and varied,

[1] 2nd, iv–v.
[2] Ibid., 104, Q.4904.
[3] Passengers' sea-stock was often very perishable, badly packed and of bad quality. It caused dirt and took up much space on the passenger deck. It also

and the vessels made entirely and specifically responsible for feeding the passengers. As to health, the committee recommended that vessels should be required to carry surgeons whenever there were 300 (instead of the current 500) passengers aboard; that this number should be further reduced when more surgeons were available; that the quality of the surgeons be improved by raising the salaries and awarding bonuses for experience; that a more efficient means of checking the physician's credentials than the emigration officer's casual evaluation be instituted; and that the commissioners *and the emigration officers*[1] be granted powers to stop emigration altogether or to require any vessel whatsoever to carry a surgeon, whenever it seemed desirable to do so. And although the committee could not well pronounce upon the technical and hotly disputed subjects of ventilation and sanitation, it was bold enough to urge the use of deckhouses for air and exercise, and between-deck water-closets in consideration of 'female delicacy'.

The problems of stowage, iron cargoes, ship's instruments and the manning of vessels were considered next. The committee admitted again that in the first three cases no scientific certainty had been established, but none the less recommended that masters be compelled to follow the latest scientific line at all times. The regulations might be changed when new discoveries were made, and meanwhile wherever there was doubt the officers should err on the side of safety. The committee was also profoundly disturbed by the failure of the emigration officers to use their existing discretionary powers, and recommended 'narrower', precise discretions in the hope that these might lead to 'bolder' interventions. As to the manning of vessels, the committee could not positively recommend a 4 : 100 ratio, or examinations in seamanship, in the teeth of the evidence of the executive officers. Every officer had testified that these measures were impracticable.[2] But the report certainly indicated that such a ratio was desirable, and strongly urged that the crews be tested, in some way or another, for efficiency. Finally, the committee found that conditions during the voyage would never be fully satisfactory

(according to the committee) led owners and masters to be careless about their own supplies—and was utterly exhausted if the passage were unduly long, or the vessel put back.

[1] My italics.

[2] MacDonagh, 'Delegated legislation and administrative discretions in the 1850s', op. cit., pp. 40–1.

until the joint action of the British and American governments produced 'an effective system of co-operation . . . whereby to ensure
not only returns and statistics of the transit of passengers from one
country to another, but also a similarity and certainty of punishment in the ports of either, in cases of infraction of the regulations
mutually agreed upon'.[1]

The emigration commissioners welcomed the majority of the
legislative recommendations of the select committee, although the
matter of the central depot was tactfully ignored. They pointed out
that the space, food and health proposals alone would increase fares
very greatly; and that the traditional policy had been 'not to require
anything that would increase the expense of passage unless it could
be shown to be indispensable'. But they conceded that Irish circumstances had so far improved and the volume of remittances
grown so large that there was no longer 'the same paramount
necessity' for cheapness. The only important recommendations of
the select committee which the commissioners rejected were these:
(1) further regulation of the brokers and runners, upon the ground
that local authorities already possessed sufficient powers in this field
even if the powers had not been used; (2) the proposals for improving the quality of the ship-surgeons, because this implied wholesale
state interference of a new sort;[2] and (3) the ceiling of 500 passengers
for all vessels, upon the ground that the other new restrictions
upon numbers would reduce the lawful complement by more than
20 per cent, which was quite enough to prevent overcrowding.[3] The
commissioners naturally disagreed with the select committee as
well on the retention of the officers' discretionary powers. They
wished them all, and especially those governing sanitation, ventilation and the technical subjects to be superseded by orders-in-council.[4]

A report from a committee of the United States senate which

[1] *2nd*, iii–xii.
[2] The proposals implied that the state should regulate the salaries and conditions of service of the ship-surgeons, and also perhaps the selection of the
surgeons by some state-appointed examining physician.
[3] The committee had also recommended that very large vessels be altogether
excluded from the trade, a recommendation which the United States' select
committee, which was sitting at the same time, also made. The commissioners
did not approve of the proposal. They held, rightly, that the statistics which
appeared to link high death rates and very large vessels together were insufficient
to lead to a firm conclusion.
[4] C.O. 384/92, 11344 Passenger Act, and endorsements, 30 Dec. 1854.

inquired into sickness amongst the North Atlantic emigrants in 1854 also came under consideration.[1] For the most part the senatorial committee merely recommended the raising of American federal legislation to the level of the British at various points. But it also proposed two measures which exceeded anything in force in the United Kingdom—additional penalties for winter sailings,[2] and a *per capita* fine on masters for every passenger who died during the voyage. The commissioners reported that the first was unnecessary; but strangely enough they were much attracted by the second. The argument was, of course, that it would give masters a financial interest in the health of their passengers. It is, the commissioners enthusiastically declared, '*the* remedy'.[3] Much time was spent in trying to devise machinery to enforce it. But all in vain: it was finally pronounced 'impracticable'. 'Besides', the commissioners consoled themselves at last, 'nothing could prevent masters insuring the passengers' lives, thereby neutralizing the pecuniary interest in keeping them alive'.[4]

With this as its background, we now reach the last great piece of legislation in our field, the passenger act of 1855. A major consolidation bill, it had taken many months of preparation. 'The Passengers' Bill', wrote Elliot when it was ready for parliament, 'has been prepared at the Office of the Comrs who have received numerous deputations and have matured it with great pains, reporting progress here from time to time in person'.[5] In its final form it consisted of 105 clauses (in contrast to the four clauses of the original act of 1828) and filled nearly thirty pages of the statute book. Few new subjects were opened up; but a great superstructure was added to the existing law. Relying, and for the last time, upon our old justification for minutiae, we shall first enumerate the main changes which the act brought about. The first reforms related to space. 'Short ships' were virtually abolished; almost every vessel which

[1] Cf. also *House of Representatives, 33rd Congress, 1st Session, Miscellaneous Documents, no. 14.*

[2] This proposal also received considerable support from witnesses before the parliamentary committee. It was not, however, recommended in the committee's report.

[3] C.O. 384/93, 10350 North America, and endorsement, 6 Dec. 1854.

[4] C.O. 384/92, 11344 Passenger Act, and endorsements, 30 Dec. 1854; *15th rep. C.L.E.C.*, 26 [1953], H.C. 1854-5, xvii.

[5] C.O. 384/94, passenger act, commissioners: Merivale, endorsement by Elliot, 29 Mar. 1855.

carried any passengers at all was henceforth subject to the passenger laws.[1] By three devices, the reduction of the age of a 'statute
adult' from fourteen to twelve years, the increase of the surface
space allowance to at least fifteen square feet per passenger, and the
provision of additional space upon the upper deck for exercise and
hospitals, the complement of passengers on the average vessel was
reduced by a further 25 per cent.[2] Secondly, vessels with 300 (instead of the former 500) passengers were required to carry a physician, and the food allowance was so enlarged and varied as to obviate
the need for passengers' sea-stock altogether. The new weekly
allowance was 6 lb. of flour and breadstuffs, $1\frac{1}{2}$ lb. of rice; $2\frac{1}{2}$ lb. of
pork and beef; 2 lb. potatoes, $1\frac{1}{2}$ lb. peas; 1 lb. sugar; 2 oz. tea and
various minor items.[3] A new system of messing, incorporating the
daily issue of cooked meals, was also instituted; and the number of
the passengers' cooks was increased.[4] A third set of changes involved discretions and delegations of authority by parliament. Here
the outstanding innovation was the new right of the commissioners
to issue orders-in-council requiring any class of hitherto exempted
vessels to carry ship-surgeons; or prohibiting emigration altogether
from particular ports; or reducing the number of passengers permitted; or laying down specifications for water-distilling and similar
apparatus.[5] The executive officers' discretionary powers also grew
apace with the further enlargement of the regulation. Various new
requirements, which included hospital fittings, between-decks
water-closets (for the use of women and children) and azimuth
compasses and other instruments, had all to 'satisfy' the emigration
officer. He was also authorized to reject any *mode* of stowage which

[1] All vessels carrying more than one passenger for every fifty tons (for every
twenty in the case of steamships) or more than thirty passengers all told now
came within the acts. Practically, this covered almost all passenger ships.
[2] The allowance was increased to 18 square feet if a lower deck were used, or
25 square feet if this lower deck was less than 7 feet high or allowed less than
3 per cent of the side space to portholes. An additional 5 square feet per fifty
passengers, were to be allowed for exercise and a 'hospital', respectively.
[3] Various alternatives were allowed but only in the form of one type of meat
for another, one type of cereal food for another, one type of vegetable for
another, and so on.
[4] If there were 300 passengers aboard, two cooks were to be employed, with
an additional cook for every additional 300 passengers.
[5] It was expected that the second and third powers would be used only during
an epidemic, but it was up to the commissioners to decide what constituted an
epidemic.

was 'in his opinion' dangerous, and to determine what constituted a 'sufficient' crew for each vessel. All these discretions were absolute, except the last, in which a right of appeal to two other emigration officers or other competent persons was allowed.[1]

As to the other changes, the subsistence allowance was increased from one shilling to eighteenpence (and in some circumstances to three shillings) a day; and the emigration officer was empowered to order that the allowance be paid in addition to maintenance aboard if he considered that the master deserved this further penalty.[2] Subsistence money was also to be paid—directly to the commissioners—for passengers who had been removed to a hospital hulk; and fares were to be re-paid immediately, together with compensation for the inconvenience, if the passengers were not received aboard on the stipulated sailing day,[3] or if for any reason they were unable to begin or to complete their voyage—all these moneys to be recoverable by the same summary and informal processes as the 1852 act had provided for the emigrant's benefit. In the case of shipwreck or putting back to port, owners were now liable for the expenses of forwarding passengers to their stipulated destinations to the extent of *twice* the original fares. Finally, runners were required to be licensed annually, registered and badged. The licences might be granted only upon the positive *recommendation* of the local chief constable or emigration officer, the latter being also responsible for the maintenance of a register of runners, and the issuing of official badges for a fee. It was an offence for a broker to employ an unlicensed or unbadged runner, or to fail to inform the emigration officer within twenty-four hours of any change made in his staff of runners. It was also an offence for a runner to demand or to accept money from a passenger. The number of prescribed schedules was once again increased to cover the licensing of runners and various other of the new regulations.[4]

---

[1] The commissioners were to appoint the adjudicators, and the appellant to pay the costs of the appeal, so that the dice was certainly loaded in favour of the state.

[2] What was intended was that the master should be further penalized if the emigration officer considered that the delay was his fault, and not that of wind or weather.

[3] If, however, a broker promised and furnished a passage on 'an equally eligible vessel' within ten days, he was relieved of this liability. The officer would, of course, be the sole judge of the 'eligibility'.

[4] 18 & 19 Vic., c. cxix.

The provenance of the act is clear. As filtered through the recommendations of the select committee and the emigration commissioners, it derived to a small extent from the suggestions of outside witnesses, but mostly from the experience and recommendations of the executive officers. Almost every clause had been either proposed directly or cast into a practicable form, by the executive. The commissioners were overborne at a few points—the further regulation of runners, between-decks sanitation[1] and the retention of the administrative discretions—but each of these had found some support amongst the officers. On the other hand, nothing which received no support from the officers was enacted. As usual, the Liverpool Shipowners' Association protested and proposed amendments to the bill. But there was little heart in the protests and little substance in the proposed amendments.[2] Neither was there any significant change in the bill, or any debate whatever, in its passage through parliament. Even more than in 1852, the preliminary parliamentary inquiry served as a lightning conductor for criticism and opposition. Neither merchants nor doctrinaires nor any other possible malcontents could hope to prevail against its dreadful findings and unequivocal recommendations.

In several fields the new act represented the apotheosis of the long process of gradual change. Practically every passenger vessel was now drawn into the net of regulation. In space, the original three passengers for every four tons burthen had shrunk at last to one for every five or six.[3] The food requirements had been completely rounded off. It was now obligatory even to provide the meals in normal sequence, and to furnish a diet not merely large enough to remove all possibility of want, but (it so happened) balanced in protein, carbohydrates, vitamins and the rest. Even where it was not practicable to complete a process immediately, the road to completion without further recourse to parliament was cleared ahead.

[1] The subject of between-decks lavatories was in fact one on which opinion was fairly evenly divided. Some argued that they were invariably 'pestiferous' because emigrants did not know how to use them, others that their absence led to accumulations of filth below. Cf. *1st*, 84, Q.1418–22. *2nd*, vii–viii, 6–7, Q.3308.

[2] C.O. 384/95, 1760 and 4282 Emigration, 19 Feb. and 7 May 1855. The commissioners made a few minor concessions.

[3] An exact comparison is impossible both because the space allowance was calculated quite differently in 1855, and because the system of measurement had been changed and become more rigorous. But the increase in the allowance was roughly fourfold, or a little more.

The commissioners were empowered, for instance, to allow fresh foods when refrigeration was improved, to change the water regulations when distillation machinery became effective, and to require ship's physicians for more and more vessels, according as trained men became available. Thus, one mark of the 1855 act was finality. Many of the themes which we have been tracing throughout either reached an absolute conclusion or were else firmly directed towards their logical end. One of the few exceptions to this type of development was berthing. Separate, partitioned berths, or cabins of the modern sort, were the obvious goals to be aimed at. One witness before the select committee actually pressed strongly for the first, anticipating the objection of expense by observing (doubtless correctly) that the innovation would add less than ten shillings to the fare.[1] It certainly seems curious that berthing—with all its implications for health, cleanliness and decency—should have been ignored by the select committee's report, and in the 1855 act. Part of the explanation lies in the counter-argument that the family unit should not be split up; part in the fact that the separation of single men from the rest—ostensibly the main source of the moral trouble—was already law, and needed enforcement rather than amendment. At this time, moreover, privacy could be achieved only at the expense of ventilation; and the commissioners bravely preferred ventilation from first to last. They instructed their officers to insist on louvred bulkheads, which would permit the free circulation of air, even though modesty might suffer.[2] But if the succession of passenger acts had not been halted in 1855, berthing would undoubtedly have followed the same course as food, space and various other subjects. It was after all merely a question of room and cost—there were no technical difficulties—and it is significant that a great deal of the agitation for further reform in the late 1850s and 1860s was in the 'packed-as-in-their-coffins' and 'floating-brothels' strain.

Thus far the increase in state power tended towards simplification and uniformity. But the corresponding advances in the mode of the regulation, and in the methods of enforcement, moved in the opposite direction. At some points the order-in-council was favoured, at others the executive discretion. In places, they overlapped. At some points the discretion was left general, at others rendered specific

[1] *1st*, 71, Q.1111–27 (evidence of Lieut. Hutchinson).
[2] Cf. C.O. 384/95, 116 Victoria Emigration, 4 Jan. 1856.

and exact. In one instance a new appeal to arbitrators was allowed. The explanation of this apparent eclecticism lies in the circumstances of each case. The commissioners' appeal for statutory authority to vary the regulations by order-in-council was allowed in three—but only three—types of situation. The first was emergencies, such as epidemics, in which they were given *carte blanche* to intensify the requirements of the law, or to bring emigration altogether to a halt. This was in the true 'primitive tradition' of delegated legislation. Plague and cholera had been the occasions of the famous early delegations of authority of 1710 and 1832.[1] In so far as this clause in the 1855 act was novel, the novelty consisted in the specialized field to which the new powers applied, and the relative obscurity and autonomy of the recipients. The second sort of situation in which government by order was introduced was where more severe regulations were desired but not yet practicable. The powers to reduce the statutory passengers : surgeon ratio, and to vary the food and water requirements, fall into this category. These delegations need no explanation, and perhaps no defence. They obviously met the needs of the respective situations more effectively than any other administrative device could hope to do. The Donoughmore committee might have blessed them both.[2] There was, however, another delegation, retained from the 1852 act, and deriving ultimately from the 1848 act, which that committee would certainly have anathematized for vagueness of expression and unclear intention. This was the commissioners' power to make regulations by order-in-council 'for preserving order, for promoting health and for securing cleanliness and ventilation'. This provision originated (it will be remembered) in the desire to control life between-decks after Stephen de Vere's revelation of its indiscipline and miseries. The absurd decrees governing emigrants' conduct at sea were unenforceable from the outset, but retained. The statutory authority to make these regulations may also have survived not from *vis inertiae*, but because it was seen to have unexpected uses. The clauses 'for preserving order' and 'for securing cleanliness and ventilation' would have covered passenger stewards, ventilation and

---

[1] Cf. K. MacKenzie, *The English parliament* (London, 1959), pp. 170–1.

[2] The committee observed that orders-in-council were a very important 'constantly growing' and (subject to certain conditions) legitimate form of delegated legislation. *Rep. comm. ministers powers*, 25, Cmd. 4060, 1932.

sanitation; and these were subjects which the evidence before the
select committee of 1854 had shown to be thoroughly unsatisfactory
in practice, but which the 1855 act had almost altogether ignored.
Alternatively, the statutory authority may have been continued for
another purpose. The emigration officers already possessed discretionary powers over the appointment of the stewards and the
construction and type of the water-closets and ventilation mechanisms; but, as we shall see, the commissioners had other ambitions
which the orders might serve but the discretions could not. However this may have been, it is clear that all these important topics
had, in practice, passed out of the sphere of legislation into that of
the administrative decree.

Elsewhere the order-in-council was not employed. Stowage, iron
cargoes, ship's instruments and crews—the storm-centres of 1853–4
—are interesting here. In each case the commissioners had asked for
authority to regulate the matter by periodic orders. But in each
case the officer's discretionary power was preferred. In some
respects this was a strange outcome. First, on three of the four
issues the emigration officer was confessedly incompetent to judge.
The question of the adequacy of crews followed by a straightforward course. Like the seaworthiness of a vessel, the minimum
number and the seamanship of a crew were matters on which an
experienced sailor might reasonably have been expected to deliver
a sound opinion; and in each case human error was allowed for by
the right of appeal to a small committee of other experienced
sailors. But stowage, iron cargoes and ship's instruments were new
and very different issues. Here the opinion of a half-pay naval
officer was prima facie little better than that of any layman.[1] Unquestionably, expert or professional knowledge was demanded;
only 'scientific officers' could speak intelligently here. Why, then,
the award of absolute discretionary powers to the emigration officers?
The answer lies in the fact that it had proved extremely difficult to
wrest the salary of even one 'scientific officer' for Liverpool from
the treasury. It was hopeless to look for a sufficient number to cover
all the ports where they might be needed. Since someone had to
adjudicate these dangerous subjects, the emigration officer must
still bear the yoke. Because he was incompetent, his power had to

[1] The board of trade 'experts' stated that iron cargoes were by now decidedly
a 'specialist matter', C.O. 384/93, 9074 Emigration, 4 Oct. 1854.

be rendered absolute; otherwise, he might not escape the consequences of the inevitable mistakes. And since, aware of his incompetence, he might still hesitate to act, he was encouraged by the select committee and instructed by his superiors to err on the side of safety and severity, whatever the commercial loss. Once again, the very parsimony of the state begot administrative power and privilege. And once again, the burden of proof, so to say, was shifting. The normal assumption that what was not demonstrably unsafe was safe was, in effect, replaced by the assumption that what had not been demonstrated to be safe was dangerous.

The second remarkable feature of the business is that, from the standpoint of 'the-watchdog-of-the-constitution', the worse evil was preferred to the lesser. The order-in-council was rejected, the discretionary power confirmed. A petty and (strictly speaking) ignorant official was presented with unlimited authority in matters which might involve hundreds of pounds, while delegated legislation, which would at least have secured the publication of the rules which were being applied, was refused. How is this outcome to be explained? It is not clear whether it was the political or the permanent heads of the colonial office, or the cabinet, or the crown lawyers, who were responsible for the rejection of the commissioners' order-in-council proposal; or why this decision was made.[1] From all we know, it seems very improbable that constitutional propriety entered the discussion in any way. Certainly, constitutional propriety would scarcely have operated *against* the order-in-council in the circumstances. The most rational explanation is that it was realized that an instruction to the executive officers (when they possessed discretionary power) would achieve the same results as an order-in-council, but achieve them more expeditiously, flexibly and informally.[2] This is, in fact, substantially what happened. The commissioners circularized their officers with technical advice and instructions on iron and instruments from time to time. Had orders-in-council been the solution, these would have had to have been published, would possibly have been more cautious and less frequent,

---

[1] The internal evidence suggests that Peel, the parliamentary under-secretary, may have been responsible. But this evidence is not conclusive.

[2] Whatever the constitutional form, the actual interpretation and application of the rule depended, or would have depended, altogether upon the officer himself: the nature of the business left no alternative.

and might even have invoked public criticism.[1] Alternatively, the same feeling which inspired the select committee of 1854 to prefer the executive discretion may also have governed those responsible for preferring it in the draft legislation. This was the feeling that an absolute discretion might lead the executive officer to act more boldly and ruthlessly 'in the interests of human life'. It is significant that no right of appeal was given in the cases of iron cargoes and instruments, lest it might lead to 'weakness' in enforcement. Published orders from superiors may well have been rejected on the same reasoning. But whatever view we take, the upshot of it all was that the shipper was placed entirely at the mercy of the unqualified executive officer. Thus innocently might the forms, at least, of arbitrary government grow from the mere intractability of problems.

The 1855 act also exhibited all the various characteristics of state growth with which we are familiar. Instances of the systematic increase of the loads upon the trade, of the systematic reinforcement of weak clauses, of the effortless passage from administrative necessity to statutory requirement, of the progressive informality of the legal processes, and similar themes, can be found throughout. They need no further elaboration here. But three minor features of the statute and its aftermath, which have not hitherto been noticed, are worth some comment. One is the ultimate fate of contract in the subject. By the mid-1850s contract was reaching the zenith of its glory as a concept. The world was soon to learn that progress should be measured by the degree to which it had superseded status.[2] But by this yardstick the passenger act of 1855 represented a decided retrogression. From the outset of emigrant protection the 'free contract' had lost ground, and (in one sense of the word, at least) status was elevated. Prescribed forms and processes, and warranties and conditions of all kinds, favouring the passenger as a protected person, had been built up over the years. But one essential element of the 'common law contract' had survived every purge. Where the broker or owner or charterer had committed no mis-

---

[1] The subject of the effect of iron upon compasses and other instruments aroused great interest among mathematicians and scientists, and was lectured on at mechanics' institutes and widely noticed in the newspapers.

[2] Sir Henry Maine's *Ancient Law*, which proclaimed that the movement of all progressive societies was a movement from status to contract, and that this was an inevitable social trend, was first published in 1861.

demeanour or civil wrong against the passengers he was liable only to the extent of the original fares.[1] As late as 1853 the commissioners agreed that this was but equitable. 'Nor do we think', they wrote, 'that the imperial treasury could properly be relieved of all charges in forwarding shipwrecked passengers to their destinations by throwing the whole expense on the ship-owner or charterer, since it would be impossible for him to protect himself by insurance against an unlimited risk; and since he has no authority over the officer by whom the expense of sending on the wrecked persons is to be regulated'.[2] But the 1855 act rendered owners and charterers liable to *twice* the amount of the original fares; and in order to encourage promptness of departure, it doubled or trebled the amount of detention money in certain circumstances. It was still a limited liability—the limit being 200 or 300 per cent—but none the less an interesting new departure, because 'contracting out' of this statutory obligation was forbidden. By now, the passage contract bore practically no resemblance to the ordinary contract at common law.

A second noteworthy feature of the 1855 act was the new judicial functions of the executive officer, especially his powers over runners (they could not act at all unless recommended by him or the chief constable), and over the rate of detention money to be paid. Judicial or quasi-judicial functions for the officers were not new. All the discretions implied some judicial element;[3] and powers such as those of approving or disapproving surgeons or stewards or interpreters were decidedly judicial. But no one who understood the trade would have expected these last powers to have been exercised extensively, or perhaps exercised at all. It was very different with runners and detention money. These raised day-to-day issues of first importance which could not be avoided by any reasonably conscientious officer; and although in carrying out such duties, he could not but affect people's livelihoods—even to the extent of destroying them upon occasions—no appeal from his decision was

[1] There was one exception to this rule. Shipwrecked passengers returned to the United Kingdom were entitled to compensation for inconvenience. But this was calculated on the same basis as detention money, and was always a trivial amount.

[2] *14th rep. C.L.E.C.*, 33 [1833], 1854, H.C. xxviii.

[3] Despite the heroic efforts of the Donoughmore committee to arrange categories of 'judicial', 'quasi-judicial' and 'administrative' decisions, it is often impossible to divide them satisfactorily, cf. *Franklin* v. *Minister of Town and Country Planning* (1948), A.C. 81.

allowed. Once again, this was a remarkable conclusion to the process of regulation. To appreciate it to the full, we must recall that whereas the context of the Franks committee of 1957, and of the tribunals and inquiries act of 1958, was judicial or quasi-judicial powers exercised by a minister of state,[1] the context here is the corresponding powers exercised by a minor and practically unsupervised official. It is perhaps an apt note on which to end the critique of this astonishing branch of mid-Victorian legislation.

Finally, when the 1855 act was safely on the statute book the commissioners at once attempted to extend the regulation radically in one direction. Inevitably, they had been appalled by the accounts of life between-decks in the evidence before the 1854 committee. They well realized that emigration officers sailing on the vessels, or state-appointed surgeon superintendents, were the obvious and the only sufficient answer to the problem. But because of the supposed expense of such a service it received but passing commendation as a desirable impracticability. What the commissioners proposed instead was to arm masters (or ship-surgeons if they were employed) with immediate punitive powers over the passengers. Their draft order-in-council provided that passengers who misbehaved might be gaoled aboard or put on short rations by the master.[2] This was certainly a strange measure. None of the executive officers had been consulted; the commissioners themselves admitted that it would be in the master's interests to save food; and the evidence before the 1854 committee, not to say thirty years' experience of emigration, had shown that many masters, if not masters as a class, were quite unfit to be entrusted with these powers. The explanation of this apparently wanton piece of despotism lies possibly in the sense of frustration generated by the gulf between what needed to be done and what was 'practicable'. As in 1848, even the most unpromising activity or illusion of activity may have seemed preferable to inaction. But, in the event, the draft order was never promulgated. The crown lawyers pointed out that the reduction of the passengers' diet would infringe their statutory rights, and the proposal had to be abandoned.

[1] See G. Marshall and G. C. Moodie, *Some problems of the constitution* (London, 1959), pp. 124–42.
[2] C.O. 384/94, 11088 Miscellaneous Passenger Act, 30 Nov. 1855.

14

THE LAST PHASE

1855–65

THE last decade under review, 1855–65, was comparatively tranquil. There can be no doubt that the 1855 act contributed to the improvement of the trade, following the familiar pattern of partial fulfilment and achievement. Chastened as they were by former disappointments, the commissioners' hopes were modest. 'Looking to the result of former amendments in the same direction', they wrote in their annual report for 1855, 'it may be assumed that those now introduced will tend to make the emigration healthier and more satisfactory'.[1] This was fair and reasonable. The standard of the trade did not leap forward overnight, but another substantial layer had been added to the protective structure. 'The greater space and ampler dietary'[2] alone constituted major improvements which could be readily enforced even by the current inspectorate, and which decidedly promoted health. The death-rate of July–December 1853, 2·11 per cent, fell to ·33 per cent in 1855, to ·22 per cent in 1856, ·36 per cent in 1857 and ·19 per cent in 1858;[3] and ·1 per cent was perhaps an irreducible minimum in the circumstances.[4] The 1855 act was certainly not the sole cause of this decline. 'This result', the commissioners rightly observed, 'is due in a great degree to the improved accommodation and dietary on board ship; but it is mainly attributable to the absence of epidemic disease at the ports of embarkation. . . . When epidemics are prevailing at the port of embarkation or in the homes of the emigrants, it is next to impossible to prevent their introduction on board ship, where they

---

[1] *16th rep. C.L.E.C.*, 19–20 [2089], H.C. 1856, xxiv.

[2] The phrase is the commissioners', *17th rep. C.L.E.C.* [2249], H.C. 1857, xvi.

[3] *19th rep. C.L.E.C.*, 13 [2555], H.C. 1859, session 2, xiv. These figures, because of their method of compilation, under-estimate slightly the mortality at sea and do not include the mortality in the ports of disembarkation. ·1 per cent added to each figure below ·4 per cent would probably correct the errors.

[4] The commissioners claimed that the mortality among the same classes ashore would not be less than ·2 per cent, ibid., 13. But this would work out at nearly 2 per cent per annum, which is probably too high to justify the claim.

assume an aggravated form'.[1] None the less the improvements of the 1855 act, superimposed as they were upon half a dozen earlier reforms, cannot be denied some credit. From both the United States and British North America came tributes to the efficacy of the new legislation. Buchanan reported in 1857 that its stringency had materially benefited not only the health but also the general comfort of the passengers; and that only one clause, that which required the passengers to be supplied with cooked food, had proved difficult to enforce. Buchanan added that the act 'operated unfavourably' upon Canadian emigration by raising the fares by some twenty-five shillings to a total of £5: 'the masters of several vessels, who have always hitherto brought out a full complement of passengers, have informed me that their owners have preferred to send them out in ballast, rather than subject them to the increased liability imposed by the Act'.[2] Year after year the commissioners gathered similar appraisals, and although it might be possible, it would be ungenerous to quarrel with their moderate judgment of 1858 that the 1855 act 'has been as effective as any measure of that kind can be'.[3]

At the same time, the new legislation could scarcely have come into operation in more favourable circumstances than it did. First, like the great reform of 1842, it coincided with a drastic fall in the volume of emigration, and particularly in the volume of Irish emigration. More than two million Irish, more than one-quarter of the total population of the country at its highest point, had emigrated in the years 1841–54. The consequence was relative prosperity and full employment at home, and a diminution in the outflow—to less than half its former level, in fact—in the years 1855–64. Real wages had risen in Ireland by 25 per cent since 1845; there was a shortage of labour in several counties; thousands of small farmers, formerly part-labourers themselves, were now part-employers; even the country towns revived. 'It is not astonishing', the commissioners wrote, 'that under these circumstances emigration should have

---

[1] *18th rep. C.L.E.C.*, 13–14 [2395], H.C. 1857–8, xxiv.

[2] *Copies despatches rel. emigration N.A. colonies*, 6–7, H.C. 1857, session 2 (125), xxviii; see also ibid., 12, H.C. 1857 (14), x; *17th rep. C.L.E.C.*, 20–21 [2249], H.C. 1857, xvi.

[3] *18th rep. C.L.E.C.*, 24 [2395], H.C. 1857–8, xxiv. On the other hand, we must not forget that each of the earlier consolidation acts had been warmly praised by the North Americans, only to have its dreadful inadequacy later exposed.

diminished; it is rather a matter of surprise that it should continue as large as it is'.[1] And there were other influences, operating more or less effectively down to 1865, which also depressed emigration. The mid- and late 1850s were marked by two sharp slumps and xenophobic outbursts (mainly directed against the Irish) in the United States; and the early 1860s were over-shadowed by the civil war. Meanwhile, the home demands of the armed services for manpower, and of the now buoyant economy for unskilled labour of all kinds, provided a powerful counter-pull. From an annual average of 260,000 in the eight years 1847–54, the North Atlantic emigration from the United Kingdom fell to an average of 100,000 in the eight years 1855–62. This extraordinary decline transformed the passenger trade—altogether to the advantage of the passenger. With the pressure of overwork removed, or at least much lessened, the executive officers could perform their functions more effectively. The change was immediately reflected in a vast increase in the number of prosecutions undertaken in the United Kingdom,[2] and a corresponding decline in the number of complaints about scamped or delayed inspections. The falling off in emigration was so large, moreover, that scarcely any vessels sailed with their full statutory complements. Most carried less than two-thirds of the legal quota.[3] This automatically increased the space allowance, with all its consequent advantages. Again, the rise in Irish living standards (and to a lesser extent the contemporaneous rise in British and German standards)[4] meant that emigrants boarded the vessels less liable to epidemics and deficiency diseases,[5] better clothed and equipped,

---

[1] *16th rep. C.L.E.C.*, 11 [2089], H.C. 1856, xxiv.

[2] The annual average number of prosecutions in the years 1851–4 was twelve; in the years 1855–8 it was fifty. There were, moreover, other indications of unwonted activity on the part of the emigration officers, amongst them considerable success in recovering money due to passengers. These sums ran into thousands of pounds a year. After 1858 the number of prosecutions dropped although the amounts recovered for emigrants increased, reaching as high as £6,397 in one year. This decline in prosecutions was normal once a trade had been brought to heel, cf. *15th rep. C.L.E.C.*, 44 [1953], H.C. 1854–5, xvii. The later annual reports of the colonial emigration officers also remarked the increased vigilance of the United Kingdom officers.

[3] Cf. *Copies despatches rel. emigration N.A. colonies*, 3–5, H.C. 1857, session 2, (125), xxviii.

[4] *17th rep. C.L.E.C.*, 12 (2249), H.C. 1857, xvi.

[5] Ophthalmia, a form of blindness, and a deficiency disease common in the late 1840s and early 1850s, disappears altogether from the records after 1854.

and with greater security against the vicissitudes of the passage.[1]
Thus, the decline in emigration, and its causes, reduced the problem of emigrant protection to much more manageable proportions,
and greatly narrowed the gap between the pretension and the
achievement of the law.

The second favourable circumstance for the passenger act of
1855 was the enactment of a counterpart by the United States congress in the same year. This was the fruit of agitation on both sides
of the Atlantic in 1854, and more particularly of coinciding pressures
at Washington from both the New York legislature and the British
government. But the Americans now found themselves in the difficulty that the United Kingdom was by no means the only, and might
soon not be even the main area of embarkation. German, French
and even Norwegian embarkation ports were rising fast, and each
had its own passenger regulations,[2] much inferior to the British.[3]
Any attempt to reconcile the United States legislation with all the
European codes would have watered it down to nothing. But to
have adopted the British outright would have imposed sudden and
intolerable burdens upon the continental outlets. Inevitably, congress compromised. At the same time, it went surprisingly far
towards approximating the United States and United Kingdom
systems. In one field the new American legislation[4] was much the
more severe: masters were required to pay a $10 'fine' for 'every
passenger who died of natural causes' during the voyage.[5] The
space allowances of the two acts were almost identical;[6] and the
congressional penalties for excess passengers, $50 *per capita* or up
to six months' imprisonment at the magistrate's discretion, were
certainly the more drastic. The American food allowance was not

[1] *17th rep. C.L.E.C.*, 12 [2249], H.C. 1857, xvi.
[2] *15th rep. C.L.E.C.*, 26–27 [1953], H.C. 1854, xvii.
[3] *19th rep. C.L.E.C.*, 23 [2555], H.C. 1859, session 2, xiv.
[4] *An act to regulate the carriage of passengers in steamships and other vessels,
1855.*
[5] Ibid., sec. 14. This was a more drastic, or at least less equitable, statutory
requirement than any which the United Kingdom legislation imposed and it was
meant perhaps not only to secure the passengers' health by identifying the
master's self-interest with their preservation, but also to provide an antidote to
the master's powers over the passengers. But if, as the emigration commissioners
alleged, the masters could insure against the liability, the practical effect would
have been merely to increase the fares.
[6] Ibid., sec. 1.

greatly inferior to the British;[1] and again the penalties for disobedience, up to $1,000 fines or one year's imprisonment, were very formidable. The ventilation, sanitary, hospital, berthing and cooking provisions were similar,[2] although the American legislation was both less onerous and less sound in every case. Certainly, the congressional act was weaker. The many other topics regulated by United Kingdom law were all ignored by congress, which also failed to provide an effective system of enforcement. Everything which concerned the voyage was specifically entrusted to the master to carry out although there were continuous complaints of masters' brutality and ignorance throughout the decade.[3] Otherwise the act was left to the customs officers to execute: no federal corps of emigration officers was as yet established. Despite all this, the American legislation of 1855 was an important step towards an international code to govern the Atlantic trade. So far as the United Kingdom was concerned, the near-identity of the major food, space and accommodation clauses (which were moreover relatively easy to enforce in the quieter circumstances of 1855–65) laid the foundation of a counter-checking protective system. From its inception, therefore, the parliamentary legislation of 1855 enjoyed teeth and force which none of its predecessors had possessed.

The third major advantage of the 1855 act was that it coincided with fundamental changes in the structure of the shipping industry which heavily favoured passengers. From 1850 on, steam power, the specialized vessel and the large and broad-based shipping company had made inroads in the emigrant business. By the late 1850s all three were advancing rapidly. Initially, the specialized vessel and the large company did not necessarily benefit the emigrant. Most shipwrecks, the heaviest mortalities and the worst scandals of the early 1850s came from the ranks of the thousand-ton vessels and the rising international lines. But in the long run the emigrants were

[1] Ibid., sec. 6.
[2] Ibid., secs. 2–5 and 7–8.
[3] One group of Norwegian emigrants wrote to warn their fellow-countrymen against sailing from Liverpool in American vessels in these terms: 'Whoever will not be treated as a mad dog, and will not let himself feel a rope's end so soon as he shows himself on deck, do not go this way. And whoever does not want, after repeated mis-handling, to be set in irons for the amusement of a ship's crew that cannot even be compared to animals, do not go there', *Morgenbladet* (Oslo), 14 Jan. 1854. I am indebted for both the reference and the translation to Mr K. M. Drake.

bound to gain from size, regularity, capital and the concentration
of the trade in three or four embarkation ports, and the hands of a
relatively few companies. By 1855 the old, small trades were certainly dying. But the act itself accelerated their demise. The
250–400-ton cargo vessel and the local port lost their last marginal
advantages in the rising costs occasioned by the statute. The great
Liverpool and New York lines could absorb much of the increases
through economies of scale;[1] the small owner or charterer was
powerless. The new and incalculable liabilities of the act, moreover, drove many of the latter to fly immediately from the trade
to the safety, if unprofitability, of ballast. Again, the sharp
competition for clients which followed the decline in emigration
favoured the companies, and the individual merchant-shipper
gradually vanished from the scene. In the years immediately preceding 1856 direct emigration from Irish ports still averaged
30,000 a year; thereafter it dwindled to 6,000 or even less. This
fall was more than twice as steep as the general decline in Irish
emigration.

Steam shared in the benefits which the 1855 act bestowed upon
the big battalions. But sooner or later it would have beaten not
merely the little vessels but even the best new sailing packets from
the trade without assistance. By 1855 the steamships had probably
captured one-sixth or more of the entire passenger business.[2] From
then on, the lowering of steamship fares and the increased prosperity
of the emigrating classes converged to reduce the sailing vessel's
sole advantage, cheapness.[3] Sail, embattled but not yet annihilated,
survived in the passenger trade to the outbreak of the American
civil war. Thenceforward, it was quickly routed, and by 1875 altogether swept away. For steam had so much more to offer passengers:
still greater space and better accommodations, fresh food, mechanical contrivances, and above all, speed. The new sailing packets of
the 1850s had reduced the average Atlantic crossing from six weeks
to five.[4] But the steamships cut the passage to a fortnight or even

[1] *Copies despatches rel. emigration N.A. colonies,* 12, H.C. 1857 (14), x.

[2] Ibid., 3–5, H.C. 1857 (125), xxviii.

[3] To a small extent, the steamship always saved on food because steam
passages were so much more rapid.

[4] Other things being equal, passages from the Irish Atlantic ports were three
or four days shorter than those from Liverpool, *Rep. select comm. colonization
Ire.,* 342–4, Q.3302–13 [737], H.C. 1847, vi.

less.[1] The changes wrought by steam and iron in the size and character of vessels inevitably raised the standards in most respects.[2] But it was the change in the time-scale which was really revolutionary. A two-weeks' voyage resolved many of the old difficulties automatically.

The last phase of our subject was, then, relatively quiet and buoyant, with the new legislation blessed on every side by increasingly favourable conditions. But it is not to be supposed that further regulation was no longer needed. On the contrary, the trade cried out for more reform. The commissioners readily admitted the persistent evils. Such of their old complacency as remained had been destroyed forever by the revelations of 1854, although it tended to be supplanted by fatalism rather than zeal.[3] They did not dispute that in two important stages of his journey, from home to port lodgings,[4] and during the passage, the emigrant was practically unprotected; and that various other problems were yet unsolved. On several occasions in the years 1856–60 the familiar cycle of scandal and intensified regulation seemed on the point of being repeated. It was in 1857 perhaps that it came closest to realization. A Dublin ship physician, Custis, who had made six Atlantic crossings, published a series of articles entitled 'Floating Brothels' in the *Mona Herald*, which were widely noted in other newspapers and periodicals. In much the same terms as the witnesses before the 1854 committee had employed, Custis complained that the passenger act generally was disregarded at sea. But he selected two evils for particular condemnation, the brutality of ship's masters and crews, and sexual immorality. The first, he wrote, bred bullying and terrorization all round, the second consisted in the demoralization of 'innocent' girls, some very young, and sprang ultimately from the berthing system. Seduction and even rape were common.[5] The commissioners would not accept these charges at their face value. They

---

[1] By 1857, in fact, the Liverpool–Quebec steamers had reduced the average length of the crossing for the season to eleven days, *18th rep. C.L.E.C.*, 43 [2395], H.C. 1857–8, xxiv. The steamers carried over 4,000 passengers, nearly 3,000 of them in the steerage.

[2] Cf. R. L. Schuyler, *The fall of the old colonial system*, pp. 171–2.

[3] Cf. the case of the *Oliver Lang*, C.O. 384/95, 116 Victoria, 4 Jan. 1856.

[4] The commissioners, in effect, washed their hands of responsibility for this stage, *2nd rep. select comm.* emigrant ships, 45, Q.3817–19, H.C. 1854 (349), xiii.

[5] C.O. 384/99, 10207 Emigration, 11 Nov. 1857.

found it hard to believe that 'virtue could be completely corrupted' during the voyage, or 'that if the scenes of profligacy, violence and indecency described by Dr Custis had actually taken place—still more if, as is alleged, they are of common occurrence—no appeal or complaint should be made by the emigrants on their arrival'.[1] It is true that Custis's accounts were hardly credible as they stood. His purpose was serious enough—he had made official complaints at New York and Quebec[2]—but the letters were, in the terms of today, decidedly 'lurid' and 'sensational'. Many a modern newspaper would have paid him richly for his labours. On the other hand, forty years' experience went to show that the emigrant's capacity for not complaining, after he had disembarked, was almost infinite; and the evidence delivered only three years earlier to the emigrant ships committee amply confirmed that there was underlying substance in the general allegations. Moreover, two very reputable witnesses, Vere Foster (of the *Washington* case) and Sir Frederick Foster, in letters to the main London and Dublin newspapers in the autumn of 1857, insisted that the dangers to morality during the voyage were very real. The commissioners, impressed particularly by these last interventions, determined upon action at last.

Once again, they set aside the obvious solution, emigration officers aboard the vessels, as impracticable. It would, they wrote, be most expensive, and lead to conflict over jurisdiction upon the American ships. Actually, the cost of a full service at this stage might have been as little as £10,000 a year;[3] and it is possible to think of means whereby some at least of the difficulties over jurisdiction might have

---

[1] *17th rep. C.L.E.C.*, 16 [2249], H.C. 1857, xvi.

[2] Ibid., 15–16. When Custis complained to the commissioners about the *St Patrick*, Liverpool to Quebec, at the end of 1855, they asked Buchanan and Douglas to investigate the case. They found nothing on which a prosecution might be based, but this is not surprising when all the 'plaintiff's' witnesses had long since dispersed. Custis explained his failure at New York by legal difficulties (and in fact the conduct would not appear to have contravened the U.S. passenger act as such) and by the reluctance of the injured parties to testify.

[3] This is my own estimate based upon the facts that less than 250 vessels were currently engaged in the passenger trade, and the emigration 'season' was now spread throughout the year. Forty, perhaps even thirty, officers would have sufficed: and this was the time when the commissioners were busiest in reducing the number of the corps. If state-appointed physicians had been employed, with their stipends saved wherever they were required by law, the cost would have been much lower.

been overcome.[1] But the commissioners dismissed this solution without a backward glance, and sifted the less hopeful alternatives. Two were eventually proposed. First, that all masters be required to enter 'a bond for morality'. The object was to ensure the punishment of foreign masters, if they returned to the United Kingdom, for permitting misconduct on their vessels. For various reasons, this was unlikely to prove effective.[2] The second recommendation was much more promising. At an outlay of £600–£800, the commissioners proposed to 'test' twenty vessels by sending out 'secret' government agents as steerage passengers to gather full and accurate information on conditions between-decks, from which the necessary reforms could be riddled out in course. This was by no means the bizarre, 'cloak-and-dagger' business which it might at first appear. No public servant had ever reported, formally or informally, upon the passage: so far as we know none had ever experienced it. It is true that a decade's lay testimonies, some from intelligent, dispassionate witnesses, had produced an overwhelming convergence of probabilities upon the main points. But the conclusions were general, incapable of scientific or statistical arrangement and naturally disputed by owners and masters. The state could not well implant an imprimatur under these conditions. Executive experience was the foundation, and the irresistible justification, of the regulation which had slowly been erected at the ports of embarkation. What the commissioners now proposed was to secure the equivalent experience of the Atlantic crossing; and to do this secrecy was indispensable. A master who knew that his doings would sooner or later be reviewed in bluebooks was bound to be on his best be-

[1] It was not impossible, under the new good relations between the United Kingdom and American authorities, that some arrangement leading to prosecutions in the United States for infringements of the congressional act might have been reached. And apart from this, even *ex parte* testimony by deposition backed by the direct evidence and authority of a state officer might have sufficed often enough in British courts to have acted as a general deterrent. As to the difficulty of foreign masters not returning to the United Kingdom, the passenger trade was now such a specialized business that all were practically obliged to do so, unless they changed their occupation.

[2] The one circumstance in which it was likely to operate effectively was when foreign ships were obliged to put back to or into British ports after they had cleared. Otherwise, the difficulties of securing satisfactory evidence to enforce the bond were practically insuperable. Cf. *17th rep. C.L.E.C.* [2249], H.C. 1857, xvi. Moreover, 'morality' in this context was, to say the least, difficult to formulate legally.

haviour during the voyage. Thus, the commissioners' proposal was
the logical administrative response in all the circumstances. But
there is more to government than governing. Unerringly, Elliot
revealed the insurmountable obstacle. He had, he wrote, 'an almost
insuperable dislike' of spying.[1] There can be little doubt that this
would also have been the common Englishman's reaction. The
emotive powers (to employ again the jargon of today) of such a
phrase as 'secret government agent' in the 1850s would have been
disastrously great. The proposal was dropped immediately, never
to be revived by the administrators.

In the event nothing was done. The commissioners privately
determined to investigate all complaints, and to tighten the system
of controls.[2] But this was a meaningless, if pious, aspiration. They
already 'investigated complaints' to small effect, and there were no
controls to tighten. Publicly, they admitted in their annual report
of 1857 that the conditions between-decks were conducive to indecency; that profligacy was common; that the passenger act was
'constantly, perhaps generally, disregarded on the voyage, and that
emigrants are sometimes treated with neglect and possibly with
violence'. Nor, the report continued, was it only at sea that the act
was flouted by foreign masters. Foreign vessels commonly took on
what the officer deemed to be a sufficient crew, or a surgeon or a
steward if they were required by British law, for the purposes of
passing the inspection, and then re-landed them up-river or along
the coast.[3] The explanation of this startling frankness was, of course,
the commissioners' blanket defence that they had no jurisdiction
over foreign vessels after they had been cleared. Many remedies,
the report laconically concluded, had been suggested, but none with
any prospect of success.[4]

In fact, the age of large reforms and overhauls was done. In the
spring of 1859 the commissioners successfully resisted the last considerable attempt to open up the subject as a whole. An Irish M.P.,
MacEvoy, proposed yet another select committee to investigate the

[1] C.O. 384/99, 10207 Emigration, Elliot's endorsement, 16 Nov. 1857.
[2] Ibid., commissioners' endorsement.
[3] The commissioners pointed out that the emigration officer's inspection had
to be made before the ship got under way; that it was very easy to drop men at a
river like the Mersey; and that the only alternative, a second inspection by a
man-of-war at the river mouth, was obviously objectionable.
[4] 18th rep. C.L.E.C., 16–17, 24 [2395], H.C. 1857–8, xxiv.

operation of the passenger act. But Bulwer-Lytton, the colonial secretary of the day, rejected the proposal, upon Murdoch's strong recommendation. Murdoch admitted that there was still much 'sharping' at the embarkation ports, still frauds by brokers, still insufficient protection for the female emigrants. But even these evils, he claimed, were being reduced; and he had learned his lesson of Elliot well enough to point out the difficulty of persuading 'respectable men' to act as 'virtual spies', if a current suggestion of employing the ship's physician as a government agent were adopted.[1] Murdoch's insouciance was unjustified. But he was certainly right in believing that a third select committee would not have added significantly to knowledge of the problems or of the potential remedies. The 1854 committee had exposed almost everything. Thereafter, the resources of the parliamentary inquiry were exhausted—so far at least as the gathering of information was concerned.[2]

Meanwhile, the covert governmental processes continued, albeit at a much diminished pace. Two cases will suffice to show how and why their operation still persisted. As a first instance, the responsibility for runners which the 1855 act had laid upon the officers led to a fresh understanding of the gravity of this problem, especially at Liverpool. The making out of registers and recommendations in itself revealed the hordes of unregistered and unrecommended runners who had survived all purges. After the 1855 act had been in operation for fifteen months, the commissioners dolefully confessed that it had failed to secure its objects in this field, although they still 'trusted that if due strictness is enforced by the magistrates, the runners will be brought sufficiently under control to prevent the abuses which formerly prevailed'.[3] The magistrates proving broken reeds, the Liverpool dock trustees were asked in 1858 to use their statutory powers to exclude unlicensed runners from the quays where the Irish steamers berthed; and when the dock trustees refused to act, the commissioners appointed Sam Povey, a police detective, as 'special emigration officer' with charge of runners.[4]

---

[1] C.O. 384/99, Murdoch: Bulwer-Lytton, unmarked, 17 Mar. 1859.
[2] An inquiry might, of course, have generated sufficient pressures to procure improvements where they were still most needed, in the system of enforcement.
[3] Ibid., 21.
[4] C.O. 386/118, pp. 446–8, 457–8, 22 Mar. and 25 May 1858; *18th rep. C.L.E.C.*, 25 [2395], H.C. 1857–8, xxiv.

We do not know who suggested this appointment;[1] possibly the chief emigration officer himself.[2] As to the new salary, the commissioners had already 'saved' five stipends (one of them at Liverpool) by the reductions in the corps in 1856-8: even after Povey's appointment, they could argue, there was still a net saving of £85 15s. 0d. a year in the Liverpool establishment.[3] The scheme was certainly successful.[4] 'Experimental' in the first instance, it was continued for several years. But even after twelve months Murdoch reported joyfully that the problem of the unlicensed runner at Liverpool was at last being solved, and the volume of complaints declining.[5] Here again is a case of legislative demand tending ultimately to create its own supply. The 1855 act not only rendered the executive officer wholly responsible for the runners. By the sub-section requiring records and recommendations,[6] it ensured (though unintentionally, of course) that the problem would not drop out of sight once more. If a special police officer at such a port as Liverpool was not the only remedy, it was certainly the most obvious one, and much the most likely to be effective.

The repercussions of New York reforms of 1854-5 furnish an example of administrative momentum of a different type. In 1855 the New York emigration commissioners set up a central immigrant station at Castle Garden in an effort to supersede entirely the crimps, runners and lodging-keepers who infested the quays.[7] Although Castle Garden remarkably resembled the depot which had been proposed some years before for Liverpool, its origin was probably

[1] From about this time there is a gap in the manuscript records of the commission for several years. Hitchens, op. cit., p. 81, n. 69, plausibly accounts for the disappearance. When the commission was wound up in 1877 many of the records were 'Destroyed under Statute', and he believes that the relevant series may have been amongst them.

[2] Schomberg was a man of initiative; and he had also kept this problem to the forefront, and was actively involved in it himself, C.O. 384/99, Murdoch-Bulwer-Lytton, unmarked, 17 Mar. 1859.

[3] For details of stipends and dates of transfers and appointments, see Hitchens, op. cit., pp. 169-75.

[4] Cf. *Hans.*, 3rd, clxxxiv, 1618-25, 27 July 1866 (Adderley).

[5] C.O. 384/99, Murdoch: Bulwer-Lytton, unmarked, 17 Mar. 1859; *19th rep. C.L.E.C.*, 18 [2555], H.C. 1859, session 2, xiv.

[6] See also C.O. 384/98, 2065 Emigration, 7 Mar. 1857; *Return of licensed passenger brokers and licensed runners in Liverpool*, H.C. 1857 (103), xxviii; ibid., H.C. 1857-8, (150), x.

[7] *10th rep. New York commissioners emigration* (New York, 1856); Purcell, 'The New York commissioners of emigration', op. cit., pp. 28-42.

independent. It needed little experience of the trade in the largest
ports to discover that nothing less held out any prospect of complete
protection. But one incidental result of its establishment was the
discovery that a fraudulent trade in 'inland tickets' (rail or canal
tickets from the port of arrival to the destination) existed in Ireland,
Liverpool and aboard ship. Even if the tickets were genuine, they
placed 'the emigrant at the mercy of the runners, lodging-house
keepers, and others, who make a livelihood out of the money they
can extort from emigrants'.[1] The New York authorities pressed
continuously for the total prohibition of the sale of 'inland tickets'
in the United Kingdom. This was never done;[2] but the United
Kingdom commissioners did issue a *Caution* and a leaflet of *Information* to be distributed to all passengers to North America. These
warned them in very strong terms of the various frauds which had
come to light, and recommended the use of the station at Castle
Garden 'where you will obtain, free of charge, good accommodation
and instructions as to the best mode of reaching your destination
. . . and . . . every facility for obtaining "Inland Passage Tickets,"
by railroads and steamboats, to all parts of the United States and
the Canadas'.[3] The United Kingdom commissioners also took up
the complaints forwarded by their New York counterparts, and
recovered all the moneys due in fifteen cases in 1858.[4] In this way,
new, or rather, neglected abuses came gradually under surveillance,
as the protective systems on both sides of the Atlantic began, practically, to interlock.

Minor amendments of the requirements also accumulated during
the concluding phase. Further orders-in-council and circulars of
instruction, which covered the dietary scale, launching mechanisms

[1] *Caution to emigrants to North America. By order of H.M. Emigration Commissioners*, March 1857.

[2] The United Kingdom commissioners argued that the prohibition would be
impossible to enforce, and that the 'honest' sale of such tickets in the United
Kingdom was a great convenience, *19th rep. C.L.E.C.*, 19 [2555], H.C. 1859,
session 2, xiv.

[3] *Caution*, op. cit.; *Information for emigrants to the United States. By order of
H.M. Emigration Commissioners*, March 1857. See also C.O. 386/84, pp. 17919,
11 Mar. 1857. 'Beware of buying "Inland Passage Tickets" in this country or on
board ship', the *Information* continued, 'as you will obtain them cheaper and
run less risk of imposition by getting them at Castle Garden. Do not trust to
strangers, whose object in offering you assistance is probably only to gain your
confidence for the purpose of defrauding you of your money'.

[4] *19th rep. C.L.E.C.* 19 [2555], H.C. 1859, session 2, xiv.

for ship's boats, ventilation and distilling machinery and similar matters, were issued.[1] The systematic collection and interpretation of statistics began to be undertaken in 1854, with the double justification of an urgent request from the registrar-general, and the demonstration of the want of much relevant data during the crisis of the winter of 1853.[2] The surgeon-superintendents of the Australian vessels were required to submit regular reports on various new devices for health and safety. 'We are unable', wrote the commissioners in 1857, 'without further experience, to speak confidently on this subject [ventilation]. The reports, however, which we have directed our surgeons to make will afford a valuable body of evidence, not for our use only, but for the information of all who may be interested in the matter, than which none can be more important to the health of emigrants':[3] and the observation is typical of a latter-day abandonment of the facile *post hoc propter hoc* explanations, so characteristic of the report and statistical inquiry in early nineteenth-century reform. By 1862 the commissioners considered that enough evidence of deficiencies in the 1855 act had been gathered to justify an amending statute;[4] and the bill which they drafted was passed, virtually unchanged and unchallenged, by parliament in 1863. The new act[5] altered the dietary scale again; closed some gaps in the 1855 act which experience had revealed; and brought cabin passengers and steam-powered vessels more fully within the regulation.[6] Mail boats and cabin passengers were no longer exempted from the acts: so far from passengers and vessels growing out of the ring of statutory restraint as standards rose, the acts were applied more widely. The most interesting provisions were those which raised the bond

[1] Cf. *17th rep. C.L.E.C.*, 15, H.C. 1857 [2249], H.C. 1857, xvi; *18th rep. C.L.E.C.*, 25, 109–10 [2395], H.C. 1857–8, xxiv; *19th rep. C.L.E.C.*, 19, 117–18 [2555], H.C. 1859, session 2, xiv.

[2] C.O. 386/117, pp. 322–3, 13 Dec. 1853.

[3] *17th rep. C.L.E.C.*, 15 [2249], H.C. 1857, xvi. The extraordinary emphasis on ventilation (which was also a feature of congressional and New York state legislation) was probably due to the still generally accepted atmospheric theory of infection.

[4] *23rd rep. C.L.E.C.*, 14 [3199], H.C. 1863.

[5] 26 & 27 Vic., c 51. For the debate on the bill, see *Hans.*, 3rd, clxxi, 1275–7, 13 July 1863.

[6] The statutory definition of 'passenger ships' was, however, slightly narrowed. Cf. Section 10 of the congressional legislation of 1855 subjected steam vessels to the same restrictions as sailing vessels notwithstanding an earlier act of 1852 which had treated them preferentially.

required of *foreign* masters to £5,000, and which empowered the commissioners to issue orders-in-council governing morals between-decks. This was an oblique but ingenious attempt to deal with the issues raised by the Custis letters. Foreign masters rarely returned to the United Kingdom in circumstances which made it possible to enforce the bond for breaches of the passenger acts or orders-in-council. But occasionally they were forced to do so;[1] and none of them could guarantee that this would not, sooner or later, happen. If (the argument doubtless ran) the penalty were sufficiently heavy, it might deter American masters, even though the chances of its being imposed were but one in a hundred, or even less.

With this statute, essentially minor reviewing legislation of the 1847 or 1851 type, the line of reforming passenger acts petered out.[2] In 1855 the stage had seemed set for a fresh revolution in government. Legislation had outstripped the capacity of the executive to enforce it; and in many fields, where administrative experience or technical knowledge were deficient, the patent need to legislate had outstripped the capacity to formulate appropriate legislation. But the final revolution did not happen. The flow of major statutes ceased in 1855, and the dwindling corps of emigration officers merely continued (with shifts and struggles still though better fortune) to enforce the more practicable of their statutory duties. Fundamentally, this was so because the problem of emigrant protection shrank suddenly to different dimensions. In 1856–7 the annual average emigration from the United Kingdom dropped abruptly to little more than half the level of the preceding decade, and in 1858–62 much lower. Thus, the tremendous pressures which had driven the state forward up to 1855 fell away almost overnight; and this weakening in pressure coincided with still greater austerity in state expenditure and the absence of that powerful detonator of reform, epidemic disease. It was not until the 1870s that emigration again reached nearly to its former height, and by that time the situation had been transformed. The passenger trade had shifted entirely from sail and wood to steam and iron, and steam had long passed its initial period of experimentation. The great shipping lines, moreover, now ruled the seas; and from their large resources, their instincts of self-

---

[1] *18th rep. C.L.E.C.*, 24 [2395], H.C. 1857–8, xxiv.
[2] A further amending act, 33 & 34 Vic., c. 95, was passed in 1870. But this was merely to enable passenger vessels to carry military and naval stores as cargo.

preservation and their scale of operations, they began to develop regulatory systems of their own which included medical inspection, compulsory de-lousing and bathing before embarkation, and separated sleeping places and discipline at sea. This postponed for some time the need for further legislation, in much the same way as another rising corporation, the trade union, temporarily superseded the state in the regulation of hours and terms of labour. Neither race was over; but for the next stage the batons had changed hands. Finally, the character of the emigrants had altered. Doubtless, they were still poor, but the continued growth in the remittance system and the vast changes in both the British and the Irish economies had removed forever the extremities of destitution and inexperience which had been the pre-condition of the early revolutions in administration. For all these reasons our story lacks, if not an ending, at least the grand culmination which events seemed to have had prepared. But to the limit to which it can be unravelled, 1863, and despite all the depressing agencies by then in play, the inherent momentum of governmental growth still worked, below the surface.

Under the merchant shipping act of 1872[1] passenger legislation and the corps of emigration officers were transferred to the board of trade in the interests of 'economy as well as efficiency'. It was argued that emigrants were no longer so vulnerable a class that a separate commission to guard their interests was necessary; and from the outset steamships had been subjected to board of trade regulation and inspection as well as to the passenger code.[2] Undoubtedly, efficiency in inspections and uniformity of practice were served. As to economy, the first step was to deprive London of two officers and Liverpool of one. It took memorials of protests from the ports and a tedious correspondence with the treasury to secure pensions (the first ever to be awarded) for the officers who had been dismissed.[3] Five years later the vestigial remains of the colonial land and emigration commission were transferred to another branch of the colonial office, and the commission itself wound up.[4]

[1] 35 & 36 Vic., c. 73.
[2] Cf. Prouty, op. cit., pp. 59–62.
[3] For details, see Hitchens, op. cit., pp. 176–7.
[4] Ibid., pp. 84–96.

15

CONTEXTS

IT remains to place the developments which we have described and analysed in their various contexts, and to draw what lessons we can from the analysis.

First, the general historical setting. Most historians take it for granted that the function and structure of executive government changed profoundly in the course of the nineteenth century. If pressed, they would probably allow as well that the change was one of both kind and quantity, and sufficiently drastic to justify the employment of that volatile but indispensable term, 'revolution'. But if these assumptions are in fact made, they are (it seems fair to say) made casually. Little thought is given to their internal implications, still less to their bearing upon other fields. In particular, it is not clearly realized that what we have here is a 'revolution' transcending the historian's shorthand for 'great change'—a 'revolution', in fact, of the same general type as the industrial or scientific. The scale may be very much smaller, the accidents much less spectacular. But there is no difference in essence. In each case a leap was made to wholly new forms of organization or behaviour which sooner or later affected, and ultimately reshaped the entire society. Mr Elton has already distinguished and named an 'administrative revolution' of the sixteenth century by which personal and household government was replaced by impersonal, bureaucratic and continuous rule.[1] However we estimate the intervening shifts in government, the nineteenth-century transformation of the state was certainly as complete a break with older forms as had been the Tudor development of bureaucracy. It was moreover a highly articulated process in which (the present author at least would argue) internal dynamism played a crucial part. This then, the context of a major 'governmental revolution', is the first in which to fit our story.

If the nineteenth-century revolution in government has been

---

[1] G. R. Elton, *The Tudor revolution in government* (Cambridge, 1953).

ill-recognized, its causes have, equally, received too little attention. Such reasons for the change as are commonly adduced have not been analysed or classified systematically. Comparatively little has been done towards 'weighting' these one against another or entering them upon a time-scale. And—to complete the circle—the whole complex of causation is misconceived in so far as there is no clear understanding that the new sort of government gathered its own momentum as it went along. More specifically, where the nine-teenth-century metamorphosis of government has been generally discussed, the discussion has been pretty much in terms of three types of factors: what men thought, and what men felt, contem-porary practices should be (doctrines and sentiments, if one wishes); and what external or overt events, such as acts of parliament or the judgments of courts of appeal, directed the current of affairs deci-sively, or made men fully conscious of the tendencies of their time. Clearly each of these factors is important, and was in fact influential. But they neither cut deeply enough nor extend sufficiently wide to furnish a full explanation. Further, their inherent limitations are worth noting. Two of them, doctrines and sentiment, deal with abstractions—the first with abstractions of the ideological kind, such as utilitarianism; the second with abstractions of the *Zeitgeist* kind, such as humanitarianism. We should proceed warily when we set out to show, simply, that notions were translated into fact. Here the fallacy of *post hoc propter hoc* is especially beguiling. There is, for example, an obvious danger that all 'useful' and 'rational' nine-teenth-century reforms may be ascribed indiscriminately and un-critically to the utilitarians. And there is an equivalent danger of humanitarianism being credited with various pieces of merciful legislation, without any recognition of the corollary that merciful legislation itself contributed to the spread of humanitarianism. As Dicey has so wisely observed, law itself is the creator of law-making opinion. The third element of explanation, the concrete single event or series of events relative to governmental change, is in itself straightforward. But it is often taken to explain more than it actually does. Generally, the historian dealing with this sort of event does not examine the connexions between the event which he describes and either administrative practice or the character of the state. Thus, for example, a political historian investigating the waning of the in-fluence of the crown may discover some pertinent change in the function or distribution of patronage, or in the relationship of the house of commons to executive government, without concerning himself with whether public servants were the same sort of persons, or adopted the same sort of procedures, or did the same sort of things, before and after. Or an administrative historian may analyse the civil service reform of 1853–5 without considering when it bore fruit or whether the results were what the authors intended or even if it influenced in any way the character of contemporary or later government.

This is, of course, no criticism whatever of the historians concerned. The political historian is not making it his business to look for or explain changes in the mode of government. The administrative historian does not choose to add a second field of inquiry to his first. But for our present purpose it is important to draw attention to the omission of these other issues. It is (to continue with our two examples) all too easily assumed that when we know that patronage lost its old political function or when we know how and why it came to be outlawed, we also know a great deal more about the origin of the modern state. The answers to the ulterior questions are supposed to be implicit in the facts themselves. A very little reflection teaches us that this is by no means the case. The discoveries which we have mentioned open up rather than exhaust fields of inquiry in the history of nineteenth-century government. They locate and define the problems more exactly. But location and definition do not supply the answers. Thus, the third element of explanation has pitfalls of its own. In particular, what might be termed (if the barbarism is allowable) a *propter hoc post hoc* fallacy tends to creep in unless we guard specifically against it.

Nor is the range of the ideological, sentimental and political factors (however they may be handled) sufficient to explain the transformation. At least two other—and largely neglected—factors are indispensable. One is the underlying social and economic pressures, and the scientific, medical, mechanical and engineering potentialities, of the time. The nineteenth century produced at once social problems of an unprecedented scale and intensity, and methods of measuring them with unprecedented exactitude, and of tackling them with unprecedented assurance and success. This constantly repeated convergence and intersection was of primary importance in advancing collectivism. The second vital and neglected factor is the momentum of government itself, and especially the consequences of building up executive corps in the field.

Not that these latest elements of explanation are free of pitfalls and difficulty. The fourth, that which looks to the pre-conditions of change, moving back into the vast social and economic hinterland to estimate the problems calling for solution, cannot be simply applied. The correlation between social problem and administrative remedy was seldom, perhaps never, exact. Of the several qualifications which must be borne in mind, one, that of time and timing, may serve sufficiently to illustrate the possible discordance. We have seen how crucial the press of parliamentary business might be in fixing the date of legislative amendments; and we all know (though historians, more perhaps than any others, need to remind themselves) that people live not in the long run but in the present. Moreover, the impulse was always prone to be distorted by accidents of personality or politics, of finance or the state of expert opinion, at the moment when the remedy is debated. Professor Finer describes, for example, several points in Chadwick's career when the iron was hot, but the 'reformer's' failure or inability to strike allowed a fatal growth of irremovable opposition. Conversely, there were occasions when the iron was struck too soon, when the postponement of the striking for a decade would have avoided the erection of elaborate administration upon erroneous or irrelevant scientific theory. Sometimes, in fact, the mere timing of the effort to reform had an important (perhaps even a decisive) effect upon the whole course of subsequent administration. Just as industries which have developed 'too far too early' may find themselves heavily committed to yesterday's processes of production, and others which enter late upon the field may reap the benefit of a more advanced technology, so also there is a significant element of 'investment' in altering old or in setting up new government. English local government might be very different today had not the first major reforms in that field been carried before a really effective system of national communications and transport had developed. The educational system might be very different today had (as could conceivably have been the case)[1] the cause of national education been seriously taken up in the early, and not the late, Victorian age. Correspondingly, while there may not

[1] Cf. Halévy, op. cit., pp. 53–59.

be any peculiar error or likely fallacy to guard against in the last factor we have introduced, the metamorphosis of government itself, there is certainly the simple—but immense and endless—difficulty of achieving exactitude and definition in a world of half-lights, of gradual and silent shifts and growths. Despite these reservations, however, it will hardly be disputed that the two new elements are integral parts of the explanation of the governmental revolution, even perhaps that they are primary and general explanations in a sense in which no others are. At any rate, the second context of the present book is one in which they are not only taken into reckoning but made the very basis of the inquiry.

Third, the bibliographical context. Writings upon the nineteenth-century state, down to the present day, are divided fairly sharply between general surveys of the change in the character of the state and particular studies of various departments, measures, administrators, philanthropists, reform movements, lobbies and the rest. The general view of the problem has, I think, been dominated by Dicey's *Law and public opinion in England*, first published in 1905. *Law and public opinion* is a work of great originality, energy and imagination. It virtually uncovered and specified for the first time the developments which it attempted to explain. It avoided—many years before Professor Butterfield issued his famous caution—anything in the nature of a whig interpretation of the subject. Deeply as Dicey deplored the trend of his own and earlier times, he eschewed human heroes and villains in his story, and fixed attention upon the unrecognized *Zeitgeist* of collectivism. Collectivism came, he insisted, not because people strove for it as such, but they failed to perceive that it was the necessary implication of parts of their theories or some of their legislative acts. Finally—and most acutely of all—Dicey recognized the cumulative effect of apparently isolated and ad hoc measures. In doing so he described an important mechanism for the transference of state intervention to new fields. There is, he observed, an inherent tendency in laws to reproduce themselves. Willy-nilly, every law expresses and endorses a principle or principles. In so far as it does, it reshapes, however slightly or imperceptibly, the general opinion from which further laws derive. This was a bold stroke; and one which opened up the way for new advances by historians even if few have chosen this particular path. But despite all this *Law and public opinion* should not be taken as providing either a comprehensive explanation[1] or a history proper of the change in the nature of the state. It is essentially the work of a lawyer and student of political ideas rather than that of an historian. Dicey marks change in terms of changes in the law. He does not ask how or whether a law was enforced, or how or whether it changed people's lives. And he finds reasons for the legal changes almost exclusively in terms of abstractions. Even if he holds that it was not what men intended or anticipated or even perceived which operated, it is none the less their ideas and prejudices which engross him. To regard the matter from another angle, no public servant is mentioned from beginning to end of *Law and public opinion*, unless he were also a political economist or 'thinker'. No reference is made to parliamentary investigations or departmental inquiries or reports from the inspectorates. Simply, practical government does not exist for Dicey. In the same fashion, the extent to which legislation was actually applied and the effects of attempting to apply it are ignored. Nor is the development of the experimental sciences so much as mentioned; while a few generalized paragraphs provide the only description of the changes in the size and distribution of the population, and in the domestic and occupational conditions of life. In short, it is political doctrine, trends in articulate opinion, specific statutes marking changes in principle, and the corresponding decisions of the law courts which hold the stage for Dicey. From the historian's standpoint, he legalizes and intellectualizes the problem altogether.

Law and public opinion has been considered at such length because Dicey's is the sole effort to offer on a really large scale an explanation of nineteenth-century collectivism as such. Since 1905 no considerable and sustained attempt has been made to formulate an alternative to Dicey's thesis. In the interval, several penetrating surveys of the modern state have appeared. But none has treated the governmental revolution as a distinct and individual problem in nineteenth-century history, involving a distinct and individual process of its own. Most of them are (like *Law and public opinion*)

[1] Whether or not Dicey himself intended it, his work has commonly been taken to offer such an explanation. The preface to the first edition says, rather vaguely, 'It has been written with the object . . . of drawing from some of the best-known facts of political, social, and legal history certain conclusions which, though many of them are obvious enough, are often overlooked, and are not without importance', Dicey, op. cit., viii–ix.

heavily ideational in bias, and all interpret growth, if they consider it at all, in an arithmetical and accumulative rather than an organic sense.[1] Hence, from our present standpoint, they take us little farther forward.

The other sort of writing upon the nineteenth-century state, the special studies of administrators, movements and departments, has on the contrary advanced very rapidly in recent years. The general views presented by the Webbs, the Hammonds and the other pioneers have been significantly corrected and extended. More and more tracts of nineteenth-century government are being surveyed, and (still more interesting) the conduct of important public servants and groups scrutinized, often for the first time. There is already a body of major works of discovery such as Mr Thomas's *Early factory legislation*, Professor Finer's *Chadwick* or Mr Lewis's *Chadwick and the public health movement*. In some respects, the present book is of this family, even if, remote and inglorious in subject, it must sit below the salt. But there are other respects in which it is markedly dissimilar. First, it is primarily concerned with the inherent momentum of government, whereas this is not specifically noticed or discussed elsewhere. Secondly, while emigrant protection was a representative social problem, its history differed, in some ways, from most of the social problems which, so far, have been examined. Although, as we observed at the outset, several of the characteristic Victorian media of exposing evils and procuring reforms appear in our story, one predominated. It was the everyday practice of government which really signified. Except in the very earliest years, no organized pressure group, after the fashion of the Anti-Slavery, Health of Towns, Peace or Aborigines Protection Societies or Associations, concerned itself with the safeguarding of

[1] There is a very brief but interesting mention of the question in H. R. G. Greaves's *The civil service in the changing state* (1949). Mr Greaves distinguishes three stages of development, the 'oligarchic maladministration and interfering paternalism' of the eighteenth century, the regulatory stage' of the nineteen, and 'the social service democracy of the twentieth century'; and argues that the last was born before the first was dead, and that the second never existed except in men's minds. It is certainly true and pertinent to observe that on occasions 'eighteenth century' forms of government merged imperceptibly into 'twentieth century', But it seems misleading to draw a fundamental distinction between the eighteenth- and nineteenth-century concepts of the state, except in so far as notions of efficiency in, and methods of, conducting state business are concerned. However, Mr Greaves does not define his categories or elaborate his thesis in any detail.

voluntary emigration. There was but one occasion on which an influential newspaper conducted a campaign for reform. Only twice did individual philanthropists contribute significantly to the improvement. Emigrant protection rarely engaged the attention of public men or parliament, and never entered party politics. Three investigations by commissions or select committees, in 1837, 1851 and 1854, had important consequences; and one colonial secretary, Stanley, took a vital step towards further regulation on, more or less, his own initiative. But generally speaking parliament and politicians counted for very little. Theory counted for nothing, at any rate for nothing positive. The only plausible doctrinaire influence whatever was that of Sydenham's memorandum of 1841; and even if we waive the questions of whether Sydenham was still a doctrinaire, and whether doctrine influenced his observations in the slightest, we are left with the fact that none of his proposals was ever translated into law. Generally speaking, the agents of the change were the professional administrators, and the lesser and least distinguished administrators at that. The colonial office had its eminent Victorians. James Stephen, Henry Taylor, Frederic Rogers and Herman Merivale are of moderate celebrity, at least. But none of these played a significant part in our story except the first—and Stephen's part was altogether negative and resistant. The men who made the revolution were the humdrum executive officers, and career civil servants who never rose above the height of assistant undersecretary.

Does this absence of master-bureaucrats, philanthopists and reformers, ideologues and pressure groups, newspapers and novelists, mean that emigrant protection was a most exceptional field? No: what it means is that the genus to which emigrant protection belongs has as yet received relatively little attention. Dramatic or political themes, and especially those linked with great persons or ideas, are naturally the first to catch attention. Inevitably, and also rightly, the early tendency was to enter the field of nineteenth-century administration through the gates of biography or politics or public sentiment. Inevitably, in this branch of history as in others, the analysis of inherent growth and structure is slow to be undertaken. Hence it is not to be lightly assumed that if a field of social reform lacked ideologues, schools, pressure groups, philanthropists and administrative Caesars, it is a-typical and unrepresentative. Nor is it to be assumed that the fields which were bestridden by a Colossus, or trampled by the battle of interests or nostrum-mongers, have nothing to show independent of these activities. For my part, I have no doubt that subjects amenable to the sort of treatment which emigrant protection has been given exist and even abound. Especially is this likely to be the case where humanitarian reform was married to an executive corps, or where safety or health or any other aspect of the public welfare was efficiently connected with the findings of experimental science, or even with technicalities of any kind. Because the object of our search is the interior momentum of government in nineteenth-century circumstances what matters in emigrant protection is not so much its 'typicality' or otherwise, but its degree of freedom from exogenous factors;[1] and while there may be many other fields in which outside pressure counted for as little as in ours, there can be few in which it counted for less. But for all that it is well to remember that the nineteenth-century administrative landscape may in the end look very different.

Such, then, is the general bibliographical setting. It follows that this book falls between—as it also endeavours to connect—the two main lines of inquiry which have so far predominated. It also follows that it is profoundly indebted to all this earlier work. Not only did Dicey map the country, he set out an important principle of growth: while his comments on nineteenth-century theorists have been developed, corrected and vastly improved by later writers. Correspondingly, the generalizations of this book would have been still more tentative—if they could have been made at all—without the large body of comparative material which has been built up in recent years.

The fourth context is the ingredients of the subject. For the purpose we have set out, the presence of certain characteristics and forces is as valuable as the absence of others. Emigrant protection contains almost all the useful features. It involved at least three key issues: the statutory supersession of ordinary contract; state protection of (amongst others) adult males; and the intimate regulation of a form of ordinary commerce. From Adam Smith's tautologous

[1] Professor Burn has pointed to the importance of Ireland in this respect. It formed, he observes, 'a social laboratory. . . . The most conventional of Englishmen were willing to experiment in Ireland on lines which they were not prepared to contemplate or tolerate at home', W. L. Burn, 'Free trade in land: an aspect of the Irish question', *Trans. Royal Hist. Soc.*, 4th series, xxxi, p. 68.

anodyne, 'Government activity is natural, and therefore good, when
it promotes the general welfare, and is an interference with nature,
and therefore bad, when it injures the greatest interests of society',
downwards, one finds refinements and reservations amongst the
political economists which may—though sometimes it is jesuitically
—be construed as endorsing or advocating state intervention. But
this should not blind us to the essential fact that the preponderant
bias of contemporary theory, and still more of its popularizations,
was dead contrary to this development. Instead, it was directed
towards a society based, so far as might be, upon individual contractual relationships. Hence our three issues form fair and critical
tests of the overthrow of major accepted principles. Secondly, emigrant protection involved technical—and in its later stages also
scientific—issues. That is to say, it involved marine, dietary,
engineering and medical matters, over which there could be no
argument, save such as arose from insufficient knowledge or understanding of the technicalities. A-political or supra-political issues of
this type are a most important constituent of modern government,
and go far towards explaining its development and nature. Here
again our subject, while not so perfectly matured as many others,
is certainly rich enough to serve. It is moreover extraordinarily apt
in the very wide range of the technical matters which, in one way or
another, it embraced. All transport and nautical problems apart,
ship-board life formed a microcosm—or perhaps a momentary
intensification—of existence in overcrowded, unventilated and ill-
appointed rooms, and of deficiency and epidemical diseases. Thirdly,
emigrant protection involved various pertinent qualities and difficulties of legal enforcement and legislative formulation. The character
of the beneficiaries was such that little or nothing could be left to
their own unassisted efforts. The character of the trade was such
that only instant remedies, prescribed schedules and administrative
discretions were likely to prove effective. The elements of the problem were so complex and interlocked that none could be dealt with
once for all or in isolation. The consequent type of reforming
statute inevitably tended to transfer ultimate control—even of
law-making, to an extent—from the legislative to the executive. All
this anticipates other vital constituents of modern social regulation, and also helps to explain their growth. Here our subject may
be unusually good for purposes of elucidation. In a small and

manageable compass there is a wonderful concentration of relevant data, because the extremes inherent in the particular problem acted, as it were, as a burning glass upon the legal issues.

Fifthly, the subject introduces us to humanitarianism in its simplest and least adulterated form. In one sense, humanitarianism was responsible for all the happenings which we have described. At least, there was no other incentive of any power in operation. Passenger legislation served no one's interest save that of the inarticulate and politically insignificant masses, and—intermittently and indirectly—that of un-influential colonists. On the contrary, it appeared to injure the interests of both the central government and the trade. It was generally assumed that it was in the government's interest to reduce, as rapidly and far as possible, the number of Irishmen in Ireland, and in the trade's interest to exact the utmost profit and to undergo the least restraint. But the general level of compassion in contemporary English society overswept policy and commerce. Our case is all the more interesting, and the better pressure-gauge, in that we are dealing not with organized or self-conscious and deliberate humanitarianism, or with sects or groups, but with the raw and immediate reactions of a variety of ordinary and thoroughly representative people. It also provides (to apply the words used recently by Professor Jacob Viner of the Irish economic problem of the nineteenth century) 'a striking illustration of the possibility that a greater prevalence of uncalculating compassion and sympathy with suffering may at times be a better instrument of reform than the most carefully reasoned weighing of prudential pros and cons . . .'[1]

Next, the administrators themselves need to be placed in their setting. We have two different sets of actors here, the superior and the executive officers. Practically, we may define the superiors as Stephen, Elliot and Murdoch. On the whole, the politicians had no permanent and important influence upon the development; and the minutes show that no other colonial office servant counted here for much. The decade or so of difference between the ages of Stephen, Elliot and Murdoch made slight, but, I think, perceptible and interesting differences of attitude from case to case. To each part-generation, active central government appeared less curious and

[1] Introduction to R. D. Collison Black, *Economic thought and the Irish question, 1817–70* (Cambridge, 1960), p. vii.

painful. But a more important distinction was perhaps that Stephen and Elliot were lawyers by training, where Murdoch was from the start a career civil servant. The son of a London-Scots physician, he had joined the civil service in his eighteenth year, after a short period as an undergraduate at Cambridge. In 1846 after a service of twenty years at the colonial office he became chief clerk, and at the end of 1847 succeeded Elliot, as we saw, as chairman of the commission.[1] Murdoch equalled or even excelled the others in his respect for 'trade' as an interest and a part of the staple fabric of the community, and in his obeisance to competition and self-help. (Here perhaps the difference in generation pulled the other way.) But he lacked the sheet anchor of 'constitutional principle' and the powers of political analysis with which the lawyers were equipped. When the wind rose, he was much the more liable to be blown about. In crisis, his regard for trade and individualism might count for nothing. Murdoch's and Elliot's respective reactions in the Liverpool depot, Cork hospital hulk and stowage cases are interesting illustrations of this contrast in qualities. All this may have some general application. It is easily, if not always, forgotten that lawyers formed a large and most important component of the nineteenth-century civil service. Inevitably, they brought to it habits of mind which must have contributed significantly to its colouring. Conversely, it is all too easily assumed (*pace* Hewart and Dicey) that the case for constitutional propriety was never made, except— so to say—posthumously and too late; and that had the case been made in time, the offences and divergencies might never have occurred.[2]

Again, if James Stephen was too unusual a person to be classified in any general type, Elliot and Murdoch were patently—and despite their individual differences—run-of-the-mill Victorian public servants of the higher grades: intelligent, immensely experienced in their own lines of administration, conscientious but, personally,

[1] *D.N.B.; Alumni Cantabrigiensis.*
[2] James Stephen himself recognized very clearly the revolutionary implications of colonial legislation when, in effect, he presided over the liquidation of the first British empire in the years 1815–40. He painstakingly pointed out, and deplored, the probable legal and political consequences of what was being done; deriving, however, a perverse satisfaction from the unfailing fulfilment of his forebodings. Cf. P. Knapland, *James Stephen and the British colonial system* (Madison, Wisconsin, 1953).

passive and uncreative. It may be a valuable corrective to set the work of men like this against that of the empire builders and the zealots in bureaucracy. It is not merely that the Elliots and the Murdochs predominated in number. They also contributed essentially, if unsystematically, to empires and expertise in the subjects under their charge. They were indispensable to the advance of modern government—in providing direction, uniformity and permanence in executive practice; in creating and sustaining a continuous, impersonal official memory; in constituting a repository of 'case-law'; in acting as the necessary middleman between the field-work and the parliamentary review; above all, in the winnowing of proposed reforms and the framing of legislation meant to be executed. In short, it was they who canalized the pressures, and enabled them to be harnessed profitably. There is perhaps as much to be learned from the administrative behaviour of this numerous, anonymous second rank of nineteenth-century public servants as from the conduct of the handful of creative (but also often obstructive) geniuses whose names were familar to the world at large.

It is, however, the emigration officers, the most vital element, who engage our interest closest. They were unquestionably representative of a new and small, but immensely creative, class of nineteenth-century civil servants, the field executive. The clumsy term 'field executive' has been deliberately chosen for this precise context. The more straightforward 'inspectorate' has confusing connotations. To give one example, the famous first factory 'inspectors' were as much professional magistrates and independent commissioners as field workers. This conflation was due to the initial doctrinaire failure to understand the bias of England's political system towards a hierarchy and division of administrative responsibility, and an independent exercise of the judicial function—*eo nomine* at least. Naturally, the three-headed animal did not long survive in the very uncongenial environment.[1] But this—and similar early anomalies and ambiguities—means that the word 'inspectorate' has certain implications for the nineteenth-century historian which render it inappropriate to the type of officer whom we are trying to describe, when the description has to be as exact as possible. Of course, many

[1] The factory act of 1844 corrected these eccentricities.

entitled 'inspector'—the inspectors of the board of works, of the marine or railway departments of the board of trade, or of mines, are instances—belonged to the same genus as the emigration officers. So, too, did the first factory superintendents of the 1830s, the public health officers and sanitary engineers of the medical department of the privy council and the local government act office of the 1860s,[1] or (to use a modern case) the divisional officers and managers of the labour exchanges in the 1900s.[2] What we are concerned with, then, is subordinate officers charged with the direct execution or supervision of some regulation up and down the country. Such men were usually recruited from some other original profession close or as close as possible to their new work. Initially, they were not and could not have been experts in their administrative work. But neither were they altogether amateurs. These royal, civil or marine engineers, physicians, army and naval officers, chemists, policemen, business or colliery managers and the rest—and pride of place must surely go to the ubiquitous royal engineers—were for the most part practically or scientifically trained in the discipline most relevant

[1] Dr R. J. Lambert's admirable study 'Some aspects of state activity in public health, 1858–71' (an unpublished dissertation, University Library, Cambridge) has recently brought the work of these men to light.

[2] 'The Divisional Officers, in addition to J. B. Adams [Divisional Officer of Labour Exchanges in the North Midlands], included Richard Bell, General Secretary of the Amalgamated Society of Railway Servants; W. S. Cohen, who had been engaged for some time in the Land Settlements Departments of the Orange River Colony; T. W. M. Fuge, an Irish J.P. who had held a number of posts chiefly with police in South Africa from 1900 to 1908; Carlton Hackney, a barrister for a time working in H.M. Office of Works; J. T. Homer, leading member of a Local Authority in the Midlands, but claiming also at one time to have run a labour exchange in Chicago, with a revolver provided as part of his office equipment in the drawer of his desk; G. W. Irons of the Education Department of the London County Council; W. E. Long, a soldier by profession, who had acted as Assistant Commissioner of Police in Cyprus; Colonel A. M. Murray, another professional soldier; O. W. Owen, of the Mines Department of the Transvaal and with ten years' banking experience in Britain; S. W. Scott, with a varied experience of municipal administration and finance; R. F. Williams, who had been secretary to a colliery in South Wales.

'Most of the labour exchange managers were described as drawn from among men who had experience of industrial conditions, either as works managers and foremen on the one hand, or as trade union officers on the other', Lord Beveridge, *Power and influence* (London, 1953), pp. 76–7. Conversely, some of the early special magistrates resembled the field executives in many ways, and had much of the same effect and influence. A particularly interesting and instructive case is the West Indian special magistracy in the 1830s and later. See W. L. Burn, *Emancipation and apprenticeship in the British West Indies* (London, 1937).

to their executive task.[1] They were, that is to say, half-professionals in their fields, if decided intruders to mere administration. Largely because of the contemporary 'economy' they are to be numbered in tens and twenties, and not in hundreds. But they were the leaven of the Victorian state. The attempt to enforce a regulation in the field bred rapidly new knowledge of the subject of reform, and a new pressure to legislate afresh. Perhaps the nineteenth-century field-executives may also be regarded as the earliest of those saving infusions of outside talent, experience and obstinacy (of which the intake of 1909–13 or of the two world wars are recent counterparts) which set off new ferments in old government.

As a group of persons, the emigration officers were direct, and moderately intelligent and educated men, distinguished, however (after the manner of Anne Elliot's encomium of His Majesty's sailors) for their humane no less than their martial virtues. Their original view of their functions was simple. The emigrants required protection; the trade required discipline; and they themselves required legal sanctions, official support and above all comprehensive and summary powers to achieve their ends. Surprisingly, the officers did not succumb, to any significant extent, to the corruption of the world's slow stain. Nearly all the convenient compromises with the shippers were practical necessities. But neither did their view of their functions change to keep pace with the legislative development, although it was their own efforts which were largely responsible for the eventual complex regulation. This was not surprising: the officers were, as a whole, active and practical, and not reflective men. The outcome was, however, both ironic and instructive. Though chance burked this conclusion in our particular story, the quasi-expert and the single-handed half-professional were, in the nature of things, paving the way for their own

---

[1] In this respect, it may ultimately prove that there is a further dividing line to be drawn *circa* 1860. The line I have in mind is one marking the beginning of a deliberately experimental approach to various problems on the part of trained scientists employed permanently by government: that is to say, when subjects for experiment were defined and systematically worked, and no administrative action taken until the findings were established scientifically. There are various earlier precedents for this, even (as we have shown) in our own subject; and occasional work of this kind, such as that of Graham, Hofmann and Redwood on original gravities in beer (*Journal Chem. Soc.* (1853), v, pp. 229–56) date back to 1845. But as a regular and large-scale feature of administration, its starting point may be found to have been in the 1860s.

supersession. Their work ensured that they would be replaced, in part at least, sooner or later, by the complete specialist and the great administrative machine.

The remaining contexts need not detain us long. First, emigrant protection in the United Kingdom had little relation to outside departments or agencies until its concluding phase, and its development owed nothing to the passenger codes of other nations. It was only in the 1850s that external influences were of any real significance. By the second half of the century, the level of regulation had risen so high, and parts of the regulation become so technical, that it overlapped certain activities of the board of trade, admiralty and other official or lay specialists. Conversely, this sort of scientific or specialist work had not developed far at all before 1850. The cross-reference and cross-fertilization was, however, peripheral until the 1860s. Thenceforward, it became important as the steam-powered vessel came to command the passenger business. From the outset, the marine department of the board of trade had specialized in this field; and their inspectors were much more competent to tackle the mechanical, and engineering problems which were involved, than the emigration officers. As steam gained ground, so also did the interpenetration of and need to marry the marine inspector's and the emigration officer's skills and functions; and this eventually issued, as we have seen, in an amalgamation. So far as the development of emigrant protection was concerned, however, all this was virtually an epilogue. It did not assume serious proportions until after the main line of reforming legislation had petered out. Much the same was true of the commissioners' own work on assisted emigration to the Antipodes. For the most part, it was irrelevant to their other problems. Australian emigration involved a trans-equatorial passage three times as lengthy as the Atlantic, and a different sort of vessel. Money for equipment, provisioning and other things, and state officials for ship-board, were readily available. The assisted emigrants (the overwhelming majority) were selected by the government, and subjected to a rigid discipline from the time they left their homes. Only after 1850 was the Atlantic emigrant protection sufficiently developed to be able to profit from the lessons or example of the Australian: and even then it did so only in a minor way, in some dietary and mechanical issues.

Again (so far as we can tell) the emigration department owed nothing in structure and organization to outside example. It was, of course, confined and characterized by the fundamentals of the political system, which sooner or later impose themselves on every element in the state. But otherwise it grew naturally enough, and certainly with little premeditation. Nor had foreign legislation any significant influence upon the development of emigrant protection in the United Kingdom. There is a simple reason for this. The United Kingdom was confronted with the problem of mass-emigration much earlier and in a more acute form, and responded to it more fully and carefully, than any other European country. The later continental legislation was, in general, a pale reflection. At certain stages American legislation was more advanced than British, in the sense of more repressive or demanding. But the two only overlapped in part; and the task of the congress and the state legislatures was both simpler than, and different from, Westminster's. The Americans had not to worry—on the contrary, from time to time—about reducing emigration by statutory restraints or higher fares. Nor could any of the American measures, before 1854, at any rate, compare in legal or executive quality with the British. They were short, crude prohibitions or requirements, after the fashion of the United Kingdom act of 1828. They lacked the variety and flexibility (designed to combat evasion) and the concern with practical execution which marked their counterparts on this side of the Atlantic. Again, there is a simple reason, the absence of an effective, co-ordinated inspectorate. When this was at last provided, as at New York in 1848, the state legislation rapidly came to resemble that of the United Kingdom in both type and detail, subject to the general difference in character between British and American draftsmanship. In general the New York protective system of the 1850s and 1860s corresponded closely to, and even improved upon, that which had developed at Liverpool, London and the Irish ports. But if there was any direct inspiration from without at work, it was exported from and not imported to the United Kingdom.

16

CONCLUSIONS

I

IN spite of its tightly knit fabric, the story of emigrant protection divides into several distinct parts. The opening phase lasted from the first efforts at reform at the turn of the eighteenth century to the recommencement of regulation in 1828. This was essentially a prologue. It had also two curious features: one, that the very first piece of legislation in the field was more mature and apt than any of its successors for more than thirty years; the other, that instead of an intensification, there was an erratic decline in both rigour and comprehensiveness, down to the total repeal of passenger legislation in 1827. Despite these curiosities, the first phase belonged to a recognizable type of rudimentary social reform through legislation. Three corresponding and more or less contemporary cases were the pioneering endeavours to alleviate the sufferings of pauper children in the cotton mills (by Sir Robert Peel's act of 1802),[1] of the 'climbing boys' or chimney-sweeps (by Hanway's act of 1788)[2] and of the coalwhippers at the port of London (by the coal trade act of 1807). The first passenger act, marked by considerable legal sense and a fair working knowledge of its field, was a more thorough and 'professional' measure than any of these counterparts. But it suffered from the same fatal defect—the very hallmark of 'first phases'—the want of any special agency to examine or enforce it. The protected classes being what they were, first reforming legislation of this type was inevitably barren. In fact, it may even have been deleterious in so far as it spread an illusion of activity and success. Another uniform weakness, the corollary of the first, was the reliance upon the existing arms of government to carry out the new measure. In

---

[1] See above, p. 59.
[2] Jonas Hanway died before the act was passed, but it was essentially the fruit of his agitation and preparations. Dolben's act, regulating the slave trade, was passed in the same year, 1788. For its early workings, see *Parl. Hist.* (1792), vol. xxix, p. 1126.

general, the 'authorities'—navy, customs, magistrates and the rest —had no interest in, and carelessly neglected, the extraordinary obligations laid upon them by social legislation. To pursue our three examples, factory legislation was altogether ineffective until the introduction of inspectors and superintendents in 1834; the climbing boys act (despite improvements in the law through amending legislation in 1834 and 1840) was ineffective until direct executive control, by register and licence, was instituted in 1875;[1] and the coalwhippers remained unprotected until commissioners and registrars were set up in 1843 to supervise their employment.[2] The same pattern was repeated as late as 1867–76. When workshops, as distinct from factories, were first subjected to state regulation in 1867, the execution of the relevant acts was entrusted not to a special central agency but to the local authorities, with the familiar consequence of non-enforcement until this error was corrected. Similarly, the first food and drugs act of 1860 achieved little until it was supplemented by a requirement in 1872 that all counties and boroughs with police forces should appoint professional public analysts. Hence, the 'prologue' was a fairly common feature of early social improvement in the nineteenth century; and so far emigrant protection followed a common course.

The six years 1828–34 may be taken as our second phase. The 1828 act marked an altogether fresh start. Only twenty-five years divided it from the original interference. But the political atmosphere in which it was passed was worlds apart from the antique airs of 1803. The great difference was that legislation of this type now tended, or was soon to tend, to be the responsibility of the cabinet rather than the private member, and to be drafted and controlled by some branch of the permanent central government rather than by outside persons or associations. This silent constitutional revolution of 1815–35 whereby the cabinet began to engross the formulation of legislation, and willy-nilly—as head of the executive— responsibility for its enforcement, inevitably changed the character of statutory social reform. A second major change in politics in the quarter-century 1803–28 sprang from the growth in voice

---

[1] Shaftesbury observed that the law had been inoperative for a century, and systematically disobeyed, because of the hostility of the magistracy, both unpaid and stipendiary, and public indifference, S. Gordon and T. G. B. Cocks, *A people's conscience* (London, 1952), pp. 99–100.

[2] Cf. Prouty, op. cit., pp. 78–80.

and influence of political economy and other social 'sciences'. This meant the emergence and application of new sorts of ideological criteria of reform. The implications of the 1803 act for the trader in his business, or the individual conducting his affairs, or contract or government or law, went altogether unremarked. But the subsequent contraction of passenger legislation was fairly in step with the rise of the doctrinaires. For these reasons alone, the 1828 act marked the beginning of a new venture rather than the revival of an old.

Certain features of the 1828 act have been emphasized already. It was a deliberate and fully conscious recoil from laissez faire. It was a precedent of the utmost significance in drawing adult males into the notional ring (or what was later to be defined as such) of protected persons. It provided a new case of, if it did not actually introduce, statutory limitations upon contract. We need not traverse this ground again, except perhaps to emphasize the sudden reaction to unrestrained individualism. The immediate practical consequences of de-control seemed appalling, were pronounced intolerable; and the doctrinaires had no choice but to re-state the doctrine to accommodate the retreat, and concentrate upon securing the 'minimum' requirements. The 1828 act then took up a place in the line of 'precedents' for state regulation. Like other social reforms of the second generation, its own most powerful 'precedent' was the regulation of the slave trade. 'Why should we deny our fellow citizens the securities which slaves are guaranteed by law?' was the effective question—just as a corresponding demand was to enfeeble the resistance to further factory control. 'The House', said William Smith in a debate on the cotton mills regulation bill in 1825, 'has heard much of the condition of slaves in the West Indies. No one can reprobate the system of slavery more than I do; but the labour performed by the negroes in the West Indies is actually less than is exacted from these poor children at Manchester'. 'The children are not free agents', said Gordon in the same debate, 'and require the protection of the legislature as much as the slaves of the West Indies, for whom regulations have been made, not only as to what work they should do, but what allowance of food they should receive'.[1] And this was, of course, the form of appeal employed again

[1] *Hans.*, 2nd, xiii, 1008–10, 31 May 1825. The gist of the bill was that the labour of child operatives in cotton factories should be limited to twelve hours on weekdays. It was not enacted.

in the celebrated Oastler letters, 'Slavery in Yorkshire', of 1831. We should also note that once enacted, new measures like the passenger act themselves formed 'precedents' for qualitative as well as quantitative enlargements of state activity. Cases were never quite the same. Often they were essentially different. Novelties did in fact accumulate under the plea that nothing really new was being done.

Immediately, the significance of the passenger act of 1828 was altogether formal. It made little difference to the conduct of the trade; it was not, and would not be enforced, at the outports until there were state officials to enforce it. 1834 has been selected as the terminal date of the second phase because it was not till then that the executive corps was securely established. The first, indirect step towards an executive was taken when Buchanan was made immigration agent for Canada in 1828. This mattered because of the man himself. Buchanan had participated in the drafting of the statute; he was personally interested in its execution; and he became, in effect, a member of the colonial office. He could achieve comparatively little in Quebec. But his struggles may well have influenced Low's engagement as emigration officer in 1833.[1] Certainly they foreshadowed the enforcement of passenger law by direct state action. But it was the Liverpool experiment which was decisive. Unlike Buchanan's, Low's specific and primary function was emigrant protection. Unlike Buchanan, Low was professionally qualified and stationed at the great source of troubles. His appointment therefore marked the real beginning of central control, especially when it was confirmed and acclaimed within a year by the institution of a corps to cover, so far as might be, the United Kingdom. The field executive was not so much a sudden or deliberate creation as a development. Nor was it a very marvellous innovation. It needed but common sense and first-hand knowledge of the realities to understand the necessity for official intermediaries. The practical and experienced Robert Owen had told Peel's committee on child labour in factories in 1816 that reforming legislation would remain inoperative until paid and qualified inspectors administered the acts. Had the expected 'Gibraltar fever' broken out in 1805, the new board of health would probably have included a medical inspectorate. Fifty years earlier still, Fielding's Bow Street runners antici-

---

[1] Buchanan's brother was one of those who proposed a superintendence of passengers at embarkation to the colonial office in 1832.

pated several of the features of central and professional enforcement, including the provision of a free public service.[1] Nor can we
certainly claim that the emigration officers constituted the first
modern field executive, although they did precede those commonly
chosen for the honour—the factory superintendents which Owen
had suggested years before. Here all depends upon the definition of
terms, and argument is not likely to be profitable. What we can say
is that the emigration officers were among the very earliest representatives of this new force which was to change the whole character
of social regulation and even, in the long run, of society. Like their
fellows in other fields, they were to provide not only a first bridge
between law and actuality, but also the principal dynamic of governmental growth.

The intrusion of the executive corps set off, then, a process of real
change in place of the old formality and immobility. But it did not
do so completely, all at once; and the interval of adjustment,
1834–42, may be taken as our third phase. The entry of the executive upon the scene was firm and final by 1834, but eight years were
to pass before it was harnessed to full effect. One consequence of its
gradual, unconsidered origin was that neither the existing legislation nor the existing administrative arrangements were geared to
the new force; and so much of the old order or perennial inertia
survived at the colonial office that this weakness was not eradicated,
or even seen, for several years. Thus at the start the field executive
was a relatively alien, unexploited and uncomfortable body in
government, and bound to remain so until the necessary modifica-
tions in its administrative environment were complete. Much the
same was true of, for example, the poor law assistant commissioners
between 1834 and 1847.

At the same time, the existence of a body of persons, however
few, professionally charged with carrying the passenger act into
effect inevitably transformed the situation. It meant, as we have
seen, a certain level of practical achievement instead of a general

[1] The runners were paid in part from public monies, the Secret Service Fund;
they investigated crime free of charge; and they encouraged the public to call
on their services by the regular issue of advertisements to report robberies, &c.
John Fielding's first 'flying squad' in 1754 was, in his own words, 'always ready
to set out to any part of this town or kingdom'; and the cost of these journeys
was met out of public funds. P. Pringle, edit.: *Henry Goddard's Memoirs of a
Bow Street runner* (London, 1956), pp. xi, 73.

neglect, some measure of regulation where before there had been none. It also meant, through the hard experience of the officers, a much fuller and more concrete revelation than any other of the manifold deficiencies in both the restrictive and the executive clauses of the statute. This led at once to demands for legislative amendment in a large number of particulars. These demands were made, moreover, with a new and ultimately irresistible authority. For incontrovertible, dispassionate first-hand evidence was accumulating, for the first time, in the officers' reports and correspondence; and there was both a large measure of unanimity in their practical proposals and complete unanimity in their insistence upon the urgency of the reform. Finally, side by side with the imperative demand for further legislation, there came an equivalent demand for centralization. This too arose as a matter of plain necessity from the actual day-to-day difficulties of an ill-regulated inspectorate. The 1828 act was meagre and imprecise, and framed before the executive was contemplated: the customs boards were its nominal executors. Nor had the original appointment of the emigration officers supplied the omissions: their powers and discretions were undefined. Therefore, without a definite and authoritative superior, the executive officers tended towards exorbitance or timid inactivity. The door was open to arbitrary or ineffective government. The Liverpool and other early imbroglios sprang directly from this deficiency. And the superior was needed not merely to discipline the corps, but also to define their status and the law, and to protect and support them against the anarchic 'public'. Moreover, it was very soon demonstrated that centralization was indispensable for two other purposes, the systematic collection and collation of evidence and proposals of reform, and the establishment of a link between parliament and the executive in the field.

Again the adjustment to what was needed was gradual and unplanned. The amendment act of 1835 was in part the product of the early agitation of the emigration officers. But it left them still without statutory authority for their interference; and not only were they not consulted during its formulation, their recommendations were partially ignored. In short, there was still no effective junction between executive and ministry. Elliot's appointment as United Kingdom agent-general in 1837 was a major forward step. But he had not the undisputed status or undivided time or office organization to fill the position of superior successfully. His further duties, the preliminary planning of a vast state-aided emigration from Ireland and the management of assisted emigration to Australia, engrossed his energies, and in certain other ways conflicted with his responsibilities for the corps. The really critical change was the establishment of the colonial land and emigration commission in 1840. As with Elliot's appointment, the better ordering of the executive was by no means the sole object of the new departure. The reduction of the colonial office estimate, a relief from the bickering and rivalry of the agent-general and the South Australia commissioners, and some apparent response to the clamour raised by the Durham report, were also aimed at. But it was now clearly established that setting passenger legislation to rights, and constituting an authoritative and regular intermediary between parliament and the practical administrators, were amongst the duties of the commissioners; and this was enough to harness the powers of the executive. Amongst the first-fruits of the new arrangements was the great passenger act of 1842. The experience of the field workers was at last capitalized, and their functions defined and standing secured, substantially as they had demanded. This brought the third phase to a close. The mechanics of government and the body of law were now such that the new type of direct social regulation could proceed with reasonable efficiency in this field.

To the contemporaries concerned this seemed to bring the matter to an end. The great deficiencies revealed had been corrected. The superintending central body was in harmony with constitutional principle and practice. The consolidation act was so sweeping and matchless in its severity that its permanence was easily assumed. That the growths which had begun would continue and accelerate was not dreamed of in 1842. In less than a decade, however, the attitude of the administrators had changed completely—a development which constitutes a fourth phase in our subject. It was quickly borne in upon the executive officers, and through them upon the central authority, that even the new amending legislation did not provide a solution to the problem. Of course it embodied many, perhaps even most, of their recommendations of the 1830s; and it did effect substantial practical improvements. But instead of ending, it initiated change. Experience soon showed that it was possible—almost endlessly possible—to devise means of evading some at

least of the new requirements, and each disclosed evasion implied
further regulation; and this in turn often carried government beyond
its original objective. Experience showed that the practical effect, or
the lawyers' interpretations, of the various clauses could not be altogether or always predicted: and again the necessary remedies sustained the forward momentum. Experience showed that what
seemed self-evident when the measure was prepared required in
fact glosses and instructions; and almost without fail the gloss, instruction or enabling action found its way into the next amendment.
More important still was the change in the administrators' perspective which the possession and daily working of even so large a
measure of government as the 1842 act brought about. What had
hitherto seemed almost unattainable in its boldness came in time to
look ordinary and then inadequate. Imperceptibly, the range of the
apparently possible and practicable extended. Moreover, the mere
conduct of administration steadily threw up new problems calling
for solution, and new evidence of the need for tackling problems
which had been postponed. All this meant that the original limitations of the field of regulation—we might add the very assumption
that there were fixed boundaries to such a field at all—came to
appear much too narrow; and in the process the outlook of both the
officers and the commissioners was transformed. Gradually they
ceased to regard their difficulties as resolvable once for all by some
grand piece of legislation. Instead, they began to see improvement
as a slow, uncertain process of closing loopholes and tightening the
screw ring by ring, in the light of continuing experience. Correspondingly, experience rendered them more expert, and the exercise
of practically unchallenged power rendered them more authoritative. The fact that the corps and their superiors were both forced by
circumstances and allowed by the colonial office to act autonomously
also transformed their attitude in time. The supersession of parliamentary processes by delegations of legislative and judicial powers
ceased to seem extraordinary, but came to be regarded as the mere
formalization of the inevitable and indispensable. To sum up, what
this fourth phase witnessed was a profound change in the pre-
suppositions and bearing of the administrators. In place of a static
and purely executive, they developed a dynamic, creative and expert
concept of administration. It is impossible, in the nature of the
matter, to provide an exact date for the maturity of this new outlook.

We have seen that there is some evidence of the shift as early as 1845. Certainly it was complete at the end of the 1840s.

It is clear thereafter that we have moved into a new world of government. The more or less conscious Fabianism, which had grown up since 1842, was by then working itself out in modes of regulation which resemble, often astonishingly, our modern systems. The officers and commissioners not merely requested and secured, they even anticipated legislation which would award them the widest discretions and independence. These discretions governed not merely the application of many clauses in the passenger acts but even the imposition of penalties and the framing of rules to meet hypothetical contingencies. There could be no doubt now that the limit of state activity was imposed, not so much by individualism, contract, free trade or any other notion, as by the paucity of the human and physical resources at the executive's disposal. There was now small concern about the multiplication of controls. As needs arose, they were simply satisfied—in so far as legislation or instructions might serve this purpose. Again the change is shown by the new type of experimentation and the new desire for forms of administration and law sufficiently flexible to accommodate the eventual findings of experiments. Gradually, it came to be accepted—and this was a vital break with earlier nineteenth-century government—that the collection of statistics or other evidence might lead, not to sure answers, but to new questions and the prolongation or enlargement of the inquiry. Gradually it was accepted—the second vital break—that new mechanisms might require lengthy tests before their utility was established, and that the natural sciences must proceed at their own empirical pace, and government shape itself according to that often irritating progress. Spasmodically, at least, the commissioners and the best of their leading officers strove to get and keep in touch with the inventions, new techniques and foreign practices relevant to their field. They even called upon medicine and engineering and the infant research professions to find answers to intractable difficulties in composing or enforcing measures. All these developments were rudimentary; and their growth was checked abruptly by the fall in emigration, the advance of the steamship and the emergence of the great shipping company. But each trend is clearly and diversely exemplified in the legislation and administrative practice of the

1850s. Equally, the need for their institutional corollary, the extensive division and specialization of administrative labour, was already patent. In all these last developments towards autonomy and delegation, towards fluidity and experimentation, towards fully professional and scientific government, the shape of the present state may be discerned. Essentially, it is our own society which is foreshadowed.

II

We have then a completed or virtually completed process of governmental growth. It was a process because there was a logical progression in the whole, and each step followed naturally from its predecessor. It was not, in absolute terms, an inevitable process: there are no inevitable processes in history. But there was certainly a very high degree of inherent likelihood in the general movement. Every development was necessary for the better fulfilment of the primary aim; as a whole the sequence constituted a purposeful and orderly advance. Through it all ran what might be termed contingent necessity, the 'contingent' being—if emigrant protection were to be realized. Because the emigrants could not protect themselves, special statutory protection was required: there was no alternative to legislative interference. Without a field executive, the legislation could not be enforced. Without properly constituted superiors, the corps could not operate effectively. The articulated administration was bound to secure further reform and its own extension. The comparative failure of each advance, and the comparative ease of its attainment, inevitably bred new attitudes in both parliament and the administration which opened the door to practically limitless and continuous intervention. In absolute terms none of this had to happen. But not only did it follow successively from the humane object. It was also inherently probable in the circumstances of the early and mid-nineteenth century. It was very likely that legislation to stamp out the 'intolerable' miseries and mortalities of the Atlantic passage would sooner or later be enacted: 'intolerability' would sooner or later open any door. It was very likely that someone would sooner or later discover the simple truth that, to operate, such laws as these required their own executors. And it was very likely, to say the least, that a special branch of government working directly on the problems and specifically charged with their solution would generate a further process of regulation, a professionalism and an expertise.

The other forces which aided the growth of government, and counteracted passivity or self-satisfaction on the part of the administrators, were also data of the period and the matter. It was intrinsically likely that the public of 1820–60 would be shocked, repeatedly, by fresh demonstrations of the 'intolerable' sufferings of the emigrants. Like the actual happenings within government itself, the shipwrecks and epidemics, the interventions of the humanitarians, and the institution of the parliamentary inquiries, sprang naturally from the circumstances of the time and case. Their incidence and form were, of course, random and unpredictable. But their occurrence and influence were not. Marine disasters and great (and equally important, sensational) mortalities were inevitable in such a business as the early nineteenth-century passenger trade. The law of averages alone ensured as much. And the middle quarters of the century formed the hey-day of both the humanitarian investigator and the select committee charged with the unravelling of social evils; and voluntary emigration was a very apt subject for their attentions. All that surprises is that so ready a field attracted so few philanthropists or agitators—or rather it would surprise us if we did not know the early date of the first official intervention. The humane reaction to the disclosure of abuses and the publicization of calamities was certainly a constant.

After 1850 there were two significant additions to the general circumstances. First, we have entered a new technological age, in which scientific method was both exploited and applied in an unprecedented fashion. Secondly, treasury control and public economy had become more systematic, effective and intense. Whether or not, these developments were themselves predictable, their various effects upon the administration might surely have been foretold.

III

In spite of the very modest limits of its subject matter, this study may have some general bearings. The mere fact that (speaking not loosely but exactly) a prototype of present-day government can be found in the 1850s is arresting. It is often supposed that this is, almost of necessity, a recent phenomenon.[1] But the way in which the prototype emerged is still more interesting. Its growth was self-explanatory. The development owed nothing, either directly or indirectly, to contemporary theory. This is significant because it is sometimes assumed that the early modern state was essentially the creature of applied ideas. Whatever else, the present study shows that it was possible, and even easy, for the new type of government to have developed independently. There was no stage at which further advance was impossible until some *a priori* administrative invention, or some fresh theory of the state, provided a release. These facts may also have some bearing upon the general approach to the creation of nineteenth- and twentieth-century collectivism. If we are not obliged to accept the more complicated explanation, Occam's razor may come into play. *Essentia non sunt multiplicanda praeter necessitatem.* Other things being equal, the explanation with the least and simplest parts is to be preferred. An explanation in terms of natural inclination and momentum is precedent to one which predicates an artefact. This does not mean, of course, that it will necessarily prove to be the correct explanation in any particular instance: undoubtedly, the contribution of ideas and ideologues was very large in certain fields. But it does imply a transference of the burden of proof. If a change can come about without, so to say, a 'special creation', it may perhaps be taken that it did so, until this presumption is rebutted. Apart from these more abstract uses, the process which we have elucidated may also help us over some very awkward gaps in the development. It is obvious that there must have been some multipliers, some mechanisms of intensification and increase, in central government in the nineteenth century. These were essential for the results achieved. But we cannot look to political economy or utilitarianism or any other of the prevailing doctrines of the first three-quarters of the nineteenth century to supply them. On the contrary, all implied, at best, a static view of social regulation. The professed object of each was to correct, in

[1] One of the most recent and penetrating works to touch this field contains these sentences: 'The legislative activity of the twentieth century stands in sharp contrast to that of the nineteenth. Of statutes passed since 1900 probably a majority are enactments which either create new statutory bodies or confer powers of regulation on existing authorities', Marshall and Moodie, op. cit., p. 108. In general this book is exceptionally shrewd and well informed.

one way or another, supposed deviations from a norm. Thenceforward, the natural, or artificially adjusted, workings of social, economic and political relations would automatically resolve the problems. When the necessary calculations had been made and expressed in legislative and executive rules, when the 'natural' state of things had been created or recreated, the state's role was purely one of maintenance. Even the most likely form of doctrinaire radicalism in this respect, tutelary Benthamism, went no further. It assumed that the felicific calculus could, and would, embrace all that the administrator-legislator needed to know; that his laws would encounter no unforeseeable or novel obstacle or fact; and that the sum-total of his work was the initial adjustment of a social unbalance, and, subsequently, the sustaining of the equilibrium. All this was the very antithesis of multiplying, intensifying and fermenting government.[1] But the pattern which we have found shows one way at least in which the state not only could but was even impelled to develop in these directions. The enforcement-inspection-amendment and the various other cycles which have been disclosed certainly supply in our particular case, and would possibly supply in many others, several of the missing pieces of the puzzle.

These points are all the more pertinent, perhaps, because the growth of passenger regulation was so largely a matter of the most commonplace actions and reactions. The accumulative effects, and the interactions, may surprise. But each individual movement was ordinary, even banal. This is true not only of the main stages, of the steady passage from simpler to more complicated forms, of the quantitative differences breeding qualitative change, or practice the elaboration of principles of administrative action. It is also true of the least and most technical portions of the pattern. To take examples almost at random, the history of the survey or stowage clauses, of the schedules of the passage contract, of the licensing of runners, and the projected depot, shows an inevitable slide towards specialist government, delegated legislation, a permissive and contingent commerce and direct state management. But the triviality of the instances, and their immediate derivation from the particular

---

[1] It is also true, of course, that all the various forms of doctrinaire radicalism threw direct obstacles of one kind and another in the way of the development of the modern state. For a brief discussion of these effects, see O. MacDonagh, 'The nineteenth-century revolution in government: a re-appraisal', *Historical Journal*, I (1958), 62–66.

circumstances of the case, do not mean that these trends were in any way peculiar or mysterious. On the contrary, they are of the most general application. That the enlargement of the body of exact knowledge leads towards specialization; that it proves convenient to delegate responsibility for the framing and amendment of numerous and technical regulations to the professionals; that a desire for uniformity, and for security against evasions, in contracts favours the utmost possible formalization; that a demonstrable social need, which is not met and cannot be met by voluntary activity, tends to become the responsibility of the state—these are not, to say the least, startling observations: they are almost truisms. But the everyday character of its phenomena also means that the lessons of this book may extend far beyond its own small confines, and perhaps even, here and there, to the world in which we live.

APPENDIX

Yearly totals, in thousands, of Emigration from the United Kingdom to North America, 1815–72

1815	2·0	1832	99·4	1849	267·3	1866	180·8
1816	12·5	1833	58·5	1850	268·8	1867	181·5
1817	20·6	1834	73·4	1851	314·4	1868	183·5
1818	27·8	1835	42·6	1852	281·0	1869	243·1
1819	34·8	1836	72·3	1853	268·5	1870	239·9
1820	26·7	1837	67·0	1854	240·2	1871	240·2
1821	18·3	1838	19·2	1855	124·5	1872	279·4
1822	20·6	1839	46·5	1856	132·0		
1823	16·5	1840	75·0	1857	151·6		
1824	14·0	1841	86·0	1858	74·7		
1825	14·4	1842	119·8	1859	89·4		
1826	20·0	1843	53·8	1860	104·1		
1827	27·3	1844	68·4	1861	68·0		
1828	25·0	1845	92·7	1862	79·4		
1829	29·1	1846	127·5	1863	217·7		
1830	55·8	1847	253·3	1864	168·0		
1831	81·6	1848	224·0	1865	172·4		

The above figures are deduced from statistics furnished in *33rd rep. C.L.E.C.*, appendix I. Few, or none, of the small number returned as 'Destination Not Stated' in these statistics can have been Australian emigrants (the only non-American category taken into account). The bulk of the Australian emigration was government-assisted, and the rest was closely checked.

It should also be noted that the figures set out above probably under-estimate the true totals of emigrants for North America. The collection of emigration statistics became successively more efficient after 1833, after 1851 and after 1855. But even down to 1860 there were illegal embarkations and unrecorded sailings of emigrants. Before 1833, and in isolated seasons of great pressure thereafter (such as 1847 or 1849), the under-estimation must have been considerable. Perhaps as much as 5 per cent should be added to the grand total for 1815 to 1872 to compensate for the embarkations which were not returned.

SELECT BIBLIOGRAPHY

I. PRIMARY SOURCES

1. MANUSCRIPT

Public Record Office
Colonial Office Papers, files 42/–, 43/– 324/–, 384/– and 386/–.
Russell Papers.
Various printed *Circulars* to the emigration officers, and *Cautions* to emigrants, amongst the Colonial Office Papers.
Home Office Papers, file 122/–.

State Paper Office, Dublin Castle
Registered Papers, cartons 698–700.

National Library of Ireland
Larcom Papers.
Monteagle Papers.

In Private Possession
Correspondence relating to Dr Edward Mulligan's appointment as ship-surgeon, 1851.

2. PARLIAMENTARY PAPERS

Survey and report by Thomas Telford, 1802–3, iv.
First report of the committee on the survey and report by Thomas Telford, 1802–3, iv.
Report of 1826 of the select committee on emigration, 1826, iv (404).
Report of the commissioners of emigration, 1831–2, xxxii (724).
Act levying a tax on emigrants, 1831–2, xxxii (730).
Report of Mr Richards respecting the wastelands in Canada, and emigration, 1833, xxxii (334).
Correspondence with the governors of colonies, 1833, xxvi (141).
Correspondence with the same, 1835, xxxix (87).

Correspondence with the same, 1837, xlii.

First report of the poor inquiry commissioners, Ireland, 1836, xxx.

Further report of the same, 1836, xxxiv.

Annual report of the agent-general for emigration, Canada, 1837, xlii (132).

Annual report of the same, 1837–8, xl (389).

Report of the agent-general for emigration, United Kingdom, 1837–8, xl (388).

Letter from N. W. Senior on the third report of the poor inquiry commissioners, Ireland, 1837–8, li (376).

Report of the select committee on shipwrecks of timber ships, 1839, ix (333).

Second report of the select committee on emigration, Scotland, 1841, vi (333).

Correspondence relative to emigration to Canada, 1841, xv (298).

Seventh annual report of the poor law commissioners, Ireland, 1841, xi (327).

Papers relative to emigration to British North America, 1842, xxxi [373].

Annual reports of the agents-general for emigration, Canada, 1844, xxxv (181).

Report from Her Majesty's commissioners of inquiry into . . . land in Ireland (Devon commission), 1845, xix-xxi.

Papers relative to emigration to British North America, 1847, xxxix [777].

Report of the select committee on colonization from Ireland, 1847, vi [737].

Papers relative to emigration to British North America, 1847–8, xlvii (50).

Further papers relative to the same, 1847–8, xlvii [932].

Further papers relative to the same, 1847–8, xlvii [964].

Further papers relative to the same, 1847–8, xlvii [985].

First report of the select committee on colonization, Ireland, 1847–8, xvii (415).

Second report of the same, 1847–8, xvii (593).

Third report of the same, 1849, xi (86).

Seventh report of the select committee, poor laws, Ireland, 1849, xv, part i (237).

Papers relative to emigration to British North America, 1849, xxxviii (593.11).

Papers relative to the same, 1849, xxxviii [1025].

Papers relative to the same, 1851, xl (348).

Reports from the select committee inquiring into the operation of the passenger acts, 1851, xix (632).

Letter detailing the treatment of passengers on board the *Washington*, 1851, xl (198).

Papers relating to the North American colonies, 1852, xxxlii [1474].

Copies or extracts of despatches relative to emigration, 1852–3, lxviii [1650].

First report of the select committee on emigrant ships, 1854, xiii (163).

Second report of the same, 1854, xiii (349).

Reports on loss of vessels carrying emigrants, 1854, xlvi (429).

Report on the re-organization of the civil service, 1854–5, xx [1870].

Copies or extracts of despatches relating to emigration to the North American colonies, 1857, x (14).

Copies or extracts of the same, 1857, session 2, xxviii (125).

Report of the committee on ministers' powers (Donoughmore report), 1932, Cmd. 4060.

* * *

Copies of the commissions appointing the colonial land and emigration commissioners, 1840, xxxiii (113).

Report of the colonial land and emigration commissioners on the necessity of amending the passengers' act, 1842, xxv [355].

General report of the colonial land and emigration commissioners, 1842, xxv [567].

Second annual report of the same, 1842, xxv (567).

Third annual report of the same, 1843, xxix (261).

Fourth annual report of the same, 1844, xxxi (178).

Fifth annual report of the same, 1845, xxvii [617].

Sixth annual report of the same, 1846, xxiv [706].

Seventh annual report of the same, 1847, xxxiii [809].

Eighth annual report of the same, 1847–8, xxvi [961].

Ninth annual report of the same, 1849, xxii [1082].

Tenth annual report of the same, 1850, xxxii [1204].

Eleventh annual report of the same, 1851, xxii [1383].

Twelfth annual report of the same, 1852, xviii [1499].

Thirteenth annual report of the same, 1852–3, xl, [1647].

Fourteenth annual report of the same, 1854, xxviii [1833].

Fifteenth annual report of the same, 1854–5, xvii [1953].

Sixteenth annual report of the same, 1856, xxiv [2089].

Seventeenth annual report of the same, 1857, xvi [2249].

Eighteenth annual report of the same, 1857–8, xxiv [2359].

Nineteenth annual report of the same, 1859, session 2, xiv [2555].

Twentieth annual report of the same, 1860, xxxix [2696].

Twenty-third annual report of the same, 1863, xv [3199].

Thirty-third annual report of the same, 1873, xviii, Cmd. 768.

A return of the names of emigration officers; with a copy of instructions, 1854, xvi (255).

A return of the passenger brokers and licensed runners in Liverpool, 1857, xxviii (103).

A return of the same, 1857–8, x (150).

3. STATUTES

Collections of Statutes, Public and General, and Private and Local.

Acts of the Congress of the United States, and of the Legislatures of the States of New York and Massachusetts.

4. PARLIAMENTARY DEBATES

Hansard, first, second and third series.

House of Commons Journals.

5. PUBLISHED SELECT DOCUMENTS AND LETTERS

Abbott, E., *Historical aspects of the immigration problem: select documents* (Chicago, 1926).

Bell, K. N. and Morrell, W. P., *Select documents on British colonial policy, 1830–60* (Oxford, 1928).

Benson, A. C. and Esher, Viscount, edit., *The letters of Queen Victoria* (London, 1908).

Doughty, Sir A. J., edit., *The Elgin–Grey papers*, 4 vols. (Ottawa, 1937).

Gooch, G. P., edit., *The later correspondence of Lord John Russell, 1840–1878*, 2 vols. (London, 1888).

Knapland, P., edit., *Letters from Lord Sydenham to Lord John Russell* (London, 1931).

Walrond, T., edit., *Letters and journals of James Bruce, 8th Earl of Elgin* (London, 1872).

6. NEWSPAPERS AND PERIODICALS

Cork Constitution

Cork Examiner

Economist, The

Edinburgh Review

Evening Post (Dublin)

Freeman's Journal (Dublin)

Health of Towns Journal (London)

Illustrated London News

Limerick Chronicle

Limerick Reporter

Liverpool Courier

Londonderry Sentinel

Morning Chronicle (London)

Nation (Dublin)

Northern Whig (Belfast)

Quarterly Review

Saturday Review

Times, The

Tipperary Vindicator (Nenagh)

Westminster Review

7. CONTEMPORARY PRINTED SOURCES

Annual reports of the Emigrant Protection Society (Dublin), from 1850 . . .

Annual reports of the New York commissioners of emigration (New York), from 1847 . . .

'A Passage Broker', *Letter to Lieutenant Low, R.N.* (Liverpool, 1838).

Chisholm, Mrs. C., *Emigration and transportation relatively considered* (London, 1847).

Colquhoun, P., *A treatise on the wealth, power and resources of the British Empire* (London, 1814).

Davin, N., *The Irishman in Canada* (Toronto, 1877).

Document No. 48 Legislature of the State of New York, 1848 Session.

Durham, *The report and despatches of the Earl of Durham*, 3 vols. (London, 1839).

Godley, J. R., *Letters from America* (Dublin, 1844). *Observations in an Irish poor law* (Dublin, 1847).

Greville, C. C. F., *The Greville memoirs: first part*, 3 vols. (London, 1887).

Grey, H. G., 3rd Earl, *The colonial policy of Lord John Russell's administration*, 2 vols. (London, 1853).

Maguire, J. F., *The Irish in America* (London, 1868).

Mills, A., *Systematic colonization* (London, 1847).

Miscellaneous Documents, No. 14, House of Representatives, 33rd Congress, 1st Session.

O'Donovan, J., *A brief account of the author's interviews with his countrymen* . . . (Pittsburgh, 1864).

O'Brien, W. S., *Emigration* (London, 1840).

Peyton, A. J., *The emigrant's friend* (Cork, 1853).

Senior, N. W., *Journals, conversations and essays relating to Ireland*, 2 vols. (London, 1868).

Stephen, F., 'The characteristics of English criminal law', *Cambridge Essays, 1857* (London, 1857).

Stephen, J., 'Colonization as a branch of social economy', *Trans. Social Science Assoc., 1859* (London, 1859).

Transactions of the Highland Society of Scotland, annual from 1802.

Trench, W. S., *The realities of Irish life* (London, 1868).

Trevelyan, C. E., *The Irish crisis* (London, 1848).

Walkinshaw, E., *A vindication of Edward Walkinshaw* (Liverpool, 1834).

II. SECONDARY SOURCES

Adams, W. F., *Ireland and Irish emigration to the new world from 1815 to the famine* (Yale, 1932).

Albion, R. G., with the collaboration of Pope, J. B., *The rise of New York port* (New York, 1939).

Beveridge, Lord, *Power and influence* (London, 1953).

Bindoff, S. T., 'The unreformed diplomatic service', *Trans. Royal Hist. Soc.*, fourth series, xviii.

Brebner, J. B., 'Laissez-faire and state intervention in nineteenth-century Britain', *Jour. Econ. Hist.*, supplement, viii, 1948.

Burn, W. L., *Emancipation and apprenticeship in the British West Indies* (London, 1937). 'Free trade in land: an aspect of the Irish question', *Trans Royal Hist. Soc.*, fourth series, xxxi.

Cohen, E. W., *The growth of the British civil service* (London, 1941).

Collison Black, R. D., *Economic thought and the Irish question, 1817–70* (Cambridge, 1960).

Conroy, J. C., *A history of railways in Ireland* (London, 1928).

Cousens, S. H., 'The regional distribution of emigration during the great Irish famine', *Trans. Inst. Brit. Geographers, 1960*.

Cowan, H. I., *British emigration to British North America, 1783–1837* (Toronto, 1928).

Dicey, A. V., *Lectures on the relation between law and public opinion in England during the nineteenth century*, second edition (London, 1914). 'The development of administrative law in England', *Law Quart. Review*, xxxi.

Dunaway, W. F., *The Scotch-Irish of colonial Pennsylvania* (Chapel Hill, 1944).

Edwards, R. D., and Williams, T. D., edit., *The great famine: studies in Irish history, 1845–52*, a symposium (Dublin, 1956).

Ferenezi, I., edit., *International emigrations*, 2 vols. (New York, 1929).

Finer, S. E., *The life and times of Sir Edwin Chadwick* (London, 1952).

Flick, A. C. and Fox, D. R., edit., *History of New York*, 7 vols. (New York, 1937).

Garis, R. L., *Immigrant restriction: a study of the opposition to and regulation of immigration into the United States* (New York, 1937).

Gordon, S., and Cocks, T. G. B., *A people's conscience* (London, 1952).

Greaves, H. R. G., *The civil service in the changing state* (London, 1949).

Halévy, E., *The age of Peel and Cobden* (London, 1947).

Hammond, J. L., and B., *The age of the chartists* (London, 1938).

Handlin, O., *Boston's immigrants, 1796–1865* (Harvard, 1941).

Hitchens, F. H., *The colonial land and emigration commission* (Philadelphia, 1931).

Keep, G. R. C., 'The Irish congregations in nineteenth-century Montreal', *Irish Ecc. Record* (December, 1950).

Kiddle, M., *Caroline Chisholm* (Melbourne, 1948).

Knaplund, P., *The British empire* (New York, 1941). *James Stephen and the British colonial system* (Madison, Wisconsin, 1953).

Madgwick, R. B., *Immigration into Eastern Australia* (London, 1937).

MacDonagh, O., The various monographs cited or referred to in the text, and 'Emigration and the state, 1833–55: an essay in administrative history', *Trans. Royal Hist. Soc.*, fifth series, v.

MacKenzie, K., *The English parliament* (London, 1959).

Marshall, G. and Moodie, G. C., *Some problems of the constitution* (London, 1959).

Monypenny, W. P., and Buckle, G. E., *The life of Benjamin Disraeli*, 6 vols. (London, 1920).

Morehouse, F., 'The Irish emigration of the forties', *Amer. Hist. Review*, xxxiii.

Morrell, W. P., *British colonial policy in the age of Peel and Russell* (Oxford, 1930).

Prouty, R., *The transformation of the Board of Trade* (London, 1957).

Purcell, R. J., 'The Irish Emigration Society of New York', *Studies*, xxvii; 'The New York commissioners of emigration', *Studies*, xxxvii.

Reynolds, L. J., *The British Immigrant: his social and economic adjustment in Canada* (London, 1935).

Schneider, D. M., *The history of public welfare in New York state, 1603–1866* (New York, 1938).

Schuyler, R. L., *The fall of the old colonial system: a study in British free trade* (New York, 1945).

Thomas, M. W., *The early factory legislation* (Leigh-on-Sea, 1948).

Walpole, K. A., 'The humanitarian movement of the early nineteenth century to remedy abuses on emigrant vessels to America', *Trans. Royal Hist. Soc.*, fourth series, xiv.

Walpole, Sir S., *The life of Lord John Russell*, 2 vols. (London, 1889).

Ward, W. F., *Aubrey de Vere: a memoir* (London, 1904).

Wrong, E. M., *Charles Buller and responsible government* (Oxford, 1926).

MISCELLANEOUS

Herman Melville's novel, *Redburn*, gives a dramatic and remarkably accurate account of conditions in Liverpool and on the North Atlantic emigrant ships in the mid-nineteenth century.

INDEX